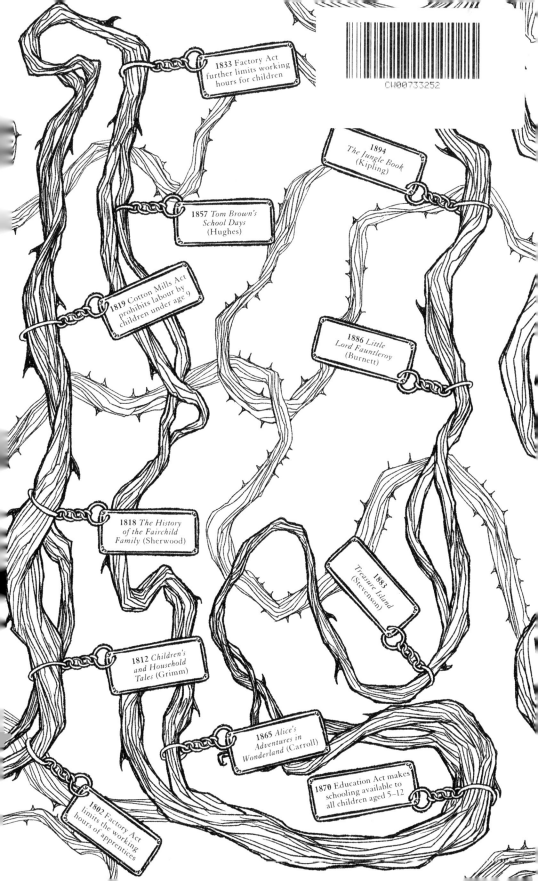

1833 Factory Act further limits working hours for children

1894 *The Jungle Book* (Kipling)

1857 *Tom Brown's School Days* (Hughes)

1819 Cotton Mills Act prohibits labour by children under age 9

1886 *Little Lord Fauntleroy* (Burnett)

1818 *The History of the Fairchild Family* (Sherwood)

1883 *Treasure Island* (Stevenson)

1812 *Children's and Household Tales* (Grimm)

1865 *Alice's Adventures in Wonderland* (Carroll)

1870 Education Act makes schooling available to all children aged 5–12

1802 Factory Act limits the working hours of apprentices

'Scholarly but wholly accessible and written with such love, *The Haunted Wood* is an utter joy.'

LUCY MANGAN

'A gorgeous, loving and, most of all, learned guide to the stories that make us who we are.'

HADLEY FREEMAN

'How children imagine the world and how the world imagines children are questions of perennial interest. The process by which "children's literature" came to be a distinct phenomenon is central to understanding the issues; and here is an exuberant, very wide-ranging, irrepressibly funny, consistently insightful survey of that story, as much a delight to read as the best of its subject matter.'

ROWAN WILLIAMS

'A history as beguiling, peculiar and immersive as the field it describes – and the alluring, creepy woods into which it leads us, never to return…'

LEMONY SNICKET

'From Wordsworth to Wonderland, and the Hundred Acre Wood to Hogwarts, Sam Leith's history of children's literature is as surprising and playful as the stories themselves. Written in punchy, energetic prose, this isn't only a set of love letters to the authors who have shaped generations of readers. It's a reminder that their books continue to be little time machines that can transport even the most jaded of adults back to the imaginative world of childhood.'

ROBERT DOUGLAS-FAIRHURST

THE

HAUNTED
WOOD

A History of Childhood Reading

SAM LEITH

ONEWORLD

A Oneworld Book

First published in the United Kingdom, Republic of Ireland
and Australia by Oneworld Publications Ltd, 2024

Copyright © Sam Leith, 2024
Illustrations copyright © Rowan Daniel Eason, 2024

The moral right of Sam Leith to be identified as the Author of this work has been
asserted by him in accordance with the Copyright, Designs, and Patents Act 1988

ISBN 978-0-86154-818-7
eISBN 978-0-86154-819-4

Typeset by Tetragon, London
Printed and bound in Great Britain by Clays Ltd, Elcograf S.p.A.

Oneworld Publications Ltd
10 Bloomsbury Street
London WC1B 3SR
England

Stay up to date with the latest books,
special offers, and exclusive content from
Oneworld with our newsletter

Sign up on our website
oneworld-publications.com

MIX
Paper | Supporting
responsible forestry
FSC® C018072

James Leith (1946–2022)
O Best Beloved

Contents

Faces along the bar
Cling to their average day:
The lights must never go out,
The music must always play,
All the conventions conspire
To make this fort assume
The furniture of home;
Lest we should see where we are,
Lost in a haunted wood,
Children afraid of the night
Who have never been happy or good

W.H. AUDEN,
'SEPTEMBER 1, 1939'

A Note on the Text

Children's books are, like children, unruly things. Eccentric or transatlantic spellings and quirky punctuation have been kept as far as possible, faithful to the edition under discussion. The odd particularly extravagant outburst of random early-modern italics and capitalisations (looking at you, John Newbery) are per the originals, too.

As for Peter Pan, the tangled publication history through which he came into our imaginarium – book section; play; novella; novel; revised and retitled novel, and so on – means keeping the title of the works in which he appears straight is about as easy as ruling on how to spell Neverland. That's the devil in Peter. The fullest prose version – *Peter and Wendy*, later *Peter Pan and Wendy* – now mostly goes by *Peter Pan*.

PROLOGUE

JUST SO

MY FATHER GREW UP IN AFRICA. HE LOVED RUDYARD Kipling, and the *Just So* stories especially. On his shelves there was a handsome uniform edition of Kipling's works, with dark burgundy dust jackets. My father was an actor, for a while – and when he read to me from Kipling you could hear something of the actor he had been in his voice. He relished the cadences of those stories.

Was he remembering his childhood, his own father reading to him in 1950s Johannesburg, or the landscape of Africa, while in 1980s Surrey he invoked 'the great grey-green greasy Limpopo River, all set about with fever trees' or described Yellow-Dog Dingo's skittering pursuit through the bush? Was he remembering being playfully so cautioned, himself, when in 'How the Whale Got His Throat' he admonished his small audience: 'You must not forget the suspenders, Best Beloved.'

'Best Beloved.' The phrase that describes how every child, wrapped in a story read by a parent, will feel in that moment. It is handed down: generation to generation. My father to me. His father to him. Somewhere, far behind that, is Rudyard Kipling – not a figure in the late-Victorian literary firmament, but a man, miles from the place of his birth, reading fondly to his daughter.

We pass these stories, hand over hand, voice to voice, as stories have always been passed. Each generation reads the old ones and finds new ones that will in turn be passed on. As a child, I was read *The Tiger Who Came to Tea*, *Mog the Forgetful Cat*, *Alexander and the Terrible, Horrible, No Good, Very Bad Day*,

Dogger, Burglar Bill, Green Eggs and Ham, Burnie's Hill. I read those same books to my own children. They in turn added to our family canon the works of Julia Donaldson and Jon Klassen, the *Harry Potter* series and *Diary of a Wimpy Kid,* S.F. Said's *Varjak Paw* books, Piers Torday's *Last Wild* series, Katherine Rundell's *The Wolf Wilder.* Will they read some of those books to their own children? I hope so.

I still cherish the photograph I took of my son, then aged four, sitting with Judith Kerr, then aged ninety-four, at her home in Barnes. (I went to interview her, and the childcare fell through.) Judith's gone now, but Mog and that hungry tiger are still with us – and will be for many decades to come.

Martin Amis, a writer I revere, once said something uncharacteristically foolish. Talking to the novelist Sebastian Faulks in 2011, he said: 'People ask me if I ever thought of writing a children's book. I say, "If I had a serious brain injury I might well write a children's book," but otherwise the idea of being conscious of who you're directing the story to is anathema to me, because, in my view, fiction is freedom and any restraints on that are intolerable. I would never write about someone that forced me to write at a lower register than what I can write.'

The idea that children's writing is a lower form – a brain-injured version of writing for adults, as Amis caricatured it – is as persistent as it is misguided. Children's literature isn't a defective and frivolous sidebar to the grown-up sort. It's the platform on which everything else is built. It's through what we read as children that we imbibe our first understanding of what it is to inhabit a fictional world, how words and sentences carry a style and tone of voice, how a narrator can reveal or occlude the minds of others, and how we learn to anticipate with excitement or dread what's round the corner. What we read in childhood stays with us. No less a figure than G.K. Chesterton was to say in 1924 that the children's fantasy *The Princess and the Goblin* had 'made a difference to my whole existence'. It really matters.

So what do we mean by children's literature anyway? Most children's books have children or adolescents as their protagonists; but not all of them. Most children's books are simpler in their language than books for adults; but not all of them. Most – as time goes on – have come to be very directly addressed to child readers; but not all of them. Many of the classics, it strikes me, and I include *Alice's Adventures in Wonderland* in this, are scarcely books for children at all. The boundaries are extraordinarily blurry. And the question of what children's literature is *for* is a question that haunts the whole history of children's writing, and to which every book finds a different answer, or dares to find no answer at all.

The idea that there is a distinctive literature for children has come and gone over the years. Some of the greatest children's writers are firm in disavowing the very categorisation. Many classics of what we'd now call children's literature weren't seen as such when they were first published. We might think of fairytales, in the same breath as nursery rhymes, as being a basic form of children's writing – but the great collectors of fairytales like Perrault and the Grimms originally targeted their texts at sophisticated *salonnières* or cultural historians.

A full account of the childhood reading of the past would take in sensation literature and penny-bloods as much as educational chapbooks. In the nineteenth century, there was nothing to say that *Heidi*, or *The Swiss Family Robinson*, or *Little Lord Fauntleroy*, were for children, and nothing to indicate that adults weren't reading them with enthusiasm. There was no children's section of the bookshop. It wasn't until the early twentieth century that children's publishing really became a distinct sector of the industry.

Over the years it has segmented, as established markets do, drawing lines between learn-to-read books, read-aloud books, chapter books, books aimed at pre-teens and young teenagers. Those distinctions acquired a vocabulary: professionals now, for instance, talk of MG ('middle-grade': 8–12) and YA ('young adult': 13–18). But age ranges have always been fuzzy approximations of the contract between individual writers and individual readers. Some nine-year-olds will read Homer or Charlotte Brontë; some seventeen-year-olds will be happy with Harry Potter. A comprehensive history of children's *reading*, as opposed to children's writing, would likely include, too (at least for my generation), such treasures of the parental bookshelves as Agatha Christie, Wilbur Smith, Jackie Collins and the smutty bits of Shirley Conran or Harold Robbins. I try not to fuss too much here about these distinctions. In our own age, the growth of YA has further blurred the boundaries; a significant sector of audience for so-called YA is now women in their early thirties. This returns us, perhaps, to the situation of more than a century before.

To state something obvious but easy to lose sight of, what all children's books have in common is that they are not written by children.* They are written for, or about, children. That makes them more psychologically complex and culturally interesting artefacts than their grown-up counterparts. They come to be a document not of how children are, but how adults imagine children to be, or how they imagine they want them to be. They very often, particularly in their early years, had a design upon their readers: they wanted to educate first, and offer delight (if at all) only incidentally, as a means to that end. But even when they did not have so palpably didactic a design, they have inescapably reflected adult anxieties about childhood – our sentimental projections, our recuperative fantasies.

So a children's book will often address more than one audience. It will be written from an adult to a child, from an adult to the adult who will be reading to that child, and, in some sense, from

---

* Daisy Ashford's *The Young Visiters* (1919) is the obvious exception; but its enduring charm, in part, is that it clearly aspired to be a book for adults written by a nine-year-old child, rather than a book for children. It's a literary curiosity, and one that will strike some readers as charming and others as nauseating, but it doesn't belong in this study.

the child that the author once was to the adult that they now are. There's a lot at stake. Wordsworth minted the phrase 'the Child is Father of the Man', but the sentiment it expresses is much, much older. Human beings are storytelling animals, and it is out of the stories we tell ourselves that we make sense of the world. The books of our religions, and the founding narratives of our civilisations, are storybooks.

The awareness of storytelling's power, and the sense that children are particularly vulnerable to it at a vital stage in their development – 'impressionable', as the wax tablet metaphor descending to us from Plato via Locke has it – is a central theme of this history. Moral anxieties over the contents of children's books are as old as children's books themselves. Children's writing tells us not only how children experience the world, but also how adults conceive the world of children. It tells us about childish aspiration and adult fears and longings. And it shapes the adults that the children who delight in it are to become.

A note about the scope of *The Haunted Wood*. I'm aware, and I became ever more aware as I wrote this book, of how indescribably vast this subject is. I'm humbly conscious of (and grateful for, where I lean on it) the work of the many scholars who dedicate entire careers to this subject. I could spend ten, fifteen or twenty years writing this book, and countless thousands of pages, and there'd still be more omissions than there are inclusions. I would still read a chapter covering a decade or two and notice, reproaching me, the absence of this writer or that book. So, for the partisans of a particular writer who are mortified to see them ignored or relegated to a passing mention, I apologise.* We all feel strongly about this subject because the

---

* Unless it's the *Mr. Men* you're complaining about. Nuts to the *Mr. Men*.

stories we read and loved as children mean something to us all our lives.

My ambition is to discuss the books and writers that I think are important – whose influence has been unignorable or whose quality is unimpeachable – and the ones I think have something original, something special, something magical about them. I wanted, in the role of literary historian, to see how these books have shaped each other; in the role of literary critic to ask whether they're any good, and why; and in the role of social historian to understand how these books are involved with the story of childhood itself in Britain.

I have set out to trace the history of children's stories from their prehistory in the deep past of the oral tradition to, roughly, the turn of the millennium.* Love or loathe the stories as you may, the Harry Potter phenomenon provides an inflection point in the recent history of the genre. Its sheer popularity transformed the publishing industry, rewrote the rules of who children's books were for, and shaped the ecosystem in which the children's and young adult stories of the last two decades were to exist.

The book's movement, chapter by chapter, is chronological; but with wide latitude to muddle chronology a little to group writers by genre, or to slot writers in according to their most important works or phases of popularity. Enid Blyton, for instance, was first published in 1922 – but she seems to me in her essence, and in her success, to belong to the post-war period. P.L. Travers, if we were going to be strict about publication dates, could be stitched into any decade from the 1930s to the 1980s – but it would test the reader's patience to find Mary Poppins descending with her parrot-handled umbrella at random points in a whole series of consecutive chapters. The apparently dry question of taxonomy – of eras and dates – pushes us towards something more slippery and more fruitful; a question that's central to this project. Children's books, from *Alice's*

---

* Though I make no apologies for breaking my own rules where I see fit.

Adventures in Wonderland onwards, have been deeply preoccupied with time. Why would they not be? When you're a grown-up, the years go by like telegraph poles glimpsed from the window of a high-speed train. When you're a child, a summer takes a decade. Children's stories are time machines. They give us, most famously in J.M. Barrie but also in any number of his successors, children who never grow up, or children who somehow stay eleven years old when the world about them hurtles through the decades. And they give us, mournfully, children who, by growing up, are locked out of timeless spaces, just as their adult authors are locked out of childhood itself.

On a prosaic level, the visual iconography of children's books is often almost comically out of date. A is for Aeroplane; and here you'll see something with a propeller on its nose. T is for Train; and there is a stout little engine with a chain linked to a bell on the roof and a tall smokestack from which a plume of steam proceeds. T is also for Telephone, an apparatus with a handle linked to its body by a curly cable and a rotary dial. Yet landline telephones with rotary dials were last sighted when I was a teenager, most planes haven't had propellers on their noses for decades, and the last passenger steam train to run in these isles delivered its valedictory 'choo-choo' in the summer of 1968. It's not just a reluctance to face up to the horrors of industrial agriculture and animal husbandry that fills the landscape of children's literature with farms that belong to the 1920s or even the 1820s rather than the 2020s.

Comics like the *Beano* have modernised, but only slowly. In my 1980s childhood, Teacher still had his cane and mortarboard; public spaces were the province of uniformed park wardens with sharp elbows, a stick with a spike on it and a fanatical obsession with keeping off the grass. The Bash Street Kids are still basically 1930s schoolchildren, with their collars and ties and Danny's trademark peaked cap. Minnie the Minx still wears a tam-o'-shanter. Fish and chips still appear in newspaper, teachers use blackboards and catapults and conkers are as likely to feature as Nintendo Switches.

Fairy stories and nursery rhymes have always plunged children into a medieval Albion or a heavily forested Mitteleuropean never-was. Here are worlds where spinning wheels are commonplace; water comes from wells; princes are expected to marry princesses; woodcutter, rat-catcher and huntsman are honourable lower-middle-class occupations; and bears and wolves – rather than, say, off-road motorbikes – are the main thing to be nervous about encountering in the woods.

Emotionally, children's stories have what I sometimes think of as baked-in nostalgia. That makes sense when you think about how they come about. They're written by adults, and the resource on which those adults draw for their understanding of what it is to be a child is their memory, however distorted and partial, of their own childhood. The fuel that drives the reactor has been in storage for twenty or more years. More than that, the literary models on which they draw for inspiration will as often as not be the books that they read in their own childhoods.

So even when you see children's books whose trappings are contemporary with their publication, you are in some sense seeing, say, a 1950s childhood in 1980s drag. Jacqueline Wilson's taboo-busting 1990s treatment of broken families and children in care is full of the detailed flotsam and jetsam of 1990s childhood – McDonald's, karaoke machines, mobile phones, labels from high-street fast-fashion chains – but it's also reacting against the petty snobberies and social stigmas that troubled the author's own childhood in the 1950s and 1960s.

Remembered joys and defining traumas – above all, perhaps, the impact of war on childhood and family life – come out, often in slightly different forms, decades later. A.A. Milne was writing about late-Victorian childhood in the interwar years. C.S. Lewis's most personal Narnia book, *The Magician's Nephew*, is a mirror of his own Edwardian childhood. Richard Adams, as his daughter Juliet pointed out to me, set *Watership Down* in the English countryside he remembered from his own childhood, one that was already all but vanished in the 1960s of his great novel's composition. Those who lived through war as young adults often wrote children's stories in which the experience is conspicuous only by its absence; those who experienced it in childhood wrote books, years later, in which that trauma is alchemically configured into something else.

The long history of children's writing has thrown up an inexhaustible resource of archetypal characters and situations: orphaned protagonists with portentous destinies, portals to other worlds, exotic monsters and talking animals, midnight feasts, cosy hearths, perilous journeys, enchanted objects, dark forests, thuggish bullies and evil wizards. It has seen long swerves between versions of realism and wild fantasy. And it has always, always, drawn on its predecessors.

'Intertextuality' – that buzzword of the literary theory departments of universities, referring to the way texts refer to other texts – is all over children's writing. Homages and tributes and echoes, the wholesale pinching of plots and situations and jokes, and even the outright reworking of earlier stories, are the stuff of which this tradition is made. It's extraordinary, and seems to me telling, how many of the best-known children's writers, from Carlo Collodi, E. Nesbit and Enid Blyton to Jacqueline Wilson, Michael Morpurgo and J.K. Rowling – have also been anthologists and retellers of fairytales and myths.

This book has a British emphasis; not from some post-Brexit chauvinism, but because it seems to me that we do have a distinct tradition, and that it is rooted in a specifically British cultural and literary and social history. It's one that has had an outsized impact on the world. British children's literature was – along with more predictable fare such as Routemaster buses, James Bond and Her Majesty the Queen – one of the central themes of Danny Boyle's London 2012 Summer Olympics opening ceremony.

The first few minutes of the programme, 'Journey along the Thames', included a glimpse of the riverbank creatures from Kenneth Grahame's *The Wind in the Willows*. Later in the show, in a section called 'Second to the right, and straight on till morning', British children's literature shared space, and by implication a place in our national pride, with the NHS. The segue was a troupe of dancing NHS nurses and doctors in white coats tucking pyjama-clad children up in hospital beds. Under the sheets of those beds, TV viewers saw the children lighting torches and peering into the pages of an old-fashioned copy of *Peter Pan*, open to a picture of Captain Hook.

'But some would prefer a bedtime story...' came the voiceover. Standing in the spotlight, J.K. Rowling started to read. 'Of all delectable islands Neverland is the snuggest,' she announced. 'It's not large and sprawly, you know, with boring distances between one adventure and the next. It's nicely crammed. When you play at it by day with the table and chairs, it's not a bit frightening. But in the two minutes before you go to sleep, it is real.'*

At once, circling the arena, the Child Catcher from *Chitty Chitty Bang Bang*† processed on his black carriage-cum-mobile-cage as the children in their beds looked up in alarm. Soon after, giant puppets of the Queen of Hearts (from *Alice's Adventures in Wonderland*), Cruella de Vil (from *The Hundred and One Dalmatians*), and Lord Voldemort (from the Harry Potter books) rose on stage. A little girl, in her bed, was hoisted into the sky while a two-storey Voldemort towered menacingly over her, sparks shooting from his wand. Guitars squealed. Black-clad, hooded, tufted minions with glowing green eyes danced. Then, brollies decorated with points of light, a couple of dozen Mary Poppinses – a flock of Poppinses – descended

---

*   This is an approximate quote from J.M. Barrie's *Peter and Wendy*, abbreviated and simplified for the occasion.
†   The 1968 movie, to be pedantic; the character doesn't feature in the 1964 novel by Ian Fleming on which it was based.

from the heavens and the puppets of the villains deflated. Lord Voldemort collapsed. The green-eyed monkey-creatures scuttled off. The ceremony had enacted the journey so many of the children's stories it celebrated describe: a pleasurable frisson of fear; a reassuring return to safety.

A focus on Britain doesn't mean that all the writers I consider are British, by any means. I've come to think of it this way: the remit I set myself is to look at the history of children's writing through the history of a British nursery bookshelf. I don't think you can ignore Maurice Sendak or E. B. White or Dr. Seuss on the grounds of their being American; nor can you exile Frances Hodgson Burnett as an expatriate. British children have read Tintin and Asterix, Pippi Longstocking and the Moomins.

Nevertheless, American children, at least until the arrival of the digital age, have had a slightly different canon. Every American eighth-grader could be expected to know *Little House on the Prairie*, *Little Women*, *Anne of Green Gables*, *The Adventures of Tom Sawyer* and the Uncle Remus stories. Many British children will have grown up reading them – these books are enduring international classics – but I don't think they are a central part of the canon here, any more than the Famous Five or Just William stories are staples of a childhood in rural Idaho. But these are judgement calls. You may disagree. I hope you do.

Britain gave the world what you might call the ground zero of modern children's literature in the middle of the nineteenth century. It also produced some distinctive and enduring genres – such as the boarding-school story, still going strong after nearly three centuries; and, for better or worse, the tale of colonial adventure – that could only have emerged from these islands. The British canon hangs together. These books speak to each other, and their gradually shifting furniture of Kensington townhouses and Highland castles, nannies and cooks, public parks, school holidays, English or Scottish or Welsh landscapes, speak to their audience directly of a world they will recognise or aspire to. That audience changed over the years – and that, too, is part of the story. The rise (and changing form) of education, urbanisation, immigration, the experience and the idea of travel, changing ideas of social class, changing gender roles, the experience of war, the rise of new sciences and technologies, the shifting place of religion in our national life: all these are mapped, obliquely and directly, in the history of our children's literature.

That literature is peculiarly omnivorous in its subject matter. History is repackaged in children's writing as it is in children's playground games. The settling by Europeans of the American West in the eighteenth and nineteenth centuries, much mythologised in the yellow journalism of the time, entered the British childhood imaginary as 'cowboys and Indians'. Children play at bandits, at pirates, at cops-and-robbers, at highwaymen, at smugglers, at explorers, at Robin Hood and his merry men, and these playground games all take shape and are in turn shaped by children's stories. Never mind that these versions of history are mythologies built on previous mythologies, repackaged as archetypes and tropes that bear little or no relation to the historical grounds on which they are erected.

Children's stories are deeply involved in the creation of a British imaginary. That imaginary, like its real-world counterpart, has its nanny-staters and its libertarians. The instinct to shape and instruct children has always wrestled with the instinct to entertain them. The history of children's literature is in one respect the history of how those aspects of stories that were initially introduced to sugar the pill *became* the pill.

Over the centuries, as more children were able to read books to themselves and still later to *buy* books for themselves, what children wanted to read influenced what was written for them. The authors of children's stories came to speak directly to the children they were writing for. The basic direction of travel over three centuries or so has been from capsules of cod-liver oil to Bertie Bott's Every Flavour Beans, though the cod-liver merchants have been always with us.

Take, just as one example, the way that children's books have mapped the idea of naughtiness. Through much of the eighteenth and nineteenth centuries, the prime virtue of the child was obedience to its parents. To be 'naughty', as in the older sense of the word, was to be sinful, and the wages of sin are death. But even the most basic accommodation with reality recognises that children *are* naughty. What had been a term of disapproval became a central virtue of children's stories. Naughtiness – provided it was accompanied by a good heart – was okay, even to be celebrated. Some rules were made to be broken.

Bunking off school, sneaking out of the window at night, raiding the larder, pranks and practical jokes: these are the meat and drink of the child protagonist. The magic phrase that activates the 'Marauder's Map' in *Harry Potter and the Prisoner of Azkaban* is: 'I solemnly swear I am up to no good.' Having started out as a tool for cementing adult authority, children's stories came to allow children to imagine worlds in which they resisted or subverted it more daringly than they could possibly do in real life. And they allowed adults to indulge that fantasy – to wink at naughtiness.

Another thing that Martin Amis said in the interview I quote – 'fiction is freedom' – seems to me to be especially apposite. In the narrative spaces that these books create, adults and children meet each other travelling in opposite directions. These spaces offer different sorts of freedom. For the child reader, it is a fantasy of (to borrow Isaiah Berlin's 'Two Concepts of Liberty') positive liberty: freedom *to*. A child is given the chance to identify with a protagonist who has freedom to act in the world in a way that few children do in their own lives. That's why, one way or another, and with only relatively rare exceptions, the parents have to be got out of the way. You'll meet in these pages any number of orphans, or children severed from their parents by circumstance – whether something as worldly as a colonial posting overseas or a place in the dormitory of a boarding school, or as unworldly as a portal to a fantastical universe. The child reader can dream of a temporary, but usually safely bounded, version of adulthood.

For the adult reader or, perhaps more pressingly, the adult writer, the imaginative spaces of children's stories represent negative liberty: freedom *from*. Freedom from adult responsibility, freedom from loss and sorrow, freedom from the drudgery of the workaday round. The children's writer is able to imagine him or herself as a child again: to recreate the childhood they remember, or, as often, to concoct a compensatory version of it that will be braver, happier, less dull, less loveless. That's the core of this strange territory. The most effective writers for children almost always seem to be the ones who have most invested in it emotionally. Often, they are writing from a wound – whether a wound sustained in childhood, or the wound of having had to leave it behind in the first place.

That's why a surprising constant in a literature associated with ideas of freedom and innocence is grief. Many of the most enduring and most moving of these stories have a pulse of sadness in them or behind them. To be a child is to know that you have to grow up. To be an adult is to know that you have to die. And to be a parent is to be in a permanent state of mourning: as you watch your son or daughter grow up, you are saying an irreversible farewell to the child that they were, day by day, month by month, year by year.

There's grief in the back-story of many of these books, too. It's not brain damage that makes you a children's writer – but for a lot of them, there was damage of another sort. This isn't purely a literary-historical book but, here and there, a biographical one. I wanted to look at the often strange and often troubled and sometimes sad lives of the people who have written for children. Creation serves a need, and it's seldom just a need for a royalty statement.

Many of the great children's stories started their lives being addressed to particular children. The origin myth of *Alice's Adventures in Wonderland* has it addressed to ten-year-old Alice

Liddell. Barrie's Peter Pan stories were directed at the childless author's friends' children, George and Jack Llewelyn Davies. *The Wind in the Willows* started life as the improvised bedtime stories Kenneth Grahame told his son Alastair. *Watership Down* had its origins in the tales Richard Adams spun to his daughters to beguile long car journeys. And sometimes the child whom the writer was addressing, the child the writer yearned to preserve and protect, was him- or her-self.

Those children, as children do, outgrew the images of themselves fixed in the pages. It often cost them their happiness. Sometimes, it cost them more. In disconcertingly many cases, they would not live to find out what it would cost them. The *Just So* stories were originally told by Rudyard Kipling to his first child, Josephine or 'Effie'. 'There were stories meant to put Effie to sleep, and you were not allowed to alter those by one single little word.'[*] Effie was 'Best Beloved'. Effie died when she was six years old.

Yet the stories that were told to Effie, and Christopher Robin, and Alastair Grahame and all those real children like them, have outlived their original audiences and outlived their authors. They remain, even if shadowed by sadness, bright objects. There is adventure in them, and love, and laughter, and fun; they place their readers in each generation on the brink of new worlds, new possibilities. So let's move on to look in more detail at how those worlds and possibilities came into being.

---

[*] *St Nicholas* magazine, December 1989.

I

ONCE UPON A TIME

Anonymous · Aesop · Apuleius · Vladimir Propp ·
Joseph Campbell · Philippe Ariès · Lawrence Stone ·
John Locke · Jean-Jacques Rousseau · William Blake ·
William Wordsworth

THE PREHISTORY OF
CHILDREN'S WRITING

'ONCE UPON A TIME...' THESE FOUR WORDS HAVE been uttered by English-speaking parents to their children for hundreds of years. They connect the act of storytelling to the past; and, as successive generations utter those syllables, they affirm a connection to the past of storytelling itself. The first children's literature wasn't literature – and it wasn't for children. Storytelling begins for humanity as it begins for individual human beings, in the spoken word.

So I want to begin by considering the deep roots of a distinctive literature that is surprisingly young – and to give a sense of the soil in which it germinated. The fairytales that you read to your children at bedtime, or that have taken canonical form in Disney movies, were in existence millennia before anyone wrote them down. Scholars tracing the linguistic ancestry of stories have argued that the folktale known as 'The Smith and the Devil' – an archetypal Faust story – goes back five thousand years, to the Bronze Age.

We can speculate that there will have been rhymes and stories that parents or nurses told specifically to children, but none of those survive. How could they? What descends to us of the folktales and myths of prehistory is only fragments of their narrative DNA: the shapes of stories. No nursery, no nursery rhymes. The audience around that proverbial fire in the mouth of a cave didn't differentiate between stories for adults and stories for children; they were just stories.

You might think of the history of storytelling in terms of a river system, flowing from prehistory to the present day. Broad watercourses – archetypal stories, which appear in many forms in many cultures – carve deep channels into the landscape. There are tributaries and diversions, meanders, eddies and currents. At this stage it's a process as collective and unauthored as nature – the tribal unconscious in action, the stories passing through generations of anonymous storytellers.

But there comes a point at which folktales and oral myths start to pass into the written language. Tribal myths find their way into the foundational texts of religions. Homer's epics start to be written down. People like the Grimms collect folktales, and edit or shape them, and adapt them – or, as in the case of Hans Christian Andersen, invent new variations. Poems become prose. Songs and ditties, many of them increasingly gnomic or surreal as they become corrupted or their original points of reference dwindle to obscurity, turn into nursery rhymes.

The great rivers of oral storytelling are canalised, dammed and diverted. They are domesticated and put to the use that a given writer in his or her own age finds for them. Individual inventiveness creates fixed genres and particular tales: you start to be able to pick out lines of influence between individual authors rather than the chaotic cataract of the oral tradition. Here, at last, are ponds and pools and ornamental fountains. But it's the same force, upstream, that feeds them.

For children's writing to become the genre that we now recognise, several things needed to happen. I mean to trace them in the pages that follow. The first was that childhood itself needed to be conceptualised as a separate space. In pre-modern societies for whom survival was a priority, that will have been a dangerous luxury. Children were adults-in-waiting: to be protected, raised and trained as soon as possible to become productive members of the tribe.

Looked at from this point of view, the history of children's literature – as the oral tradition became a written one, and as that written one speciated to form a sub-tradition that would address the experience of children directly – is the history of childhood. It was through telling stories that we originally explained the world to ourselves (the sun and moon, the creation, the cycles of nature) and, in turn, it was through telling stories that we came to explain childhood to ourselves.

At the same time, children's writing didn't just need a scheme of ideas. The basic law of supply and demand means that it also needed an audience. That is, you needed the means of reproducing it at scale: which meant the printing press. You needed the spaces in which it would be told: which meant schoolrooms and nurseries and playgrounds. And you needed readers: which meant the spread first of adult, and then of child, literacy.

Excavating the Past

ANONYMOUS

I F YOU GO LOOKING FOR CHILDREN'S STORIES IN THE earliest examples of the written word that come down to us, for the most part you look in vain. But not entirely. In 1896, a pair of archaeologists were digging in the rubbish dumps of a ruined and all-but-forgotten city, now called Oxyrhynchus, in a backwater of the then Ottoman Empire. Here, among the detritus, they discovered a cache of papyri, perfectly preserved for a millennium and a half, that have been exercising scholars non-stop for the 150 years since.

As well as innumerable bureaucratic bits and pieces – census returns, wills, bills of inventory and so forth – the rubbish heaps of Oxyrhynchus have yielded lost poem-fragments of Sappho, Pindar and Homer, diagrams from Euclid's pioneering mathematical work, scraps of Plato and an unknown play by Sophocles, Old Testament apocrypha and some of the earliest surviving Greek texts of the New Testament. But also found there, just under twenty-five by ten centimetres in size, is what concerns us here: Volume XXII, Papyrus 2331.

On this fragment, yellow with age, are a few lines from a third-century CE poem in Greek about the first labour of Heracles, the killing of the Nemean lion. The poem is an 'elementary text written in simple style and diction and crude meter', and the words, unusually for the classical world, are written with spaces between them rather than squashed up together. The whole presentation seems designed to make the text easy to read and, perhaps, memorise or declaim out loud. Also, again unusually, it is illustrated. There are three little cartoons embedded in between the lines of the text – and in the best-preserved you can still see the green of the grass on which the lion stands; flashes of yellow in the hero's hair as he wrestles the beast.

Is this the very distant ancestor of a modern children's picture book? The literary historian Seth Lerer* writes of this fragment: 'It is, perhaps, something of a children's book itself: a little illustrated drama for the reader weary of rhapsodes and grammarians.' Over a difference of seventeen centuries, in other words, it may just be possible to detect a quality coming off that text like light reaching us faintly from a distant star. It's a quality that is present in all the children's writing worth talking about – and that is often present even when it is not intended by the author. That quality: delight.

But let's not go overboard. Here was a text that was, probably, aimed at children. Yet it was still not a children's story so much as an adult story truncated, simplified, adapted for the attention span and reading or listening comprehension of a child. The delight is there, but it's incidental. And it's all but a one-off. As Lerer writes, in the classical world 'the two poles of early learning were memorisation and recitation. Students would be given passages from poets and dramatists and would be expected to learn and then recite them.'† Therefore 'the study of children's literature in this period is not the study of particular works written for children, but the study of how pre-existing texts were adapted for children: how Homer gets excerpted into schoolbooks, how Virgil was parsed, how plays and lyric poems could be reread and retaught with increasing complexity of grammatical, stylistic and ethical analysis.'

Documents have survived that look a lot like primers. One, a Greek-language scroll discovered in Egypt, was described by the

---

*   Seth Lerer, *Children's Literature*.

†   Ibid.

Egyptologists O. Guéraud and P. Jouguet as *'un livre d'écolier du IIIe siècle avant JC'*,* 'a schoolbook from the third century BC'. It begins with tables of letters, numbers and syllables, names of the gods of Olympus, rivers and mythological heroes, moves on to two passages of Euripides 'designed to teach word division and the caesura', and in the second half is an anthology of poetry including passages from *The Odyssey*, epigrams and extracts from comic plays. The classical canon was clipped down for educational purposes – and the emphasis would have been more on the grammatical or rhetorical parsing of bits of text than on imaginative engagement for the sake of it. Texts were adapted to children's capacities, you could say, but not their dispositions.

In other words, there wasn't a distinct children's literature because there wasn't a distinctive idea of childhood as we have today. Children were apprentice adults, and the defining virtue of the adult Athenian (or, later, Roman) was rhetorical excellence. Children – male, obviously – were being prepared, as quickly as possible, for the duties of citizenship. And citizenship meant eloquence. Indeed, one Greek word for child, *nepion*, translates as 'no word': a child was a person who didn't know how to speak.

But the pleasure principle will always, somehow, win through – and perhaps it is for that reason that the abrupt reverses, anthropomorphic animals, sharp (if, to us, sometimes eccentric) morals and trickster antagonists of Aesop's fables have cast so long a shadow over the history of children's writing.

---

* O. Guéraud and P. Jouguet, 'Un livre d'écolier du IIIe siécle avant J.-C.,' *Publications de la Societé Royale Égyptienne de Papyrologie; Textes et Documents II* (Institut français d'archéologie orientale, 1938).

Fables and Morals

AESOP · APULEIUS

Fables; The Aesop Romance; The Golden Ass

ESOP, LIKE HOMER, IS ONE OF THOSE AUTHORS WHO tends to disappear in a cloud of smoke the closer you get. Perhaps, if one of the most influential accounts of him is to be trusted, that's for the best. He wasn't, according to his anonymous first biographer in *The Aesop Romance*, a pretty sight:

> The fabulist Aesop, the great benefactor of mankind, was by chance a slave but by origin a Phrygian of Phrygia, of loathsome aspect, worthless as a servant, pot-bellied, misshapen of head, snub-nosed, swarthy, dwarfish, bandy-legged, short-armed, squint-eyed, liver-lipped – a portentous monstrosity. In addition to this he had a defect more serious than his unsightliness in being speechless, for he was dumb and could not talk.

Tradition places him as having lived at some time in the sixth century BCE. But was he a slave, or an adviser to the king? Was he Phrygian, a Thracian, a Lydian or an Ethiopian? Was he black, or white? Did he even exist? The sources vary. Most accounts of him that survive are from a century or more after his birth, and *The Aesop Romance* seems to have been composed six centuries later and is agreed by scholars to be entirely fictional. Even the earliest written versions of the works that are ascribed to him date from centuries after his death.

Aesop, you could say, is something of a fable himself. Versions of his stories are to be found all over Europe, India and the Far East, and the lines of transmission remain unclear to this day. But the literary genre associated with his name has proved inextinguishable. Quintilian's rhetoric handbook *Institutes of Oratory* calls Aesop's fables 'the natural successors of the fairy stories of the nursery' and says pupils should learn to paraphrase them as the first step in rhetorical training.* Caxton published an English version in 1484. And you can see the footprint of Aesop in Brer Rabbit, Marie de France and La Fontaine, Rudyard Kipling, Beatrix Potter, Kenneth Grahame and Richard Scarry.

The genre's distinguishing characteristics were its talking animals, who are now everywhere in children's writing, and its morals. On a very basic and obvious level, they show the didactic roots of children's literature: storytelling is a way of giving children a sense of their place in the world, of power relations and right conduct, and of the fickleness of fate. But they're interesting, I think, because they sweeten the didactic pill with imaginative engagement.

The fables we now remember best – 'The Hare and the Tortoise', say, or 'The Town Mouse and the Country Mouse' – seem to speak straightforwardly to our own age. We can still agree that the race is not always to the swift, and that a boost to your social status isn't worth being eaten by a cat. Over the years in which the rambunctious, various, semi-apocryphal canon of Aesopica descends to us – rolling downhill like a snowball and gathering fresh apocrypha – its strangeness and the alterity of its worldview has been quietly adapted, version by version, to the age in which its stories are consumed. The more congenial of the fables come to the fore; the more riddling and obtuse of them slide quietly into obscurity. And they are subtly adapted to a contemporary purpose. The blackly funny 'The Murderer and the Nile' – which tells the

---

* Quintilian, *Institutes of Oratory*, Bk 1 Ch.9 (around 95 CE).

story of a murderer fleeing justice who climbs a tree to avoid being eaten by a lion, jumps out of the tree into the river to avoid being bitten by a snake, and is duly eaten by a crocodile – was given a Christian moral (about the inexorability of God's justice) in post-classical versions.

The essence of Aesop, then, can be thought of not so much as a fixed body of work, but as a way of doing things: a style. The tales get their allegorical force from their simplicity. Their directness is unmuddied by realism. Yet much of their attractiveness, like the attractiveness of any successful allegory, comes from the way the reader ascribes human character to their allegorical animals: the humble and industrious ant, the sullen and devious fox, the ingenious crow, the boastful hare.

Also, they are characterised by a stripped-down, vernacular* style. Aesop was a slave's-eye view of the world, and both explicitly political fables (such as 'The Frogs Who Desired a King', which warns the common folk to be careful what they wish for) and more general fables (such as 'The Lion's Share' or 'The Wolf and the Lamb') are pointed in their depiction of the depredations of the powerful. There is vivid and recognisable life in Aesop's telegraphic little stories – and that is surely one of the reasons that the Aesopic style has survived. There's more than a touch of Aesop in Julia Donaldson's delightful *The Gruffalo*, where the bewildered monster of the title follows a mouse through the forest and marvels to see predators scattering in apparent terror of the rodent. It's a riff, you could say, on the Aesopic fable of the fly perching on a chariot wheel and marvelling at what a lot of dust it's kicking up.

There are other ways in which what children read in classical antiquity trickles down to us. Many scholars see the story of Cupid and Psyche – as written down in Apuleius's second-century *The Golden Ass* – as being the first fairytale in the Western tradition. It

---

*   From the Latin *verna* – a female slave.

certainly contains many of the elements, from jealous sisters and (in Venus) a vengeful fairy, to magical helpers in the form of the ants who help Psyche sort the grain, that will reappear in subsequent stories. It looks like the template, too, for what were later called the 'monster groom' tales – outstandingly 'Beauty and the Beast'.

The connection between Aesop's archetypal stories and European folktales is a vital one to grasp. Coming out of the oral tradition, changing form as they go to fit local circumstances, the stories that were to become folktales and the folktales that were to become fairytales – and which in turn set the pattern for so many children's stories – have an enormous amount in common.

The Shapes of Stories

VLADIMIR PROPP · JOSEPH CAMPBELL

Morphology of the Folktale;
The Hero with a Thousand Faces

V LADIMIR PROPP WAS A RUSSIAN SCHOLAR OF FOLK-
lore who, in a 1928 book called *Morphology of the Folktale,*[*]
advanced an extraordinarily bold and suggestive idea. He
thought that the vast number of different folktales to be found in
different traditions and languages all over the world are, at root,
just variations on a theme: 'All fairy-tales, by their structure, belong
to one and the same type.' 'Morphology' means the study of shapes.
Propp argued that you could look under the surface and find that
the bones of all these different stories were the same.

In effect, he argued that folktales had evolved just like animals
from a common ancestor, and that you could classify them just as
you classify species of fauna. If you X-ray a bat's wing or a whale's
flipper, you can recognise in them the same pattern of bones as
you see in a human hand. So it would be with folktales: Propp
believed that, by looking rigorously at their structures, a 'given
class [of story] may be discerned from others absolutely accurately
and objectively'.

What might that common ancestor be? 'A "single source",'
Propp writes, 'does not positively signify, as some assume, that all

---

[*] Vladimir Propp, *Morphology of the Folktale.*

folktales came, for example, from India, and that they spread from there throughout the entire world, assuming their various forms in the process of migration. The single source may, as well, be a psychological one.'

It's quite an idea. To suppose a depth-psychological origin to these stories is to ask serious and fundamental questions about human nature – about the meaning of storytelling and even, which may be related, the religious instinct. If folktales are, as we might conjecture, the primal form of storytelling – a basic set of patterns that underpin the narrative shapes we give to a chaotic world – then the patterns that persist in them are wired deep into the species.

Propp's work, that said, can seem almost comically dry. A so-called structuralist, he was not remotely interested in the human stories and social worlds of the folktales he studied. All those are historically contingent – random set-dressing, as far as he was concerned. He talks, instead, of 'functions' and 'moves' in the narrative; of developing a 'grammar' of storytelling. The idea of a grammar is a suggestive one. Language allows us to create a limitless number of meaningful utterances from a very restricted set of things – the twenty-six letters of the alphabet or the forty-four phonemes in English. So, narratologists like Propp say, it is with stories. For the twenty-six letters of the alphabet, to follow the metaphor, you might substitute what Propp called 'functions', by which he meant elements of plot: bricks in the storyteller's Lego box. He decided that there were just thirty-one of them, and he abbreviated them as a series of symbols, so the stories he studied could be boiled down and reduced to their essences.

Once Propp had gone to work on a story, it would end up looking more like a mathematical equation than something that would hold your toddler spellbound over warm milk. Yet Propp's basic insight – that the same patterns recur again and again across stories in every culture and at every time – is sound. 'Folktales possess one special characteristic,' he says. 'Components of one tale can, without any alteration whatsoever, be transferred to another.'

A story starts, say, with a safe and stable situation that is disrupted. There is an 'absentation': the hero leaves the safety of home, or the princess is kidnapped. There will be an 'interdiction' – don't take your eye off the baby; don't open the door to the special room – which will be violated. The protagonist will be tested – asked to capture a unicorn or spin straw into gold. Magical agents will be enlisted to help. The hero will find the antagonist's lair – Baba Yaga's chicken-footed hut; the giant's castle in the clouds; the Green Chapel – triumph over the villain and return home with the prize. There may be further challenges to overcome – pursuit, a false hero to displace. At last there's what Propp called 'the wedding': the hero gets his final transformation, marrying the princess or taking the throne or both, and lives, well, happily ever after.

In story after story we find some combination of Propp's seven basic characters. There's a hero, a villain, a 'dispatcher' who will set the hero on his quest, the object of the quest (often a princess), a 'false hero' (who will attempt to usurp the hero), a 'helper' or sidekick, and a 'donor' who gives the hero a magical object to help him overcome his challenges. If this sounds a little schematic – you'll probably have noticed that many stories have more or fewer than seven characters – it's worth mentioning that these roles can be played by more than one character at once; and that some characters will take on more than one of the roles. Again, the point is about the roles that any given character takes in the story.

The *Shrek* franchise, of which Vladimir Propp would I suspect have very much approved, plays gleefully with these categories. Prince Charming appears, there, in the role of the 'false hero', while the ogre is the true hero. Donkey and Puss in Boots are helpers. The fairy godmother – whose cottage must be ransacked for a love potion – plays the role of donor as well as of villain. And Fiona, defying the patriarchal traditions of the fairy story (in which, in Propp's words, princesses are 'obtained' and brides 'either earned or given in reward'), is sometimes hero and sometimes helper, not just the object of the quest.

When Propp writes of one folktale that 'the enchantment of a boy is not followed by the breaking of the spell, and he remains a little goat for life', the modern reader might immediately be put in mind of Roald Dahl's *The Witches* – in whose closing pages the narrator/protagonist is still a mouse. Propp's 'deceitful proposal' is there as the White Witch seduces Edmund with Turkish Delight in *The Lion, the Witch and the Wardrobe*. When Propp describes function XXIII – 'the hero, unrecognised, arrives home or in another country' – you will perhaps think of Odysseus reaching Ithaca.

By dwelling on the abstract formulations of a long-dead Soviet academic, and in looking back through centuries and even millennia to the roots of storytelling, we can glean one of this book's themes. Children's stories remain close to those aboriginal forms of storytelling – myths, fairy stories and folktales. They draw their force from them. Where the 'literary novel' may, with various degrees of success, seek to do away with quest narratives, happy endings or heroes and villains, the canon of children's literature is far more ready to draw on these archetypal story-shapes and characters.

Propp's argument has been taken up by subsequent writers about narrative: most influentially, perhaps, the Jungian Joseph Campbell in *The Hero with a Thousand Faces* (1949). The idea that there are only 'seven basic stories' has become common wisdom; and, indeed, gives its name to the UK's pre-eminent museum of children's literature, Seven Stories in Newcastle upon Tyne.*

In the pages that follow we'll meet such patterns again and again: departure, challenge, combat, transformation and reward. And yet, just as in the history of the folktale, they will come dressed in the clothes of their own era and be given shape by the peculiarities and affinities of the individual storyteller. The abstract becomes concrete. The 'function' becomes a dragon so real you can smell the sulphur and scorch of her breath.

---

*   Oxford's Story Museum runs it a gallant second.

I make a distinction between folktale, fairy stories and myths – and I should set out a little what I mean by those three things. They are categories that substantially overlap. But folktales are what descend to us through the oral tradition: versions of the same story, as folklorists have painstakingly discovered, can be found all over the world in different forms, their accidental aspects local to the area where that version has developed. Fairytales are not just a subset of folklore, and they don't have to involve fairies; rather, they are what you get when folktales are domesticated and written down.

It's possible, too, to make a distinction between folktale and myth. What's characteristic of both these things is that they aren't single stories – in the sense that there's a single immutable thing called, say, *Daisy Miller* by Henry James – but frameworks for stories, patterns for stories, fields of stories.

In a fairytale or folktale, the framework – the irreducible thing – is the basic shape of the plot. The plot stays the same and the characters are indistinct. What makes Cinderella 'Cinderella' is not the protagonist's name or hair colour, or how many stepsisters she has, or whether it's a glass slipper or a wooden clog. It's that a put-upon drudge goes in disguise to a party, snags the handsome prince and lives happily ever after.

Myths, in the way I understand them, are slightly different. There's one distinction you can draw to do with the sheer gravity of meaning. Myths often deal with the doings of gods and superhumans; they can include explanatory accounts of the universe itself. Folktales and fairytales, though they contain magic, operate at the ordinary-folk level, with woodcutters and suchlike at the bottom and royal personages at the top. But the distinction I'm interested in here is a narratological one. With a myth, the plot changes and the characters – or the constellations of characters – stay the same. The core of the Greco-Roman mythologies is their pantheon of gods and heroes, whose qualities are instantiated in a great cloud of different stories. The fixed points are the attributes of, and relationships between, the characters.

Comic book universes are profoundly mythological. What actually happens in any given issue of *The Avengers* or *Fantastic Four* or *X-Men* couldn't matter less, except to diehard nerds. The same villains will escape and come back. Nobody ever dies for good. The stable elements are the characters. Their accidental details will be reinvented, their costumes redesigned. But Spidey will always recognisably be shooting webs – 'thwip' – and wisecracking; Wolverine will – 'snikt!' – always have his adamantium claws; Shadowcat will always have a brother–sister relationship with Colossus; Hulk will always, finally, be alone.

Myths are narratologically open-ended. Fairytales and folktales – bookended as they conventionally are with the phrases 'once upon a time' and 'happily ever after' – come to an end. Children's stories, as we'll see, draw deeply on both the narrative shapes of fairytales and the timeless resonance of myth.

Pre-Modern Childhood

PHILIPPE ARIÈS · LAWRENCE STONE

Centuries of Childhood; The Family,
Sex and Marriage

OMETHING ELSE NEEDS TO HAPPEN TO THE PATTERNS we see in these stories for them to turn into children's literature, though. They need to start speaking to a distinct concept of childhood; and it's a concept that has been and remains a site of fierce contestation. We'll see in the following chapter how folktales became fairytales – and how at the same time they competed for space with another model of storytelling for children, one rooted in Puritan anxieties and concerned with moral rather than practical education. Is the child naturally innocent, or is the child dangerously amoral or even evil? What, and when, is a child?

There was no real distinction, much before the middle of the eighteenth century, between what children would have read, or had read to them, and writing for adults. There were grammars, books of religious instruction, bestiaries, catechisms and the like – educational books, primarily – and, at the higher end, a child's literary diet would include simplified versions of adult classics.

The first half of the eighteenth century alone saw half a dozen different editions of *Robinson Crusoe* ('epitomised' or 'abridg'd') and cut-down versions of *Gulliver's Travels* started appearing as early as 1727. Other staples included the *Morte d'Arthur*, *Reynard the Fox*, the *Geste of Robin Hood*, *Aesop's Fables*, *The Pilgrim's Progress* and *Foxe's Book of Martyrs*. Their heads, if not their bookshelves, would be well furnished with fairytales and nursery rhymes. And at the less exalted level, children are known to have been a significant market for sensation literature – chapbooks that retailed lurid versions of the real-life adventures of highwaymen, bandits and rogues.

You might say that what made children's literature, at this stage, was more to do with a way of reading than a way of writing: that a child would enjoy *Gulliver's Travels* or *Robinson Crusoe* on the level of a fantastical adventure story without much attending to Swift's political satire or Defoe's theology and economics. A child might thrill to the adventures of Dick Turpin or Robin Hood while paying even less lip-service than an adult reader to the moralising *sententiae* in which the story was wrapped. Some children may have been reading, but very few adults were writing for children.

Why did that change? There's one theory, which became fashionable in the 1970s, that implies the reason we didn't have children's literature until the early modern period is that we didn't have children – or, at least, not in the way that we think of them now. In his influential study of the history of childhood the Spanish historian Philippe Ariès made the notoriously bald claim that 'in medieval society, the idea of childhood did not exist'.*

His case was that childhood as we currently understand it – an extended period that runs from infancy to late adolescence, and that takes a particular place in our family structures and in our ideas of human inwardness – was not something for which medieval Europeans had either a firm conceptual framework or a vocabulary. The rise of an idea of childhood came as the flip side of a civilising process where adult behaviours were codified as a matter of etiquette, and where the family as a private unit started to be hived off from the rest of society.

---

* Philippe Ariès, *Centuries of Childhood*.

In the medieval and early modern worlds, for most people, there was no expectation whatever of privacy as we now think of it. Families were mixed and woven into the rest of society. Upper-class households would have had servants whose presence extended into the most intimate settings of dress and toilet; the peasantry lived cheek by jowl with each other in multigenerational families. Life was overwhelmingly communal. The historian of childhood Hugh Cunningham writes: 'Living conditions in medieval houses gave little opportunity for privacy, whether for adults or for children, and in the outside world children were immediately part of a society in which the ages mixed, and in which neighbours played their part in looking after children.'[*]

All of that has implications for the literature of childhood. If you're going to have a special category of storytelling that's 'suitable' or 'unsuitable' for children, you're going to need a special separate space in which the stories can be told. You're going to need an idea of the child's persona and inner life as something distinct from that of an adult. And, for a written children's literature, perhaps it goes without saying, you're going to need children (or, first, adults) who can read.

Ariès argued that children would tend to join the adult world as early as seven or sooner. The horror with which we now view the sexualising of children is historically specific: children were frequently married off before adolescence. And children worked. Especially for poor families – and long before even the most rudimentary forms of contraception were available – a child was a potentially catastrophic drain on the exchequer. Parents couldn't afford to keep them economically unproductive – which is, in modern terms, almost a defining characteristic of childhood. Children would leave the family home to be apprenticed to a trade, or would be expected to help with work conducted in the

---

[*] Hugh Cunningham, *Children and Childhood in Western Society Since 1500.*

home or to look after younger children, as soon as they were physically able.

The British social historian Lawrence Stone, in his *The Family, Sex and Marriage in England 1500–1800* (1977), developed a similar case when considering the early modern period. He thought that 'affective individualism' – aka loving marriages and doting parenthood – didn't really come in until the eighteenth century for practical reasons. He went so far as to claim that the enduring high levels of infant mortality meant that parents didn't even name their children until they were two or three years old, did not mourn dead children in the way we do now, and would breezily reuse the name of a child who died in infancy for a younger sibling who looked like having a better chance of making it.

The evidence for all this is, at best, circumstantial, not least because child mortality continued to be horrifyingly high until long after the rise of affective individualism: in Manchester's slums in 1840, infant mortality was at 57 per cent. And there has been a distinct pushback in recent decades against the strong versions of these arguments. As critics of Stone have pointed out, reusing a name could just as easily be evidence of deep grief as of cold pragmatism; and common sense tells us that it's unlikely that, even all those years ago, people didn't love their children in much the way that we do and mourn them when they died.* I think of Chaucer's dedication of his 1390s *Treatise on the Astrolabe*, to 'litil childe Lowys my sone'. It is impossible not to read paternal tenderness in those words.

Yet childhood certainly was an often brutal and distinctly limited phase of life from the classical period right up to the nineteenth century. Children weren't, as they are now, seen as something intrinsically precious. Much as we might like to think that child

---

* Not to mention the findings of primatologists and sociobiologists – who observe that all great apes including humans need a certain amount of protection and loving care to develop normally, and that parents will tend to try to supply same.

abandonment was a unique cruelty of the ancient world, it continued right into the modern period. In Western Europe between the
sixteenth and eighteenth centuries, rates of abandonment seemed
to fluctuate between about 10 and, in some places, as much as 50
per cent – and the availability of orphanages or foundling hospitals
correlated with a rise in these figures. Medieval and early modern
people may have loved their children, after their fashion. But an
affectively bonded nuclear family with the care of children at the
heart of its endeavours was for most people for most of history
economically unsustainable. Childhood was a luxury children
could not afford.

What changed? Perhaps the most important historical shift
was the steady spread of universal education. This was important
because it started to create the space for, and the idea of, a childhood
that would run from infancy to mid- or late adolescence. For the
ancients, education was not something specially associated with
childhood. By the end of the nineteenth century, it was its defining
characteristic.

The alternative to school was not play: it was work. From medieval times, children in peasant societies had been involved in seasonal
agricultural and domestic labour, and child labour continued to
be seen as completely natural and, indeed, desirable right into the
nineteenth century. When Daniel Defoe toured England in the
early eighteenth century, he reported approvingly from Norfolk
that 'the very children after four or five years of age, could every
one earn their own bread'.*

From the late eighteenth century – as the grimness of some of
that bread-earning came to public attention – the excellence of this
norm started to be questioned. Jonas Hanway's 1766 *An Earnest
Appeal for Mercy to the Children of the Poor*, for instance, made the
(admittedly weak sauce) appeal that, if children did have to work,

---

* Daniel Defoe, *A Tour Thro' The Whole Island of Great Britain* (G. Strahan, 1724).

we should at least make it nicer for them: 'it should be considered
how to make labour as pleasant […] as little *irksome* as possible, and
with a tender regard to the measure of a young person's strength
of body or mind.'*

That tendency was to go further. Attention started to be paid
to the physical harms involved – particularly of children involved
in the manufacturing of cotton, where by 1835 nearly half the
workers were under eighteen. The Industrial Revolution had made
the child labour problem (as we would think of it now but they
did not think of it then) worse rather than better. Children were
cheaper to employ, and the competitiveness of many eighteenth-
and nineteenth-century industries depended on them. A Yorkshire
man, Richard Oastler, petitioned Parliament in 1833 to complain
that he lived in

> a district of England, where *Infants* labour for their *Parents'* food; –
> labour for their own sustenance; – and die, – absolutely *die*, in their
> efforts to *live*! […] It is notorious that the health of the negro slave,
> of the adult felon, of the horse, of the ass, of the hare, of the rabbit,
> of the partridge, of the pheasant, of the cabbage and of the straw-
> berry, is protected by law; but at the same time the children of the
> poor are unprotected by the law, – are treated by their employers
> with a rigour unheard of in the most barbarous regions; and are
> absolutely, sometimes worked to death.†

It became a commonplace in what we'd now think of as liberal
circles that child labour bore comparison to slavery in the colo-
nies – which, in the 1830s, was the subject of popular emancipation

---

* Jonas Hanway, *An Earnest Appeal for Mercy to the Children of the Poor*
(J. Dodsley, 1766).
† Richard Oastler, *Eight Letters to the Duke of Wellington: A Petition to the House
of Commons: and a letter to the Editor of the Agricultural and Industrial Magazine*
(James Cochrane & Co., 1835).

campaigns. Samuel Taylor Coleridge, who campaigned for an Act of Parliament to protect children in the workforce, talked of 'our poor little White-slaves, the children in our cotton Factories'. Coleridge mocked the so-called 'free labour' of children (a term for children not formally apprenticed and so still living with their parents): 'If the labour were indeed free, the contract would approach, on the one side, too near to suicide, on the other to manslaughter.'*

The emblematic figure of the child labourer came to be the chimney-sweep – and it's scarcely surprising that it did. Sweeps were prone to diseases of the lungs, injuries from falling, could be encouraged up chimneys by having their feet pricked or fires lit under them, and – according to Hugh Cunningham – 'if they avoided death by suffocation they were peculiarly liable to cancer of the scrotum'. It wasn't a nice job. In 1785 the same Jonas Hanway wrote *A Sentimental History of Chimney Sweepers in London and Westminster, shewing the necessity of putting them under regulations, to prevent the grossest inhumanity to the climbing boys.*†

Five years later the first part of William Blake's 'The Chimney Sweeper' appeared in *Songs of Innocence:* 'When my mother died I was very young / And my father sold me while yet my tongue, / Could scarcely cry weep weep weep weep. / So your chimneys I sweep & in soot I sleep.' The poem presents a dream of 'thousands of sweepers Dick, Joe, Ned & Jack [...] all of them lock'd up in coffins of black'. There's a resonant echo, there, of Cinderella sleeping in soot – and Blake's visual contrast of the soot-blackened sweep with the angelic image of a 'naked & white' child in a state of innocence is one whose symbolic and theological implications were irresistible. A mythology of the child chimney-sweep, then, of industrial dirt versus the purity of childhood in nature, was

---

* Coleridge, Samuel Taylor, *Remarks on the Objections which have been Urged against the Principle of Sir Robert Peel's Bill* (privately printed, 1818).
† Jonas Hanway, *A Sentimental History* (J. Dodsley 1785).

getting on for a century old by the time Charles Kingsley came to write *The Water-Babies* (1862).

It was not until the nineteenth century, though, that the English state started to take a serious legislative interest in child labour, with the first half of the century seeing a succession of interventions to protect children in the workforce. The Health and Morals of Apprentices Act of 1802, inspired by an outbreak of fever in a Lancashire cotton works, sought to protect apprentices working in cotton mills by requiring minimum levels of ventilation and cleanliness. In 1819 Robert Peel sponsored an Act that forbade children under the age of nine from being employed in cotton mills, limited the working hours of children and stipulated that they could not be made to work at night. Subsequent inquiries looked at conditions in mining and other industries that heavily employed children.

The effect of these and other Acts of Parliament was to recognise that pre-adolescent children had rights, and deserved protections, that could supersede the authority of their parents or the economic needs of their employers. They moved towards a recognition that childhood had a span, and a much longer one than had been previously acknowledged: puberty, 'at or about the fourteenth year', was when 'the body becomes more capable of enduring protracted labour [and] they cease to be under the complete control of their parents and guardians'. At the same time as opinion moved against the idea that children should be expected to work, it moved gradually instead towards the notion that children – all children – should be educated.

These changes in law and society did not emerge spontaneously. From the Enlightenment onward, the idea took hold that a child had its own properties and was more than just an adult-in-training. Something changed. And the change took place both in the realm of ideas and in the shape of day-to-day life.

The Child Is Father of the Man

JOHN LOCKE · JEAN-JACQUES ROUSSEAU ·
WILLIAM BLAKE · WILLIAM WORDSWORTH

An Essay Concerning Human Understanding;
Some Thoughts Concerning Education;
Emile; Songs of Innocence and of Experience;
Ode: Intimations of Immortality

THIS IS WHERE LOCKE AND ROUSSEAU AND THE Romantics come in. In his 1689 *An Essay Concerning Human Understanding*, John Locke (1632–1704) advanced what has become one of the most influential ideas, or you could say catchphrases, in history: that the human mind at birth is a *tabula rasa*, or 'blank slate'. It's an idea so powerful that you can still find Steven Pinker arguing against it* more than three hundred years later. Locke didn't in fact use the expression 'blank slate', taking instead a more contemporary image of the infant mind as 'white paper, void of all characters'. But the phrase (versions of which go back to Aristotle) has attached itself to his argument. Locke said that at birth human beings have no innate knowledge. What writes on this white paper, he argued, is experience of the world.

Here, if you like, is one pole of the nature/nurture debate. Though Locke didn't press the point explicitly, the idea of the mind

---

* Steven Pinker, *The Blank Slate: The Modern Denial of Human Nature* (Viking, 2002).

as a blank slate is one that has strong implications for religious tradition. A blank slate will not only be unmarked by a facility for differential calculus; it will be unmarked by the knowledge of good and evil. No innate knowledge: no original sin. And that – in terms not only of the nature of children, but also of its implications for what education might usefully do – signalled a momentous shift.

Locke advanced the implications of this idea in *Some Thoughts Concerning Education* (1693). Originally written as a set of letters to some friends who had solicited his advice on childrearing, its modest title belies the scale of its influence. If the human child really is a blank slate, then childhood experience, directed by a programme of education, is everything. He sets out his stall in Part One:

> Of all the men we meet with, nine parts of ten are what they are, good or evil, useful or not, by their education. 'Tis that which makes the great difference in mankind.

Accordingly, he sets about trying to show how a boy (it is mostly a boy – though he speaks out against the negative effects on girls of tight-laced bodices and foot binding) may be built into a virtuous and reasonable man.

Despite his great learning and his fervent enthusiasm for rationality, Locke spends the first of the three sections of the book on the question of how to encourage physical health. *Mens sana in corpore sano*. He was keen on cold baths, disapproved of children being coddled by wrapping them too warm in winter, and had firm if eccentric views on the wholesomeness of various fruits: children should be kept at all times from melons, peaches, 'most sorts of plums, and all sorts of grapes in England' ('very unwholesome'), though strawberries, cherries, gooseberries and currants could be eaten safely when ripe, and apples 'never did anybody hurt, that I know of, after October'.

He sums up his prescriptions thus: 'plenty of open air, exercise, and sleep, plain diet, no wine or strong drink, and very little or no physick, not too warm and strait clothing, especially the head and feet kept cold, and the feet often used to cold water, and exposed to wet'. Locke's Fungus-the-Bogeyman insistence on children benefiting from squelching around in wet shoes (he's very particular on this one) is one of the aspects of his treatise that has aged least well – but much of what he writes would sit quite comfortably in a modern childrearing manual. He may spend more time worrying about regular bowel movements (the prime concern of the first twenty-five pages of his book) than we do now, but Locke's idea that good health in childhood is of prime importance is one that has only deepened.

Locke's basic idea here was that *habit*, more than anything else, shaped a child's character. Rather than chastise a child with physical blows and force them into a particular set of socially appropriate behaviours, he said, you were better off nourishing the root than pruning the tree. If a child does what it's told because of fear of punishment, it will not internalise the principles underlying the rules – and, indeed, it'll develop a habit of dishonesty to avoid being punished for its transgressions.

Rather, you want to cultivate a child's willing assent to behaving well by modelling the behaviour you'd wish the child to reproduce, rewarding honesty and encouraging in the child as early as possible the habit of restraint: 'the great principle and foundation of all virtue and worth is placed in this: that a man is able to deny himself his own desires, cross his own inclinations, and purely follow what reason directs as best, though the appetite lean the other way'. Here, as we'll see, is where he differs from his great successor Rousseau.

Blank slate man or no, Locke didn't think we are all born identical. Rather, what is required of a child 'should be adapted to his capacity, and any way suited to the child's natural genius and constitution [...] God has stamped certain characters upon men's minds, which like their shapes, may perhaps be a little mended, but can hardly be totally altered and transformed into the contrary.' You find throughout Locke's essay a genial pragmatism. He acknowledges the basic disposition of children to delight: 'Recreation,' he says, 'is as necessary as labour or food.'

So when he comes to the question of what we'd now call education, i.e. book-learning, Locke upsets convention and (as he seems to think) surprises his audience by counselling against cramming children with the grammar of dead languages and abstract philosophy. A child's natural love of liberty and play, he argues, is the best ally in the quest for academic excellence. Reading, and learning, will be easier if it's fun: 'a child will learn three times as much when he is in tune, as he will with double the time and pains when he goes awkwardly or is dragged unwillingly to it.'

Why not teach the alphabet with toys? 'There may be dice and play-things,' he suggests, 'with the letters on them to teach children the alphabet by playing; and twenty other ways may be found, suitable to their particular tempers, to make this kind of learning a sport to them.' When it comes to children's literature, he prescribes

> some easy pleasant book, suited to his capacity [...] wherein the entertainment that he finds might draw him on, and reward his pains in reading [...] I think Aesop's Fables the best, which being stories apt to delight and entertain a child, may yet afford useful reflections to a grown man [...] If his Aesop has pictures in it, it will entertain him much the better, and encourage him to read.

He adds that some Bible stories – those with 'easy and plain moral rules', such as David and Goliath or Joseph and his brothers – are more suitable for children than others. Locke recognised that simple stories were most appealing to children – and, being a man of his time, it made sense to him that those stories would carry a moral. In 1703 he went on to prepare for publication an edition of *Aesop's Fables* of his own; and it was handsomely illustrated. Here we are again, almost, with Heracles and his lion; before the novel was even thought of, myths and fables were the introduction to narrative for children.

Locke established a way of thinking about childhood. Children had their own propensities and impulses, chief among them a natural love of freedom and an instinct for play, which needed to be acknowledged and celebrated rather than suppressed by force. The business of education was to work with the grain of those propensities. Locke knew that you catch more flies with honey than vinegar.

In the great one-two punch of early modern theories of childhood, the second boxing glove belonged to the French philosopher Jean-Jacques Rousseau. Rousseau's *Emile, or On Education* (1762) went into English the following year and has been incalculably influential on Western European thinking about childhood ever since. It's an unusual sort of book; not quite a how-to, and more a philosophical meditation dressed up as a *Bildungsroman*. In it, Rousseau imagines that he's the tutor to a child called Emile, whose life from childhood to young manhood the action of the book traces. 'This is,' he admits in his Preface, 'not so much a treatise on education as the visions of a dreamer with regard to education.'

Rousseau's view was that the mistake educators had always made was 'they are always looking for the man in the child, without considering what he is before he becomes a man'. The idea that children were merely defective or incomplete adults, adults-in-waiting who were to be forcibly chivvied to the finishing post, was to miss the distinctiveness of childhood itself.

That distinctiveness, in Rousseau's account, was what we would later call innocence. Children were not, as the Church had long contended, innately evil and in need of leading to salvation. Rather, they were neither good nor evil – the very concepts belonged to the sort of adult reasoning of which children are incapable: 'Wholly unmoral in his actions, he can do nothing morally wrong, and he deserves neither punishment nor reproof.'

Rousseau was in conscious dialogue with Locke. Where Locke exalted reason as the guiding light of a programme of education, Rousseau turned this aspect of his argument upside down:

'Reason with children' was Locke's chief maxim; it is in the height of fashion at present, and I hardly think it is justified by its results; those children who have been constantly reasoned with strike me as exceedingly silly. Of all man's faculties, reason, which is, so to speak, compounded of all the rest, is the last and choicest growth, and it is this you would use for the child's early training [...] You begin at the wrong end; you make the end the means.

For Rousseau, nature was what guided the proper growth of a child. The thing was to allow them to grow according to their own natures, and according to nature in general: 'The child's individual bent [...] must be thoroughly known before we can choose the fittest moral training.' The teacher should learn from the pupil how to teach them. In this, Rousseau resembles Locke more than the crude 'blank slate' reading of Locke would have it. The differences between them, it seems to me, are often in emphasis more than they are in kind. Both took the view that, as Wordsworth was later to put it, 'the Child is Father of the Man', both were broadly in favour of sparing the rod, and both asked educators to work with the grain of a child's nature rather than against it.

But where Locke wanted to encourage an adult consciousness (and specifically an adult conscience) in children as soon as possible – he wanted us to treat children as reasonable beings even before they were able to reason – Rousseau took a slightly different tack. He thought that, rather than immiserate the child in the hopes of making them happy as an adult, educators should grasp the present moment and encourage the children to thrive *as children* – a consideration all the more urgent given the infant mortality rates when he was writing: 'Of all the children who are born scarcely one half reach adolescence, and it is very likely your pupil will not live to be a man. What is to be thought, therefore, of that cruel education which sacrifices the present to an uncertain future, that burdens a child with all sorts of restrictions and begins by making him miserable, in order to prepare him for some far-off happiness which he may never enjoy?'

As Rousseau saw it, nurture – or civilisation – was where it all went wrong. 'Our wisdom is slavish prejudice, our customs consist in control, constraint, compulsion. Civilised man is born and dies a slave. The infant is bound up in swaddling clothes, the corpse is nailed down in his coffin. All his life long, man is imprisoned by our institutions.' Rousseau extolled, and somewhat romanticised, the wisdom of rural life against the unnatural affectations of urban elites.

Accordingly, and two hundred years ahead of his time, he was strongly in favour of breastfeeding and thought the widespread practice of swaddling infants was an abomination. He argued that a mother's unconditional love was vital to a child's proper development – that the maternal relationship was the primary one – and that stern or absent fathers were neglecting their natural duties too:

> Poverty, pressure of business, mistaken social prejudices, none of these can excuse a man from his duty, which is to support and educate his own children. If a man of any natural feeling neglects these sacred duties he will repent it with bitter tears and will never be comforted.

Mind you, Rousseau was on the face of it a do-as-I-say-not-as-I-do kind of guy. Notoriously, when young and penniless he bullied his mistress Thérèse into turning the children she bore him over to a foundling hospital rather than raise them himself (he got her mother to help pressure her into it because she 'feared the inconvenience of a brat'). Passages like the one I quote above could be, and often have been, adduced as evidence of Rousseau's hypocrisy. But I wonder if there's a kinder way to see it. He wrote those words a decade or so after abandoning his own children. Could they not rather be a token of his repenting that failure with bitter tears?

Rousseau associated childhood with happiness. Reason may have been necessary for human prospering, but it was also the source of all human misery: 'We pity the sufferings of childhood; we should pity ourselves; our worst sorrows are of our own making.' There's a voltage of feeling when he writes: 'Love childhood, indulge its sports, its pleasures, its delightful instincts. Who has not sometimes regretted that age when laughter was ever on the lips, and when the heart was ever at peace? Why rob these innocents of the joys which pass so quickly, of that precious gift which they cannot abuse?'

Here, then, is the fountainhead of much of how childhood came to be understood: as a time associated with happiness, innocence, freedom and the natural world; and as a rebuking antithesis to the corruptions of urban civilisation and the chiselling miseries and compromises of adult life. Like many theorists of childhood, Rousseau's way of thinking was blissfully uncompromised by much in the way of hands-on experience with actual children. This idea of childhood, then, as ever, served a rather adult need – and it's worth noticing, too, that it circles round to a Christian schema by the back door. Childhood is Eden; adulthood our fallen state.

In the decades after its publication, *Emile* spawned countless imitators. The scholar Peter Coveney[*] estimates that there were more than two hundred treatises on education published in England alone before the end of the eighteenth century; across the channel Madame de Staël reported in 1788 that 'everyone has adopted Rousseau's physical system of education'. And even if we don't now use *Emile* as a childcare manual (its injunctions on toughening kids up would no longer pass the safeguarding test),[†] its way of thinking about childhood is the air we all still breathe.

---

[*] Peter Coveney, *The Image of Childhood*.

[†] The eighteenth-century writer Thomas Day, for instance, an enthusiastic Rousseauian, adopted an eleven-year-old girl from an orphanage and attempted to bring her up in the approved manner – including pouring hot wax on her arms to inure her to physical pain. She didn't thank him for it.

Rousseau's idea of childhood was taken further by the writers of the Romantic era. Childhood innocence was sacralised. For Blake, reason was 'mind-forg'd manacles'; for Wordsworth, in his 'Ode: Intimations of Immortality from Recollections of Early Childhood' (1807), 'Heaven lies about us in our infancy!' The binary division of William Blake's most accessible work, *Songs of Innocence and of Experience* (1794), lodged in the Western mind.

Children came to be seen as closer to God, and more alive to beauty and wonder, than adults; the 'inner child' (as it was not then called) was not just the father to the man but the heart of his creative and moral faculties. One scholar reckoned Wordsworth's view to have had 'as powerful an influence on nineteenth-century ideas of childhood as Freud has had on present-day ones'.[*] And it was under the influence of such ideas that many of the social changes I describe above were taking place.

If children were more than just apprentice adults, if childhood was a distinctive and special category of existence, then the stage was set for the emergence of a distinctive literature that would speak to children. But it was one shaped at every turn by the hopes, nostalgia, moral schemes, class prejudices and sentimental imaginings of the adults who created it.

---

[*]   B. Garlitz, 'The Immortality Ode: Its Cultural Progeny,' *SEL Studies in English Literature 1500–1900*, vol. 6, iss. 4, 1966.

II

'COME, BOY, LEARN TO BE WISE'

John Amos Comenius · James Janeway · John Bunyan ·
Isaac Watts · John Newbery · Sarah Fielding ·
Anna Laetitia Barbauld · Sarah Trimmer · Martha Mary
Sherwood · Charles and Mary Lamb · Giambattista Basile ·
The Brothers Grimm · Charles Perrault ·
Hans Christian Andersen

MORALISTS AND FABULISTS

Lessons from the Puritans

JOHN AMOS COMENIUS · JAMES JANEWAY ·
JOHN BUNYAN · ISAAC WATTS · JOHN NEWBERY

*Orbis Sensualium Pictus; A Token for
Children; The Pilgrim's Progress; A Book for
Boys and Girls; Divine Songs; A Little Pretty
Pocket-Book; The Lilliputian Magazine;
The History of Little Goody Two-Shoes*

THE TUG OF WAR BETWEEN INSTRUCTION AND DELIGHT in children's literature goes right back to the very beginning. The dawning of the so-called Golden Age, smackbang in the middle of the nineteenth century, with *Alice's Adventures in Wonderland*, *Tom Brown's School Days* and *The Water-Babies*, set children's writing on a path to modernity. But it didn't come from nowhere, and it was preceded by two distinct traditions that, in varying ways, it responded to or assimilated. The first of these traditions was instructive; the second narrative. And it's to the first that what's generally described as the world's first children's book belongs.

Orbis Sensualium Pictus (1658) is a bit like an illustrated encyclopaedia. The Enlightenment was just getting under way, Knowing Things was in fashion, and its author, a Moravian educationalist called John Amos Comenius (1592–1670), saw no reason children shouldn't be part of it. Originally published in German and Latin, it became popular throughout Europe and was in English* within a year of its original German publication: 'It is a little book, as you see, and no great bulk, yet a brief of the whole World, and a whole language: *full of Pictures, Nomenclatures, and Descriptions of things.*'

Comenius was not kidding about the whole world: *Orbis Pictus* is a wildly ambitious omnium-gatherum, which can still be read with pleasure and curiosity, covering everything from animal noises (we learn that 'the Lamb blaiteth', 'the Goose gagleth', 'the Duck quaketh', 'the Bear grumbleth', 'the Chicken peepeth' and, mindful perhaps of all this good eating nearby, 'the Dog grinneth') to comparative religion.

Here, in true Enlightenment style, is an attempt to gather information about the world about us and organise it into categories ('Flying Vermin' are differentiated from 'Crawling Vermin', for instance, and freshwater from marine fish). The reader learns about animals, vegetables, minerals and natural processes, and then about Man – inside and out. There's even an agreeable chapter on 'Deformed and Monstrous People', illustrated by pictures of a giant, a dwarf, 'One with two Bodies' and 'One with two Heads' – the last two categories, possibly for reasons of space, being combined into one very amusing illustration. Our students are invited to consider the 'jolt-headed', the 'goggle-eyed', the 'blubber-lipped' and the 'wry-necked' among us with the dispassionate eye of the scientist.†

In due course Comenius turns to Man's social organisation and effect on his environment, from gardening and agriculture to fishing and hunting to butchery and brewing. Different shops,

---

* Translated by Charles Hoole as *Visible World, or a Picture and Nomenclature of all the chief Things that are in the world, and of Men's Employments therein.*

† You could see this material as presaging the weird and wonderful gallimaufry of human extremity to be found in the annual *Guinness World Records* books, still a perennial Christmas bestseller.

domestic spaces and professions are quite charmingly described in simple language. In a reflexive twist, it even offers introductions to the history of the written word ('The Ancients writ in Tables done over with wax, with a brazen Poitrel, with the sharp end, whereof Letters were engraved, and rubbed out again with the broad end'), paper-making, printing and bookselling. It all reminds me, just a little, of the educational excursions 'through the Round Window' in the *Play School* of my own childhood.

Like that *Play School* slot, its educative project is advanced by the appeal to pleasure and curiosity. Its preface argues that the key to getting knowledge of the world into children's heads is to make it concretely available to their senses – 'not obscure, or confused, but apparent, distinct, and articulate, as the Fingers on the Hands. The ground of this business is that *sensual objects be rightly presented to the senses*. I say, and say it again loud, that this last is the foundation of all the rest.'

Eye-catching pictures are accompanied by parallel descriptions in Latin and the reader's own vernacular, in order to associate these images and words firmly together: not 'torment to be in the School, but dainty-fare'. Its 'Symbolical Alphabet' – associating letter-shapes and letter-sounds with images – will help children learn to read without 'troublesome torture of wits'. There are the stirrings, here, of a sort of intuitive cognitive science.

But *Orbis Pictus* also, in form and content, evinces a sense of the structures and hierarchy into which the child is expected to fit. It is bookended by images of a master and his pupil standing in the countryside outside a city. The opening image is headed 'The Invitation', and the text begins with the master's words: 'Come, boy, learn to be wise.' The envoi is marked 'The Close': the same child stands in the countryside outside a city. His teacher is gesticulating with one hand. It looks now as if he might not be beginning a lecture so much as offering one last word of advice to his charge before the boy sets off on a journey. Comenius intends to send a child on the journey from childhood to adulthood, and from foolishness to wisdom.

The closing words of the book are addressed to the child reader:

Thus thou hast seen in short, all things that can be shewed, and hast learned the chief words of the English and Latin Tongue.

Go on now and read other good Books diligently, and thou shalt become learned, wise, and godly.

Remember these things; fear God, and call upon him, that he may bestow upon thee the Spirit of Wisdom.

Farewell.

There's a touching tenderness to the image Comenius presents of a child's proper place and the road to adulthood, but the watchwords are conventional: piety, labour, chastisement, reverence and service; all under the aegis of duty to parents and, above them, duty to God and gratitude for His grace. Where Comenius is forward-looking is in tipping his floppy seventeenth-century hat to the pleasure principle. Not all who followed, particularly not the English writers in the century or two after, did. In the unimprovable formula of another critic, children's literature through most of the seventeenth and eighteenth centuries was dominated by 'Calvinists of unrelenting severity'.[*]

Severest of the lot was the Puritan hellfire preacher James Janeway (1636–1674) – now forgotten by all but scholars of this sort of thing, but rivalled only by Bunyan and the Bible for popularity in his own era. His best-known work, *A Token for Children: Being an exact account of the conversion, holy and exemplary lives, and joyful deaths of several young children. In two parts* (1671) was going into edition after edition hundreds of years after his death. John Wesley published an edited and updated version of it in the following century, and, in the US, that notorious fun-sponge Cotton Mather produced a home-grown knock-off called *A Token for the Children of New England.*

---

[*]   Percy Muir, *English Children's Books 1600–1900* (Batsford, 1985).

Janeway's *A Token* is your basic snuff-fiction anthology: thirteen supposedly true stories of piteous infants rolling a seven and going gladly, but painfully, to their Maker. Its purpose was not to entertain so much as to scare the willies out of its young audience, taking a shock-and-awe approach to the business of converting them to Janeway's austere Puritan creed. 'Sarah Howley' dies before she turns ten, but finds time to warn her schoolmates: 'O make use of time to get Christ for your souls; spend no time in running up and down in playing.'

The stories all follow a similar pattern: conversion, astounding protestations of faith, copious tears and self-reproach, and a peaceful death. Janeway lends them authenticity by including dates, names and details of their parents' employment or circumstances, and often descriptions of how the stories came to him. He boasts in his first preface that 'several passages are taken *verbatim* in writing from their dying lips'. But what's absent, however they are differentiated in their labelling, is any real novelistic detail that makes the children sound or seem like human children: they are paragons, exemplars, mash-ups of Bible verses and pious sayings. Writing for children, in this account of it, is designed to affect rather than to reflect its audience.

Janeway prefaced it with a note 'To Parents, School Masters & School Mistresses, or Any concerned with the Education of Children' (as with Comenius, whose book comes with a preface addressed to adults, children were the secondary addressees) making clear what was at stake:

> Remember, the devil is at work hard, wicked ones are industrious; and corrupt nature is a rugged, knotty piece to hew [...] Is not the duty clear? And dare you neglect so direct a command? Are the souls of your children of no value? Are you willing that they should be brands of Hell?

He moves on to address his child readers – 'my dear lambs' –in a second preface:

How art thou affected, poor Child, in the Reading of this Book?
Have you shed ever a tear since you begun reading? Have you
been by your self upon your knees; and begging that God would
make you like these blessed Children? or are you as you use to be,
as careless & foolish and disobedient and wicked as ever?

If this sounds hair-raising, it was. But if, as Janeway undoubtedly
did, you believe children are born in sin and will burn in hell if
they die without the mercy of their redeemer, you can be expected
to set about the matter with some urgency. As he tells his young
readers, 'I fain would do what I can possibly to keep thee from
falling into everlasting fire.'

Janeway connects, as a long line of successors were to do, the
hierarchy of the family with heaven's authority. The devil, he says,
is 'father' to naughty children, and he warns his readers that 'O!
Hell is a terrible place; that is worse a thousand times than whipping. God's anger is worse than your father's anger.' Naughtiness,
in Janeway's account, consists of most of the things that we would
now think of as natural and enjoyable childhood activities ('play';
'idleness'; 'to run up and down upon the Lord's Day') and many
things (fibbing, bad language and truancy) that in later children's
writing came to be winked at as minor sins or positively celebrated.

Janeway himself lived fast and died young. When the government tried to get England's post-Reformation religious turbulence
under control with the 1662 Act of Uniformity – imposing the new
Book of Common Prayer on the church – Janeway was one of the
refuseniks, kicked out in the so-called 'Great Ejection'. He set up
shop as a nonconformist preacher in east London, attracting so huge
a congregation that it has been claimed the Church, un-Christianly,
put out a hit on him. (I can't find a reliable source for the claim
that in one of two attempts on his life he was shot through the hat,
but I pass it on because the image is too good to waste.) Certainly,
it's a matter of record that his meeting house in Rotherhithe was
burned to the ground. He died of tuberculosis in 1674.

His contemporary John Bunyan (1628–1688) was a more attractive figure. His *The Pilgrim's Progress* (1678) was to become another constant in early modern children's reading, and that it has survived longer in the canon than Janeway speaks to its narrative satisfactions. Bunyan's introduction to the first edition says he produced the work 'mine own self to gratify' and 'to divert myself': having fun was a feature of its make-up.

It's a good story, following its protagonist Christian's journey from his unfortunately named hometown 'The City of Destruction' to the 'Celestial City' via all sorts of strange and wonderful encounters. Its curious and rather enchanting quest narrative dramatises the theological message. Where Janeway offered something purporting to be reportage, Bunyan was writing a medieval-style allegory in dream-vision form, whose 'dark and cloudy words [...] do but hold / The truth, as cabinets enclose the gold'. He knows that stories are more memorable when filled with 'what doth our imaginations please', and in his defence of its approach he points out that fowlers, in order to catch birds, will 'pipe and whistle', and that some fish need to be tickled to be caught.

Even if it was to become a staple of nursery bookshelves, though, Bunyan didn't write *The Pilgrim's Progress* as a children's book. He made a direct contribution to children's literature in 1686, however, in the form of *A Book for Boys and Girls, or, Country-rhimes for children*. The verse introduction gives you a sense not only of his didactic project but of his method – and how the now-clichéd tagline 'for children of all ages' really did indicate how blurry the distinction between childhood and adulthood was.

He announces that the book's 'proper Subject' is 'Boys and Girls of all Sorts and Degrees / From those of age to Children on the Knees', before conceding that 'we now have Boys with Beards, and Girls that be / Big as old Women, wanting Gravity'. That is to say: childhood is a state of mind, and the untrained or childish soul can be found in a fully grown (and, perhaps, uneducated or un-evangelised) body.

After an instructional section on spelling and grammar, the book consists of a series of allegorically minded rhymed verses on a range of subjects, beginning with the Ten Commandments in heroic couplets ('From Fornication keep thy body clean / Thou shalt not steal, though thou be very mean') and moving on through such curios as 'Meditations Upon An Egg', 'Of the Boy and Butter Fly', 'Upon the Sight of a Pound of Candles falling to the Ground', 'Upon the Kackling of a Hen', and 'Upon a stinking Breath'.

Even as Bunyan allegorises, though, there are glimmerings of actuality; glimpses of what childhood was in the real world. That boy chasing a butterfly, for all that he stands as a symbol of the foolish love for worldly fripperies, is instinct with human detail: 'He hollo's, runs, and cries out here Boys, here, / Nor doth he Brambles or the Nettles fear: / He stumbles at the Mole-Hills, up he gets, / And runs again'. A boy with 'a Paper full' of plums is seen pulling them out of their wrapping 'with joy'. Bunyan's allegorical imagination lights on ordinary objects, the furniture of his world – a whipping-top, a penny loaf, the unwound watch that a boy has inherited from his father. The poem on a swallow opens: 'This pretty bird, oh! How he flies and sings!' Even when pleasure and irresponsibility in childhood is described to serve a didactic purpose, the life of it peeps through.

Writing in the same evangelical vein was Isaac Watts (1674–1748), whose *Divine Songs Attempted in Easy Language for the Use of Children* (1715) was a collection of pious poems seeking to bridge the gap between the jangle of the nursery rhyme and the sonorities of the hymnal. It hoped to 'furnish [children's] memories and beautify their Souls'. It's these days best known for being spoofed by Lewis Carroll in *Alice's Adventures in Wonderland*.

That Watts was so obvious a target for mockery in the middle of the nineteenth century was a compliment of sorts: indicative of how universal these poems still were in the Victorian nursery and schoolroom, at the same time as hinting that, by then, readers might be open to giggling at their fustiness. Carroll wasn't the only one to do so. Dickens has a schoolmaster quote Watts sententiously in *David Copperfield* (1850), and in *Moby-Dick* (1851) a pious little old lady goes round the *Pequod* before it sails leaving copies of Watts on the sailors' bunks in the hopes of weaning them off vulgar sea-shanties.

It was towards the middle of the eighteenth century that the idea children should enjoy what they read rather than being corrected by it was gaining a real foothold. John Newbery (1713–1767) is sometimes called 'The Father of Children's Literature'. He was an entrepreneurial publisher who spotted a gap in the market and piled in to exploit it. Over the course of a nearly thirty-year career he produced more than a hundred children's books in all sorts of genres, starting to shape the very idea of children's writing as a separate domain; and he launched, in *The Lilliputian Magazine* (first published 1751), the first children's periodical. When the world's first prize for children's literature was established in 1922, it was named for him. The Newbery Medal continues to be awarded to this day.

His career in children's publishing started with 1744's *A Little Pretty Pocket-Book*. It came with quite the subtitle: 'Intended for the Instruction and Amusement of Little Master Tommy and Pretty Miss Polly: With Two Letters from Jack the Giant-Killer; as also A Ball and Pincushion; the Use of which will infallibly make Tommy a good Boy and Polly a good Girl. To which is added, A Little Song-Book, being a new Attempt to teach children the Use of the English Alphabet, by way of Diversion'.

Facing the title page is an engraved frontispiece showing a well-to-do woman sitting in a comfortable room with a fireplace. Standing in front of her chair are two children, a periwigged boy in a smart little suit and a slightly older girl in a bell-like dress, both apparently attending to her with animated interest. The lady's right hand rests on an open book on her lap; her left is raised in gesticulation. The motto below reads: '*Delectando Monemus*', which is glossed: 'Instruction With Delight.'

It really is a pocket-book. It sits very comfortably in the palm of your hand, not much bigger than two or three inches by four, and it's a properly loveable object. It had, in its original edition, a brightly coloured cover, and almost every page is livened by attractive simple woodcut pictures. This very Lockean principle, that instruction and delight, or teaching and 'diversion', go together, runs through the production. There's even a pointed shout-out to 'the great Mr Locke', from whom these precepts are lifted.

Only once several pages have been spent on setting out the programme for the benefits of the parents, though, does the book turn to address its primary audience. There follow two letters (all but identical in wording; the first to Tommy, the second to Polly) from Jack the Giant-Killer, in which the noted mythological mass-murderer addresses little Tommy and little Polly with warm affection. Those gimmicky free gifts of the ball and the pincushion – which, perhaps, we could see as ancestors of the cover-mounted toys on children's magazines – are not just for play, either.

As the letter from Jack tells the children, these balls and pincushions are for keeping score: 'I have [...] sent you a Ball; the one Side of which is Red, the other Black, and with it ten Pins; and I must insist upon making this Bargain, that your Nurse may hang up the Ball by the String to it, and for every good Action you do, a Pin shall be stuck on the Red Side, and for every bad Action a Pin shall be stuck on the Black Side. And when by doing good and pretty Things you have got all the ten Pins on the Red Side, then I will send you a Penny [...] But if ever the Pins be all found on the Black Side of the Ball, then I will send a Rod, and you shall be whipt'. He signs off; 'Your Friend, JACK the GIANT-KILLER.'

Carrot and stick, then. Prefaces all dispensed with, we're into the fun stuff. First there's a great catalogue of children's games and pastimes, starting with 'Chuck-Farthing' and moving on through kite-flying, dancing round the maypole, shuttlecock, thread-the-needle, leapfrog, tip-cat, birds-nesting, blind-man's buff, peg-farthing, hop-step-and-jump, marbles, cricket, fishing, and any number of others, many of them still recognisable today. Among its many distinctions, the *Little Pretty Pocket-Book* contains the first mention of 'Base-ball' in the English language.

The allegorical habit is still strong: each game is illustrated with a woodcut and a rhyming quatrain pointing up the 'moral' or 'rule of life' it illustrates. There's a learn-the-alphabet section ('Great A, B and C, / And tumble-down D, / The cat's a blind buff, / and she cannot see'), a sequence of fables (one, slightly alarmingly, has a stork getting 'trepann'd by a crane' after being foolish enough to try to make friends with it), pretty pictures of children doing virtuous things, a list of proverbs and a weirdly exact 'One Hundred and Sixty three Rules for the Behaviour of Children'. 'Smell not of thy Meat, nor put it to thy Nose,' it advises its young audience. 'Throw not any Thing under the Table.' (I wish my own youngest child would take such advice.) It also states a principle that was to have a long afterlife: 'Among Superiours speak not until thou art spoken to, and bidden to speak.'

Generically speaking, then, *A Little Pretty Pocket-Book* is a wonderful mess: part etiquette manual, part light verse anthology, part songbook, part picture book, part commonplace book – a ragbag such as you might find in a children's comic annual in the present day, and a document that abundantly follows its stated intention to educate through play. More than that, there's a sense in its tone of address of how intimate and affectionate parents could be with their children. Is the lady in the frontispiece Nurse, or Mother? The preface suggests it could be either. The teasing addresses from Jack the Giant-Killer have a playful quality, and it affirms that good behaviour will be rewarded not just in heaven but in this world – 'This Character, my Dear, has made every Body Love you'. Home-fires, not the fires of hell.

It was a roaring success – not only or even especially, as far as we know, with the children who were encouraged to read it, but with the adults who were buying it. Newbery published more and more into the market, and he made the books attractive: 'Neatly

Bound, Gilt and Glaz'd'. By the 1760 tenth edition (the earliest that survives, according to the British Library) it was a thriving retail space. The closing endpapers of the book contain advertisements for further reading, as '*printed for and sold by* John Newbery, at the Bible and Sun *in* St. Paul's Church-Yard.'

They included *The Royal Battledore; or, First Book for Children* – an ABC 'laid down in a plain, easy and entertaining manner, in order to Induce Children to learn their Letters'; *The Royal Primer* ('an Easy and pleasant guide to the Art of Reading'); an educational game-set – 'A Set of Fifty-Six Squares'; spelling books; picture books of beasts and birds ('To which is added, the History of little *Tom Trip* himself, of his Dog *Jouler*, and of *Woglog*, the Giant'); *Food for the Mind; or, a new Riddle Book*; two different poetry volumes – *A Collection of Pretty Poems, for the Amusement of Children Three Foot high,* and the indispensable sequel *A Collection of Pretty Poems, for the Amusement of Children Six Foot high*; a volume containing 'fables in verse' by one Abraham Aesop *Esq*, with additional fables in verse and prose apparently contributed by the aforementioned Woglog the Great Giant; books of improving maxims; a collection of 'Letters on the most common, as well as important Occasions in Life' (anthologising everyone from Cicero to Dryden); not to mention an illustrated and annotated abridgement of the Bible 'illustrated with notes and adorned with Cuts, for the Use of Children'.

That lively salmagundi of material is full of whimsical characters, and emphasises illustrations, pretty bindings and 'amusement'; yet at the same time it promises homiletics, education in letters and morals. That gives you a sense of how children's books were conceived; depending on how you looked at them, they were learning under the cover of play or they were play under the cover of learning. A spoonful of sugar helped the medicine go down. Newbery knew all about that too: he combined his publishing business with a side-hustle selling patent medicines, and he was not shy about exploiting potential synergies by advertising them in the backs of his books.

The endpapers of *The History of Little Goody Two-Shoes* (1765), a sentimental fable of the progress of its orphan heroine Margery Meanwell, listed no fewer than ten pills and potions, and there were even product placements in the text. Its tragic story is kicked off by the non-availability of one of the medicines advertised in the back. 'Care and Discontent shortened the Days of Little *Margery's* Father,' opens the first chapter. 'He was forced from his Family, and seized with a violent Fever in a Place where Dr. *James's* Powder was not to be had, and where he died miserably.' Fortunately, Little Goody Two-Shoes makes out all right without the help of Dr James's powder. She goes from childhood destitution to adult eminence and pious death, accruing along the way a long roll of good works done and homilies pronounced (the death of a dormouse is the occasion to deliver 'a Lecture on the Uncertainty of Life, and the Necessity of always being prepared for Death'). She plants free potatoes for all who want them, gives poor parishioners the price of a loaf for coming to church, and offers financial incentives to promote the honourable state of matrimony. She's a one-woman National Conservative nudge unit. After her death a stone in the local churchyard is, we're told, 'ever bathed in tears' because of the incessant weeping of the poor when they pass by it.

She gets her nickname ('Goody' is short for 'goodwife' – an old-fashioned form of address, something like 'Missy'), by the way, when a kindly benefactor buys her a pair of shoes. After her father goes to the grave and her mother dies of a broken heart, Margery and her brother are destitute and own only three shoes between them: 'Tommy had two Shoes, but Margery had but one.' That nickname survives in playground taunts long after the book that popularised it has fallen into obscurity.

Respectable Ladies

SARAH FIELDING · ANNA LAETITIA BARBAULD · SARAH TRIMMER

The Governess; Lessons for Children; Hymns in Prose; Evenings at Home; Fabulous Histories; The Ladder of Learning

AFTER NEWBERY, THE EVANGELICAL LINE CONTINUED through the eighteenth century with a whole run of authors who produced improving texts and who tended to be known by the austerely respectable sobriquet 'Mrs' rather than their first names: Mrs Trimmer, Mrs Barbauld, Mrs Sherwood and Mrs Fielding. The latter of these was notable for giving us the first novel written for children, and the first entry in what was to become a major genre of English children's fiction, the boarding school story.

Sarah Fielding's *The Governess; or, the Little Female Academy* (1749) tells the story of the widowed Mrs Teachum, who after her own two children drop dead of a fever and her fortune is lost to the 'unforeseen breaking of a banker' makes ends meet by setting up as a schoolmistress. 'About forty years old, tall and genteel in her person, though somewhat inclined to fat', she takes in nine pupils, all but one of them under twelve.

The Governess is, like other early novels, a higgledy-piggledy and hybrid work – not so much a continuous third-person narrative as a pre-teen *Decameron*: a collection of tales set in a frame story. It begins with a fantastic scrap, when the girls fight over a basket of apples: 'they fell to pulling of caps, tearing of hair, and dragging the clothes off one another's backs; though they did not so much strike, as endeavour to scratch and pinch their enemies'. The sulks and recriminations are realistically described; as is the mumbled apology: 'Miss Sukey did indeed stammer out some words, which implied a confession of her fault; but they were spoke so low as they could hardly be heard.'

What does *The Governess* tell us about eighteenth-century childhood? It is a reminder, above all, of how big a part bereavement could be expected to play in it. The deaths in *A Token for Children* were a conventional aspect of its devotional programme; it's a collection of saints' lives in all but name. Here, though, they are a bit closer to realism. Before it even starts, Mrs Teachum has lost her husband and two children to illness. Sukey's mother died when she was too young to remember. Dolly lost a beloved sister 'just before I came to school', as did Betty. Jenny Peace, when she tells her story, describes matter-of-factly how her father died when she was one, and only one of her five siblings survived beyond their first year.

The religious and instructional tradition continued in the work of Anna Laetitia Barbauld (1743–1825), a hugely popular writer for adults in her own age who has fallen dramatically out of fashion since her death. Her children's books were written, originally, for her son (not her biological son: she persuaded her brother to let her adopt one of his after despairing of having children herself).*

Her first such books were *Lessons for Children*, a series of reading primers published from 1778 onwards: 'It was found that, amidst the multitude of books professedly written for children, there is not one adapted to the comprehension of a child from two to three years old.' She insisted on 'good paper, a clear and large type, and large spaces', and did so on the warrant not of an idea of children

---

* The Barbauld marriage was not a huge success. In later life her husband went off his onion, was prone to fits of 'insane fury' and tried to stab her to death. She jumped out of a window to escape. In 1808 he drowned himself.

but the experience of a real one: only those 'who have actually taught young children, can be sensible how necessary these assistances are'. She insisted that writing for children mattered: 'The task is humble, but not mean; for, to lay the first stone of a noble building, and to plant the first idea in a human mind can be no dishonour to any hand.'*

There's charm in the way she goes about it: the lessons are offered in the form of a dialogue between mother and son. 'Come hither, Charles,' the first book begins, 'come to mamma. Make haste. Sit in mamma's lap. Now read your book. Where is the pin to point with? Here is a pin. Do not tear the book. Only bad boys tear books…' There's a touch, I fancy, of Joyce Grenfell in there. As the texts continue, the sentences become more complicated. Natural objects, vocabulary items, the way things work; they're all introduced not in dry lists but as part of a conversation. Glow-worms, ladybirds, the point of a compass, the carnivorous predilections of cats, the names of carpentry tools. It's at once old-fashioned, and recognisable as the antecedent of any number of board books for toddlers to this day. *Hymns in Prose for Children* (1781), and the co-written short-story collections that followed (*Evenings at Home: Or, the Juvenile Budget Opened*, published between 1792 and 1796) all aim to meet the child reader on his or her level. Though some contemporaries cavilled at a writer of Barbauld's reputation spending her energies on writing for children – a form of snobbery that has never gone away – others were inspired by her example. Sarah Trimmer (1741–1810) was one such. She was an educational philanthropist, who in addition to educating her own twelve (twelve!) children set up a Sunday school for poor children in Brentford in 1786. She captured the zeitgeist of benign class condescension – hoping to encourage cleanliness, godliness and literacy in working-class children and equip them for respectable lives in service.

---

* Mrs Barbauld, you may notice from this, was another student of Locke.

Her *Fabulous Histories, Designed for the Instruction of Children Respecting their Treatment of Animals* (1786) stayed in print for more than a century, and anticipated the association of childhood with anthropomorphic animals. It describes the relationship between the Benson children Harriet and Frederick, and a family of robins (Robin, Dicky, Pecksy and Flapsy are the names of the fledglings) that set up home in their garden. The human and avian households present two parallel models of benevolent parenting. Her *The Ladder of Learning* (1789) (subtitled 'A Select Collection of Fables; consisting of words of one, two and three syllables; with original morals') is an illustrated series of beast fables with morals, many taken from the Aesopic tradition. It follows Barbauld's pattern of Christianised practical pedagogy, right down to the syllable-counting. The first part of the book confines itself to one-syllable words, the second to two, and the third 'admitting but very few that exceed Three Syllables'. Here, in its way, is the distant ancestor of *Biff, Chip and Kipper.*

For all her embrace of fable and allegory, though, Mrs Trimmer was vocal in her disapproval of fairytales. Charles Perrault, whose *Tales and Stories of the Past with Morals, or Tales of Mother Goose* went into English in 1729, and *The Arabian Nights* (1706) were becoming general even as Mrs Trimmer and co were writing strait-laced stories of Christian virtue. Of *course* she didn't trust them. A world in which you could go from pauper to prince by luck or magic was not one whose values accorded with what Weber called the Protestant work ethic.

Rectitude and Romanticism

MARTHA MARY SHERWOOD ·
CHARLES AND MARY LAMB

*The History of Little Henry and his
Bearer; The History of the Fairchild
Family; Tales from Shakespeare*

EVANGELICAL MORALISTS AND THE FAIRYTALE merchants, nevertheless, coexisted in the literary ecosystem for decades, and their two worldviews tangle in the genre to this day. Still, at this stage, both traditions were talking slightly past children rather than directly to them. The moralists aimed to idealise and reproach children; and fairytales may have appealed to children, but they weren't necessarily *about* them.

As the nineteenth century dawned, literature for children aimed at evoking – as Roger Lancelyn Green put it – 'the child of fact' rather than 'the child of wishful thinking' was still just barely glimmering on the horizon.[*] The best-selling work of Mary Martha Sherwood (1775–1851) is one of the most notorious inheritors of the Janeway line of doing things.

Martha Mary Butt, whose vicar father was at one point chaplain-in-ordinary to George III, learned her severity young. Looking back on her childhood, for instance, she described without any apparent ill feeling having spent seven years or so locked into a set of stocks:

---

[*] Roger Lancelyn Green, *Tellers of Tales*.

It was the fashion then for children to wear iron collars round the neck, with back-boards strapped over the shoulders. To one of these I was subjected from my sixth to my thirteenth year. I generally did all my lessons standing in stocks, with this same collar round my neck; it was put on in the morning, and seldom taken off till late in the evening… And yet I was a very happy child, and when relieved from my collars I not unseldom manifested my delight by starting from our hall-door and taking a run for half a mile through the woods.*

I daresay most of us would 'not unseldom' bolt off into the woods at the end of a school day if we had spent it strapped into a medieval torture device, but *autres temps, autres mœurs*.

She married a cousin, Henry Sherwood, when she was in her mid-twenties and they had a daughter before, in 1805, his military career took the family to India. Mrs Sherwood had to leave her child, Mary Henrietta, back in England with her mother. Their son Henry, with whom she had been pregnant on the voyage to India, died of whooping cough when he was two – and not long afterwards Mrs Sherwood got God, and in a big way. She went on to have another five children, as well as adopting foundlings in India and starting an orphanage there.

Can it be coincidence that Henry was the name of the protagonist of her breakthrough book, *The History of Little Henry and his Bearer* (1814)? It's a contribution to the popular evangelical genre sometimes called the 'Obituary Tract' – in which, as we've seen, a pious tot goes gratefully to Jesus leaving all around moved and reproached by his precocious holiness. But within that paradigm – and here is where she starts to move things forward – there's more going on with little Henry.

---

* Quoted in Mary Palgrave's introduction to a 1931 edition of *The Fairchild Family*.

The poor mite, born at Dinapore in eastern India, is briskly orphaned on the first page and taken in by a philanthropic lady of the sort whose charitable engagement ends with the writing of a cheque. She takes him in to her large pukka house, instructs her servants to give him whatever he needs, and 'would not afterwards suffer Henry to give her the least trouble'.

Henry is, instead, brought up by a native bearer called Boosy, who 'attended him night and day, warmed his pap, rocked his cot, dressed and undressed and washed him, and did every thing for him as tenderly as if he had been his own child'. Henry doesn't speak English, but 'he could talk with Boosy in *his* language as fast as possible; and he knew every word, good or bad, which the natives spoke. He used to sit in the *verandah* between his bearer's knees, and chew *paun*, and eat *bazar* sweetmeats'. The grand lady having neglected his religious education, Henry at the age of five had conceived the idea (from observing Boosy and remembering his mother's trips to church) that there were 'a great many Gods, and that the God that his Mamma went to pray to at Dinapore was no better than the Gods of wood, and stone, and clay, which his bearer worshipped'. Henry's loving relationship with Boosy – tenderly if sentimentally evoked – has turned him into an opium-chewing little pagan.[*]

The pivot comes when a clergyman's daughter from England comes to stay, equipped with 'a box of Bibles, and some pretty little children's books and pictures'. Gradually winning Henry's trust, she tries to give him the basics of Christian instruction, declaring that there is only one true God, and warning of the 'dreadful hell, prepared for those who die in their sins'. His first reaction is indignation, but she wins him to monotheism when she takes 'one of the Hindoo Gods made of baked earth' and throws it on the floor

---

[*]   Mrs Sherwood glosses paun as 'an intoxicating mixture of opium & sugar etc'. The active ingredient of paan, which is still widely chewed today, is actually betel nut rather than opium, though.

to shatter into 'an hundred pieces': 'Henry, what can this God do for you? It cannot help itself. Call to it, and ask it to get up. You see, it cannot move.'

Henry is brought to God – and made crushingly conscious of being steeped in sin, and the eternal death that is its reward. He becomes pious, charitable, modest, humble and studious. The very recognisably natural child – devoted to Boosy, potty-mouthed, shy, a little naughty, fond of sweets – turns into a little evangelist. Henry's adoptive mamma is later to complain that their visitor has 'made a Methodist, a downright canting Methodist, of the boy'. Yet Henry's dearest companion is still Boosy. I don't think it's too much to say that Mrs Sherwood's doctrinal rectitude tugs, at times, against her instincts as a novelist.

The book's best, its most living, passages aren't its catechistic exchanges and its solemn scriptural precepts (she quotes chapter and verse – literally) but its descriptions of Indian life and landscape. There's a lovely mention of the 'creaking of the *punkah* and the guggling of the water in the *hookah*', and out in the open air:

On their left-hand was the broad stream of the Ganges winding round the curved shore, till it was lost behind the *Raja-mehal* hills. The *budgerow,* gayly painted, was fastened to the shore just below them […]. Before them, and on their right hand, was a beautiful country, abounding with corn-fields, *topes* of trees, thatched cottages with their little bamboo porches, plantain and palm trees; beyond which the *Raja-mehal* hills were seen, some bare to their summits, and others covered with *jungle,* which even now affords a shelter to tigers, rhinoceroses, and wild hogs.

To an English reader the story would have the attractive quality of the exotic. To children in India – Sherwood's calling to missionary work had her set up schools there – they would be relatable in a way that books set in England might not.

In due course the machinery of the genre cranks into action. Henry is taken ill and turns up his toes, at the age of eight, amid a flurry of damp-eyed biblical quotations. His last thoughts are prayers for the conversion of Boosy – and, though readings from the Bible in Hindi while the boy was healthy didn't do it, emotional blackmail gets there in the end. After Henry is gone, Boosy joins the household of a pious Mr Smith, 'renounced *cast*, and declared himself a Christian'. The book went into seven languages and remained in print for most of the nineteenth century. My hunch is that it's the human sympathy in the characterisation of Henry's relationship with Boosy, and the novelistic touches in the descriptions of India, rather than the formal piety, that gave it its enduring appeal.

Yet the work for which Mrs Sherwood is now most remembered, and most pilloried, came after the family's return to Britain in 1816: *The History of the Fairchild Family* (1818).* Its distinguishing virtues are its unflinching piety and its surprisingly high body count. The day-to-day adventures of an English family are presented as lessons in the perils of sin and the necessity of repentance. Divine and parental authority are echoes of one another: 'I stand,' Mr Fairchild says at one point, 'in the place of God to you, whilst you are a child.'

The godly and respectable Mr and Mrs Fairchild live in a house in the country with a pleasant garden. They have three children between the ages of nine and six (Lucy, Emily and Henry), two servants (Betty and John) and neighbours with Bunyanesque names such as Friendly, Trueman, Goodwill, Noble and Cutshorter. Each chapter closes with a prayer and a hymn appropriate to the story that precedes it, and the Fairchild children are all prone to saying things like: 'Oh! I wish I could love the Lord Jesus Christ more

----

*   The full title lets you know plainly what it's about: *The History of the Fairchild Family, or, The Child's Manual; being a collection of stories calculated to shew the importance and effects of a religious education.*

than I do; but my wicked heart will not let me.' Punishment is frequent and severe. Sometimes it comes from a parent: when Henry is falling behind in his Latin prep, for instance, Mr Fairchild 'took a small horse-whip, and, making John hold him, he flogged him well, and sent him to bed'. Sometimes it comes from the Almighty. The prideful and disobedient Miss Augusta Noble (apple-thief, mocker of God, all-round show-off) is burned to death: 'a warning to all children how they presume to disobey their parents'. Emily nearly dies just from stealing 'damascenes'* – she spills juice on herself, washes her frock to cover it up, puts it on wet and gets a fever as a result.

The most notorious episode comes in 'Story on the Sixth Commandment'. Mr Fairchild finds the kids squabbling about who gets to play with a doll. He steps in, takes away the doll, and whips the hands of all three children with a rod 'till they smarted again' while reciting a poem about the wickedness of children fighting. They are made to stand in the corner of the room, don't get breakfast, and an educational outing is proposed for the early afternoon, to a broken-down old brick house set in an overgrown garden. It's not the house that Mr Fairchild wants to show them, though.

> Just between that and the wood stood a gibbet, on which the body of a man hung in chains: it had not yet fallen to pieces, although it had hung there some years. The body had on a blue coat, a silk handkerchief round the neck, with shoes and stockings, and every other part of the dress still entire: but the face of the corpse was so shocking, that the children could not look at it [...] Whilst Mr Fairchild was speaking, the wind blew strong and shook the body upon the gibbet, rattling the chains on which it hung.

---

*   Damsons.

Beneath this decaying corpse, Mr Fairchild tells them the story of the man hanging in the gibbet – a fratricide who had lived in the adjoining house before killing his brother and being hanged. The traumatised children resolve to stop quarrelling. When a neighbour dies Mr Fairchild announces, as if suggesting a donkey-ride at the beach: 'Should you like to see the corpse, my dears? You never saw a corpse, I think?'

All this may read like black comedy, but it's a faithful picture of a world in which death was more present, and more present to children, than it is now; and one in which the besetting fear of mortal sin was a real thing. In its own era, it was admired for its realism – which, compared to its seventeenth-century ancestors, is justified praise. Stiff-backed though Mrs Sherwood may be, there is a proper sense (albeit often a disapproving one) of the lives and characters of real children in this book. That squabble over the doll has a recognisable childhood energy, and there are lovely descriptions of the children feeding parsley to the family's tame pet hare.

You see them playing on a swing ('Swing me higher! Swing me higher!'), the joy in play feelingly evoked – even though the consequences of such immoderation, this being Mrs Sherwood, are two teeth knocked out, a grotesquely swollen eye and lip, and blood pouring from a bashed nose. Emily's train of thought while she's sneaking into the pantry for another of those near-fatal damsons is novelistically inhabited – 'I will not take any more damascenes; I will go back, I think. But yet, as I am come so far, and am just got to the closet, I will just take one damascene – it shall be the last; I will never come here again, without Mamma's leave.'

One episode of delinquency sees the children failing to make their beds, scoffing 'a large quantity of toast and butter' before dirtying their clothes chasing a pig out of the garden, then repairing to a kindly neighbour to eat cake and drink cider. *Just William* on the road to perdition.

Mrs Sherwood's work and that of the tradition she inherited was one of the things that needed to be got past to reach the mid-Victorian Golden Age. As Peter Hunt has written, 'evangelistic attitudes dominated children's books until the end of the eighteenth century, and influenced, directly or in reaction, attitudes almost to the end of the nineteenth'.[*] But it was hugely popular in its own era – and it looked, sometimes despite itself, forward as well as back.

So to see children's literature moving uniformly from didacticism to delight, then, would be to oversimplify. As seen from the end of the eighteenth century, the earnestness of Mrs Barbauld and Mrs Trimmer had been a step backwards from the playfulness of Newbery. Charles Lamb, writing to Samuel Taylor Coleridge in 1802, complained of going to the bookshop in search of a copy of *Goody Two-Shoes*. His complaint, and it was a Romantic's complaint, was that the Gradgrinds had taken over:

> Mrs Barbauld's stuff has banished all the old classics of the nursery; and the shopman at Newbery's hardly deigned to reach them off an old exploded corner of a shelf, when Mary asked for them. Mrs. B.'s and Mrs Trimmer's nonsense lay in piles about. Knowledge insignificant and vapid as Mrs. B.'s books convey, it seems, must come to a child in the *shape of knowledge* [...]
>
> Science has succeeded to Poetry no less in the little walks of children than with men. Is there no possibility of averting this sore evil? Think what you would have been now, if instead of being fed with Tales and old wives' fables in childhood, you had been crammed with geography and natural history? Damn them! – I mean the cursed Barbauld Crew, those Blights and Blasts of all that is Human in man and child.[†]

---

[*] Peter Hunt, *An Introduction to Children's Literature*.

[†] Letter to Samuel Taylor Coleridge, 23 October 1802, in E.V. Lucas (ed.) *The Letters of Charles Lamb, to which are Added Those of His Sister Mary Lamb* (J. M. Dent & Sons, Methuen & Co, 1935).

This is a little unfair to Mrs Barbauld. Nevertheless, Mary Lamb (1764–1847), she of the thwarted bookshop trip,* combined with her Barbauld-sceptical brother Charles (1774–1834) to produce another of the era's classics of children's literature. Their *Tales from Shakespeare* (1807) was, in its way, an educative work – a work with a design on its audience – but it was interested in educating its readers to appreciate artistic rather than moral excellence; it is 'submitted to the young reader as an introduction to the study of Shakespeare'.

They aren't seeking to create an abstract of Shakespeare's work, but to give 'as much of Shakespeare's own words as possible' (this was much easier in the tragedies than the comedies, apparently, the former being Charles's bailiwick and the latter Mary's) so as to offer 'a few hints and little foretastes of the great pleasure which awaits them in their elder years'. They also direct it towards young women in particular – noting that boys will tend to 'have the use of their fathers' libraries at a much earlier age than girls are' and can be expected to have the best scenes from Shakespeare by heart before their sisters. An inequity in education marked; and an effort made to rectify it.

It was a harbinger of what was to come. The Lambs' ambition doesn't omit moral improvement – the preface closes by assuring readers that Shakespeare's plays are 'enrichers of the fancy, strengtheners of virtue' and teach 'courtesy, benignity, generosity and humility' – but it's one of the first children's books in the English canon in which God doesn't play any obvious role. And it has never been out of print.

---

* And, possibly more traumatically, of the 1796 episode of mental illness that caused her to stab and kill her own mother; her brother wrested the knife from her hand. A bit like something from the Brothers Grimm.

Glass Slippers

GIAMBATTISTA BASILE ·
THE BROTHERS GRIMM · CHARLES PERRAULT ·
HANS CHRISTIAN ANDERSEN

Il Pentamerone; Children's and Household Tales;
One Thousand and One Nights; Tales and Stories of
the Past with Morals; Fairy Tales Told for Children

F OR ALL THE DISAPPROVAL OF THE SHERWOODS AND
Trimmers of the world, there was no gainsaying the appeal
of fairytales to children. Even as the roundheads held the
field, the cavaliers were charging in. Blowing like a warm breeze
from the Continent and the wider world beyond it came the
fairytales, bringing into the nursery the buttery whiff of Perrault's
croissant-crumbs, the umbrageous forests of the Grimms, and a
scent of myrrh and spice from *One Thousand and One Nights*. Just
as the early Puritans thought reading for pleasure was a dangerous
subversion of the gift of reading, Mrs Trimmer inadvertently pays
tribute, in her mistrust of it, to the essential unruliness of the storytelling instinct. It's that unruliness which was to come to the fore as
children's literature really hit its stride. What children wanted and
what adults thought they needed were always uneasy bedfellows.

Yet fairytales, to complicate the story a little further, weren't
children's stuff to start with. The idea that they were is one that's
encouraged, strangely, by the titles of early written collections. The
first significant collection of fairytales in the West, for instance, is the
posthumously published *Il Pentamerone* by the poet Giambattista

Basile (1556–1632).[*] Its subtitle is *Lo cunto de li cunti overo lo trat-
tenemiento de peccerille*, which is translated as 'The Tale of Tales: or,
Entertainment for Little Ones'. But, as Nancy Canepa writes in the
introduction to her recent translation, 'the collection is decidedly
not for little ones':[†]

> Basile's work signals [the] passage, from the oral folktale to the
> artful and sophisticated 'authored' fairytale. Despite its subtitle,
> 'Entertainment for Little Ones,' *The Tale of Tales* is not a work of
> children's literature, which did not yet exist as a genre, but was
> probably intended to be read aloud in the courtly conversations
> that were an elite pastime of the period and whose dynamics we
> can find described in the frame tales of many novella collections
> (Basile's included).

Born into the Neapolitan minor gentry, Basile was an urbane
soldier-turned-courtier, well plugged in to the literary and
political ferment of the Renaissance and Counter-Reformation.
His *Pentamerone,* whose stories include prototypical versions of
'Cinderella' and 'Rapunzel', is bawdy, vulgar, full of toilet humour
and eye-stretching invective. Canepa suggests that the subtitle,
rather than signalling a child audience, is a semi-apologetic way
of acknowledging the low status of the artform. Its frame story
is hectic and profane, involving colourful exchanges of insults
and a peasant woman flashing her private parts at a courtier. It's
cartoonish, but not obviously childish; more like *South Park* than
Dora the Explorer.

The main artery through which the modern Western fairytale
canon passes down to us, though, is the Grimm Brothers. They

---

[*]   His book was published under the pseudonym Gian Alesio Abbatutis: 'the
dejected one'.
[†]   Giambattista Basile, *The Tale of Tales: or, Entertainment for Little Ones*, trans.
Nancy Canepa (Wayne State University Press, 2007).

came a little later. But, as with Basile (whose work was known to the Grimms), the title of their canonical work is misleading. The first, two-volume edition of their fairytale book (1812 and 1815) is called, in German, *Kinder- und Hausmärchen* – that is, *Children's and Household Tales*. But still, these were not for children. The Grimm Brothers were, in their pioneering and slightly haphazard way, professional folklorists.

Their project, slightly ironically, given how internationally and cross-culturally tangled folktales turn out to be, was to build an archive of old German literature with a view to, as Jack Zipes has put it, 'recovering the "true" nature of the German people'.[*]

In fact it's not until a decade later, in 1825, that an audience of children was specifically sought in the pared down 'small edition' – containing only fifty stories, stripped of its scholarly apparatus and embellished with illustrations. There was a market emerging – as Newbery had established a few decades earlier in England – for a distinctive literature for children, and the desire to start to cater to these children was an editorial influence on the Grimms' progressive reshaping of their tales.

It's a commonplace that, especially compared to Disney's versions, the Grimm Brothers' originals are rather darker than we're accustomed to.[†] Immediately following 'Cinderella', in the first edition, are two versions of the tale called 'How Some Children Played at Slaughtering'. In its least embellished form, it runs as follows. Two brothers watch their father slaughter a pig. That afternoon, they decide to 'play at slaughter' and one slits the other one's throat. Their mother, bathing a younger child upstairs, hears the screams and rushes downstairs. She takes the bloody knife and stabs the surviving brother in the heart. Meanwhile the child she

---

[*]   J. Zipes, *The Original Folk and Fairy Tales of the Brothers Grimm* (Princeton University Press, 2014).

[†]   I hope the reader will appreciate the strength of character it has taken to avoid punning on their name.

left unattended drowns in the bath. She hangs herself. On returning from the fields her husband dies of grief. It's hard to imagine that becoming a Disney movie.

The fairytales we know now have almost all made a long journey from what in the US is called a 'hard-R' to PG certificate. In the process these stories have been refined in such a way as to fit our social set-ups and our notions of childhood as neatly as Cinderella's foot fits into her slipper. Take, for instance, the evolution of that very story.

Cinderella is to be found in countless traditions all over the world – there are Chinese, Khmer, Tibetan and Ancient Greek stories about humble and put-upon girls whose footwear ends up rescuing them. The Greek geographer Strabo reports that the Egyptians told the story of Rhodopis ('rosy-cheeks'), a pretty slave girl whose sandal is stolen by an eagle and dropped in the lap of the Egyptian king, who seeks her out and marries her. In China, where a version is attested as early as the mid-800s, Ye Xian is dressed for the ball by magical fish-bones – and it's a golden slipper that finally connects her to her prince.

The earliest European written version of the story is Basile's 'Cenerentola', translated by Nancy Canepa as 'The Cinderella Cat'. As the story opens, the heroine has a doting father and a wicked stepmother; but she also has a kindly sewing teacher who becomes her confidante: 'the poor little thing was always complaining to the teacher of her stepmother's ill-treatment, saying, "Oh, God, couldn't you be my little mommy, you who give me so many smooches and squeezes?"'

But this sewing teacher does not, as you might have expected, stand in for the fairy godmother. She persuades Zezolla (as Cinders is called here) to murder the wicked stepmother by slamming the lid of a chest shut on her head. Zezolla then talks her father into marrying the sewing teacher in the hopes that, as she was promised, they'll live happily ever after. After only a week, the scheming seamstress turns into a wicked stepmother herself: she produces 'six daughters of her own whom she had kept secret up until then', installs them in the household, and Zezolla, now renamed Cinderella Cat, 'ended up being demoted from the royal chamber to the kitchen and from a canopied bed to the hearth, from sumptuous silks and gold to rags, from the scepter to the spit'.

The supernatural agent that dresses Cinderella for the ball, in this version of the story, is not a fairy godmother but a magical date tree. And what in the best-known versions is a golden or glass slipper is, in Basile's Neapolitan dialect, a *chianiello*, which can mean a cork-soled patten, or an overshoe designed to stop a long dress trailing in the filth of the street; but which has the penumbral association of the chopine, a platform shoe associated with prostitution.

The moral and emotional set-up here is treacherous. Cinderella herself is steeped in blood before the main section of the tale even starts. Her apparent protector turns out to be her principal antagonist. Her supposedly doting father, when the prince turns up searching for the owner of the lost slipper, admits, 'I have a daughter, but she looks after the hearth and is an unworthy wretch and does not deserve to sit at the same table at which you eat.' There's even a suggestion that it was Zezolla's neediness that turned the sewing mistress to scheming in the first place: 'she chanted [her complaints] so incessantly that she planted a wasp in the teacher's ear' so she was 'blinded by evil spirits'.

The story ends with a curiously opaque and generalised moral. The ambitious sisters, now forced to curtsey to their new queen as Zezolla is crowned, 'nearly died of anger, and [...] quietly stole away to their mother's house, confessing in spite of themselves that *those who oppose the stars are crazy*'. Zezolla has, in her apotheosis, somehow sidled out of the story – it's for the stepsisters to learn the lesson of the tale, and the lesson is one that effectively chalks up all that has happened, all the moral reverses and psychological cruelty, to the operations of impersonal fate.

That is almost the opposite of what we now expect from children's literature proper: most children's stories place their stress on the possibility of agency and the value of moral responsibility. Virtue is rewarded and vice punished – and you expect a certain integrity of character. Villains, though they might feign virtue, will always be villainous under the mask; heroes and heroines will be, though flawed, pure of heart. Courageous or ingenious action, rather than blind fate, determines the outcome of the story.

That framework of morality and individual agency is the one on which even more sophisticated stories play knowing variations. Yet that framework is a historically contingent one. It is shaped in the West, as we'll go on to see, by a pervading cultural Christian sensibility, by Enlightenment individualism and by developing notions of what childhood meant and what sort of moral creatures children are. As these notions develop, as stories develop, they leave traces of what they were before: in their patterns and structures as well as in their 'morals', in their worldviews as well as in their worlds.

Cinderella, meanwhile, proliferates. Later in the seventeenth century, Charles Perrault published the version that gives us the pumpkin and the glass footwear: 'Cinderilla; Or, The Little Glass Slipper' appeared in Perrault's 1697 *Tales and Stories of the Past with Morals, or Tales of Mother Goose* – along with 'Sleeping Beauty', 'Bluebeard', 'Puss in Boots' and 'Red Riding Hood'. His 'Cinderilla' is quite a different proposition to the earthy, almost feudal world of Basile's: it is something more like a high-society romance.

Writing his fairytales as exercises in whimsy for the literary sophisticates of Paris in the age of Louis XIV, Perrault goes to town on fashionable details. We encounter in one scene alone 'plaited ruffles', 'red velvet suit with French trimming', a 'gold-flowered manteau', 'double pinners' and 'a diamond stomacher'. And, of course, it introduces those glass slippers – *pantoufles de verre* – which may have been an inspired creative mishearing: medieval versions of the story have her in *pantoufles de vair*, or grey squirrel fur. The ending is distinctly civilised, too. No speechless rage or podiatric mutilation for the stepsisters. 'Cinderilla, who was no less good than beautiful, gave her two sisters lodgings in the palace, and that very same day matched them with two great lords of the court.' The moral: 'The fairies' gift of greatest worth / Is grace of bearing, not high birth.' Grace, rather than beauty or nobility, is what is most to be admired. The Grimms' version of the story – 'Aschenputtel' – is, like most of their tales, more grounded in peasant life, or at least in a recognisably domestic life where the unfortunate heroine sleeps in the embers of the fire. As in older versions of the story, it's not a fairy godmother but a magic tree that grants Cinderella's wishes – this one having been planted on Cinderella's mother's grave. The ugly sisters aren't ugly, incidentally: 'they had beautiful features but proud, nasty, and wicked hearts'. The tasks they set Cinderella to get on with while they're at the ball – separating lentils and peas – descend from the story of Cupid and Psyche, as do the magical animal helpers (ants in that story; pigeons in this one) who allow the task to be accomplished. The bloody conclusion, in which each of the sisters attempts to fit into the slipper by mutilating her own foot with a knife, is a world away from the suavity of Perrault: 'The prince looked down and saw that the stockings of the bride were coloured red and that her blood was streaming out of the slipper.'

The sanguinary part of the Grimms' version is now, quietly, forgotten. What we're seeing, in the progress of stories like 'Cinderella' from the oral tradition into a literary or written one, is something feral being tamed. They are given a particular place and style according to the worlds of their tellers and their audience: and in due course they make their way from the literary salon to the nursery, the bedside table and eventually the Disney box set. They became children's stories.

Their roots in orality also mark another of the distinctive inheritances that folktales pass on to children's writing. The basic world of the Eurasian fairy story is one that is soaked in fantasy and magic – but, paradoxically, also close to the human life-world. Magic, in these stories, is not the exclusive property of remote and abstract divinities. It is a widespread technology. Witches and wizards, giants and ogres, fairies and dragons are familiar if dangerous aspects of the world to its wary human inhabitants.

The protagonists of these stories are not gods and heroes: they are woodcutters and huntsmen, blacksmiths and farmers, merchants and tinkers. Kings and princes sit atop the social hierarchy as they did in medieval Europe. And what stands for the numinous and unknown in the fairytale is what stood for the numinous and unknown in the superstitious world in which they were told: the wolf-patrolled forest at the centre of which you might find a gingerbread house, or Baba Yaga's hut standing on chicken-legs; the haunted wood.

The special appeal of so much children's writing is that it encompasses that paradox. It tells stories of adventure – often magical or fantastical – but it roots them, at least to start with, in worlds familiar enough to invite its readers to imagine that the protagonists could be them. We could all be Charlie Bucket, or Alice lazing on a summer afternoon by the river before she first catches sight of the white rabbit.

So, despite their difference in register, Basile, the work of the French authors of *contes de fées*, the Grimms (not to mention the Russian folklorists, and the orientalising fabulists who made *One Thousand and One Nights* a European literary sensation at the beginning of the nineteenth century) all had something more important in common. They drew from each other as well as from oral and classical tradition – and they were, originally, writing tales for an audience of literary adults.

It's possible to speculate that the European folklore craze might have burned itself out. It might have, from this distance, looked like the folding of an ancient form of storytelling into a literary framework, to be in turn superseded by more sophisticated narrative forms as the novel itself started to get going around the late eighteenth and early nineteenth centuries. Yet something else happened. These tales started to be recast as stories for children – and as templates for the more sophisticated and individual children's stories that were to come.

A bridging figure was Hans Christian Andersen (1805–1875). He was the odd one out, in a way, because most of the stories he produced were invented rather than adapted. It is testament to the continuing popularity (and high literary status) of fairytales in the nineteenth century that having started as, in his words, a 'poor washerwoman's son who ran about with wooden shoes', he became one of the most celebrated European authors of his day. His work was to go from Copenhagen around the world. His writing became popular in India in his own lifetime, in China he is still revered as 'Antushun', and his stories such as 'The Little Mermaid' and 'The Snow Queen' are now core components of the Disney canon (the latter as *Frozen*).

Andersen grew up in a one-room home, which doubled as his shoemaker father's workshop, in the slums of Odense on the island of Funen in central Denmark. His grandfather had struggled with mental illness, one grandmother had been locked up for having three children out of wedlock and his aunt was the madam of a brothel. He was a shy, awkward boy – physically ungainly (adult acquaintances were to remark on the 'grotesque ugliness of his face and hands' and Elizabeth Barrett Browning said he was 'rather like his own ugly duck') and bullied by his peers.

Even in adulthood he was socially gauche: when he visited Charles Dickens, he overstayed his proposed two-week visit by three weeks. Dickens's daughter Katey remembered him as 'a boney bore who stayed on and on', while Dickens himself complained to a friend, as if his houseguest was a disease, 'we are suffering very much from Andersen'.* He had fierce, unreciprocated crushes on women and men alike – 'I long for you as though you were a beautiful Calabrian girl,' he wrote to a male friend – but likely died a virgin. He never fitted in.

Yet his childhood was suffused with magical thinking and, nourished by the stories that his father read him from *One Thousand and*

---

*   Michael Slater, *Charles Dickens* (Yale University Press, 2009).

One Nights, the fantasies of escape and transformation that were later to emerge in his work. He himself escaped and transformed. After his father's death, he left home to make his way in the world alone at the age of fourteen, and on reaching Copenhagen he finagled a place in a ballet school (he was cast as a troll) and moved from there to a miserably Gradgrindian grammar school.

Yet by his early twenties, with the help of a philanthropic high society patron, he started to make a literary career – and in 1835 he published the first of a three-booklet collection (the third booklet came out two years later) called *Fairy Tales Told for Children*. That collection included 'The Princess and the Pea', 'Thumbelina', 'The Emperor's New Clothes' and the story that was to make his name, 'The Little Mermaid'. The high literary reaction to these was at very best lukewarm: the *Danish Literary Gazette* sniffed that 'it is no empty convention that one must not put one's words together in the same disorderly fashion as one may do [...] in oral speech'.

What affronted critics was precisely what was to make the stories so popular with children: their idiom was that of ordinary speech, their fantastical elements spun out of recognisable domestic scenes and objects (ducklings, tin soldiers, tinderboxes and candles) and they had an unruly and sometimes opaque moral order. Andersen drew on the orality and moral unpredictability of the original folk-tales – but harnessed them in the service of a distinctive children's literature, not inherited but invented, and grounded in fear and longing, wonder and delight.

———

So as the middle of the nineteenth century approached, those two lines of inheritance – the earnest didacticism of Christian moralists, and the unpredictable whimsy of the fairytale, a religious form and a secular one – were in place. What came next was to twist and tangle them out of all recognition, gleefully mocking the first thing and taking the second in a surreal new direction.

III

DOWN THE RABBIT-HOLE

Lewis Carroll · Charles Kingsley · Thomas Hughes ·
Boy's Own · W.H.G. Kingston · Captain Marryat · G.A. Henty

THE DAWNING OF
THE GOLDEN AGE

LOOKED AT IN ONE WAY, THE MID-NINETEENTH CENtury was a time of worldliness, prosperity and unprecedented national self-confidence. The Anglican Church marched in lockstep with the Crown. Empire was in its pomp; and the fruits of that pomp had never been more visible at home. At mid-century, marvels of technology and global exotica flowed into the Great Exhibition of 1851.

The very venue – Joseph Paxton's Crystal Palace, thrown up in London in less than a year – was a scintillating image of technological ingenuity. Inside it were the most advanced telescopes in the world, daguerreotypes, cutting-edge home appliances, demonstrations of steel-making and advanced agricultural technologies. Colt's new revolvers spoke of growing technologies of war, while the Koh-i-Noor diamond and artefacts from New Zealand whispered of riches beyond the sea. The launch of the yacht race that was to become the America's Cup spoke of the ever-greater ease of getting there.

England was outward-looking. It was powerful. But at the same time, the prosperity was not spread evenly. The poor –not the picturesque rural sort but the rootless and putatively criminal urban poor drawn to the towns by the Industrial Revolution – aroused those good Aristotelian emotions, pity and fear, in the middle and upper classes. Charles Dickens – not a children's writer, but one whose concern with children and childhood shadows all the children's writers of the second half of the nineteenth century – had close-up experience of the wretchedness of debt. He was twelve in 1824 when he was consigned to the blacking factory. He never forgot it.

Though Church and state were harmoniously married in the person of the sovereign, the new sciences were starting to chip away at old theological certainties. Is it significant that of the three writers whose work is credited with starting the new era of children's writing two – Lewis Carroll and Charles Kingsley – were churchmen? Carroll's radically disruptive *Alice in Wonderland* stories imagine a world in which religious certainty, indeed any certainty, is unobtainable; Kingsley's *Water-Babies* offered a queasily pantheistic attempt to marry religion with his scientific fascinations. Meanwhile the third, Thomas Hughes, in *Tom Brown's School Days*, offered a story whose 'muscular Christianity' linked body and soul in the trainee servants of Empire.

Curiouser and Curiouser

LEWIS CARROLL · CHARLES KINGSLEY

Alice's Adventures in Wonderland;
Through the Looking-Glass; Sylvie
and Bruno; The Water-Babies

'ALL IN THE GOLDEN AFTERNOON / FULL LEISURELY we glide...' The story of the birth of *Alice's Adventures in Wonderland* has itself passed into legend. A stretch of the Thames at Oxford; a golden afternoon; and a young clergyman extemporising a wild and silly fantasy story over his shoulder to the little girl coxing the boat. It was 4 July 1862. That little girl was ten-year-old Alice Liddell, daughter of the Dean of Christchurch. The man was Charles Dodgson, who had taken her and her two sisters out on the water for a day-trip.

The story she was hearing would eventually become *Alice's Adventures in Wonderland*: the story of a little girl who follows a white rabbit into an underground fantasia where nothing behaves as it does in the workaday world above. The creation myth of the *Alice* books isn't just an incidental piece of background trivia: it's part of the story itself.

Alice – which ends with its heroine waking up on the riverbank – is a dream-narrative in a waking-world frame. That frame story is itself given yet another frame story: the story of the creation of *Alice's Adventures in Wonderland*. It's a big part of their place in the culture. 'Alice's Day' is still celebrated in Oxford every July, and Alice Liddell's place in literary history as the 'original' of Alice followed her to her death. By the time she toured the US in 1932 (by then she was Alice Hargreaves, a wife and mother) she could be prevailed on to sign her name 'Alice in Wonderland'.

Supplying her recollections for the first full biography of Carroll around the turn of the century, she described that day as a 'summer afternoon when the sun was so burning that we had landed in the meadows down the river, deserting the boat to take refuge in the only bit of shade to be found, which was under a new-made hay-rick'. The story was already halfway to fiction. The hayrick played no part in an account later provided by the other adult in the boat, Dodgson's friend Robinson Duckworth, who recalled in 1899 that 'the story was actually composed and spoken over my shoulder'.

Carroll himself had already long since mythologised the story behind the story – not only in the prefatory poem from which the words that open this chapter are taken, but in his own journal. It was six months after the fact that he went back and altered his diary entry for that day to insert an account of his composition of the story. If we're going to be pedantic, even that 'golden afternoon' was nothing of the sort: meteorological reports have it that the afternoon of 4 July 1862 was in fact 'cool, and rather wet'.

Yet the succession of retellings of that afternoon came to swaddle the actual history of the story's composition in a layer of fiction. The 'dreamy weather' was just that: not literal, but dreamy, part of a dream-narrative that spilled out to encapsulate its own creation. It came to stand in the book, and in its readers, not just for the after-noon the story was born but for the golden weather of childhood itself – the irrecoverable sunshine of a world lost to adults.

So when you're dealing with *Alice's Adventures in Wonderland*, you need to keep in mind that it isn't just a fairy story itself: it's a fairy story within a fairy story. Even its author – that weedy, tweedy young man pulling at the oars and telling a story over his shoulder – is a creation of the imagination.

The flesh-and-blood Charles Lutwidge Dodgson, the creator, was born in 1832, the son of a Cheshire clergyman and the oldest of four brothers in a family of eleven children. Charles had a life-long stammer but an outgoing temperament – his letters home and the jokey magazines he edited for family consumption as a child showed an energetic character and a puckish sense of humour. At Rugby School he won academic prizes and was especially notable for his facility in mathematics. He wasn't sporty. A contemporary inscribed the words 'C.L. Dodgson is a muff' in one of his school-books. When he followed his father to Oxford the direction of his talents became clearer: in his mid-career exams he got a first in mathematics, and scraped only a third in greats.

He seemed destined to follow his father into the priesthood. That was the presumption that accompanied his being given a stu-dentship at Christ Church – a post that came with lifetime tenure and rights of residence at the college. The recipient was expected to join the clergy and to remain unmarried. Yet though Dodgson remained unmarried – he seems to have been largely untroubled by conventional romantic attachments – he was never ordained: he became a deacon but refused, at the risk of expulsion from the college, to take the final step to become a priest.

Does this point to a wavering of faith – as can seemingly be found in the almost nihilistic flavour of parts of the *Alice* books? Was it, as has also been suggested, that he feared stammering in the pulpit (less likely, given he went on without apparent trouble to deliver lectures)?* Instead he became a tutor in mathematics and, later, a rather pernickety sub-librarian at the college. Meanwhile the less conventional side of his character flourished. He contributed comic squibs to literary magazines and pursued an infatuation with the young art of photography.

Lewis Carroll, the creation, was born in 1856 after the editor of a magazine to which Dodgson contributed asked him to come up

---

* A lot has been ascribed to that stammer. Not only his failure to become a man of the cloth, but his preference for infant company: it was said that he stammered less noticeably among children.

with a pseudonym. Carroll was a looking-glass version of his creator, transformed by the strange verbal logic-of-association that was to characterise his books. Charles became (in Latin) Carolus, which became 'Carroll'; Lutwidge became Ludovicus, which became Lewis. A shadow-self was born.

The 'dry and perfunctory' lecturer in mathematics – the pedant who kept a meticulous 'Register of Letters Received and Sent' that at his death ran to nearly 100,000 entries, the productivity-fanatic who mapped out his working day in half-hour increments – acquired a more ebullient alter ego. The doubleness never abated. Queen Victoria, as one story goes, once made it be known she'd enjoyed *Alice's Adventures in Wonderland* so much that she'd like a copy of the author's next book. She in due course received a package containing *An Elementary Treatise on Determinants: With Their Application to Simultaneous Linear Equations and Algebraical Geometry*.

What that creation in turn created was at once hugely influential and entirely *sui generis*. It's almost impossible to overstate what strange books *Alice's Adventures* and its sequel are. That they are nonsense, and that they are the account of a dream, or a nested series of dreams, is relevant. From these premises they get their giddy transitions and shifts of scene, their doublings and their longeurs (there can have been few readers, I think, who have wished that the *Alice* books contained more puns). Their heroine's progress through Wonderland proceeds more like a string of static tableaux or set-pieces than a continuous narrative.

There's a strong case to be made that they aren't really – or aren't primarily – even children's books at all. The current of feeling that animates the myth of their creation, and animates the books themselves, is an adult one. They contain mathematical conundrums,*

---

* How many children, or even adults, will have clocked that when Alice struggles with her multiplication tables it's because she's working in base-18 and base-21 rather than base-10? Or taken on board that the Mad Hatter's Tea Party is sending up the theory of quaternions?

theological echoes and philosophy-of-language jokes, and admit of psychoanalytic and mythological readings, many of which seem quite an unusual bill of fare for what Carroll himself called 'a fairy-tale'.

The books are haunted by anxieties about identity, meaning, death and the passing of time – though they approach those anxieties through jokes and riddles and paradoxes. It takes an adult to really apprehend the ways in which they are frightening. Think of Humpty Dumpty's demise, for instance, just glimpsed offstage ('a heavy crash shook the forest from end to end. The next moment soldiers came running through the wood, at first in twos and threes, then ten or twenty together...'), or of Tweedledum and Tweedledee's battle being interrupted (as it is fated to be) by the arrival of the crow, which seems to belong to Ted Hughes as much as to Lewis Carroll: 'What a thick black cloud that is! And how fast it comes! Why, I do believe it's got wings!'

Early in the first book, as she shrinks, Alice worries that the process might end '"in my going out altogether, like a candle. I wonder what I should be like then?" And she tried to fancy what the flame of a candle is like after the candle is blown out.' Shades, perhaps, of a smile without a cat. The image is reprised, in still more alarming form, in *Through the Looking-Glass*, when Tweedledee points out the sleeping King and tells Alice: 'Why, you're only a sort of thing in his dream!' Tweedledum chimes in: 'If that there King was to wake, you'd go out – bang! – just like a candle!' Suddenly, we're in what's sometimes called a *mise-en-abyme*, an infinite corridor of mirrors: Alice's dream contains a dream-character for whom Alice is herself a dream-character.

But in dreams, as Yeats said, begin responsibilities: here's nonsense to serious effect; here are real figures and feelings transfigured by what Freud many years later would call the 'dream-work'. Explanations get knotted into meaninglessness or break off with another jump-cut. The floor, so to speak, is constantly dropping away. They are full of little loops of frozen time: the Mad Hatter's constantly rotating tea party; the Queen running at top speed just to stand still. Time, indeed, could be said to be the books' deep theme. It's their treatment of time that gives them both the surface fizz of paradox and a strong and very adult undertow of plangency.

The books may be concerned with childhood but their protagonist is an odd, and not very childlike, child. Alice is pragmatic, good-natured and a little proud – though often also frequently bewildered and frightened or upset. Both books end with violent tantrums. But she doesn't noticeably develop; such changes as she undergoes are changes of mood (and size). Rather, she's there as an interlocutor, a foil to the succession of peculiar individuals and situations she meets: a proxy, in some way, for the rational reader wondering what on earth is going on. In most respects, she's more adult than the characters she meets on her adventures. You could even see Wonderland as an externalisation of her childishness.

Her sense of her own identity is unstable, almost fugal. There's a dismaying episode in the first book, when Alice loses a sense of herself altogether:

> Dear, dear! How queer everything is today! And yesterday things went on just as usual. I wonder if I've been changed in the night? Let me think: was I the same when I got up this morning? I almost think I can remember feeling a little different. But if I'm not the same, the next question is, Who in the world am I? Ah, *that's* the great puzzle! And she began thinking over all the children she knew that were of the same age as herself, to see if she could have been changed for any of them.
>
> 'I'm sure I'm not Ada,' she said, 'for her hair goes in such long ringlets, and mine doesn't go in ringlets at all; and I'm sure I can't be Mabel, for I know all sorts of things, and she, oh! She knows such a very little! Besides, she's she and I'm I, and – oh dear, how puzzling it all is!'

It's silly and funny – we should not lose sight of its declared status as nonsense (the term 'nonsense poetry' was minted in 1851, and

Edward Lear's *Book of Nonsense* was published in 1846) – but it's also alarming and, in a slant way, plausible. A child is a creature in a constant state of change, with a shaky sense of selfhood. Alice's transformations – as she closes like a telescope or stretches to fill the White Rabbit's house – are alarming to her and frightening, even dangerous, to some of the creatures in Wonderland. When the caterpillar (another creature, of course, destined for transformation) asks, 'Who are *you*?', Alice confesses: 'I – I hardly know, sir, just at present – at least I know who I *was* when I got up this morning, but I think I must have been changed several times since then.'

The passage of writing in which Alice is most vividly evoked as a flesh-and-blood-child, rather than the telescopic foil for a succession of bizarre vaudeville routines, comes right at the end of the first book. Alice leaves Wonderland at a moment of crisis. She's about to get into a fight with a pack of cards. 'Who cares for you?' she exclaims. 'You're nothing but a pack of cards!' The pack of cards 'rose up into the air, and came flying down upon her'. Before they can exact their revenge, she wakes up to find her head in her sister's lap and her sister brushing dead leaves from her face.

'Oh, I've had such a curious dream,' she says. She recounts her adventures – and then her sister, in turn, starts to dream:

> First, she dreamed of little Alice herself, and once again the tiny hands were clasped upon her knee, and the bright eager eyes were looking up into hers – she could hear the very tones of her voice, and see that queer little toss of her head to keep back the wandering hair that would always get into her eyes...

There, as nowhere in the body of the book, is the tender and exact recollection of an authentic mannerism, that head-toss. Though it's ascribed to Alice's sister (Alice Liddell's older sister Lorina was only thirteen) that is surely a Carroll's-eye, an adult, gaze. A grown man, more than a thirteen-year-old girl, would be struck by 'little Alice', her 'tiny hands', and the eyes 'looking up into hers'.

A lot of ink has been spilled over the years considering the question of whether Carroll's interest in children was sexual; and, if it was, whether he'd even have recognised it as such. Certainly, throughout his life, he cultivated what he called 'child-friends' ('they are three-fourths of my life,' he told Isa Bowman, a child actress who played Alice on stage) and did so in a way that looked an awful lot like what we'd now call grooming. He found excuses to talk to them in public places, befriended their parents, beguiled them with toys and tricks,* and sought permission from their parents (some of whom, latterly, would have been impressed by his fame) to meet and photograph them. Some of these photographs depicted the children naked.

It's hard to come down firmly on one side of this debate, though. Among other things, four volumes of Carroll's diaries have vanished from the record, and crucial pages from the extant diaries – apparently detailing a falling-out that Dodgson had with the Liddell family – have gone missing. But the conscious idea that children might be sexually aware, or sexually vulnerable, was largely in the future. They were the incarnation, rather, of innocence: the assumption would be that the conjunction of an adult with a naked child would purify the former rather than corrupt the latter. Child nudes were a wholly conventional Victorian interest. They even appeared on Christmas cards. At the same time, the question of when children became adult – i.e. sexual beings – was earlier than we are accustomed to thinking of it. Until 1865, the age of consent was twelve, and it didn't reach sixteen till 1885. It was quite ordinary for sixteen-year-old girls to be engaged, and even married.

The file in which Carroll kept his nude images of children was marked '*Honi Soit*', from the Anglo-Norman motto '*Honi Soit Qui Mal Y Pense*': shame on him who thinks evil of it. That at once

---

* One former child-friend, Ethel Arnold, said his Christ Church rooms were 'an El Dorado of delights', cupboards full of 'mechanical bears, dancing dolls, toys and puzzles of every description'.

evinces an anxiety that evil *might* be thought; and seeks to affirm that the only evil can be in the eye of the beholder. That the naked body of a prepubescent child might be seen as a sexual object – decades before the 1903 edition of Krafft-Ebing would introduce 'paedophilia' to our vocabulary – was unthinkable. It'd be nearly fifty years before Freud would be around to introduce such sentimentalists to the idea of the Return of the Repressed.

Yet whatever judgements we might make about Carroll's private feelings, the tenor of the *Alice* books has a fascination with childhood that is not sexual, or not knowingly so. It rather more smacks of an adult, preoccupied with the passing of time and finding the universe more unstable than he'd like, wanting to preserve an *idea* of childhood – catching Alice, a specimen child, like a fly in amber. He's in the position of creating that secret garden and looking at it, as Alice does when she opens a tiny door with a golden key, down a corridor through which he can't fit, and longing to visit 'the loveliest garden you ever saw'.

The flesh-and-blood Alice will grow up and leave Wonderland behind. She'll get married and bear children of her own, grow portly and knowing: but the Alice of whom she's an impression will remain frozen in time between the covers of those books. Writing in 1887, Carroll declared that adults 'look before and after, and sigh for what is not; a child never does this [...] it is only a child that can utter from her heart the words [...] "I am all happy now!"' Carroll's interest in photography – another means of capturing a moment out of time – answers the same impulse.

Alice makes the standard folktale journey from the safety of hearth and home into a space where she's tested before returning. But there's another journey taking place too: the reader's, through the portal of the book's pages, into an idealised moment of carefree childhood bliss. A draft of an article ghostwritten for Alice Hargreaves by her entrepreneurial son Caryl – who managed her US tour and wrung all the profit from the myth that he could – described Dodgson/Carroll as a 'fairy godfather'. More even than usually in the genre, this is a book that speaks to adults, childishly, about childhood.

Are the books creating, as many children's books can be supposed to do, an imagined or compensatory fantasy childhood for the author? Hardly. The fictional Alice they create is not a proxy for the author. She's hardly, indeed, a proxy for her original. It was Tenniel's illustrations that gave her what we now still call an Alice-band and her long blond hair; Alice Liddell had a dark-brown bob and was three years older than the story's heroine. Rather, the books – and in that I include the myth of their creation, as it is inscribed within them – preserve an idealised fantasy of an adult–child relationship. The fictional Alice is the perfect child-friend, one who will never grow up. The confiding, arch, unstable voice of the narrator – now indulging Alice, now teasing her; arguably a more vivid character in the book than Alice herself – shades the whole story like a watercolour wash.

At the same time, it points to the passing of that relationship and mourns its loss even as it seeks to fix it. The heroine is always headed, one way or another, for the eighth square, where she will become a queen – and her grown-up friend cannot follow. Alice's encounter with the White Knight – with his battery of silly gadgets and his 'mild eyes', here is Carroll's self-portrait – is a valediction. He reassures Alice that she will get her desire and become a queen: 'So you will, when you've crossed the next brook. I'll see you safe to the end of the wood – and then I must go back, you know. That's the end of my move.'

Before they part ways, the White Knight sings her a song:

As the Knight sang the last words of the ballad, he gathered up the reins, and turned his horse's head along the road by which they had come. 'You've only a few yards to go,' he said, 'down the hill and over that little brook, and then you'll be a Queen – But you'll stay and see me off first?' he added as Alice turned with an eager look in the direction to which he pointed. 'I shan't be long. You'll wait and wave your handkerchief when I get to that turn in the road? I think it'll encourage me, you see.'

'Of course I'll wait,' said Alice: 'and thank you very much for coming so far – and for the song – I liked it very much.'

'I hope so,' the Knight said doubtfully: 'but you didn't cry so much as I thought you would.'

Is that last retort self-mocking? Is it a little passive-aggressive? Or is it, perhaps, a painful acknowledgement that children aren't nearly as sentimental about childhood as adults are? I read it as all three.

Right at the end of the book, once Alice has woken from her reverie, and is debating with her kitten whether she dreamed the Red King or he dreamed her, we encounter another valediction. This one is a poem. The initial letters of its lines spell out ALICE PLEASANCE LIDDELL in acrostic form, and it is saturated with *saudade*:* 'Still she haunts me, phantomwise. / Alice moving under skies / Never seen by waking eyes.' That stands for a whole history, in the literature of childhood, of broken relationships and Edens to which there is no return.

Dodgson never went so far as to repudiate the works of Carroll; indeed, he was an incredible fusspot when it came to tinkering with details of punctuation and typography in later editions. But as more than one critic has pointed out, there does seem to have been a growing disjunction, especially in later life, between the conventional proprieties of the former and the debunking imagination of the latter.

Subsequent editions of the *Alice* books came prefaced with twee poems. An 1876 'Easter Greeting to Every Child Who Loves Alice' is practically a sermon, inviting children to look forward to that 'great morning when the "Sun of Righteousness shall arise with healing in

---

* An unimprovable Portuguese word for the wistful yearning for a past happiness that is irrecoverable or that may never have existed.

his wings'". Carroll even admits that some might find this 'a strange letter to find in a book of nonsense'. A later work, *Sylvie and Bruno* (1889), is described by the critic Humphrey Carpenter as 'one of the most muddled, sentimental, drearily pious works ever produced in the Victorian age'.* How do we reconcile that with the ironist who has the Duchess, in *Alice's Adventures in Wonderland,* declaring unconvincingly: 'Tut, tut, child! Everything's got a moral, if only you can find it'?

Like Alice, Dodgson/Carroll couldn't be exactly sure that he was the same person who woke up that morning. It's as if one half of this remarkable writer cleaved to every mid-Victorian conventionality, while the other set out to kick the stilts from under them. As much as *Alice* is sentimental, it's also aggressive.

Carpenter made the case that the Alice stories dramatised Carroll's religious doubts, and there's a lot in the text to support his position, even if you hesitate to see the size-transforming consumables ('EAT ME' and 'DRINK ME') that Alice encounters early in the story as a blasphemous parody of holy communion. Religious texts are in its make-up. Carpenter draws out its antecedents in the medieval tradition of dream visions, such as *Piers Plowman* and the *Roman de la Rose*, that begin with the speaker lying drowsily down to sleep. He notes the resonances with Dante – the White Rabbit, as it were, a Virgil taking Alice into an underworld where she finds a succession of characters caught (as the Inferno's damned souls are) in tableaux of eternal repetition.

Many of the nonsense songs that fill the story are spoofs of pious nursery staples. Isaac Watts's 1715 *Divine Songs* are a particular favourite target.

> How doth the little busy bee
> Improve each shining hour,

---

* Humphrey Carpenter, *Secret Gardens: A Study of the Golden Age of Children's Literature* (Allen & Unwin, 1985).

And gather honey all the day
From every opening flower.

Becomes

How doth the little crocodile
Improve his shining tail,
And pour the waters of the Nile
On every golden scale!

'Twinkle, Twinkle, Little Star' gets the treatment ('Twinkle, twinkle, little bat!' trills the Mad Hatter), as does Robert Southey's sententious 1799 poem 'The Old Man's Comforts and How He Gained Them'. That poem ends:

'I am chearful, young man,' Father William replied,
'Let the cause thy attention engage
In the days of my youth I remember'd my God!
And He hath not forgotten my age.'

Carroll's version has its elderly protagonist incessantly standing on his head, balancing an eel on his nose, and trying to sell his younger interlocutor a jar of ointment, before declaring:

'I have answered three questions, and that is enough,'
Said his father; 'don't give yourself airs!
Do you think I can listen all day to such stuff?
Be off, or I'll kick you down stairs!'

The reverential relationship between father and son in Southey's poem is transformed into one between impertinent whelp and crotchety oldie.

That's a sign of just how revolutionary Alice was – and how its assault on the conventions of its age may have taken in religion but didn't end there. A central pillar of the relationship between adults and children in Victorian society, the hierarchy of authority, is relentlessly undermined in the books. In her argument with the Lory, the latter tells Alice: 'I'm older than you, and must know better' – but 'this Alice would not allow without knowing how old it was, and, as the Lory positively refused to tell its age, there was no more to be said.' Anything with rules – from a game of croquet to a criminal trial – turns out to be nonsensical or arbitrary: it doesn't matter, seemingly, whether the jury writes 'important' or 'unimportant' on their notebooks. Nothing is stable. A baby turns into a pig. A cook flings pots and pans with startling violence at her employer. The Queen of Hearts storms around demanding, seemingly at random: 'Off with their heads!'

It's not just religious or social hierarchy that Carroll is turning on its head. The books' project of parody and undermining is addressed at the existing body of children's writing. Tweedledum, Tweedledee, Humpty Dumpty and the Knave and Queen of Hearts are characters from established nursery rhymes, turned to new and unexpected purpose by the text. Carroll takes the mick, too, out of the dry lessons of the schoolroom. While she's falling down the rabbit-hole, Alice starts to speculate that she must be approaching the centre of the earth: '"Let me see: that would be four thousand miles down, I think–" (for, you see, Alice had learnt several things of this sort in her lessons in the schoolroom…)'.

After Alice and her animal companions nearly drown in a pool of tears in the opening pages of the first book, the Mouse attempts to dry them all out with a historical lesson on the Norman Conquest, 'the driest thing I know'.

All this is subversive. But it is also, looked at from another angle, more than that: it is a way of entering into a childlike mode of apprehending the world. The fact that some of the episodes in these books resemble psychedelic experiences has not gone unnoticed. We have lit on the hookah-smoking caterpillar, the drinks that make you bigger and smaller, the magic mushroom, the unstable sense of self and other, the way familiar people and objects become strange. In Jefferson Airplane's 'White Rabbit', Grace Slick commands in a rising howl: 'R*emem*ber... what the dormouse said! Feed your head!'

But there's no reason at all to suppose that the strait-laced Dodgson was off his head on laudanum. To see the dream-narrative of Alice as a trip is to put the cart before the horse: being a child is trippy enough. Neuroscience backs this up. Adult minds are focused like spotlights – they have learned to ignore extraneous sensory input and fit the world into established categories and hierarchies of meaning – but children have what the developmental psychologist Alison Gopnik has called 'lantern consciousness'. They are overloaded with external stimuli and form original and unusual connections and hypotheses. Fantasy and counterfactuals are how children run. 'Children,' writes Gopnik, 'are the R & D department of the human species.'[*] What makes established, running-on-rails adult cognition behave like that? Psychedelic drugs. It's no coincidence that Michael Pollan, in his book about the developing science of such drugs, quotes Gopnik.[†]

The *Alice* books are bizarre, then, but they're not random: they simply obey different rules. They don't discard a priori the supposition that a smile could survive the disappearance of a cat, or that you might be somebody totally different from the person you were when you woke up this morning. Like a child's consciousness, they make unexpected connections, following the sort of logic – of linguistic coincidence, for instance – that adult thinking has learned to discard as irrelevant. As the literary critic Robert Douglas-Fairhurst puts it, 'What links these childhood games

---

[*]   Alison Gopnik, *The Philosophical Baby: What Children's Minds Tell Us About Truth, Love and the Meaning of Life* (Bodley Head, 2009).

[†]   Michael Pollan, *How to Change Your Mind: What the New Science of Psychedelics Teaches Us About Consciousness, Dying, Addiction, Depression, and Transcendence* (Allen Lane, 2018).

and fictional experiments is Carroll's desire to unpeel some of the layers of cliché and habit that muffle ordinary life.'* That dovetails, too, with the Romantic way of thinking about childhood – the notion that children experience the world in a profoundly different, fresher, more vivid way than adults: that the doors of their perception are cleansed.

So what did Alice give to children's writing in particular? At the time Carroll was writing, we'd had a century or more of dry books of facts and history, and moralistic fables – books that sought to improve children's minds or their souls. Both had in common that they were, one way or another, trying to shape children in an orderly way, to inscribe neat lines on the blank slate. Carroll ridiculed both these projects, and instead made a knight's move: the books repudiate a moral and rational order in favour of the chaotic play of paradox and whimsy. He took the blank slate and doodled on it.

That made available a new mode of writing for children. One in which fun and silliness was an end in itself, and the sheer otherness of a child's apprehension of the world could be acknowledged. It smashed up the old conventions, showing how children's writing could be silly, and mysterious, and magical, and entirely uninterested in preparing its readers either morally or informationally for adult life. It marked one position in a negotiation between realism and fantasy that has been going on in the bookshelves of our childhoods ever since. One tendency tracks the path of the novel itself towards the high-water mark of nineteenth-century naturalism you find in George Eliot or Flaubert; the other hews closer to the folktales and fables that are our basic narrative inheritance.

In children's literature, as in childhood itself, growing up is a matter of negotiating between fantasy and reality, magic and

---

* Robert Douglas-Fairhurst, *The Story of Alice*.

disenchantment, the latter steadily gaining the upper hand. Children's books simultaneously seek to prepare us for the real world – offering lessons in courage or friendship or virtue – and to offer a marvellous escape from it. Often, again following the model of *Alice*, they contain elements of both by supplying a rabbit-hole, a magical wardrobe or a curiously permeable railway platform that creates a portal between two worlds. As any student of folktale will know, magic mirrors and underground kingdoms aren't original to Carroll – but he made them his own. A vast body of subsequent children's fantasy writing takes its protagonists through some form of portal into a world populated by fantastical creatures and whose rules are not like our own.

Even the books' emphasis on food anticipates a thread of gustatory wonder that runs through subsequent children's stories – with their midnight feasts, their fabulous picnics and their bags of sweets. Alice's potion, before Bertie Bott's Every Flavour Beans or Willy Wonka's three-course-dinner chewing gum were thought of, before lashings and lashings of ginger beer, or a rat's picnic containing 'col dtonguecoldhamcoldbeefpickledgherkinssaladfrenchrollscress-sandwidgespottedmeatgingerbeerlemonade-sodawater', Alice's 'Drink Me' elixir tastes of 'cherry-tart, custard, pineapple, roast turkey, toffee, and hot buttered toast'.

But at the same time, *Alice* has a place in literary history more like that of *Tristram Shandy* than that of *Tom Jones* or *Clarissa*. Vital elements of its outlook go through subsequent children's writing like the lettering through a stick of rock, but it doesn't establish a genre. There aren't any other books remotely like it. It's more, to mix metaphors in what I hope will pass as a Carrollian way, like a catalyst than a foundation-stone.

There's no denying, anyway, that children as well as adults adored it, and quickly. Five hundred copies of *Alice* were sold in the first three weeks after publication and a 3,000-copy reprint was made in September of the following year. By 1869 it was still selling more than 500 copies a month and had gone into French and German translations.* The 1871 publication of *Through the Looking-Glass* fixed Carroll in the firmament: within two months of its appearing in print 15,000 copies had been sold, and a review in the *Athenaeum* thought it 'had the power to bring happiness to countless children of all ages'. In 1898, the *Pall Mall Gazette* conducted a poll entitled 'What Children Like to Read'. In first place, which the magazine described as a result 'so natural that it will surprise no normal person', was *Alice's Adventures in Wonderland*.

By the end of the century in which they were published, then, these books dominated the children's literary landscape. Manuscripts and early editions have routinely set record prices at auction, and *Alice* became the first multimedia children's franchise. There were theatrical productions, cash-in imitations (when *The Adventures of Pinocchio* found its way to the US, one edition billed it as *Pinocchio's Adventures in Wonderland*), multiple new versions† and even merch. There were Alice stamp-cases, 'Alice in Wonderland Biscuits' and advertising tie-ins. A 1919 pamphlet called 'Alice in Fi-co-land' had Alice sipping from a bottle (marked 'Drink Me') of a patent laxative called Ficolax.

The success of *Alice* represented an unimaginable transformation in only thirty-odd years: a transformation of reading tastes and of the widely accepted idea of what children's literature could be for. The pious tracts of the previous century had given way to wit and silliness, to that most vital ingredient of children's writing and of the modern idea of childhood: *play*.

⸻

Charles Kingsley (1819–1875) was a strange man, and he had the distinction of writing perhaps the only book in the history of

---

* An appealing piece of trivia is that, in 1923, a young Vladimir Nabokov made the first translation of *Alice* into Russian: his fee was a single five-dollar bill.

† As Robert Douglas-Fairhurst points out, the 1905 version *Retold in Words of One Syllable* 'posed a challenge for important words such as "Alice" and "Wonderland"'.

children's literature as weird as, if not weirder, in its original form, than *Alice's Adventures in Wonderland*. When I say 'in its original form', I mean to acknowledge that the long survival of *The Water-Babies* (1863) as a childhood classic may be in part down to the fact that it hasn't always been consumed in its original form: the very many theatrical adaptations and edited versions have tended to flatten its vast digressions, theoretical in-jokes and wild swerves in register to focus instead on the innocent sort-of-love-story and its hero's aquatic adventures.

Impressively bewhiskered, chauvinistic, philanthropic, and worryingly keen (from the other side of the twentieth century, at least) on the Nordic purity of the Anglo-Saxon race, Kingsley occupied a very prominent place in Victorian public life. He was influential in the cultural, religious, scientific and imperial worlds and was chaplain to Queen Victoria and tutor to the Prince of Wales: deeply embedded in the establishment. His oddities and contradictions tell you something about the oddities and contradictions of his age. He was volubly concerned with the plight of the poor, for instance, but mortified by the threat to the established order that the Chartists, demanding votes for the working classes, represented. He even wrote an open letter urging them to 'turn back from the precipice of riot' and urging on them spiritual reform rather than the vote.

By the time he wrote *The Water-Babies* he was a successful novelist for adults (the uniquely punctuated seaside town of Westward Ho! was named after his 1855 bestseller), a social reformer campaigning to improve the condition of the urban poor, Canon of Westminster and Regius Professor of Modern History at Cambridge. For the latter job he hadn't the slightest qualification, having originally graduated in classics and mathematics. A contemporary historian, perhaps a shade jealous, remarked that they might as well have asked him to command the Channel Fleet. No matter. This was, after all, the last great age of the amateur.

But Kingsley was no sort of self-complacent grandee. His most enduring work emerged not from confidence but from anxiety.

He wrote *The Water-Babies* after a series of nervous breakdowns, and in a state he characterised as 'dark nameless dissatisfaction and dread'. There's something queasy even in its humour: a sense that at the heart of it there are a series of contradictions it is trying and failing to reconcile. As Humphrey Carpenter argues, the book is like 'a prospectus for future genres of children's fiction' – not one but several: 'It is like a plan for things to come; but it remains only a plan, because Kingsley no sooner tries out one mode than he is drawn aside into another.'*

Still, at least its aquatic theme played to his strengths. Kingsley had a psychosexual/religious thing about cold water – as Carpenter puts it, something that would 'both purify him and give him a kind of compensation for sex'. He was fanatically averse to dirt, and believed cold baths were vital instruments for improving the character of the working classes. Cold water wasn't the whole of it. While he was courting his wife he scourged himself, rolled naked in thorn-bushes and made presents to her of home-drawn religious pornography in which scantily clad female saints were tortured by monks. Here, perhaps, we start to stray outside the remit of this book – except inasmuch as we establish a theme. Kingsley, like Carroll, and like very many distinguished authors of children's literature, was Not Like The Other Ducks.

Like *Alice*, *The Water-Babies* was in dialogue with established ideas about children's education – though the satirical targets in this case were not primarily Christian homilists but Gradgrindian encyclopaedists. It also participated in ideas about class and exploitation, and in the scientific and religious debates that had opened up around Darwinism.

Realism and fantasy seldom exist as isolated absolutes – and that is blazingly obvious in this case. The book opens with a proto-Dickensian portrait of the life of its chimney-sweep protagonist

---

*   Carpenter, op. cit.

Tom: soot-black, unlettered, 'who had never heard of God, or of Christ, except in words which you never have heard, and which it would be well if he had never heard', and enduring daily beatings from his master Grimes with the sort of stoicism that regarded violence towards him as 'the way of the world, like the rain and snow and thunder'. The book is popularly credited with influencing the Act of Parliament making it illegal to send children up chimneys, though there's a wan wit to Kingsley's framing of Tom's situation that suggests he's playing it, at least in part, for laughs.

But soon it swerves off into something almost indescribably wayward and disorganised. Tom is sent to sweep the chimneys of a grand manor house, gets lost in the flues, and issues from a fireplace into a pristine white room containing the sleeping form of an angelic little blond girl. He catches sight of himself in a mirror: 'What did such a little black ape want in that sweet young lady's room? [...] And Tom, for the first time in his life, found out that he was dirty.' Taking fright, he bolts across the moors pursued by a comical cavalcade of servants of the house, plunges down an escarpment, and, not long after, with church bells tolling in his ears and possessed by the desire to be clean, he throws off his clothes and slips into the 'clear, clear limestone water'.

There, he dies – or doesn't. The searchers after him 'found a black thing in the water, and said it was Tom's body, and that he had been drowned. They were utterly mistaken. Tom was quite alive; and cleaner, and merrier, than he had ever been.' Reality and fantasy part ways. That 'black thing' has a weight to it that the fantastical story that is to follow never quite shakes off,* but:

---

* It's suggested that the plangent jumping-off point for *The Water-Babies* – the brute fact that the whole fantastical narrative and its theological superstructure strives to transcend; that 'black thing in the water' – may have come from life. Kingsley's brother died – at least according to rumour – by drowning, as did a childhood friend.

Tom, when he woke, for of course he woke – children always wake after they have slept exactly as long as is good for them – found himself swimming about in the stream, being about four inches, or – that I may be accurate – 3.87902 inches long and having round the parotid region of his fauces a set of external gills (I hope you understand all the big words) just like those of a sucking eft, which he mistook for a lace frill, till he pulled at them, found he hurt himself, and made up his mind that they were part of himself, and best left alone. In fact, the fairies had turned him into a water-baby.

There follow a whole series of wacky submarine adventures in no very particular order. From his underwater vantage point Tom witnesses the subsequent drowning of the brutish Grimes – and sets out downriver and into the open ocean where, eventually, he will be washed clean of his sins, help to save Grimes's soul, and be chastely reunited with the blonde who caused all the trouble in the first place. You can see the influence of *The Pilgrim's Progress* and *Gulliver's Travels* – while at the same time Tom's sea-quest prefigures the transatlantic crossing in *James and the Giant Peach*.

It's a moralistic book – in some ways a classic story of the path of a soul to redemption; its protagonist is brought through the novel from a state of sin (or at least of ignorance) to a state of grace – that insists repeatedly that it doesn't have a moral. It's a book lovingly crammed with closely observed material about marine biology[*] and the habits of sea-creatures ('the good whales lay, the happy sleepy beasts, upon the still oily sea') yet railing against the imaginative poverty of scientific empiricism. It's a picaresque adventure story and a philosophical investigation. It insists more than once that it is 'a fairytale, and all fun and pretence; and that you are not to

---

[*] Kingsley's previous work included *Glaucus, or The Wonders of the Shore* (1855).

believe one word of it, even if it is true'.* Myth and allegory and sheer nonsense jostle in it.

Its oddest quality, especially to the modern reader, is the way that this parable of the shriving of a soul is at least as interested in Darwin's box-fresh theory of evolution by natural selection. Darwin was a friend and correspondent of the author – *On the Origin of Species* was published four years before *The Water-Babies* – and Kingsley's work is full of jabs at the hidebound scientific establishment that was so slow to accept it. He includes T.H. Huxley and the palaeontologist Richard Owen in the book by name, and offers a Swiftian spoof of a then-current argument about whether the hippocampus (as the seat of reason) was a unique feature of the human brain.

We're accustomed to thinking of Darwin's ideas – making it possible as they do to take the creator out of the picture – as having dealt a great blow to Christian faith. But faith and Darwinism coexist in Kingsley – indeed, they even complement each other. At least, the author seems to hope so. Kingsley's beef is with a science that leaves no room for enchantment. Wordsworth supplies many of the book's epigraphs; among them are the passage containing the line 'we murder to dissect'. Kingsley said plainly in a letter to a friend that he wanted to make his readers understand that 'there is a quite miraculous and divine element underlying all physical nature'.

The world of *The Water-Babies* is one, like that of *Alice* and for that matter of Victorian England, of constant transformation. When Tom first enters the river he gets involved with caddis-flies and watches a dragonfly leave its larval form. At various points in the story we're presented with creatures evolving backwards: a sniffy salmon explains that trout are salmon who, being 'lazy, and

---

* Compare the formulaic opening of the Arabic folktale: 'There was, there wasn't…'.

cowardly, and greedy', have regressed to their present degraded form; the selfish and idle human tribe of Doasyoulikes grow hairier and more ape-like with each successive generation. Tom, too, is in a state of transformation – first physical and then spiritual. Under the supervision of the two fairies Miss Doasyouwouldbedoneby and Miss Bedonebyasyoudid, the first embodying divine grace and the second divine judgement, he is, you could say, evolving. And when he finally meets the creator-aspect of this tripartite sisterhood, Mother Carey, he finds her ceaselessly 'making old beasts into new'; or, as she puts it: 'I sit here and make them make themselves.'* As with Darwinian evolution so, perhaps, with the operation of the divine plan in a world containing free will.

In keeping with the speed of its composition (Kingsley's wife claimed he'd knocked the first chapter out in half an hour), or, if we're to be more charitable, with its consistent interest in transformation, the shape of *The Water-Babies* is a mess. A bit of business with a lobster, for instance, sparks a four-page anecdote about what happened to the mayor of Plymouth involving a lobster 'eight or nine hundred years ago'. A brief encounter with a Professor Ptthmllnsprts ('a very great naturalist, and chief professor of *Necrobioneopalaeonthydrochthonanthropopithekology* in the new university which the king of the Cannibal Islands had founded'), who refuses to believe in water-babies even when he catches one, leads into a digression about the professor subsequently losing his wits and a Rabelaisian catalogue of the ludicrous quack cures that doctors attempted on him. It's by turns wearyingly whimsical and highly readable, but it is consistently as mad as a box of frogs.

---

* Kingsley borrowed the name of this sea-fairy from folklore, where she more often appears as the goddess of storms – but her name chimes perhaps not by accident with that of the Roman nature-goddess Ceres; as does her more nurturing role in the story.

Incuriouser and Incuriouser

THOMAS HUGHES · *BOY'S OWN* ·
W.H.G. KINGSTON · G.A. HENTY

*Tom Brown's School Days; Peter the Whaler; Sheer
Pluck; Out on the Pampas; With Lee in Virginia*

I F THE TWO AUTHORS I'VE JUST DESCRIBED NEGOTIATE
the religious uneasiness of the age, Thomas Hughes's *Tom
Brown's School Days* (1857) embraced the heartier and more
practical side of the mid-Victorian worldview. Here's a book that
hews more to the realist tradition than the fantastical one, and
whose author, a 'muscular Christian' of the tub-thumping school,
was not so apparently tortured as some of his contemporaries we
could mention. The story is torn between eat-your-greens moral
instruction and fun for the sake of it, but its peculiarities are, at
least, somewhat under control. When Hughes sent it to his friend
Charles Kingsley to ask his opinion before publication, the latter
urged him on: 'It will be a very great hit!' So it was.

This slantly autobiographical novel about the adventures of its
titular protagonist at Rugby School – which he attended in the days
of its celebrated headmaster Doctor Arnold – is a wryly comical
Bildungsroman about a good chap making his way through public
school and learning along the way to temper his heartiness with
piety. The side of Tom in which the child reader (and the modern
one) will tend to delight is the one that breaks rules 'for no earthly
pleasure except that of doing what they are told not to do'; but the
story also shows how Tom is reformed, or semi-reformed, by being

obliged to take a vulnerable and bookish new boy called George Arthur under his wing.

Its popularity took the school story, by then an established but not a prominent genre, and put it at the centre of the tradition. As I've argued, education, which was on its way to being a universal experience, certainly for the middle classes, who would consume fiction, had become a defining aspect of childhood: it bounded the space between infancy and adulthood. So it was a natural territory for children's writing – and, in its way, it did what Alice's rabbit-hole and all those portals to other worlds that were to follow did. It made narratives possible by taking children away from parental authority and giving them independence of action.

The boarding school was a space with its own hierarchies and rules, freedoms and opportunities. It put children into a community that was not the family – and it sat, you could say, perfectly in the sweet spot between safety and danger. Nothing too bad could happen there, but plenty could happen. It's a practice-mode version of the adult world. As he heads off to Rugby, 'The second act of Tom's life may now be said to have begun [...] None of the women now – not even his mother's maid – dared offer to help him in washing or dressing.' He has his first taste of brown stout on his way to school. He shakes his father's hand ('Tom having stipulated in the morning before starting that kissing should now cease between them'). Hughes is a good enough writer and psychologist to ironise the moment. Tom, as the book opens, is still halfway between these two worlds. A mention of his mother makes him feel 'rather choky', and he 'would have liked to have hugged his father well, if it hadn't been for the recent stipulation'.

It's further made clear that school is to be taken as a microcosmic version of life. Tom's first 'calling-over' 'rolls on somehow, much like the big world, punishments lighting on wrong shoulders, and matters going generally in a queer, cross-grained way, but the end coming somehow, which is, after all, the great point'. A defining quality of *Tom Brown* is its cheery philistinism. This goes with the grain of the then English public school system rather than against it: 'The object of all schools is not to ram Latin and Greek into boys, but to make them good English boys, good future citizens; and by far the most important part of that work must be done, or not done, out of school hours.'

Public schools saw themselves as shaping their pupils' characters rather than instilling in them the rather suspect quality, now much prized, of academic excellence. In his book *Stiff Upper Lip*, Alex Renton quotes an admired headmaster of a Scottish public school on what he aspired to produce in his pupils: 'First – Character. Second – Physique. Third – Intelligence. Fourth – Manners. Fifth – Information.'* Even in more academically minded schools it was tradition, rather than the usefulness of what was learned, that guided the curriculum. The headmaster of Eton, asked by the 1861 Clarendon Commission to say how he saw the relative values of the classics, mathematics and modern languages, declared: '15:13:1'.

Then, of course, there was sport. The cliché that the Battle of Waterloo was won on the playing fields of Eton tells us something about the way sport came to be viewed. By the late Victorian period it was seen as the testing-ground of character and a guiding metaphor for life: think of Henry Newbolt's now much derided exhortation in his 1892 '*Vitai Lampada*' to 'Play up, play up, and play the game!' *Tom Brown's School Days* doesn't just reflect that ethos (when the book was published few public schools had games fields or organised sports): it helped create it.

The book is filled with detailed and approving descriptions of sport, and violence, and there's no very ready distinction between the two. The highlight of communal festivities in Tom's native village is the 'noble old game of backsword', in which young men armed with a 'good stout ash stick' compete to break each other's

---

* Alex Renton, *Stiff Upper Lip*.

heads. The organic unity of English society, Hughes warns, depends on this sort of thing:

> Don't let reformers of any sort think that they are going really to lay hold of the working boys and young men of England by any educational grapnel whatever, which isn't [...] something to put in the place of the back-swording and wrestling and racing; something to try the muscles of men's bodies, and the endurance of their hearts, and to make them rejoice in their strength.

At Rugby, Tom initially earns the respect of the older boys in a long and energetic and almost incomprehensible football match. The school hero Brooke, head of the eleven, gives a speech ('No action, no tricks of oratory – plain, strong and straight, like his play') in which he declares: 'I know I'd sooner win two School-house matches running than get the Balliol scholarship any day.' He receives 'frantic cheers' from his audience. Here is a worldview – Brooke as 'Pater', 'football king', 'leader of the sporting interest', 'full of pluck and hope – the sort of look I hope to see in my general when I go out to fight' – that collapses the distinctions between sport, politics and warfare. Tom earns his spurs when he is charged down and flattened 'under the very feet of the advancing column'. After checking that he hasn't any broken bones, Brooke anoints him: 'He is a plucky youngster, and will make a player.'

Tom is indeed a plucky youngster. He 'had nothing whatever remarkable about him except excess of boyishness – by which I mean animal life in its fullest measure, good nature and honest impulses, hatred of injustice and meanness, and thoughtlessness enough to sink a three-decker.' This puts him in line with his kinsmen:

> In the first place, the Browns are a fighting family. One may ques-
> tion their wisdom, or wit, or beauty, but about their fight there
> can be no question. Wherever hard knocks of any kind, visible or
> invisible, are going; there the Brown who is nearest must shove

in his carcass. And these carcasses, for the most part, answer very well to the characteristic propensity: they are a squareheaded and snake-necked generation, broad in the shoulder, deep in the chest, and thin in the flank, carrying no lumber.

They never love each other more than after 'a good set family arguing bout', and 'go on believing and fighting to a green old age. They always have a crotchet going, till the old man with the scythe reaps and garners them away for troublesome old boys as they are.' These fighting Browns, Hughes says, were to be found in Agincourt and Crecy, American forests and Australian uplands. It is a 'great army of Browns, who are scattered over the whole empire on which the sun never sets [...] whose general diffusion I take to be the chief cause of that empire's stability'. It is such pugnacious but enthusiastic blockheads, says Hughes, who are the very backbone of empire.

A key point to note, against our current stereotypes of public-school life, is that the Browns are emphatically not aristocrats. They are country squirearchy: curates, solicitors, middle-ranking officers. In modern pop-sociological terms they are 'somewheres' – as against the overeducated 'anywheres' of what we'd now call the metropolitan elite. The former are, in Hughes's telling, the backbone of society; the latter are deracinated, effete and not to be trusted: 'We were Berkshire, or Gloucestershire, or Yorkshire boys; and you're young cosmopolites, belonging to all countries and no countries':

You're all in the ends of the earth, it seems to me, as soon as you get your necks out of the educational collar, for midsummer holidays, long vacations, or what not – going round Ireland, with a return ticket, in a fortnight; dropping your copies of Tennyson on the tops of Swiss mountains; or pulling down the Danube in Oxford racing boats. [...] You all patter French more or less, and perhaps German; you have seen men and cities, no doubt, and have your opinions, such as they are, about schools of painting, high art, and all that; have seen the pictures of Dresden and the Louvre, and know the taste of sour krout. All I say is, you don't know your own lanes and woods and fields.

Nostalgia suffuses *Tom Brown's School Days*. The book speaks to its readers from 1857 but is set in the 1830s, and the survey of the Vale of the White Horse with which it opens is already lamenting the vanishing of rural customs and traditions, where the 'confounded Great Western [...] carried away Alfred's Hill to make an embankment'. It is already a lament for a vanishing age of organic social unity and a national identity based on tradition, land and soil, 'the great Vale spread out like the garden of the Lord [...] sacred ground for Englishmen'.

That's not just a historical but a personal idyll – nostalgia for childhood itself projected onto nostalgia for a vanishing England (a seam that was to be enthusiastically mined for the next century or more by Hughes's successors). Even Tom's arrival in Rugby is a little Fall. Once he played with the village boys – 'Squire Brown held [...] that it didn't matter a straw whether his son associated with lords' sons or ploughmen's sons, provided they were brave and honest'. Now, he finds himself on one side of a town-and-gown divide – where young men from town are 'the louts', to be bested in combat.

Hughes seems to have been pulled in two directions. His piety as a Christian socialist, and his occasional sententiousness, is always countered by an undertow of what made the book so engaging and so popular. As much as it approves the stern wisdom of Doctor Arnold, the book can't help itself celebrating, too, the anarchic energy of his wayward charges. Boys are naughty. Boys get into scrapes. That tension in Hughes's narration is never more concisely expressed than when Harry East, the older boy who takes him in hand, is first showing Tom round the school: 'There's the chapel, you see,' he says, 'and there, just behind it, is the place for fights.'

The children are forever pelting each other with acorns, assailing passers-by with pea-shooters or being tossed in blankets by bullies – the latter activity is only notionally disapproved of as unsporting when there are two boys in the blanket at once. Still, submitting to it earns Tom further respect. 'The consciousness of silent endurance,' Hughes writes elsewhere, is 'dear to every Englishman – of standing out against something, and not giving in.' Tom, as the book goes on, will come through his interactions with the gentle George Arthur to appreciate the more peaceable Christian virtues. He overcomes his embarrassment at public prayer and daily Bible readings. But he's a natural pagan to start off with.

That tension runs through the book and animates the shifts of tone in its prose. In comic mode we have a confiding, amiable narrator with his no-nonsense jocularity – 'those that don't care for England in detail may skip the chapter'; 'I make so bold as at once to tell you the sort of folk you'll have to meet and put up with, if you and I are to jog on comfortably together'. But when he starts to talk about Doctor Arnold the writing takes on an almost sacramental quality:

> More worthy pens than mine have described that scene – the oak pulpit standing out by itself above the School seats; the tall, gallant form, the kindling eye, the voice, now soft as the low notes of a flute, now clear and stirring as the call of the light-infantry bugle, of him who stood there Sunday after Sunday [...] It was a great and solemn sight, and never more so than at this time of year, when the only lights in the chapel were in the pulpit and at the seats of the præpostors of the week, and the soft twilight stole over the rest of the chapel, deepening into darkness in the high gallery behind the organ.

Hughes wonders that as boys 'we [...] thought more of our sets in the School than of the Church of Christ, and put the traditions of Rugby and the public opinion of boys in our daily life above the laws of God', and yet the emotional energy of the book is split between those pagan boys and the doctor who represents their correction and salvation. Here's a complexity you seldom see in the pious tracts of the previous century. The evangelical Hughes shares space in the telling of his story with the boy who looking back at bedtime on his first day at school 'had quite settled that it must be the greatest day he should ever spend, and didn't alter his opinion for many a long year – if he has yet'.

You can look down the time-telescope from Hughes to Rudyard Kipling's *Stalky & Co.* (which I'll discuss in the next chapter) and on to the indefatigable Angela Brazil (1869–1947; pronounced, apparently, 'brazzle'), who produced dozens of girls'-school stories between 1906 and her death just after the war, with titles like *An Exciting Term, Jill's Jolliest School, Joan's Best Chum* and *Ruth of St Ronan's*. She established the now-cliché of jolly-hockey-sticks girls called things like Ernestine Salt and Raymonde Armitage having pashes and bust-ups in rural boarding schools ruled over by grey-haired, firm-but-fair spinster headmistresses.

Through the twenties and thirties the no less indefatigable Frank Richards – one of a score of pseudonyms under which Charles Hamilton (1876–1961) published some 100 million words; he's claimed to be the most prolific author in human history – gave us the Greyfriars School stories from which Billy Bunter emerged. These stories thrived in magazines such as the *Gem* and the *Magnet*. George Orwell was to complain in his 1940 essay 'Boys' Weeklies' that these were antiques even in the 1930s: 'The outlook inculcated by all these papers is that of a rather exceptionally stupid member of the Navy League in the year 1910.'

By the time Enid Blyton dabbled in the school genre in the 1940s, then, it was on its last legs. As well as scorn, it attracted parody.*

---

* As genres ossify, and those who consumed them as children look back from adulthood with amused condescension, that's what happens. Think of Carroll's spoofing the pious hymns of Isaac Watts; *Struwwelpeter* and *Cautionary Tales* sending up morality tales; or, in our own time, *Viz* affectionately mocking Enid Blyton, eighties photo-romance stories and seventies children's comics.

The gleefully cynical and miraculously funny *Molesworth* stories, by Geoffrey Willans (1911–1958) and the illustrator Ronald Searle, had their worldly protagonist dodging the weeds and wets of a decrepit minor public school called St Custard's. It put the tin hat on the school story as it had been.*†

Yet at the same time it threw a long forward pass to J.K. Rowling, who was to revive the school story after decades in suspended animation. The word Hogwarts first appears in the title of a non-sensical Latin play written by Molesworth as a class assignment ('The Hogwarts by Marcus Plautus Molesworthus'), and, each year on prize day, St Custard's awards a 'Scrimgeour Cup for Good Character' (a Rufus Scrimgeour appears in the Harry Potter books as a sometime Minister for Magic). The railway-platform back-to-school scene in *How to Be Topp*, its narrator's atrocious spelling aside, surely laid the groundwork for those bustling scenes on Platform 9¾. All these are Hughes's children. But I get ahead of myself. Forgive me: time travel is, as I've said, a feature of children's reading.

—

If the eighteenth century had seen children's stories that sought to prepare its young audience for the next life, then, it was in the nineteenth century that writers started to realise it might not hurt to prepare them for this one. *Tom Brown's School Days* is the story of the making not of a saint, but of a young man. The stream broadened. The Calvinists were in retreat, and into their place were stepping the Anglican evangelicals, utopian social reformers and mutton-chopped patriots whose work was to lay down and consolidate some of the enduring genres of children's writing.

---

* *Down With Skool!* (1953), *How to Be Topp* (1954), *Whizz for Atomms* (1956) and *Back in the Jug Agane* (1959).

† Searle was recruited for the project after the success of his girls' school St Trinian's cartoons.

It offered a worldview with specific roles and expectations for boys and girls, specific ideas about moral virtue and social propriety. If the child, in Wordsworthian terms, was father to the man, the man aimed for was as often as not a good Christian and an honourable servant of Her Imperial Majesty.

It was an age, to those growing up in the prosperous and privileged heart of empire, ripe with possibilities of adventure, and popular writers were quick to exploit it. In the realist style, the market was flooded with roistering stories of adventure on the high seas, the African jungle or the Argentinian pampas, or tales of the past that allowed their young readers to imagine themselves in the most exciting episodes of world history – while at the same time affirming the glories of that history and making clear who were the heroes and who the villains in the making of it. The torments and paradoxes of Carroll and Kingsley may have been influential, but they weren't the only game in town.

'Boy's Own' is a phrase that has passed into our general stock of epithets, but it has its origins in a whole slew of publications launched in the Victorian age, and the best known of which – the *Boy's Own Paper* – didn't cease publication until 1967. The phrase itself connotes old-fashioned derring-do: pluck, adventures and hijinks painted in the colours of the Union Jack. Seafaring adventures in the model of Captain Marryat (Frederick Marryat, 1792–1848) proliferated – paving the way for C.S. Forester, Robert Louis Stevenson and Patrick O'Brian – as did historical romances.

Writers like W.H.G. Kingston (1814–1880) – founder in late life of a boys' magazine called the *Union Jack* – took advantage of the liberating possibilities of foreign adventure. His first book for children, *Peter the Whaler* (1851), starred a young boy whose recidivism as a poacher has his sorrowful father consign him to sea: 'We must part with you, my son; we have no choice. You must go to foreign lands, and there retrieve your name, and, I trust, improve and strengthen your character.' There followed from his prolific pen dozens of boys' adventure novels called things like

The Three Lieutenants, The Voyage of the Steadfast and *Won from the Waves*.

The man who did most to shape the genre, which in one form or another is still vigorous today, is a now nearly forgotten figure called G.A. (George Alfred) Henty (1832–1902). His schtick was historical adventure stories set everywhere from Ancient Egypt (*The Cat of Bubastes*) to the American Civil War (*With Lee in Virginia*). The fact that he's little read now – except, apparently, among American homeschoolers of a conservative bent – should not lead us to underestimate either his importance in his own age or his influence on those who were to come.

In his heyday, his main English publisher was printing 150,000 of his books a year – and it's been estimated that there could have been as many as 25 million G.A. Henty books printed worldwide by the time he went out of copyright in 1952. In part, those staggering numbers reflect not just his popularity but his rate of work. Henty didn't half churn them out. He made Anthony Trollope look like a slacker. Between 1867 and 1906 he published 122 books, not to mention countless short stories for the periodical market.* If you care to download *The Complete Works of G.A. Henty* on Kindle, £1.99 will get you just north of 33,000 pages, which I'd call a bargain.

Educated at Westminster and Caius College, Cambridge, Henty dropped out of university to join the army medical corps in the Crimean War, and after resigning his commission in 1859 became a war correspondent. His travels took him all over the world. He witnessed the Franco-Prussian, Austro-Italian and Turco-Serbian wars, and his experiences fed into the adventure stories he was to write. Their protagonists – plucky teenage boys showing their mettle in dangerous situations – were designed for his readers, whom he routinely addressed as 'My dear lads', to identify with.

---

* The attentive reader will notice that this is four years after his death in 1902. There were that many of the things, presumably, that it took a while for his publishers to clear the backlog.

In the last year of his life he described his process in an essay
called 'How Boys' Books Are Written':

> When I get to the purely historical part I have three or four [his-
> tory] books open before me, and I insist particularly that all my
> history shall be absolutely unassailable. I dictate every word – in
> that way I think you obtain larger, finer sentences, and I smoke
> the whole time. My work is extremely rapidly done. On more than
> one occasion I have completed a book of one hundred and forty
> thousand words in twenty days.*

The haste shows in the books. The 100,000 plus word-count of
each is often padded with supplementary episodes or self-contained
adventure yarns narrated by a minor character. *By Sheer Pluck*, for
instance, deals with the third Anglo-Ashanti War in the 1870s, but
the main story is prefaced by a series of mini-adventures from its
hero Frank Hargate's youth (saves the day when a dinghy is blown
out to sea in a storm; helps rescue schoolmates cut off by the rising
tide; saves a child from a mad dog), and a yarn from an old sea-salt
who never reappears. Then, when Frank's travels as a naturalist
in the African interior plunge him into the historical events of the
Ashanti War, the book abandons its over-our-hero's-shoulder narrative stance to give us an ill-integrated military-historical account
of the Ashanti campaign.

Haste is evident in the dialogue, too. Another of his self-contained
stories-within-a-story is narrated by a well-travelled tribal chief
called Sam, whose dialogue seems to have been imperfectly fed
into Google Translate (Offensive Racial Stereotype Edition). 'I hab
observed, sar, dat de geography ob women am bery defective,' he'll
say, or 'Me trabel a good deal, and me tink dat no working people

---

* Raymond Blathwayt, 'How Boys' Books Are Written: a talk with Mr G.A.
Henty', *Great Thoughts from Master Minds, II, 5th Series*, 497, October 1902.

in de world are so merry and happy as de slabe in a plantation wid a good massa and missy.' But then Henty will forget to infantilise the diction and Sam will use phrases like 'make shift to', 'skirmishing line', 'an attack upon our vessel by an English cruiser', or declare: 'The clergyman knew something of surgery, and he managed to substract the ball from my hip.'

Among the reasons Henty has fallen out of favour, as the foregoing shows, is that his historical attitudes are distinctly of his time. Henty was a lavishly bearded Victorian patriot of the old style: a fervent fan of empire and an implicit believer in the right of the freeborn Englishman to bring the benefits of civilisation to brown people around the world; and, if they cut up rough about it, to shoot them. (The same went, roughly, for Frenchmen – who having had a revolution were not wholly to be trusted.) There's no getting around the fact that Henty's worldview was what would now be called white supremacist. The n-word appears 139 times in the *Collected Works*, and the protagonist of *With Lee in Virginia* is on what moralists will consider the wrong side in the American Civil War.

Racial hierarchies are part of the furniture of Henty's world. He describes non-white characters in the same coolly quasi-scientific tone that he describes the flora, fauna and geology of his settings. One notorious passage in *By Sheer Pluck* (1884) declares: 'The intelligence of the average negro is about equal to that of a European child of ten years old. A few, a very few, go beyond this, but these are exceptions, just as Shakespeare was an exception to the ordinary intellect of an Englishman [...] Living among white men, their imitative faculties enable them to obtain a considerable amount of civilization. Left alone to their own devices they retrograde into a state little above their native savagery.' Or, in *Out on the Pampas* (1870): 'The Indians of the South American Pampas and Sierras are a very inferior race to the noble-looking Comanches and Apaches of the North American Prairies. They are generally short, wiry men, with long black hair. They have flat faces, with high cheek bones.

Their complexion is a dark copper colour, and they are generally extremely ugly.'

That anthropological racism is, in a way, no more than an embarrassing side-effect of the basic project of the books. As well as quickening the pulse with episodes of violent derring-do, Henty's stories want to tell their readers interesting things about places (and times) remote from their own experience. They are stuffed with information as well as with action. Henty's first book for children, *Out on the Pampas*, for instance, tells the story of a middle-class English family who move to Argentina in 1851 to seek their fortune as ranchers. Much of it is taken up with enraptured accounts of how their estancia is constructed, how irrigation systems are put in, how you turn sugar cane into sugar and why you need to watch out for armadillos. Henty is actuarially specific about the profits that his characters realise from their investments, and what that will mean to their prospects and standing when they return home. In this respect Henty looks backward to the 'Robinsonades' of the previous century – Robinson Crusoe being essentially a shipwrecked accountant – and forward to the works of Willard Price (1887–1983), for whom the jungle or the veldt were alike a source not just of wonder and danger but of extractable resources.* Nature – of which 'savage' peoples are implicitly a part – is there not to be enthralled by but to be tamed, taxonomised and monetised.

The violence of the books is of a part with their settler-colonial mindset. When the 'Indians' attack, Henty takes a special, and one might think unsporting, pleasure in how heavily outgunned they are. During a siege of the estancia, a 'rain of blows with hatchet and tomahawk [...] instead of splintering the wood, merely made

---

* Price's *Adventure* series, beginning with *Amazon Adventure* (1949), followed teenage daredevils Hal and Roger Hunt as they roamed the world duffing up rare and dangerous animals and bagging them for their father's Long Island zoo. The books remained popular well into the 1980s, though their low-key racism and ecocidal attitudes belonged more to the 1880s. Cracking yarns, nevertheless.

deep dents, or glided off harmlessly. Then the blows redoubled, and then a bright light suddenly lit up the whole scene. As it did so, from every loophole a stream of fire poured out, repeated again and again. The guns, heavily loaded with buck-shot, told with terrible effect upon the crowded mass of Indians around the windows.' There's a dismaying exultation – an almost industrial satisfaction – that the white man has the superior technology. The bodies pile up, not much to be mourned.

Though it won't rehabilitate his reputation to say so, Henty is pretty good as pulp writers go. His books for children are sausage-strings of violent set-pieces interspersed with Wikipedia-style info-dumps, and their language hasn't the slightest literary distinction. But they are vigorous, pacy and direct and they answer compelling fantasies. He's a good bad writer. And his immense popularity points us in the direction of a truth worth bearing in mind. Some children's writing is of literary interest – and it's that which tends to survive and attract the attention of scholars; William Empson took a serious interest in *Alice* that you can't imagine him taking in Henty – but the heart of the successful stuff is storytelling and pace. Popular fiction tends to vanish from the record, but it shapes and reflects the culture.

That culture is evidenced everywhere in even the most fantastical children's literature of the mid-nineteenth century: the march of empire (and the attitudes and ideas, not all of them savoury, that underpinned it); the rise of the industrial cities and concerns about the conditions of the working poor; the spread and questions about the uses of education; the negotiation between the new sciences and a Christianity that remained vigorous even as it became less doctrinaire. The folktales that are many of these stories' ancestors begin 'once upon a time'. But the present moment presses on these books – even as they bathe in nostalgia. That's not a contradiction. Nostalgia *occupies* the present moment; the nostalgia of every gen-eration for an imagined past; the nostalgia of every adult for an imagined childhood.

IV

MAN-CUBS
AND NAUGHTY BUNNIES

Rudyard Kipling · Robert Louis Stevenson ·
John Meade Falkner · George MacDonald · Carlo Collodi ·
Beatrix Potter · Anna Sewell

LATE VICTORIANS

THE GREAT FILLIP THAT THE FIRST BOOKS OF THE Golden Age gave to children's writing was consolidated in the second half of that century. We were to see genres being explored and established – adventure stories, school stories, fantasy, anthropomorphic animal stories. But there was not, yet, much in the way of precedent to follow. These writers were, most of them, making it up as they went along and that is what gives the era so much of its vivacity and messiness.

Markets were opening up, and audiences widening. As the literary historian Peter Hunt notes, 'there was a rapid expansion of both the middle-class "respectable" market [...] and the penny dreadfuls'.* Changing technology – from the ascendancy of the rotary printing press to cardboard book covers and photomechanical reproduction of pictures taking the place of engravings – made books cheaper and more accessible to a wide market. By 1875, one publisher's catalogue alone contained 1,000 children's books.

The periodicals market, too, was booming. Many of the classics we still read were originally published in serial form in magazines. The *Boy's Own Paper*, which started in 1879, by the end of the 1880s was selling a quarter of a million copies a week; the *Girl's Own Paper*, founded in the same year, was thought to have had the highest circulation of any illustrated magazine. These publications sought

---

* Hunt, op. cit.

to win converts (sometimes literally: *Boy's Own* was started by the Religious Tract Society) from the exciting but morally disreputable 'gallows' pamphlets in which the poor delighted and which middle-class children read on the sly. In 1890 the conservative press baron Alfred Harmsworth launched a weekly comic, *Comic Cuts*. A.A. Milne remarked that he 'killed the penny dreadful: by the simple process of producing a ha'penny dreadfuller'[*].

The late Victorian period was also a time in which children's lives transformed: they were coming down the proverbial chimney, scrubbing up and going to school. It had not been until the beginning of the nineteenth century that the English state started to take a serious legislative interest in child labour. The follow-up was that education, rather than work, was on its way to being the defining space of childhood. England made its first public subvention of funds for elementary schooling in 1833, and in the second half of the century universal education was starting to look like more than just an aspiration.

Church schools, Sunday schools and modestly priced private schools were already becoming the norm – and by the 1870s, according to the social historian Hugh Cunningham, a 'huge majority' of English children were receiving some sort of education.[†] The 1870 Education Act mandated a school in every local area, and in 1880 attendance became compulsory for children between the ages of five and ten. As Cunningham puts it, 'the way was opened to a major transformation in both the experience and conceptualisation of childhood, the shift from a situation where children were thought of as members of the labour force to one where they were schoolchildren'.

In England and Wales, the proportion of children between the ages of five and fourteen who were in school doubled between 1870

---

[*]   A.A. Milne, 'Blood and Thunder', *The Sunday Times*, 10 October 1948.
[†]   Cunningham, op. cit.

and 1880. By 1900, it was nearly three-quarters of that demographic. The 1918 act was to raise the school leaving age from twelve to fourteen; by 1920 or so, it was accepted as entirely natural and proper that every child should be in school until adolescence. Compulsory schooling was seen not only as a means of bettering the population but of extending the hand of the state into their lives and shaping their characters. Periodic moral panics about child delinquency, truancy and what we now call 'feral children' were assuaged by the idea that universal education would help to create a cohesive national identity.

If the British state, like Whitney Houston, believed that children were the future, that future was to be courteous, obedient, and trained for its proper role in life – whether that be needlework and cookery for girls or colonial administration for boys. You can see that dynamic variously endorsed and challenged in school stories over the years. Widening education meant widening literacy. It not only supplied new situations and possibilities for the literature of childhood; it supplied new readers.

What of the country in which those readers were growing up? This was the era in which Britannia ruled the waves and a good bit of the dry land too (Queen Victoria formally became Empress of India in 1876, and the 'scramble for Africa' got going in the 1880s). The pageantry of church, monarchy and empire continued in all its pomp. But Britain's worldview was not as secure as its secular power might suggest. Urbanisation, and the squalor of the urban poor, were changing the idea of what the nation looked like. Darwin's discoveries, as they percolated into the mainstream, were quietly abrading the secure foundations of its God. The anxieties that shaded the works of the early writers of the Golden Age were only deepening. The 'melancholy long withdrawing roar' of Matthew Arnold's 1867 poem 'Dover Beach' rumbled in the background.

The Law of the Jungle

RUDYARD KIPLING

*The Jungle Book; The Second Jungle
Book; Kim; Stalky & Co.; Puck of
Pook's Hill; The Just So Stories*

A CRUCIAL FIGURE IN THE LITERARY SHAPE THAT THIS double movement between self-confidence and anxiety took was Joseph Rudyard Kipling (1865–1936): a poet who, even as he celebrated empire in his poem 'Recessional', composed for Queen Victoria's 1897 Diamond Jubilee, was able to present a vision of how: 'Far-called, our navies melt away; / On dune and headland sinks the fire: / Lo, all our pomp of yesterday / Is one with Nineveh and Tyre!'

That ambivalence runs through Kipling's titanic contribution to children's writing. Along with Beatrix Potter, he bestrode the later part of the nineteenth century, and he continued to write to the brink of the Second World War. His influence has gone far beyond that. Kipling was a poet, novelist, short-story writer and fabulist with an extraordinary range of voices and styles. He produced one of the greats in the school story genre in *Stalky & Co.* (1899). He wrote the founding classic of Great Game spy adventures in *Kim* (1901). He laid, in *Puck of Pook's Hill* (1906), the groundwork for the enchanted Englands of Alan Garner and Susan Cooper. He created the rich and resonant home-made fairytales of *The Just So Stories* (1902). Plus, as Disney would have no hesitation in allowing you to forget, he wrote *The Jungle Book* (1894).

His stories often see their protagonists caught between two worlds – Kim is half sahib,* half native; Mowgli is the man-cub who belongs half to the jungle. To be caught between two worlds and two versions of childhood was Kipling's own experience as a son of the Raj, and the experience is a defining one in his work. Born in Bombay in 1865 – his parents had met and courted in England before relocating, and he was named for a lake in Staffordshire – in his infancy he absorbed Portuguese and Hindi from the servants who looked after him. It was 'the vernacular idiom one thought and dreamed in'; he spoke English, like Kim, only haltingly.

That ended abruptly and traumatically when he was shipped back to the old country to lodge with strangers in Southsea at the age of five. Being shipped halfway around the world and left among strangers seems a startling cruelty to us now, but it was a typical experience for the children of Anglo-Indian families. A version of the same thing is described in Frances Hodgson Burnett's *A Little Princess*. The young Kipling spent the next six years, as he later recalled, miserable: bullied and neglected by the couple who had taken him in, relief only coming with Christmas visits to a kind aunt in London. After a brief summer with his mother when she returned to the country in 1877, he was sent to boarding school in Devon – an experience that was to provide the basis for the boarding-school stories in *Stalky & Co*. Is it any wonder that the old pattern in children's stories – of the simultaneous yearning for a stable home, and for transformation and independence – was so feelingly limned in Kipling's work?

I have among the books piled against the wall in my sons' bedroom a short, board-bound picture book whose cover shows a winsome, tow-haired little boy in red trunks sitting on a rock,

---

* A Hindi term of respect, not generally racialised, but which Kipling frequently uses to refer to Europeans.

companionably arrayed with a cartoon tiger, an orangutan, and a bear laying his friendly paw on a panther. The title says: *Disney, The Jungle Book* and a strapline promises: 'The Original Magical Story.' Nowhere, not on the copyright page, not on the spine, not even in small print inside the back cover, do the words 'Rudyard Kipling' appear. Not only does that Disney picture book in no sense tell the 'original story', but it amounts to the wholesale erasure of the original story – and its author.

The history of children's literature, mind you, is full of retellings, reboots, bowdlerisations and outright appropriations. Long before Walt Disney was thought of, we had PG domestications of hard-R folktales, *Robinson Crusoe* without the economics, *Gulliver's Travels* without the politics, and *The Pilgrim's Progress* without the Puritanism. To get a clear view of the originals of very many children's classics these days, there's a Disney paintjob to be scraped off first. But the Disney version of the Mowgli stories is so pervasive in the culture – your first two Google hits for 'Jungle Book' will be the 1967 film and the 2016 film – and so distorted that they really might as well be two wholly separate properties.*

To pick a few instances: Kaa the snake, in Kipling, is an ally rather than an antagonist of Mowgli; King Louie, the jazz-singing orangutan who rules the Bandar-log (the monkey-people who in one episode kidnap Mowgli), was invented by Disney and appears nowhere in Kipling's stories; Mowgli, in the original, is taken in by Father and Mother Wolf after toddling towards their cave in flight from an attack by the tiger Shere Khan, not discovered by Bagheera abandoned Moses-style in a basket; the final face-off with Shere Khan doesn't result in the tiger slinking away with a scorched tail, as in Disney, but in Mowgli killing and skinning the

---

* The Wikipedia page for the first doesn't even have the courtesy to link to a disambiguation page; though if you do find the page for the Kipling book the first thing it says, as if you might have arrived there by accident, is 'For other uses, see: *The Jungle Book* (disambiguation)'. Pff.

predator; and Mowgli's eventual return to the man-village, accomplished in the film by a saccharine meet-cute with a girl carrying a water-pot, is nothing like that in the original. Mowgli's return to his own kind, in the books, is never more than provisional. His first stint in the man-village ends with his fellow humans stoning him and accusing him of witchcraft, and he pays them back with the help of his animal allies by razing the human village to the ground. Only much later, as a young adult, does he take up cautiously with a human surrogate mother.

The original stories are more sinewy, more austere, and vastly richer thematically. Though not without Kipling's humour, they are very far from being obvious candidates to turn into animated musical comedy. Written in a high style of stately formality (there's a lot of thee-ing and thou-ing among the inhabitants of the jungle), they are concerned above all with ideas of identity, honour, law and morality. There's a gravity to them, a tenderness, and a high seriousness, that's entirely absent from the pantomime world of Disney. But they aren't dry tracts either; they are, like so much Kipling wrote, fantastic feats of world-building and narrative verve.

Also, it's easily forgotten, there isn't one *Jungle Book* but two. The first, published in 1894, and the second, a year later, are short-story collections rather than novels – and they're not all about Mowgli. Come to that, they're not all about the jungle: you're stretching any definition of the word if one of your stories is set in the Bering Strait and another among the Inuit of the Arctic Circle. Only three of the seven stories in the first book, and only four of the eight in the second, are about Mowgli – and they tell his story out of sequence. Here he's a toddler, there he's a teenager. In 'How Fear Came', he's not so much a protagonist as the audience for a prototypical *Just So* story (of which more later) telling how the first tiger got his stripes. Other stories in the collections include the classic 'Rikki-Tikki-Tavi' – about a mongoose's blood-feud with a husband-and-wife partnership of cobras – and other stand-alone fables about the relationships between humans and animals both in and outside the Raj.

Also, ironically given that the phrase 'the law of the jungle' has come to mean a primal situation of anarchy in which everyone is out for him- or herself, the jungle of the Mowgli stories is a place where law is everything. When Mowgli is first adopted by his wolf family, he must be presented formally at the Council Rock for the approval of the pack. Father Wolf pushes the man-cub into the centre of the circle, where, in a lovely image of oblivious childhood, 'he sat laughing and playing with some pebbles that glistened in the moonlight'. Baloo, 'the sleepy brown bear who teaches the wolf cubs the Law of the Jungle', speaks up for him, and Bagheera seconds the nomination and buys Mowgli's acceptance with the carcass of a bull, pointing out that though he has no standing in the wolves' assembly 'the Law of the Jungle says that if there is a doubt that is not a killing matter in regard to a new cub, the life of that cub may be bought at a price. And the Law does not say who may or may not pay that price.' Not just a law, but loopholes.

The jungle is a place of fixed hierarchies, established customs and elaborate formulaic greetings ('We be of one blood, thou and I'; 'Good hunting'). It contrasts with the untrustworthy and bewildering world of the human village, where, as Mowgli reports, 'they are idle, senseless and cruel; they play with their mouths, and they do not kill their weaker for food, but for sport. When they are full-fed they would throw their own breed into the Red Flower.'* Shere Khan is a villain not because he's a predator, but because he disrupts the orderly space of the jungle – hunting man; changing his territory unpredictably; conniving with the younger wolves to depose Akela as rightful ruler of the pack. Quite beneath contempt – almost beneath mention – are the Bandar-log, the boastful and lawless monkey people who abduct Mowgli in 'Kaa's

---

* i.e. fire.

Hunting': 'They have no law. They are outcaste [...] Their way is not our way.'*

Baloo's role as Mowgli's protector ('teacher of the Law – cub-beater') is to instil in the man-cub for his own safety the laws and languages and songs of the jungle. He teaches him the 'Master-Words', which command safe passage among other peoples (the one for the Snake-Peoples, anticipating Harry Potter's mastery of Parseltongue, is 'a perfectly indescribable hiss', and it's his ability to speak to Chil the Kite that saves him when the Bandar-log carry him off to their ruined palace). Mowgli's status, though, is at once of the jungle and not of it. He's still, and always, 'man-cub': he has no fear of fire and he has man's ability to stare down the animals, even Shere Khan. When it becomes clear that the younger wolves remain suspicious of him, he is 'furious with rage and sorrow for, wolf-like, the wolves had never told him how they hated him'.

Those wolves may be right to mistrust him. Blood will out. The savagery in Mowgli – which comes out when he takes extirpatory revenge on the men who cast him out and who threatened to burn Messua, the woman who believes Mowgli is her lost son – comes not from his animal but from his human side: 'Bagheera shivered, and cowered down. He could understand, if the worst came to the worst, a quick rush down the village street, and a right and left blow into a crowd, or a crafty killing of men as they ploughed in the twilight, but this scheme for deliberately blotting out an entire village from the eyes of man and beast frightened him.' What's scary in Mowgli is not his animal nature, but his human

---

* It's an open question, and a potentially hot one, given the charge of racism against Kipling, what if anything this distinction is meant to allegorise. Are the Bandar-log representatives of savage peoples and the jungle animals of (white) civilisation? Are the villagers feckless and superstitious because they are natives, or because they are humans? Kipling in later life did not discourage the idea that the Bandar-log could stand for American populist politicians, and the phrase 'outcaste', as applied to them, seems to differentiate them from native hierarchies rather than Western ones. Perhaps they are just monkeys.

one: the jungle is civilisation, and the village is savagery. (The English, far offstage in the Mowgli stories, are drily described as 'a perfectly mad people, who would not let honest farmers kill witches in peace'.)

Uncomprehending, often angry, the adolescent Mowgli is caught between his two mothers, the wolf Raksha and the human Messua, and two natures: 'These two things fight together in me as the snakes fight in the spring. The water comes out of my eyes; yet I laugh while it falls. Why? I am two Mowglis, but the hide of Shere Khan is under my feet.' 'Mowgli's Song' concludes: 'Ahae! My heart is heavy with the things that I do not understand.'

At the same time, Mowgli is, or becomes, a superhero – Tarzan before Tarzan. As he leaps over swampy ground 'a man-trained man would have sunk over head in three strides, but Mowgli's feet had eyes in them and they passed him from tussock to tussock and clump to quaking clump without asking help from the eyes in his head'. He goes from 'Man-cub' to 'Master of the Jungle', and 'strong, tall and beautiful [...] might easily have been mistaken for some wild god of a jungle legend'. After he razes the human village in 'Letting in the Jungle', Mowgli's state is very finely and ironically described: 'He had the good conscience that comes from paying a just debt; and all the Jungle was his friend, for all the Jungle was afraid of him.'

The writing in *The Jungle Book* is often sublime. Take, for instance, the first appearance of Bagheera at the Council Rock: 'A black shadow dropped down into the circle. It was Bagheera the Black Panther, inky black all over, but with the panther markings showing up in certain lights like the pattern of watered silk.' And here, wonderfully described in a paragraph, is Kipling's sketch of the routine of the young boys of the village at work and simultaneously at play as they mind the herd for the day:

The sun makes the rocks dance in the heat, and the herd-children hear one kite (never any more) whistling almost out of sight overhead, and they know that if they died, or a cow died, that kite would sweep down, and the next kite miles away would see him drop and follow, and the next, and the next, and almost before they were dead there would be a score of hungry kites come out of nowhere. [...] Then evening comes and the children call, and the buffaloes lumber up out of the sticky mud with noises like gunshots going off one after the other, and they all string across the gray plain back to the twinkling village lights.

Mowgli, of course, slightly struggles to fit in: 'when they made fun of him because he would not play games or fly kites, or because he mispronounced some word, only the knowledge that it was unsportsmanlike to kill little naked cubs kept him from picking them up and breaking them in two'.

The protagonist of *Kim* is, in his way, no less of an in-between child than Mowgli. The very first words of the novel place him – at play – sitting on an emblem of English rule, the great gun Zam-Zammah ('always first of the conqueror's loot'): 'He sat, in defiance of municipal orders...' The son of a nursemaid and a young colour-sergeant in an Irish regiment, Kim has been orphaned as a child after his mother fell to cholera and his father to drink and drugs. He was raised by a 'half-caste' opium addict whom his father had befriended before his death. The boy is 'burned black as any native [...] spoke the vernacular by preference, and his mother tongue in a clipped uncertain sing-song', and 'consorted on terms of perfect equality with the small boys of the bazaar'.

Kim is a sahib, but he doesn't know he's a sahib: intensely streetwise, curious and audacious; a ducker-and-diver, petty thief, errand-boy and beggar on the streets of Lahore, with a head full of cynical native proverbs and a fabulous tongue for insult. He has only a half-remembered, half-understood, jumbled-in-transmission explanation of his own history. He wears in a pouch round his neck documents that his father left him; he believes them to be magical. His father's regimental emblems – a red bull on a green field – he believes to be figures in a prophecy. Kim is, like Kipling's India, a jumble of street smarts and superstition.

He falls in with a Tibetan lama in search of a magic river that the lama hopes will free him from the 'Wheel' of earthly existence, while running an errand (though he doesn't know it) for a native asset of the British secret services. The adventure on which he embarks takes him through a dense network of powers and cultures in negotiation with each other, and – appropriately in a spy story – different levels of knowledge and different ways of knowing. When his path happens to cross that of his father's old regiment, even the regimental chaplain explains the extraordinary coincidence as '*kismet*'.

Far from being delighted to be taken in by the white man and offered his supposed birthright (a place in a Masonic orphanage, as it turns out), Kim thinks the white men are crazy. 'They cannot talk Hindi. They are only uncurried donkeys,' he explains to the lama.

> He thinks that once a Sahib is always a Sahib, and between the two of them they purpose to keep me in this regiment or to send me to a madrissah (a school). It has happened before. I have always avoided it. The fat fool is of one mind and the camel-like one of another. But that is no odds. I may spend one night here and perhaps the next. It has happened before. Then I will run away and return to thee.

For Kim, as for Mowgli, the trappings of civilisation, especially white civilisation, are temporary overlays on a more primal and variegated world: 'Sooner or later, if he chose, he could escape into great, grey, formless India, beyond tents and padres and colonels.' Kim's adoption by the white world and education in Lucknow is what sets him off on his Great Game adventures – but his connection to the lama, and his ability to move between cultures, is his defining grace.

If *Kim* gave us a hero moving from the bazaar to the world of the sahibs (and back again), *Stalky & Co.* dramatises the start of a journey in the opposite direction. The 'Coll' in *Stalky & Co.* is based on the United Services College Kipling attended: a rural private school whose graduates were expected to go on to Sandhurst to serve as officers in the army. Its trio of protagonists, Stalky, M'Turk and Beetle (the latter, a dab hand with poetic lampoons, being the stand-in for Kipling himself) are sixteen – so it's a book that is preoccupied with the liminal state between childhood and adulthood. It's a portrait of adolescent friendship, caught between ostentatiously drawling sophistication and boyish exuberance.

Stalky & Co. spoke to a relatively narrow class. It's a classic public-school story: capturing a particular strand in British social history that has taken a large part too in its literary and political history. The writer Nick Duffell, author of *Wounded Leaders: British Elitism and the Entitlement Illusion: A Psychohistory*, wrote in 2014 of boarding school pupils that they develop a 'strategic survival personality': 'separated from home and family, from love and touch, they must speedily reinvent themselves as self-reliant pseudo-adults'.* A story as old as boarding schools themselves.

The boys in *Stalky & Co.* are arrogant, worldly and fabulously cynical. They look down, socially and intellectually, on their teachers. They speak in a macaronic slang full of dog Latin, mangled French, airy quotations and misquotations from books they've read, and school abbreviations ('impot paper'; 'extra-tu'). Every character has one or more nicknames. Rather than being confined to the structure within which the school supposedly places them – subordinate to the rules and regulations, and judged by the standards, of their elders and betters – they run rings around the masters, especially their pompous housemaster Prout and the sour-tempered Mr King.

---

* Nick Duffell, 'Why boarding schools produce bad leaders', *Guardian*, 9 June 2014.

Thomas Hughes's *Tom Brown's School Days* was mostly about relations between the boys, with the headmaster a figure of remote but compelling authority. But in Kipling is a model of the school story in which the protagonists are forever getting one over on teacher. When they triumph: 'They went to their study in more or less of silence. There they began to laugh – laugh as only boys can. They laughed with their foreheads on the tables, or on the floor; laughed at length, curled over the backs of chairs or clinging to a bookshelf; laughed themselves limp.' Indeed, gloating itself is a formalised activity: '*Ti-ra-la-la-I-tu!* I gloat! Hear me!'

Doesn't that just crackle with the electric vitality of a real memory? Even the younger boys – who are generally beneath our heroes' notice except when a fag is needed[*] – are sketched with a feeling sense of what boys are like in groups, and how the time passes for them.

> The Lower Third had set a guard upon their form-room for the space of a full hour, which to a boy is a lifetime. Now they were busy with their Saturday evening businesses – cooking sparrows over the gas with rusty nibs; brewing unholy drinks in gallipots; skinning moles with pocket-knives: attending to paper trays full of silk-worms, or discussing the iniquities of their elders with a freedom, fluency, and point that would have amazed their parents.

Stalky, M'Turk and Beetle are often the cause of anarchy, but they are not exactly anarchists. Like the Jungle, the Coll is a ruly place. But there are two sets of rules – the written and the unwritten. It is the delight of its three protagonists to flout (or exploit) the former and twit its pedantic upholders among the school staff, while cleaving to the latter: the code of honour among the boys, and the determination to 'pay out' any slight or grievance in kind.

---

[*] Not a cigarette or the other thing: a temporary servant.

As one of the masters later realises, the boys plot a punishment in each case to fit the crime. They break bounds in search of somewhere to read and smoke, contriving that the masters determined to catch them at it be, mortifyingly, had up for trespass by the splenetic old colonel who owns the land on which they are skiving off. When King taunts Beetle for not bathing, and the boys in his house start calling them 'stinkers', the three arrange to deposit a dead cat in the rafters of King's house. When King turns them out of their shared study after the younger boys sneak to him with one of Beetle's lampoons, Stalky engineers the destruction of King's own study by a drunken carter. As M'Turk is heard to remark absently: 'Everyone paid in full – beautiful feelin'.'

The exception to the superiority that the boys feel over the school staff is their respect for the headmaster. He too cleaves to a higher code than the pettifogging school rules – to the extent that from time to time he gives them a good caning because they deserve it rather than because they've made it possible for him to pin anything on them. The boys seem to regard that as fair enough.

The quiet but uncompromising seriousness of *Stalky & Co.* grows as the book goes on. That the boys in Stalky are on the brink of adulthood – and that adulthood, for their school generation, means service in the army – is a gathering presence. In 'A Little Prep', a team of old boys returns to play a match against the school. Many of those old boys are now serving overseas, and these are the ones for whom 'the school divided right and left in admiring silence'. One of those young soldiers is billeted to sleep the night in his old dormitory with the boys, and tells them the story of how he saw his school contemporary die after being shot in an ambush in India: 'I gave him a drink and sat down beside him, and – funny thing, too – he said "Hullo, Toffee!" and I said "Hullo, Fat-Sow! Hope you aren't hurt," or something of the kind. But he died in a minute or two – never lifted his head off my knees…'

It's in that same story that the boys discover that the head has risked his own life by sucking the gunk out of the throat of a pupil stricken by diphtheria, thus saving the boy's life. 'Pretty average heroic,' is Beetle's high compliment. 'The Head ought to get the VC,' says Stalky. There's a sense here of how relationships and hierarchies bedded in at school will carry out into the big world – how even for the Old Boys, the head remains a father figure, and how short the distance between the rugby pitch and the battlefield really is.

Later we see the boys drilling on the parade-ground, and Kipling drops in some deadly little prolepses. One boy, Hogan, grumbles about marching in public, 'not foreseeing that three years later he should die in the Burmese sunlight outside Minhla Fort'; of another, Perowne, we're told in deadpan brackets: '(This is that Perowne who was shot in Equatorial Africa by his own men.)'

The very final story in the book jumps forward in time and finds M'Turk and Beetle (who narrates this tale in the first person) and a handful of other Old Boys in the country house of their school-mate 'The Infant'. Now in their twenties, they swap tales of their adventures. Piecemeal, through glancing encounters that those present have had with him as they rattled around the empire as soldiers or administrators, we get glimpses of Stalky in adult life.

He is a trickster and subversive in the army just as at school – 'a great man for orders – when they suit his book'. He's suspicious of the authority of the 'Politicals' who cost the lives of ordinary soldiers by making foolish treaties with forces who can't be trusted. He's defiant of command. He's brave, he's insouciant, he's ingenious – he breaks a siege by fooling two factions in the enemy force into starting to fight with each other; a version of a prank he played at school – and he's funny ('You've forgotten him playin' "Arrah, Patsy, mind the baby" on the bugle to hurry us up'). Our last glimpse of him is in a Sikh village, 'a dozen Sikh babies on his knees, an old harridan clappin' him on the shoulder, and a garland of flowers round his neck. Told me he was recruitin'.')

'There's nobody like Stalky,' says one of the company. Beetle – aka Kipling – sets him right:

'That's just where you make the mistake,' I said. 'India's full of Stalkies – Cheltenham and Haileybury and Marlborough chaps – that we don't know anything about, and the surprises will begin when there is really a big row on.'

'Who will be surprised?' said Dick Four.

'The other side. The gentlemen who go to the front in first-class carriages. Just imagine Stalky let loose on the south side of Europe with a sufficiency of Sikhs and a reasonable prospect of loot.'

Stalky & Co., then, is romantic and cynical, childish and adult, wildly funny and unexpectedly serious, in some ways propagandistic and in others savagely debunking of conventional authority and imperial chauvinism. It complicates, as does all Kipling's work read in the round, the ways in which his reputation has suffered in our own age.

One of the most memorable chapters is one in which a conceited MP called Raymond Martin hopes to make a bit of political capital by visiting the school to deliver a cantingly patriotic speech. The boys' initial scorn gives way to a more profound offence as they see their inward feelings for country, and for the male relatives who have perished in defence of that country, made the stuff of vulgar oratory: 'He profaned the most secret places of their souls with outcries and gesticulations.'

Afterwards, 'They discussed the speech in the dormitories. There was not one dissentient voice. Mr. Raymond Martin, beyond question, was born in a gutter, and bred in a Board-school, where they played marbles. He was further (I give the barest handful from great store) a Flopshus Cad, an Outrageous Stinker, a Jelly-bellied Flag-flapper (this was Stalky's contribution), and several other things which it is not seemly to put down.' It is easy to imagine what Kipling would have made of Nigel Farage.

Supporter of the imperial project though he undoubtedly was, Kipling was not the 'jingo imperialist' Orwell described him as. His is not the white-supremacist sahib's-eye view that saw the empire's subject peoples as an undifferentiated brown mass. Kipling's patriotism is mournful, mystical, and bottom-up rather than top-down, and he had a far from chauvinistic curiosity about the cultures, customs, worldviews and languages of the indigenous peoples among whom his stories are set.

At the heart of his literary gift was his extraordinary ear for different languages and forms and registers. His mythology draws on Inuit, Sanskrit, Punjabi and Afrikaans folk traditions, and his vocabulary is spackled with loan-words. Stalky, in adulthood, is marked out as an effective officer not because he scorns the natives alongside whom he serves but because he goes native. He defies or ignores orders from on high. Like Kim, it's his ability to straddle cultures that makes him what he is. In *The Second Jungle Book*, the wholly admirable protagonist of 'The Miracle of Purun Bhagat' is a British-educated, Indian-born servant of empire who opts out of the hierarchies of 'civilised' society altogether to become an itinerant holy man or sunnyasi. Purun is a greater man for putting away the pomp of empire, and it is a failing of the white world that in so doing 'as far as the world's affairs went, he died'.

If *Kim* and *Stalky* can be seen as being at the young adult end of Kipling's range – books about teenagers and young men – he also produced, in *The Just So Stories*, right at the beginning of the Edwardian age, a picture book to be read aloud for very young children, and an immortal classic of fairytale or myth. If these other books dramatised a sense of his own dislocated Anglo-Indian childhood, the *Just So* stories tell you something about Kipling as a father.

They were written, or at least collected for publication, in grief. Kipling's daughter Josephine, known as 'Effie', was the original audience for these fables – so called because when he told them to her as bedtime stories Effie insisted that they had to be told word for word, or 'just so' – which is something every parent who has tried to skip a line or two in a picture book with a punctilious child will recognise. She died of pneumonia in 1899, aged only six.

She is the 'Best Beloved' to whom the stories are narrated, and in the tenderness and wit and silliness of them you can still hear the loving connection between father and daughter, given torque by the knowledge that that connection has been severed.

The stories are origin stories or creation myths, and not noticeably Christian or even Western ones. The original trio, first in the book, were 'How the Whale Got His Throat', 'How the Camel Got His Hump' and 'How the Rhinoceros Got His Skin'. Tonally, Kipling just had incredible fun with these – it's the closest he gets to the territory of Hilaire Belloc or Dr. Seuss. This is absolutely a text intended to be read aloud, complete with rhetorical questions, skittish little digressions and interpolations, and the formulaic patterning characteristic of the folktale tradition.

There's a great aural delight in Homeric epithets – 'Dingo' is never just 'Dingo', but 'Yellow-Dog Dingo', and again and again (in 'The Elephant's Child') we meet 'the great grey-green, greasy Limpopo River, all set about with fever-trees'. Episodes and epithets fall into groups of three. Dingo is 'grinning like a coal-scuttle', then he's 'grinning like a rat-trap', then he's 'grinning like a horse-collar' as he chases Kangaroo. In 'How the Leopard Got His Spots' we meet animals visible 'like ripe bananas in a smokehouse', 'like a bar of soap in a coal scuttle', 'like a mustard-plaster on a sack of coals'. In 'How the First Letter Was Written' Taffy is 'a very wonderful child', then 'a very, very wonderful child', then 'a very, very, very wonderful child'. The patternings are those of an oral tale where half the pleasure is in anticipation: if you know what's going to happen to the whale, you're going to enjoy all the more the reminders that, among the possessions of the shipwrecked Mariner ('a man of infinite resource-and-sagacity'), 'you must not forget the suspenders, Best Beloved'.

The original and many subsequent editions contained Kipling's own very accomplished illustrations. They have a stylistic flavour of Beardsley. The pictures, and even the very lengthy picture captions, work in a dynamic way with the text. *The Just So Stories* is Kipling's contribution to the picture-book tradition that was to take such a large role in publishing for pre-school children and, unlike the linguistically challenging *Stalky & Co.* and the fey and rococo *Puck of Pook's Hill*, it has, to my ear, barely dated: it has the out-of-time quality that goes with its mythological aspect.

The pleasure in sheer language, in these stories, is undimmed by the passage of more than a century. Nobody has a meeting when they can have a 'palaver and an indaba and a punchayet, and a pow-wow'. Their jokey baby-talk (the Elephant's Child is full of 'satiable curtiosity', 'inciting' is a routine mistake for 'exciting', and 'berangement' for 'arrangement'), is that of a child's mispronunciations being fed back to her. What family doesn't have a handful of private words that survive from the faltering early language of their children?

Kipling's model of fatherhood was a doting one. Tender, teasing and affectionate father-and-daughter relationships feature in the stories. In the creation myth 'The Crab That Played with the Sea', the first Man approaches the Eldest Magician 'with his own best beloved little girl-daughter sitting upon his shoulder'. The only recurring characters are the caveman Tegumai and his daughter Taffy.* There's nothing of the remote Victorian patriarch in this caveman dad: 'From that day to this (and I suppose it is all Taffy's fault), very few little girls have ever liked learning to read or write. Most of them prefer to draw pictures and play about with their Daddies – just like Taffy.'

Perhaps the most moving line in all of Kipling comes in one of the book's interstitial poems, where he imagines how thousands of years after the events of the story, in spirit, 'comes Taffy dancing through the fern / To lead the Surrey spring again':

---

* Their names, we're told solemnly, mean 'Man-who-does-not-put-his-foot-forward-in-a-hurry' and 'Small-person-without-any-manners-who-ought-to-be-spanked'. But we're also told that, being Tegumai's Best Beloved, 'she was not spanked half as much as was good for her'.

In moccasins and deer-skin cloak,
Unfearing, free and fair she flits,
And lights her little damp-wood smoke
To show her Daddy where she flits.
For far – oh, very far behind,
So far she cannot call to him,
Comes Tegumai alone to find
The daughter that was all to him.

Adventures on the High Seas

ROBERT LOUIS STEVENSON ·
JOHN MEADE FALKNER

Treasure Island; Kidnapped; Moonfleet

THIS WAS A PERIOD IN WHICH WHOLE GENRES WERE starting to bud. The boys' adventure story, which had been chugging along in its stiff way with Henty and co., got a tremendous jolt of electricity in 1883 with the publication of *Treasure Island* by Robert Louis Stevenson (1850–1894). It's artfully structured, vigorously and pacily written, funny, alarming and exciting: as fresh on the page today as when it first appeared. It had been published originally in serial form in a children's magazine called *Young Folks;* a reminder of the crescent vigour of periodicals for children and the importance of serial publication of fiction in the Victorian age.

Stevenson's audience for early drafts of the manuscript were his father and his twelve-year-old stepson Lloyd. Their reaction gave an indication of how it might take off. 'I had counted on one boy; I found I had two in my audience. My father caught fire at once.' Not only were boys excited by adventure stories aimed at grown men, as Stevenson himself had been reading Jules Verne, Captain Marryat and James Fenimore Cooper; grown men could and would delight in stories aimed at boys. It transformed the reputation of its still-young author. Up until that point, he recalled ruefully, 'I was thirty-one; I was head of a family; I had lost my health; I had never yet paid my way, had never yet made two hundred pounds a year.'

Stevenson was, like Kipling, one of those fantastically energetic

Victorian writers who roared around the four corners of the world and didn't confine himself to one genre but wrote classics in several. Spry, moustachioed, enterprising, thirsty for travel, a bohemian and an atheist, he was an adventurer as well as a writer of adventure stories. He gave us the Gothic classic *The Strange Case of Dr Jekyll and Mr Hyde* (1886), reams of journalism, short stories, essays, poems for adults and children (*A Child's Garden of* Verses (1885) is still in print) as well as travel-writing so enduring that you can still walk the Stevenson Trail in the Cevennes, where he went on his *Travels With A Donkey* (1879). He may even have invented the sleeping bag. He roamed the Pacific in his thirties and spent the last five years of his life in Samoa before his death from a stroke at forty-four. All this from a man who had been sickly with lung disease from a very young age.

Treasure Island didn't invent pirate stories. There was an existing body of mythology in sensation literature, feeding on the golden age of piracy in the previous century. A 1724 bestseller called *A General History of the Robberies and Murders of the most notorious Pyrates* had revelled in heavily embellished biographical accounts of pirate captains such as Blackbeard, William Kidd and 'Black Bart' Roberts; Stevenson even borrowed the name of one of his characters, Israel Hands, from that book.

But there's no doubt that it was *Treasure Island* that established all the furniture of pirate cliché – buried treasure, X-marks-the-spot, parrots squawking 'pieces of eight', the Jolly Roger, the 'Black Spot' as a mark of doom, the whole peg-leg, avast-me-hearties shebang – so indelibly in the culture and, especially, in writing for children. In giving this tradition mainstream form you could see Stevenson's as a bridging work between the scurrilous 'low' ephemera of the popular press and the supposedly respectable stuff aimed at middle-class bookshelves. F.J. Harvey Darton called it the 'very apotheosis of the "penny dreadful"'.*

---

* F.J. Harvey Darton, *Children's Books in England: Nine Centuries of Social Life.*

Treasure Island has another feature that goes consistently through children's writing: this is a story that's shadowed by the idea of stories. Its young protagonist Jim Hawkins – through whose eyes the story is told, except for a peculiar interlude in the middle where, when the group is separated, another character takes up the narrative for a couple of chapters – isn't just a resourceful and courageous (and lucky) child. He's an imaginative child. In the opening section of the book, after the alcoholic captain, staying at Jim's mother's pub the Admiral Benbow, warns the boy to be on the lookout for a one-legged man, Jim recalls how 'that personage haunted my dreams [...] I would see him in a thousand forms, and with a thousand diabolical expressions. Now the leg would be cut off at the knee, now at the hip; now he was a monstrous kind of a creature who had never had but the one leg, and that in the middle of his body. To see him leap and run and pursue me over hedge and ditch was the worst of nightmares.' When Jim is in Redruth waiting to set sail, he is 'full of sea-dreams and the most charming anticipations of strange islands and adventures'. Like Catherine in *Northanger Abbey*, with her head full of Gothic literature, he adventures both in the book's reality and in his imagination.

Yet his real-life adventures in the story are just as wild as any imagination could furnish. That's, in a way, the joke. *Treasure Island* is a pure thrill-ride, and it speaks to children, in Jim's ingenuous voice, on their own level. Within just a few chapters, Jim has set out to sea with the kindly Squire Trelawney in search of buried treasure, only to discover that half the crew, led by the treacherous Long John Silver, posing as a ship's cook, plan to mutiny, do for its honest passengers and steal the treasure. Once the ship reaches the island pitched battles, desperate reverses and all stripes of derring-do follow in a cavalcade.

That's not to say that it doesn't wink, a little, at the adults too. The pirate language, like Shakespeare's nautical gibberish in the opening scene of *The Tempest*, is pure colour:

'Do you call that a head on your shoulders, or a blessed dead-eye?' cried Long John. 'Don't rightly know, don't you! Perhaps you don't happen to rightly know who you was speaking to, perhaps? Come, now, what was he jawing v'yages, cap'ns, ships? Pipe up! What was it?' 'We was a-talkin' of keel-hauling,' answered Morgan. 'Keel-hauling, was you? And a mighty suitable thing, too, and you may lay to that. Get back to your place for a lubber, Tom.'

And dear old Ben Gunn – a man marooned three years on the titular island, having lost possession of the better half of his wits and peculiarly interested in cheese ('"Was it cheese you said he had a fancy for?" "Yes, sir, cheese," I answered') – speaks the most fantastic nonsense.

The most captivating figure in *Treasure Island*, though, is Long John Silver – who starts off as something of a pantomime villain and turns into something no less villainous, but far more complex and interesting. In the world of *Treasure Island*, he has the seductive qualities of an Iago: he isn't just a baddie, but a trickster figure, a shrewd player-of-the-odds, a master-deceiver. His loyalties are gimballed and ever-shifting, and – even though he's terrifyingly physically able, crutch or no crutch – his greatest power is not brute force but persuasion.

There's a wicked bit of dramatic irony, for instance, when as the expedition is in preparation the hapless Squire Trelawney writes back from Bristol docks to report on his progress. He has acquired a ship's cook who lost his leg in his country's service, he says, and this cook has helped him assemble a crew.

Between Silver and myself we got together in a few days a company of the toughest old salts imaginable – not pretty to look at, but fellows, by their faces, of the most indomitable spirit. I declare we could fight a frigate. Long John even got rid of two out of the six or seven I had already engaged. He showed me in a moment that they were just the sort of fresh-water swabs we had to fear in an adventure of importance.

The Silver that Jim first meets – Jim having been primed by the captain to fear the worst of a one-legged man – is so charming that Jim's suspicions immediately abate: 'One look at the man before me was enough.' It's only when, once aboard ship, Jim overhears Silver flattering a co-conspirator – 'you're young, you are, but you're as smart as paint. I see that when I set my eyes on you' – with the very same words with which he flattered Jim himself, that the boy gets his first lesson in not trusting appearances. Arriving on the island, Jim witnesses from hiding how Silver first flatters and then murders in cold blood an honest crewman who refuses to take the pirates' part.

Again and again on the island – as the advantage swings between the mutineers and the crew of honest adventurers against whom they have risen – Silver feints at switching sides or plays both off against the middle. His eyes are perpetually on the prize – or, rather, two prizes: the treasure, and saving his own skin. There's an odd sort of honesty in his self-interest. Even defeated, and in quasi-captivity, Silver shrugs on a different persona and goes along to get along. As the remaining companions eat Ben Gunn's salted goat and drink a bottle of wine around the fire,

> Never, I am sure, were people gayer or happier. And there was Silver, sitting back almost out of the firelight, but eating heartily, prompt to spring forward when anything was wanted, even join-ing quietly in our laughter – the same bland, polite, obsequious seaman of the voyage out.

Rather than swing from a rope at the end of the story, as he well deserves, he slips away with a portable portion of the treasure – and Jim seems not to mind too much. This is a book quite uninterested in moralising, in delivering just deserts or even a happy ending.

The goodies and baddies alike are actuated by nothing higher than greed, after all, and there's a sense hanging over it that seamen operate according to a different and more pragmatic code than their land-bound counterparts. When Silver rejoins the group – 'Come back to my dooty, sir' – Captain Smollett replies, 'Ah!' and passes no further comment. Silver's amoral charm works on the reader as well as on the characters around him.

Stevenson's other great children's adventure, *Kidnapped* (1886), set among the Highlands and Islands of Scotland during the Jacobite rebellion, hits many of the same beats – even down to the overhearing of a black-hearted plot aboard ship. It follows its orphaned seventeen-year-old protagonist David through a series of improbably twisty adventures, and a footslog through the Scottish heather that anticipates the John Buchan of *The Thirty-Nine Steps*. As in *Treasure Island*, we're seeing the real history of the middle eighteenth century recycled in iconographic fictional form: history turning into myth.

Among the striking qualities of *Kidnapped* is its wry awareness of standing in a literary tradition, and the gleam of humour that surrounds it. The early sections, in which David's villainous uncle Ebenezer tries to kill him, swindles him out of his inheritance and then has a bash at selling him into slavery, are high-camp Gothic; and when (after much *Treasure Island*-style treachery and gunplay) David is washed up alone on an island just off the Scottish shore, he grumbles about how little his situation resembles the Robinsonades that his readership will be familiar with:

In all the books I have read of people cast away, they had either their pockets full of tools, or a chest of things would be thrown upon the beach along with them, as if on purpose. My case was very different. I had nothing in my pockets but money and Alan's silver button; and being inland bred, I was as much short of knowledge as of means.

We meet a wicked ship's captain who, nevertheless, never passes the village where his old mum lives without showing the ship's colours and ordering a gun to be fired in salute. His right-hand man Riach – vicious when sober, kindly in drink – advises young David to take life as it comes:

> 'Life is all a variorum, at the best. Look at me: I'm a laird's son and more than half a doctor, and here I am, man-Jack to Hoseason!'
> I thought it would be civil to ask him for his story.
> He whistled loud.
> 'Never had one,' said he. 'I like fun, that's all.' And he skipped out of the forecastle.

David's ally, the dashing Alan Breck Stewart, bursts into boastful song at the drop of a hat. The mood of *Kidnapped*, as of its predecessor – and perhaps this is the key to their continued appeal – is one in which the reverses of fortune and the presence of mortal peril are addressed with an almost giddy lightness.

An altogether darker flavour of adventure story was to be found in John Meade Falkner's *Moonfleet* (1898) – which gave children's writing its first full-body baptism into the Gothic tradition. It begins in a graveyard, circles the graveyard, and is in turn circled by the vast cold graveyard of the sea. Densely and atmospherically written, it has been a favourite of school curricula since before I was a child – which seems odd. It is strong meat.

The poetically named village of Moonfleet, on the Dorset coast, is by the middle of the eighteenth century a place already fallen from glory, and fallen, come to that, from grace. It's a community full of secrets and myths. The cemetery overlooks the sea, and the great family who built the town, the Mohunes, moulder in the vault under it. Their patrimony has been 'breaking up and selling piecemeal for a generation', and the manor house – in which a much-resented incomer, the local magistrate Mr Maskew, now lives – is half ruined.

Legends tell of 'Blackbeard', a Mohune ancestor a century before who obtained a priceless diamond through treachery, buried it somewhere, and went to his unquiet grave with the secret of its location. Meanwhile the people of Moonfleet connive (most of them) in the smuggling trade, and over them hangs the shadow of the gibbet. When we first meet the book's fifteen-year-old pro- tagonist John Trenchard, he's watching the local stonemason letter the gravestone of one of the sons of Moonfleet shot by Maskew when the Revenue intercepted his smuggling ship. Bad blood is everywhere.

John is an orphan, and boards in the town with his prim aunt, who he says 'was kind to me in her own fashion, but too strict and precise ever to make me love her'. Led on by his childish imagin- ings of finding Blackbeard's treasure (his head is full, among other things, of the *Arabian Nights*), John stumbles on a smugglers' cache in the vault under the church: a secret hidden under a legend; a figure, perhaps, for the book's interleaving of a supernatural atmos- phere with real-world moral murk. John is a goodie, but he's on the wrong side of the law for most of the story. Blackbeard's curse may be a story to scare children, but greed for the diamond has consequences that look a lot like the actions of a curse.

The story takes John, like Jim in *Treasure Island*, from childhood to adulthood, and from Moonfleet around the world. The Mohunes' Y-shaped family crest (which also gives the town pub its nickname, the Why Not?) is referenced in a sermon preached in Moonfleet church early in the book: 'in each man's life must come a point where two roads part like the arms of a "Y", and [...] everyone must choose for himself whether he will follow the broad and sloping path on the left or the steep and narrow path on the right'.

Under its adventure-story carapace, *Moonfleet* is a story about moral choices, and about families – the ones you choose for yourself, the ones you escape, and the weight of them. When John's aunt turns him out for delinquency, he is effectively adopted by the pub landlord and smuggler Elzevir Block. Elzevir is still mourning, and plotting revenge for, his own son David – the boy killed by Maskew in the customs raid. Romeo-and-Juliet-style, John falls in love with Grace Maskew, the daughter of the man with whom his new 'father' is locked in a blood-feud.

John's entering Elzevir's world comes at a terrible cost: he and Elzevir are soon on the run, and John goes on to be an accessory to two murders, is imprisoned, branded and shipwrecked and eventually returns to Moonfleet a grown and bearded man and, once again, an orphan. There's any amount of colourful action along the way. There are hidden caves, ancient riddles, secret passwords, crooked jewel-dealers, double-crosses – and rotting coffins reaching into which, in the dark, you might find your hand involuntarily closing on the beard of a dead man.

But what makes the story stand out – what gives it its peculiar weight and resonance – is the way it is rooted in family dynamics and in the irreversible, unforgiving march of time. When John finally returns to Moonfleet – shipwrecked, and saved from drowning by Elzevir even at the cost of the latter's life – there's a moment when he finds himself back in the Why Not?, 'alone with my dead friend, and with a host of bitterest thoughts' and with half a life behind him:

The room had not been cleaned; there were spider-webs on the beams, and the dust stood so thick on the window-panes as to shut out half the light. The dust was on everything; on chairs and tables, save on the trestle-table where he lay. 'Twas on this very trestle they had laid out David's body; 'twas in this very room that this still form, who would never more know either joy or sorrow, had bowed down and wept over his son. The room was just as we had left it an April evening years ago, and on the dresser lay the great backgammon board, so dusty that one could not read the lettering on it; 'Life is like a game of hazard; the skilful player will make something of the worst of throws'; but what unskilful players we had been, how bad our throws, how little we had made of them!

Full circle. What does *Moonfleet* say, then, to a child reader? It has some very grown-up lessons about grief, obsession and redemption; and about how family and community create their own goods. John's adventures take him far outside the law – and the reader fully roots for Moonfleet's smugglers – but they don't quite take him outside a moral and emotional framework in which loyalty to your friends and comrades is the highest virtue. Yet these virtues aren't straightforward. Elzevir doesn't kill Maskew – the magistrate is drilled through the head by a stray shot from an exciseman – but he fully intends to; and John never admits as much to Grace.

John, by the end, has been rescued both literally and metaphorically from the wreckage, but he will never be the boy he was. As John says on meeting Grace again after many years: 'we are no more boy and girl, as in times past, but you a noble lady and I a broken wretch'. The implausibly pat ending – a rushed *deus ex machina* in the closing pages means that John ends up copping Blackbeard's treasure, clearing his name, getting the girl and living happily ever after – is overlaid on something darker and sadder.

The works of Meade Falkner and Stevenson stand as forefathers of a long history of boys' adventure stories. They help bridge the gap between sensation literature and the 'respectable' children's stories aimed at a burgeoning middle class. And they do something else. All three of these books are told by first-person narrators: a feature of many of the earliest novels for grown-ups but not common in stories for children. They are establishing an intimate form of address, in which the child reader hears directly from the child (or young adult) protagonist. They don't describe the adventures of children from a distanced, adult, third-person point of view; rather, they inhabit the pre-adult consciousness of their protagonists. The mediating narrator is quietly dispensed with.

The Seeds of Fantasy

GEORGE MACDONALD · CARLO COLLODI

The Princess and the Goblin;
The Adventures of Pinocchio

IF THE EMERGENT GENRE OF BOYS' ADVENTURE STORIES was still rooted in historical situations – be they pirates, smugglers and Jacobites in Stevenson and Meade Falkner, or the Raj in Kipling – the later nineteenth century also saw the emergence of a separate strand of pure fantasy, encouraged and enabled by the romantic medievalism of the later pre-Raphaelite movement in grown-up art. The fairytale was alive and well and morphing into new shapes. Tolkien and C.S. Lewis may have popularised and formalised the quasi-medieval worlds of kings and wizards, elves and goblins, but they didn't invent them.

Behind *The Hobbit* and the Narnia stories stands the work of George MacDonald (1824–1905), a Tolstoy-looking Scots genius who twisted the generic furniture of the fairytale into fantasy as we now recognise it. His works included *Phantastes: A Faerie Romance for Men and Women* (1858), *At the Back of the North Wind* (1871) and *Lilith* (1895), but it's *The Princess and the Goblin* (1872) on which his modern reputation primarily rests. As well as being a positive gift to Freudians, this story of a malign and resentful race burrowing up from the underworld to snatch prisoners from our own echoes forward to Bilbo's adventures under the Misty Mountains in *The Hobbit*, the gnomes digging up from Underland under the thrall of the Green Lady in *The Silver Chair* and even the svart-alfar in Alan Garner's *The Weirdstone of Brisingamen*.

It starts with a classic fairytale set-up: Princess Irene has a fond but absent father and a dead mother, and lives in a castle with her nursemaid Lootie. She's a lonely and isolated child, and prone to wandering the vast castle corridors – which seem to change around her as in a dream. Shades, here, of Bluebeard – or of corridor-creeping Mary Lennox in *The Secret Garden*.

Wandering, lost, among these arcades of doors, she finds one of the rooms inhabited by another Irene – an ancient but beautiful white-haired woman who lives on pigeon's eggs, works perpetually on a spinning-wheel, and claims to be her great-great-grandmother. This ancient lady is clearly magical, though whether fairy god-mother or wicked witch isn't at this point clear.

As everyone around the princess has tried to keep her from knowing, the outside world is dangerous for Irene. A race of goblins lives under the mountains, regarding the humans in general, and the royal family in particular, as hated usurpers. According to legend, their treatment by a previous human king some generations back had driven them to retreat underground, where they became cunning and physically hideous, and have ever since cherished an 'ancestral grudge'.[*]

They mostly hide underground by daylight, but it isn't safe after dark. Outside the castle Irene encounters a miner's boy called Curdie, who helps her and Lootie find their way home when they get lost outside with the light failing. Curdie, being one of the common folk who share space with goblins and whose work in the mines sees him surrounded by them, isn't scared of them: he knows that they detest poetry and, at least out in the open, can be seen off by singing rude songs about them.

The tropes of fairytales are incorporated and subverted. Irene pricks her finger while playing with a brooch, and even swoons…

---

[*] I don't think that this children's story can be read as a straightforward allegory of antisemitic paranoia, but the overtones – a people driven out by institutional persecution, and subsequently demonised as ugly, cunning creatures hatching subterranean plots – are certainly there if you care to look for them.

but MacDonald slyly undercuts expectations. It's a normal brooch and a normal cut – though the silvery grandmother goes on to heal it with her magic. The queen of the goblins wears granite shoes. The princess has promised Curdie a kiss; and in an aside MacDonald says: 'there is some ground for supposing that Curdie was not a miner only, but a prince as well. Many such instances have been known in the world's history.' There are not one but two Ariadne threads used by Curdie and Irene to navigate the underworld: one, an ordinary spool of string that Curdie attaches to his pickaxe so he can find his way in the dark; the other, the invisible filament that Irene's magic grandmother equips her with, and which leads her into the mountain to rescue Curdie from captivity.

Curdie discovers by chance that the goblins are plotting against the upper world – first to breach the walls of the humans' mining tunnels in order to flood the mines and drown the workers there, and then to tunnel up underneath the castle itself to kidnap Irene and marry her to the goblin prince Harelip. The story comes to a climax, as the mine-flooding scheme backfires, with a near-genocide of the goblin people and 'the news that dead goblins were tossing about in the current through the house'.

There's a peculiar line of sympathy in this story, though, for the goblins themselves. Amid all this racial chauvinism ('our king would dig the mountain to the plain before he would have his princess the wife of a cob') we are insistently reminded that they originated, like H.G. Wells's Morlocks, as a surface race. Their schemes against the king and his family are rooted in revenge for what they see as ill-treatment rather than motive-less malignity.

It's a stranger story even than its outline suggests, and one that lurches between wild comedy – goblins have hard noggins and soft feet, so a battle with goblins involves a fantastic amount of stamping on their feet – and Cronenbergian body-horror. Those soft goblin feet are, like those of Roald Dahl's witches, toeless blocks. Harelip, the goblin prince to whom Irene is destined for a captive bride, announces, 'it will be nice to make her cry. I'll have the skin taken off between her toes, and tie them up till they grow together. Then her feet will be like other people's, and there will be no occasion for her to wear shoes.' Brr.

The goblins also keep pets, creatures 'so grotesque and misshapen as to be more like a child's drawings upon his slate than anything natural', and which make a noise that 'could be described neither as grunts nor squeaks nor roars nor howls nor barks nor yells nor screams nor croaks nor hisses nor mews nor shrieks, but only as something like all of them mingled in one horrible dissonance'.* One such – a creature with a cat's body and spindly 'stilt-legs' as long as a horse's – frightens Irene out of the safety of home and sends her running terrified up the mountain.

The dreamlike quality of those castle corridors is present throughout the book. The reader is never satisfactorily told how the great-grandmother fits in, or even whether she's real (Curdie can't see her; Lootie won't believe in her; Irene from time to time forgets her). The kingdom itself is a vague place of mountains and crags, the king no more than a fairy-story cut-out. Yet the narrative has a hallucinatory particularity. The goblin queen, most ferocious of all the antagonists, is a comical cartoon grotesque when first introduced:

Her nose was certainly broader at the end than its extreme length, and her eyes, instead of being horizontal, were set up like two perpendicular eggs, one on the broad, the other on the small end. Her mouth was no bigger than a small buttonhole until she laughed, when it stretched from ear to ear – only, to be sure, her ears were very nearly in the middle of her cheeks.

---

* Compare, perhaps, the climactic encounter of Julia Donaldson's *Room on the Broom*, where a composite creature issues an unworldly combination of animal cries.

In the final battle, she's much more like Grendel's mother:

> Her face streaming with blood, and her eyes flashing green light-
> ning through it, she came on with her mouth open and her teeth
> grinning like a tiger's, followed by the king and her bodyguard
> of the thickest goblins.

You can well see how this strange story has been so influential in literary terms and has stuck so firmly in the heads of those who read it as children. It has an arterial connection to the darker life of the childish imagination.

Similarly strange and similarly, bizarrely, violent was *The Adventures of Pinocchio: Story of a Puppet* (1883; translated into English by Alison Murray in 1892), by Carlo Collodi. Collodi was the pen name of Carlo Lorenzini (1826–1890), a seamstress's son from central Italy whose early literary endeavours included translating Perrault's fairytales into Italian. His best-known work, which remains the most translated work of Italian literature in history, is another one of those oddball books that children's writers produced before anyone had really agreed what they were sup-posed to be doing. It's a generic mishmash: an original fairytale, a picaresque, a coming-of-age story, a mock-epic. It has a hectic, commedia-dell'arte/Punch-and-Judy energy to it; it is full of vio-lent slapstick. Even before Pinocchio is carved, there's a series of punch-ups between Geppetto (the woodcarver, Pinocchio's 'father') and his friend Mastro Cherry (the latter is so named because of his bright red nose; Geppetto's own insulting nick-name, Polendina, comes from his polenta-yellow toupee), where each comes away with the other's wig, one clenched in a fist, the other gripped between the teeth. It's like nothing so much as a *Three Stooges* scene.

The scheming cat gets his paw bitten off. A snake bursts an artery laughing when Pinocchio takes a pratfall. A well-meaning blackbird is gobbled up by a cat two sentences after it makes its first appearance. Pinocchio is (unsuccessfully) hanged. And the Talking Cricket (chirpy, top-hatted Jiminy in Disney's animated version) is murdered with a hammer just moments after he appears in the story.

> At these last words, Pinocchio jumped up in a fury, took a hammer from the bench, and threw it with all his strength at the Talking Cricket. Perhaps he did not think he would strike it. But, sad to relate, my dear children, he did hit the Cricket, straight on its head. With a last weak 'cri-cri-cri' the poor Cricket fell from the wall, dead!

He reappears as a ghost later in the story and is pretty forgiving of Pinocchio's having killed him. The cricket is only one giver of sensible advice whom the wooden-headed marionette ignores: his main protector, a turquoise-haired fairy, reappears in a series of different forms. Secondary helpers and antagonists – a talking tuna, a mastiff, a green fisherman – appear and vanish. Allegorical settings – from the openly biblical belly-of-the-whale to the Land of Toys, Island of Busy Bees and City of Simple Simons – flash past in glimpses, related by a narrative rather than a physical geography. There's a lot going on.

The thread that runs through Pinocchio's zany adventures is a moralising one. Pinocchio sells his schoolbook for a ticket to the theatre; he is gulled by bad actors and relieved of his gold coins when he greedily buys the lie that they'll multiply overnight; he'd rather beg than do work to earn what he needs ('Aren't you ashamed? Instead of being a beggar in the streets, why don't you look for work and earn your own bread?'); and he bunks off school, even though he's doing well, on the phantasmagorical promise of a land where every day is a Saturday (except for Sundays) and 'days are spent in play and enjoyment from morn till night'.

Everyone knows *Pinocchio* tells the story of its protagonist's journey to become 'a real boy'. But here's the thing: Pinocchio is a real boy all the way through. He may be made of wood, so his feet burn if he falls asleep with them propped on the stove, but his passions and vices are human ones from the get-go. What he's really learning is how to be good. Becoming human – in the final scene, he admires himself in the mirror and sees 'the bright face of a tall boy [...] with wide-awake blue eyes, dark brown hair and happy, smiling lips' – is a reward for obedience and filial love, qualities it takes him many adventures and setbacks properly to acquire.

The qualities valued in the book are the qualities adults value in children; the qualities, indeed, that Pinocchio knows are expected of him:

> 'I promise you,' answered the Marionette, sobbing, 'that from now on I'll be good–' 'Boys always promise that when they want something,' said Geppetto. 'I promise to go to school every day, to study, and to succeed–' 'Boys always sing that song when they want their own will.' 'But I am not like other boys! I am better than all of them and I always tell the truth. I promise you, Father, that I'll learn a trade, and I'll be the comfort and staff of your old age.'

So he says, but he lies lightly, and without self-knowledge, and in the moment believes the lies he is telling. His sense of self is still unstable. Pinocchio is never going to get anywhere until he's cured of idleness, theft, disobedience and keeping bad company. He doesn't get to be a real boy until, paradoxically, he abandons those qualities that make him most boy-like. He's least a marionette when he's actually a marionette – making his own headstrong, blundering way in the world with no strings attached.

What gives the book a more than merely didactic cast, though, is the imaginative energy of its narrative and the emotional warmth that underpins it. Geppetto and the blue-haired fairy are infinitely forgiving, as parents are supposed to be. Pinocchio's desire to be good is more important than his failure. As the fairy says: 'The depth of your sorrow made me see that you have a kind heart. There is always hope for boys with hearts such as yours, though they may often be very mischievous.'

In a way, it's a book whose argument is that we all have strings attached: you don't grow up until you live amid the web of reciprocal kindnesses, obligations and responsibilities that make up society itself. To be a human being, *Pinocchio* says, is about sacrifice, selflessness and hard work.

Animal Magic

BEATRIX POTTER · ANNA SEWELL

*The Tale of Mrs Tiggy-Winkle; The Tale of Peter Rabbit;
The Tale of the Flopsy Bunnies; The Tailor of Gloucester;
The Tale of the Pie and the Patty-Pan; The Tale of
Timmy Tiptoes; The Tale of Samuel Whiskers; The
Tale of Mr Tod; The Tale of Jemima Puddle-Duck;
The Tale of Ginger and Pickles; The Tale of Little Pig
Robinson; The Tale of Tom Kitten; The Story of a Fierce
Bad Rabbit; The Story of Miss Moppet; Black Beauty*

THE LATER VICTORIAN YEARS ALSO SAW THE FLOUR-ishing of what was to become another vast subgenre of children's writing: the animal story. It's now so established a part of the imaginative furniture of childhood that it takes a moment and a step back to see how weird it is. Where *did* all those talking animals come from? Children's writing has given us countless loyal dogs, perky pigs and fluffy baa-lambs. It's fair to suppose that a number of them are echoes of the Aesopic tradition. But they're distorted echoes.

The animals in the stories of the nineteenth century both were and were not descendants of the animals that feature so prominently in the history of folktale – with their cast of bears and wolves and frogs and scorpions. Talking animals in folktales are, usually, avatars of the magical order of things. They are threats and helpers from a radically non-human world. The animal heroes of most modern children's stories came to be something a little different. They are something more like humans in animal drag. As the anthropologist Claude Lévi-Strauss put it, 'animals are good to think with.'

Caring for pets is now acknowledged as one of the ways that children learn to take responsibility for other beings. We've seen, in Mrs Trimmer's *Fabulous Histories*, how early children's writers sought to shape those interactions. Children learn kindness around animals – and cruelty; most serial killers are found to have taken their first steps into depravity by torturing animals in childhood. Yet the seemingly age-old connection between children and animals – in pets and, especially, in artificial pet-substitutes – isn't as old as all that.

Nowadays, the average child's bedroom is stuffed with cuddly toys in any number of animal shapes. Their very nappies are festooned with long-lashed crocodiles. But the 'teddy bear' didn't appear until the early years of the twentieth century, and its precursor Ithaca Kitty (a sew-your-own cat toy) only appeared in 1893. Stuffed animal toys didn't exist until the culture paved the way for them. Beatrix Potter (1866–1943) laid the broadest of those paving stones. Indeed, when she lent her permission to a stuffed Peter Rabbit toy in 1903, she created the first licensed character; the Big Bang for children's fiction merchandising.

Beatrix Potter was a woman who through a solitary childhood had found emotional and intellectual sustenance in her engagement with nature. She understood intuitively the attraction of animals to children because she felt it deeply herself as a child. Though the Potter industry is entirely centred on the Lake District, she was in her late forties before she moved there to live and most of her body of work for children had already been published.

Helen Beatrix Potter, as she was born, spent the first forty-seven years of her life in Kensington, and you could see that as the spur: she was a town-mouse who dreamed of being a country mouse. She was imaginatively nourished by holidays spent in her grandfather's elegantly landscaped Hertfordshire pile, Camfield Place, a wild Perthshire estate, Dalguise, and – from 1882 onwards – visits to the Lake District.

The family was very wealthy – her father was a barrister and her grandfather an industrialist and an MP – but their strict Unitarian faith placed them a little to one side of conventional society. She was educated by a governess, rather than sent to school ('Thank goodness,' she wrote in later life, 'my education was neglected'). Beatrix had few friends of her own age, and her close relationship to her younger brother Bertram was eclipsed when he went away to school. She was a nervous, depressive child and adolescent, pouring her heart into a diary and her imagination into the fairytales and fantasies of her childhood reading.

As a child, she and Bertram amassed a sort of domestic zoo:

> The third-floor nursery menagerie included, at various times, rabbits (Benjamin Bouncer and Peter), a green frog called Punch, several lizards, including Judy who was a special favourite, water newts, a tortoise, a frog, salamanders, many and different varieties of mice, a ring snake, several bats, a canary and a green budgerigar, a wild duck, a family of snails, several guinea pigs and later a hedgehog or two. Bertram's tastes ran to the less domesticated: bats, a kestrel, and a mean-tempered Jay.[*]

These animals were not all what you'd now think of as cuddly pets. When they died, their bones would be boiled, labelled, sketched and preserved – Potter had the double eye of an animal lover and a natural scientist. Like Charles Kingsley before her – as a child, she read *The Water-Babies* with fascination – the world of nature was to her one of scientific interest rather than sentimental rapture. She was a painter before she was a writer, and her paintings were painstakingly observed. She even went on to submit a scholarly

---

[*] Linda Lear, *Beatrix Potter: A Life in Nature*.

paper on mycology to the Linnaean Society, arising from her drawings of fungus spores as seen through a microscope. Even as her fairytale fancy built on them, she was interested in animals as animals, nature as nature.

That doubleness of eye comes out in the stories that she was to write for children, their small format modelled on the little books of Mrs Barbauld and the likewise pocket-sized *Little Black Sambo*. The original Potterverse – the name fits; the characters duck in and out of each other's stories – is a strange and unstable place. The characters, creatures of the author's uncertain fancy, flicker between two states: animals and not animals. You can see the process very clearly in *The Tale of Mrs Tiggy-Winkle*, in which a little girl in search of her mislaid hankies comes upon the titular creature, frantically washing and ironing the laundry for every animal in the vicinity. Lucie helps the washerwoman do her rounds and at last is left with her own handkerchiefs, washed and folded in a clean pinafore. She turns to thank Mrs Tiggy-Winkle:

> But what a *very* odd thing! Mrs Tiggy-winkle had not waited either for thanks or for the washing bill!
>
> She was running running running up the hill – and where was her white-frilled cap? and her shawl? and her gown – and her petticoat?
>
> And *how* small she had grown – and how brown – and covered with PRICKLES!
>
> Why! Mrs Tiggy-winkle was nothing but a HEDGEHOG.

The image that accompanies the closing words is a perfectly realist watercolour of a hedgehog, the shape of a little brown aubergine. The hint in a postscript here is that, Alice-style, Lucie has dreamed the encounter. But if so, all Potter's books are half in a dream.

At one moment these creatures are furred and feathered avatars of bourgeois propriety – Mrs Tabitha Twitchit washing and brushing her kittens, dressing them in 'elegant uncomfortable clothes' and asking them to walk on their hind legs to impress her guests at a tea party. And at the next moment, they are creatures observed with the sharp eye of the amateur naturalist. Just look at the deftness with which Potter captures the movement of Mr Drake Puddle-Duck in that same book, when he picks up Tom Kitten's torn clothes: 'advanced in a slow sideways manner and picked up the various articles'. When he puts the clothes on himself, he looks just as absurd as you might expect a duck wearing a kitten's trousers and jacket to look. Fancying himself the elegant gent – 'It's a very fine morning!' he proclaims – he waddles off with the other ducks ('pit-pat, paddle-pat! pit-pat, waddle-pat!') to the pond where the clothes tumble off and sink. The final panel – shades of a *Just So* story here – explains that the ducks have been 'looking for [the sunken clothes] ever since'. The picture shows a perfectly naturalistic scene with one duck tranquil on the water and two with their tails up and heads down.

The fineness of Potter's observation is visible in little flares of style. The delinquent cat Simpkin, in Potter's home-made fairytale *The Tailor of Gloucester*, 'sniffed and mewed' at the closed shop door behind which the mice are busy. Potter goes to town on sound-effects – these are books that are begging to be read aloud. A pony goes 'trit-trot, trit-trot'; a bumblebee says, 'Zizz, Bizz, Bizzz!' and 'Zizz, Wizz, Wizz!' The magpie doctor in *The Tale of the Pie and the Patty-Pan* says, 'Gammon? ha! HA!' Spinach? ha! HA!' In *Timmy Tiptoes*, the twittering of songbirds comes out as 'Who's bin digging up *my* nuts? Who's-bin digging-up-*my*-nuts?' and 'Little bit-a-bread and-*no*-cheese! Little bit-a-bread an'-*no*-cheese!'*

Her creatures' relationship to food is no less peculiar and incon-sistent than their relationship with clothes. Sometimes they eat what their species would be expected to eat. The badger Tommy

---

* I fancy the minute differences in the repetitions are deliberate – the hyphenation second time round, for instance, speeding the phrase up. Potter is highly attentive to the music of her words and not always grammatically conventional.

Brock in *The Tale of Mr Tod* eats 'wasp nests and frogs and worms' (though we're told, oddly, that he'll eat rabbit pie when other food is scarce), and the Flopsy Bunnies – to say nothing of their notorious Uncle Peter – are bastards for lettuce. But Pig Robinson has bread-and-jam sandwiches for his packed lunch, the Two Bad Mice fall on the plaster food in a doll's house and try to carve the tiny ham with a knife, while the horrible old rat Samuel Whiskers, in Potter's most terrifying tale, hungers for a home-cooked roly-poly pudding, and his wife has a recipe.*

The ordinary laws of predation are, for the most part, in place: the fox very much wants to eat the winningly idiotic Jemima Puddle-Duck, but he makes her fetch herbs and onion so that he can eat her in the manner a human would eat her. Jemima puts on a shawl and a bonnet before setting out to find somewhere to lay her eggs where they won't be taken from her (which is what gets her in trouble with the fox in the first place). She's saved by a foxhound from being eaten herself; but the hound's puppies eat her eggs, leaving her in tears.

Is there danger in these stories? There is. Any of the generations of children haunted by the rats in the crawlspace in *The Tale of Samuel Whiskers* will have felt as much. Potter's child-animals are vulnerable when they let go of Nurse. The Flopsy Bunnies are perpetually in peril of being eaten or turned into the fur lining for a cloak. The guileless Pig Robinson is abducted by boat just like the hero of *Kidnapped*, and comes within a whisker (he's saved by a kind-hearted cat) of being roasted.† Nobody (except Jemima

---

* The chronology of the stories isn't clear, but we also know he's partial to bacon: he runs up an unpaid tab of 22/9 on bacon alone with Ginger and Pickles before their shop goes out of business.

† *The Tale of Little Pig Robinson* (1930), one of Potter's last publications, is something of an outlier in her work, and has the additional distinction of being a conscious intertextual link between Edward Lear's 'The Owl and the Pussycat' and Daniel Defoe's *Robinson Crusoe*.

Puddle-Duck's unborn children and the Fierce Bad Rabbit) comes to real harm in her stories – but the threat of it lingers.

The stories can't quite decide whether in their universe it's normal for animals to wear waistcoats and eat like humans, or whether it's absurd – and they don't need to. They have fun with the shuttling back and forth. A mother rabbit scolds her son for losing his nice coat in pursuit of a lettuce, then gives him a spoonful of chamomile tea to settle his stomach. In the matchlessly peculiar *Tale of Ginger and Pickles,* a tomcat and a fox terrier run a shop selling sugar, snuff, galoshes and red spotted handkerchiefs. The mice are frightened of Ginger and the rabbits are frighted of Pickles – but they still, cautiously, frequent the shop, because where else is a mouse going to be able to buy snuff on tick? As it happens, Ginger and Pickles lack business brains and insist on extending credit to their customers until they run out of money altogether: the story has become a touchstone in our own day for conservative-minded newspaper columnists.

Potter's books are, to use a literary-critical term, completely bananas. But they have extreme charm, and they are excellently and consciously geared to reading to children. They are full of funny noises, exclamations, buttonholings of the reader, and typograph-ical quirks for emphasis and change of pace. The rhythms of the printed text – long before picture books for children were quite the developed art they are in our own age – work in concert with the paintings on the opposite page: 'This is a Pussy called Miss Moppet, she thinks she has heard a mouse!' And there, on the facing page, is Miss Moppet comically tensed, eyes wide with attention. The illustrations aren't secondary: the whole thing is a gestalt. And these illustrations capture the doubleness of the creatures: they do not distort or caricature their animal subjects even when they're dressed in frock-coats or bonnets.

The stories are told from an animals'-eye perspective; Mr MacGregor is seldom more than a pair of gumboots and a ter-rifying appetite for rabbit pie. Yet in *Pig Robinson* humans and humanlike animals seem to coexist – pigs are customers at (human) Mr Mumby's general store. And the reader encounters 'Miss Potter' herself, unusually, near the end of *The Tale of Samuel Whiskers*, where we learn that John Joiner (the carpentry dog; do keep up) has recently built her a wheelbarrow and has been commissioned to follow it with a brace of hen coops. Samuel and Mrs Whiskers, at this point, are legging it. The author (now speaking in the first person) is on her way to the post office when she sees them fleeing up the street 'with big bundles on a little wheelbarrow, which looked very like mine'. She adds, peevishly: 'I am sure *I* never gave her leave to borrow my wheelbarrow!' Doctoral theses, I suspect, could be written on the question of how big Beatrix Potter's wheelbarrow is supposed to be. Is Beatrix Potter, in this story, the size of a rat? Or are the rats the size of Beatrix Potter? Curiouser, as another size-shifter has it, and curiouser.

The animal community in Beatrix Potter's works is a world that exists alongside our own one. Its enmities and alliances, neighbourliness and predation, exist all around us, sometimes but not always just out of sight – they are of our world and at the same time separate. Their existence doesn't follow the orderly logic of our own, but a more dreamlike one. Is that maybe an analogue to the world of the child?

Meanwhile Anna Sewell's *Black Beauty* (1877) – in whose hoofprints came *National Velvet*, *My Friend Flicka* and *War Horse* – kicked off a strand of realist animal stories that is strong in children's literature to this day. It remains one of the best-selling books of all time. It's also, I think I'm right in saying, the first story in the Western canon to be narrated by a horse, beating Leo Tolstoy's celebrated short story 'Strider' to the punch by nearly a decade.

Black Beauty was Anna Sewell's only book – and she barely lived to see it published. Born in 1820, she was an outgoing woman of high intelligence and considerable hopes for the future. Her family were Quakers – though her formal commitment to the faith (if not to Christianity itself) wavered, she used the archaic forms of address 'thee' and 'thou' her whole life. Her mother Mary was a successful children's writer: her first book *Walks With Mama* (1824) was originally composed for her own children because the family's precarious finances (her father was a hopeless businessman) didn't run to books.

The defining moment of Anna's life was what seemed at the time like a trivial accident: aged fourteen, she slipped on wet leaves in the rain while returning home from school one afternoon and hurt her ankle. Her mother later said, 'I can scarcely bear, even now, to recall the beginnings of this life of constant frustration.' The injury, reckoned then to be no more than a 'bad sprain', never healed. (Sewell's biographer Celia Brayfield reckons that the best candidate for the injury was a fracture to the talus bone, but, since the invention of X-rays lay in the future, we have no way of knowing.)*

For the rest of her life it affected her. During good periods Anna could walk with the help of a crutch; at other times she was able to walk only a few steps and, more and more, could not walk at all. Horses were not a Thelwell-style indulgence for her, but a way to get about. She never married or fell in love, forming instead a deep and almost sisterly bond with her mother. She spent her life in good works, aid to the poor, bee-keeping, and the life of the imagination, since the life of action was barred to her.

In 1871, a doctor gave Anna – by now bed-bound and in so much pain she couldn't sleep – eighteen months to live. Anna was then in her early fifties. Was it her sense of the shortness of the time she had left that fuelled her burst of creative energy? She told her diary: 'I am writing the life of a horse.' Having been Mary Sewell's most astute critic and first reader, Anna now found the

---

* Celia Brayfield, *Writing Black Beauty*.

roles reversed. She dictated her story to her mother and, as time went on, she realised she was on the verge of 'a little book, its special aim being to induce kindness, sympathy, and an understanding treatment of horses'. *Black Beauty* was accepted by Jarrold & Sons (who had been the publishers of Mary's first book) and came out in November 1877. In April the following year, Anna spoke her last words: 'I am quite ready.'

The book tells the life story of the titular horse in his* own words, taking him through a succession of situations, a succession of owners and a succession of names (in colthood he is Darkie, and is at various times Black Beauty, Black Auster, Jack, Blackie and Old Crony). Those are, be it noted, all good old English names 'not like Marengo, or Pegasus, or Abdallah'.† Like a horsey *Tom Brown*, Beauty's story is a *Bildungsroman* infused with gentle Christian orthodoxy and a sentimentally conservative sense of the class hierarchy.

Beauty's mother tells him on the first page that 'the colts who live here are very good colts, but they are cart-horse colts, and of course they have not learned manners. You have been well-bred and well born'. Later he regrets to find himself 'handsome and high-bred, but fallen into the middle class'. His progress through life is a tour of nineteenth-century England – raised on a farm, he finds himself at other points in harness (literally) to an aristocratic family, before going on to work for a poor-but-honest London cabbie. That tour drew on Anna's own experience, as her family's fortunes had taken her from her birthplace of Great Yarmouth to the East End of London (then a town that ran on horses, many treated with extraordinary cruelty), and later to Bath and Norfolk, where she died.

---

* Yup. Black Beauty is a stallion; I'd forgotten that. Though, in deference to the extent to which horse stories were to skew female in the years that followed, he became a mare in the 2020 movie. He was played by Kate Winslet.

† The Napoleonic Wars were recent enough that Marengo would not have been a tactful name for an English horse.

For those raised on the 1970s TV series – whose theme tune swells in my ear even as I write this – it may come as a surprise that Sewell is less interested in adventure for its own sake than in instruction. *Black Beauty* is very keen on imparting information to its young readers, both moral and practical. Reading it is, at times, like clopping along a country lane with an equine Sunday-school teacher, and the episodes of the story are usually chosen to point up a moral.

Here's a careless rider taking a tumble and breaking his neck on a hunt, his lamed horse being shot where it lay: 'They were carrying young Gordon to the churchyard to bury him. He would never ride again. What they did with Rob Roy I never knew; but twas all for one little hare.' Here is an uncouth man cruelly whipping his horse when his carriage-wheels get stuck in the mud. Here are thuggish boys hurling stones at horses to make them gallop. Here's a lazy stable-hand chucking fresh straw into the stall to avoid having to clean it out properly. Here's a dishonest groom stealing oats to feed them to the rabbits he's raising as a side-hustle. Here's an ignorant rider not noticing that his mount has a sharp pebble stuck in its hoof. Here's what happens when a good man falls prey to the Demon Drink. Here's what happens if you leave a lit pipe in a hayloft. And so on. Just deserts are served up; though, piercingly, it's as often a horse that suffers for human folly as a man.

Those who are kind to animals, Black Beauty observes, are also those who are kind to their fellow man. More than once, the breaking of a horse and the education of a child are paralleled. A 'crooked little hostler' declares that horses are 'like children; train 'em up in the way that they should go, as the good book says, and when they are old they will not depart from it, if they have a chance'. Black Beauty's friend Merrylegs, a cheerful little Thelwell pony, trains children to ride and, if ill-used, isn't above bucking his young charges off: "'I am as careful of our young ladies as the master can be [...] It is not them, it is the boys," said he, shaking his mane, "are quite different; they must be broken in as we were broken in when we were colts, and just be taught what's what.'" Elsewhere: 'spoiling a horse and letting him get into bad habits was just as cruel as spoiling a child, and both had to suffer for it afterward'.

But Sewell animates and embodies her moral precepts. By taking a horse's-eye view of the world, *Black Beauty* really does help its audience's moral sympathies leap the species barrier.* That is a deft response to an age of increasing mechanisation in which, its narrator complains, there are many who 'seemed to think that a horse was something like a steam-engine, only smaller'. Not only does it touch on human social injustices – alcoholism, or the poverty-trap among cab drivers who don't own their own horses – but *Black Beauty* tells us, in some detail, how horses can suffer in being ridden (and the more so by a rider indifferent to its welfare or insensitive to its needs and capabilities):

> Those who have never had a bit in their mouths cannot think how bad it feels;† a great piece of cold hard steel as thick as a man's finger to be pushed into one's mouth, between one's teeth, and over one's tongue, with the ends coming out at the corner of your mouth, and held fast there by straps over your head, under your throat, round your nose, and under your chin; so that no way in the world can you get rid of the nasty hard thing; it is very bad! yes, very bad!

Among the book's particular bêtes noires (sorry) are the docking of horses' and dogs' tails and the clipping of the latter's ears. The parallel is angrily made: 'Why don't they cut their own children's ears into points to make them look sharp? Why don't they cut the end off their noses to make them look plucky? One would be

---

* George Eliot wrote: 'If art does not enlarge men's sympathies, it does nothing morally.'

† Wonderful piece of literary chutzpah, here. Take it from me, writes Anna Sewell: I'm a horse.

just as sensible as the other. What right have they to torment and disfigure God's creatures?' There is a Rousseauian flavour to the book's view of nurture. Mutilating an animal for fashion is against the natural order: 'as if the good God that made us did not know what we wanted and what looked best'. Beauty's childhood stable-mate, the high-strung mare Ginger, speaks of how cruel treatment can create lasting trauma: 'I wish I could think about things as you do; but I can't, after all I have gone through.'

Like *The Water-Babies*, *Black Beauty* is credited with having brought about real-world reform. A particular cruelty that Beauty and Ginger suffer is the use of a 'check-rein', which was designed to raise the horse's head to give it a more fashionable profile.

> I like to toss my head about and hold it as high as any horse; but fancy now yourself, if you tossed your head up high and were obliged to hold it there, and that for hours together, not able to move it at all, except with a jerk still higher, your neck aching till you did not know how to bear it. Besides that, to have two bits instead of one – and mine was a sharp one, it hurt my tongue and my jaw, and the blood from my tongue colored the froth that kept flying from my lips as I chafed and fretted at the bits and rein. It was worst when we had to stand by the hour waiting for our mistress at some grand party or entertainment, and if I fretted or stamped with impatience the whip was laid on.

The feeling aroused by Sewell's description led directly to the check-rein being banned in England, and it's credited with a widespread effect on animal cruelty legislation in both the UK and the United States. A sour irony is that at Anna's own funeral, and to the fury of her grieving mother, the horses showed up with check-reins. 'In a few more years,' writes her biographer, 'thanks to [Anna's] work, they would be illegal.'

The book, which sold slowly on first publication, became a bestseller only when a crusading American animal rights activist,

George Thorndike Angell, published a new edition thirteen years after first publication in the UK. The nineteenth century saw the simultaneous first flowering of animal rights movements on both sides of the Atlantic. The Society for the Prevention of Cruelty to Animals (SPCA) was founded in 1824, becoming the RSPCA we know now when the dog-loving Princess Victoria, an early patron, took the throne. Angell, who had established the Massachusetts Society for the Prevention of Cruelty to Animals, had long been seeking a book that he imagined could do for animal cruelty what *Uncle Tom's Cabin* had done for slavery. In *Black Beauty*, he found that book.

The narrative that is the vehicle for these preoccupations most often proceeds at a trot – but at certain points it breaks into a gallop. One such passage is an account by Captain, an old horse who saw combat in the Crimean War and who had his rider shot off him in the Charge of the Light Brigade. Captain, describing the eve of battle, offers an affecting and wonderfully imagined detail:

> My dear master and I were at the head of the line, and as all sat motionless and watchful, he took a little stray lock of my mane which had turned over on the wrong side, laid it over on the right, and smoothed it down with his hand; then patting my neck, he said, 'We shall have a day of it to-day, Bayard, my beauty; but we'll do our duty as we have done.'

Black Beauty doesn't escape the tug of children's writing towards nostalgia. Time has its revenges. Towards the end of the book, Beauty re-encounters Ginger and nearly doesn't recognise her. The proud animal is broken down by cruel use. Not long afterwards, a cart passes with a dead horse on it – 'a chestnut horse with a long, thin neck'.

Beauty himself has a luckier end. In the closing words of the narration – restored to his old name, and to the care of his old master Joe – he is at peace. And that peace is this book's version of the Great Good Place that so many children's stories go in quest of: a place something very like childhood itself.

> My troubles are all over, and I am at home, and often before I am quite awake, I fancy I am still in the orchard at Birtwick, standing with my old friends under the apple-trees.

There, again, for horses as for humans, is the secret garden to which so many stories for children dream of returning.

V

NEVER SUCH
INNOCENCE AGAIN

Frances Hodgson Burnett · E. Nesbit ·
J.M. Barrie · Kenneth Grahame

THE EDWARDIANS

THE FAULT LINE BETWEEN THE VICTORIAN AND Edwardian eras was also the fault line between two eras in children's writing. The last Calvinist cobwebs of the moralising tradition were being blown away. At the same time what had followed – the almost sacralistic worship of children as angels in tiny suitings – came to give way to something that looked a little like psychological realism. Writers for children were learning to represent children not as they feared they might be, or as they wished they would be, but as they actually were. It wasn't an immediate change. There were, as always, qualifiers and counter-currents. Children's stories, like children, tend to resist doing what they're told. The sternest puritan or the most worshipful romantic can't help the odd fragment of realism creeping in, and few children's stories worth reading don't allow themselves the odd splash of emotional extravagance. But a change it was.

———

Stories of childhood in the era gave the children greater freedom from adult control, and presented childhood not as a waystation on the road to maturity but as a state of value in itself; one you might want to cling on to. And as industrialisation continued to press on, as urban populations continued to grow, and as the religious certainties of the previous age started to seem more remote, childhood itself became the space into which not only individual nostalgia but the longing for an imaginary past, an Arcadian and timeless one, was projected.

At the same time as childhood's place in literature was changing, so too was it in society. Childhood, more than ever, became the concern of the state – which is perhaps a rather dry way of saying that Edwardians considered the welfare of children to be the business of everyone, rather than leaving them essentially the private property of their parents. Children, in some sense, had rights and protections. The Children Act of 1908 gave a legal delineation to those rights and protections.

Its first two sections were titled 'Infant Life Protection' and 'Prevention of Cruelty to Children and Young Persons'. It made it a requirement to register foster parents, rather than leaving the care of orphans unregulated. There were provisions for home inspections, for the punishment of abuse and neglect, for removing children from the care of 'habitual drunkards'. It mandated the establishment of 'Industrial Schools' for neglected or abandoned children. It abolished the death penalty for children and provided for separate children's courts and separate children's detention facilities: 'Reformatory Schools', or borstals. Child criminals had their wings clipped demand-side, too: you could be punished for buying scrap metal or accepting goods from children as a pawnbroker.

It became an offence for vagrants to prevent their children from having access to education. The Act forbade the employment of children under sixteen in dangerous trades and made it illegal to offer young people for prostitution or take them into pubs or brothels. You could no longer sell tobacco to children. Indeed, so draconian were its provisions that it raised the legal drinking age to five.

Here were a whole raft of provisions that were important not just because of their humanity and good sense, but because *in toto* they made a statement about how society saw children, saw childhood itself. These provisions were primarily protective, but they acknowledged childhood agency too – inasmuch as they recognised that children might have impulses and ideas that they needed protecting from. Non-state organisations, too, took an interest in how children's collective agency could be channelled. The year in which the Children Act passed also saw the publication of Robert Baden-Powell's *Scouting for Boys* (the Boy Scout movement had been founded the previous year; the Girl Guides would be established in 1910).

The Edwardian era also saw childhood becoming a commercial space. A distinct children's publishing industry started to take wing. In the later years of the nineteenth century, there was still no firm distinction between books for children and for adults. As Ann Thwaite writes, 'A list of the best-selling novels in these years is very revealing: 1884 *Heidi*; *Treasure Island* 1885 *A Child's Garden of Verses*; *Huckleberry Finn* [sic] 1886 *Little Lord Fauntleroy*; *King Solomon's Mines*; *War and Peace*. Of these titles, all except *War and Peace* would now be considered children's books. At this time there was no rigid demarcation line between adult and children's literature. Publishers did not have special children's departments. There were no children's libraries.'*

Hodder and Stoughton hadn't published children's books at all until the success of *Peter Pan* transformed their remit. There was money in it – their publicity journal *The Bookman* published seven different supplements on *Peter Pan*, and the 1905 Christmas special, with a selection of photographs from the play, was reselling for twice its cover price less than a year later. That made extracting the Peter Pan chapters from *The Little White Bird* (the novel for adults in which the character first appeared) and publishing *Peter Pan in Kensington Gardens* (1906) as a children's book with illustrations by Arthur Rackham a commercial no-brainer.

When the by-then famous E. Nesbit (of whom more shortly) promoted one of her last children's books, *The Magic City* (1910), she was able to do so at the three-week Children's Welfare Exhibition

---

*   Ann Thwaite, *Beyond the Secret Garden*.

held over the new year of 1913 in London's Olympia to 'illustrate the wonderful progress of recent years in providing for the mental, physical and social welfare of the younger generation'. It was opened by Clementine Churchill and its patrons included the then prime minister, Herbert Asquith, as well as senior figures in education and the church. It was half jamboree, half trade show: a vast space full of exhibits about educational systems such as Montessori or open-air schools, discussions of children's literature and fairy-tales, 'Stencilling for Amateurs', the Women's Imperial Health Association, promotions for the health-giving qualities of Swedish Gymnastics and evangelists for the Simplified Spelling Sosieti [sic]. The NSPCC shared an exhibition stand with Horlicks. Nesbit's presence at the exhibition testifies, too, to the way 'the author of children's literature emerges in this era as an actor and public participant in the new sciences of childhood, rather than remaining a remote moralist or simply an entertainer'.*

---

*   Jenny Bavidge, 'Exhibiting Childhood', in *Childhood in Edwardian Fiction*, Adrienne E. Gavin and Andrew F. Humphries (eds).

From Paragons to Pains

FRANCES HODGSON BURNETT

The One I Knew the Best of All; Little Lord Fauntleroy; A Little Princess; The Secret Garden

T HE LIFE AND CAREER OF THE ANGLO-AMERICAN novelist Frances Hodgson Burnett (1849–1924) embodies these changes: she started out a Victorian novelist and ended an Edwardian one. She is remembered now for three novels for children: *Little Lord Fauntleroy* (1886), *A Little Princess* (1905) and *The Secret Garden* (1906). The first two of those books represent high-water marks of the Victorian cult of the golden child.[*] *Little Lord Fauntleroy* was a bestseller on a staggering scale – as one contemporary report put it, 'it does not do to say merely that *Little Lord Fauntleroy* was a great success; it caused a public delirium of joy'. Louisa May Alcott, James Russell Lowell and the prime minister, Lord Gladstone, all praised it lavishly, and it sparked the sort of literary fashion craze not seen since Goethe set the youth of Germany to dressing up in yellow trousers and killing themselves. But it's *The Secret Garden*, which went in a quite different direction, that we now regard as her masterpiece.

---

[*]   The 1905 publication date, appearing to make it belong to the era of *The Secret Garden*, is misleading. *A Little Princess* was the revised and expanded version of a story, 'Sara Crewe, Or What Happened at Miss Minchin's', that was originally published in book form in 1888 after being serialised in a children's magazine the previous year.

Her all-but-forgotten memoir shows us the soil out of which her career as a writer grew. *The One I Knew the Best of All: A Memory of the Mind of the Child* (1893) paints a vivid picture not just of her own experience of infancy, but of mid-Victorian childhood itself. Burnett, like so many children's writers, had a remarkable and exact recall of how it felt to be a child. She describes the titular child she knew the best of all, i.e. herself, as 'the Small Person' in a way that can be gratingly cutesy; but strip that away and there's a real toughness to the picture she paints. Already, by the time she writes, childhood itself has moved on – 'I have not the remotest idea of what she looked like. She belonged to an era when photography was not as advanced an art as it is to-day, and no picture of her was ever made.'

That indistinctness is generative. She remembers, which seems to me a very modern insight, the experience of childhood not as distinct personhood so much as of being a creature shaped and buffeted by the outside world. The child, in this account of it, is not marked by special goodness or potential wickedness, but by a profound sensitivity to its environment:

> I do not remember regarding her as a personality at all. It was the people about her, the things she saw, the events which made up her small existence, which were absorbing, exciting, and of the most vital and terrible importance sometimes [...] that strange, awful problem of a little soul standing in its newness in the great busy, tragic world of life, touched for the first time by everything that passes it, and never touched without some sign of the contact being left upon it.

She goes on to write that

> even the most child-loving among us should find it difficult to realize constantly that a mite of three or four, tumbling about, playing with india-rubber dogs and with difficulty restrained

from sucking the paint off Noah, Shem, Ham, and Japhet, not
to mention the animals, is a person, and that this person is ten
thousand times more sensitive to impression than one's self [...]
One takes a fat, comfortable little body on one's knee and begins
to tell it a story about 'a fairy' or 'a doggie' or 'a pussy.' And the
moment the story begins the questions begin also.

Just as children can be hard for adults to see, in Burnett's phrase,
'from the inside point of view', so are adults hard to comprehend
for children. She speaks of a 'secret consciousness that she was so
little and that the grown-up people were so big that they could not
really understand one another's point of view': 'I do not remember
any rebellion against an idea of injustice. All that comes back to
me in the form of a mental attitude is a perfect realization of the
immense fact that people who were grown up could do what they
chose, and that there was no appeal against their omnipotence.'

The intensity and loneliness of childhood fears is vividly painted.
The fear of adult authority having been struck into her by the 'Keep
off the Grass' signs at the park, she asked a policeman whether, if
she went onto the grass by accident, he would have to 'take her up'.
The policeman tells her with a face that 'did not bear the ferocity
which would have accorded with his awful words': 'Yes, I should
have to pick you up and carry you to prison.'

She must have turned pale; but that she sat still without further
comment, that she did not burst into frantic howls of despair,
causes one to feel that even in those early days she was governed
by some rudimentary sense of dignity and resignation to fate, for as
she sat there, the short legs in socks and small black 'ankle-straps'
confronting her, the marrow was dissolving in her infant bones.

It's a remarkable feat of embodied recall. Her father's death in
1853, when she was not yet four, as she records it, made far less
impression on her than the prospect of being collared for trespassing

in the public park. And isn't that just how childhood, with what to adults seem its distorting-mirror fears and obsessions, really is?

> There came a day when someone carried her into the bedroom where the crimson-draped four-post bed was, and standing by its side held her in her arms that she might look down at Papa lying quite still upon the pillow. She only thought he looked as if he were asleep, though someone said: 'Papa has gone to Heaven,' and she was not frightened, and looked down with quiet, interest and respect. A few years later the sight of a child of her own age or near it, lying in his coffin, brought to her young being an awed realization of death, whose anguished intensity has never wholly repeated itself; but being held up in kind arms to look down at 'Poor Papa,' she only gazed without comprehension and without fear.

Death, and seeing dead bodies, was nevertheless a feature of mid-nineteenth-century English childhood in a way that it is not now. Papa was not the last – and the 'Small Person' remembers the shock four years later when what she calls 'the Strange Thing' comes to a three-year-old classmate, Selina. Again, she saw the body. Again, she was not afraid: 'she bent over and kissed her round cheek where the dimples used to play. And the coldness was only the soft coldness of a flower.'

In the 'Small Person' are the stirrings of the writer that Frances was to become. At three years old, she reports, 'she had begun a lifelong chase after the Story': 'a positively wolfish appetite for books, though no one knew about it or understood the anguish of its gnawings. It must be plainly stated that her longings were not for "improving" books.' In the middle of the nineteenth century, those improving books were still everywhere. She remembers her first book – an alphabet of flowers, with each flower described in a moralising verse typical of children's writing of the time (she notes wryly the idea that a bee should be 'improving each shining hour' – a line from exactly the poem Carroll sends up in *Alice*): 'I think one rather had a feeling of having been born an innately vicious little person who needed laboring with constantly that one might be made merely endurable.'

In those days, I think, the Children's Century had not begun. Children were not regarded as embryo intellects, whose growth it is the pleasure and duty of intelligent maturity to foster and protect. Morals and manners were attended to, desperate efforts were made to conquer their natural disinclination to wash their hands and faces, it was a time-honored custom to tell them to 'make less noise,' and I think everybody knelt down in his night-gown and said his prayers every night and morning. I wish I knew who was the originator of the nursery verse which was a kind of creed:

> Speak when you're spoken to,
> Come when you're called,
> Shut the door after you.
> And do as you're told.

The rhyme and metre were, perhaps, not faultless, but the sentiments were without a flaw. A perfectly normal child knew what happened in its own nursery and the nurseries of its cousins and juvenile friends; it knew something of the romances of Mrs Barbauld and Miss Edgeworth, and the adventures related in Peter Parley's 'Annual.' Religious aunts possibly gave it horrible little books containing memoirs of dreadful children who died early of complicated diseases, whose lingering developments they enlivened by giving unlimited moral advice and instruction to their parents and immediate relatives, seeming, figuratively speaking, to implore them to 'go and do likewise,' and perishing to appropriate texts. The Small Person suffered keen private pangs of conscience, and thought she was a wicked child, because she did not like those books and had a vague feeling of disbelief in the children.

Here, stated plainly, is the situation that Burnett and her contemporaries were to work to remedy. Her near-contemporary Kenneth Grahame's autobiographical stories in *Dream Days* contrast the joy of a child's imagination immersed in a fantastical picture book with the 'anæmic, night-gowned nonentities that hovered over the bed of the Sunday-school child in the pages of the *Sabbath Improver*'.

The situation amid which Burnett grew up – infant mortality commonplace; texts for children pious; adult authority remote; 'seen but not heard' the rule – was dissolving into what even then had started to be seen as the 'Children's Century'. The literature of this era gives us larger groups of siblings; bigger families became more common as fewer children died in infancy. It shows high spirits and naughtiness celebrated rather than deplored.

Frances Hodgson Burnett, according to *The One I Knew the Best of All,* was still in infancy when she discovered her gift for narrative, captivating her schoolmates with stories, which she wrote down on scrap paper, slates and old account books. A vital punctuation point in her childhood was the discovery, when she was seven years old, of a stash of books in her mother's secretaire. She read Scott, Fenimore Cooper and *Uncle Tom's Cabin*. Her imaginative world is full of adventure and romance. She was to go on to submit stories for magazine publication while still in her teens – a lovely story has it that she earned the money to buy paper and postage for her first submissions by picking wild grapes and selling them.

But first came what she calls the 'first great event of her life'. Manchester's cotton industry was ruined by the American Civil War, and with it the fortunes of Frances's mother Eliza. They moved in 1865, when Frances was fifteen, from shabby-genteel Islington Square in Manchester, the home of her childhood – and emigrated to Knoxville, Tennessee. From urban, sooty, built-up Manchester, she found herself in 'a curious little village – one unpaved street of wooden houses, some painted white and some made of logs, but with trees everywhere, and forests and hills shutting it in from the world. Then she lived in the Story. Quiet

English people, who, driven by changes of fortune, wandered thousands of miles and lived without servants in a log cabin, were a Story themselves.' Her childhood was British but her adult life was American. As she expresses it in *The One I Knew the Best of All*, it was the acceptance for publication of her first story that marked her arrival in that adult life; 'she had crossed the delicate, impalpable guiding line. And after that, life itself began'.

Burnett was a transatlantic writer with a transatlantic life, and you could think of *Little Lord Fauntleroy,* her breakthrough novel for children (she was already established as an adult writer by that stage), as a sort of kindergarten version of a Henry James plot: an innocent from the new world travels to corrupt old Europe. But instead of that innocent, like Lambert Strether or Isabel Archer, being undone by the moral rot of the old world, the protagonist not only fails to notice the wickedness around him but transforms it by the sheer force of his own goodness. The pendulum has swung a long way from the era in which children were conceived in literature as being in mortal peril of their souls; here, they are effortless redeemers of the corrupt souls of the adults around them.

It is horribly sentimental. Cedric's physical beauty – his golden curls, his sweet face – is an uncomplicated token of his moral beauty. We hear once of his 'loving little heart' and twice of his 'kind little heart' in the first six pages alone, and Burnett's description of Cedric's dead father Captain Errol hasn't a scrap of human specificity in it:

> He had a beautiful face and a fine, strong, graceful figure; he had a bright smile and a sweet, gay voice; he was brave and generous, and had the kindest heart in the world, and seemed to have the power to make everyone love him.

Cedric is a chip off the old block. Living with his mother ('Dearest') in genteel poverty in New York, he is beloved of everyone he meets, from the bootblack to the grocer, and he takes everyone as he finds them regardless of rank or station. If he wins a running race against another little boy on the street (of course he wins the running race) his first instinct is to console the loser: 'Even in the first flush of his triumphs, he remembered that the person who was beaten might not feel so gay as he did, and might like to think that he MIGHT have been the winner under different circumstances.'

His circumstances change when a lawyer for his grandfather, the excellently named Molyneux, Earl of Dorincourt, turns up in New York to announce that, following the deaths without issue of his two uncles, the little chap is now heir to an earldom and a vast estate. The catch is that he must come to live in a draughty castle with his grandfather – who had long ago cut off his father without a penny after he insisted on marrying Cedric's low-born and dismayingly American mother. Hating her on principle, the earl insists that though Dearest may accompany Cedric across the Atlantic she must live in a cottage at the bottom of the garden, and he will on no account be so much as introduced to her.

The novel's running joke, if joke you could call it, is that Molyneux is a selfish, bad-tempered, heartless old ratbag; but Cedric is so incapable of thinking ill of anyone that he is convinced that his grandfather is the best person in the whole world. Everyone loves Cedric on sight, and everyone loathes the earl, but in an amusingly *Gruffalo*-flavoured moment Cedric completely misunderstands this:

> As they rode through the market town, he used to see the people turn and look, and he noticed that as they lifted their hats their faces often brightened very much; but he thought it was all because his grandfather was with him.

His earnest devotion, of course, eventually goes on to thaw the earl's icy heart, and, after a bit of third-act jeopardy involving the appearance of a rival claimant to Cedric's title (seen off thanks to a blush-makingly improbable coincidence), the story manages to have its cake and eat it. The tyrannical earl becomes no less benevolent than Scrooge at the end of *A Christmas Carol*,[*] and his ingenuous little democrat of a grandson is set up to cop an earldom and a fortune.

His republican, salt-of-the-earth pal the grocer Hobbs, indeed, sells up in New York and opens a shop in the village next to the castle, where, the closing pages of the novel inform us, he 'became in time more aristocratic than his lordship himself, and he read the Court news every morning, and followed all the doings of the House of Lords'. As Burnett herself once said spryly in a letter: 'I want to be a duchess myself. I think it would be nice.' A kind heart, the book seems to tell us, is a treasure above noble breeding and inherited wealth; but if you can get all three so much the better.

Its tactful negotiation between American republicanism and British pride in the class system (or, perhaps, between American fascination with the British aristocracy and British resentment of it) earned the love of readers on both sides of the Atlantic. Long before Pottermania, there was Fauntleroy-mania. It was the best-selling novel of 1886, and by 1893 only *Ben-Hur* was in more American libraries. There was merch – you could get Fauntleroy playing cards, writing paper, chocolate, and even a Fauntleroy perfume. And, as often in this period, its reach was magnified by the success of stage productions. The first of these came in 1888 after Burnett fought and won a consequential court battle to make it impossible for dramatists to adapt works of fiction without the permission of their authors.

Most bizarrely of all, there was a craze for dressing little boys in the so-called 'Fauntleroy Suit' – a black velvet suit with a lace-collared shirt, as depicted in Reginald Birch's illustrations. The earliest photograph of A.A. Milne shows him, in 1886, aged four, done up in full Fauntleroy get-up. Not surprisingly, the

---

[*]   Oscar Wilde's fable 'The Selfish Giant', published just two years later, has a similar if more expressly Christian trajectory.

little boys forced into such suits had mixed feelings about the matter. In Davenport, Iowa, an eight-year-old boy was reported to have burned down his father's barn in protest at having to wear a Fauntleroy suit. According to Burnett's biographer Ann Thwaite,* the New York press reported that one Stephen Crane (the *Red Badge of Courage* man?) generous-spiritedly gave two little boys some money and told them to get their curly locks cut short, causing the mother of one to fly into hysterics and the other to faint dead away.

The journalist Irvin Cobb (1876–1944) described it this way in his memoir: 'A mania was laying hold on the mothers of the nation. It was a mania for making over their growing sons after the likeness of a beatific image. Little Lord Fauntleroy infected thousands of the worthy matrons of America with a catching lunacy, which raged like a sedge fire and left enduring scars upon the seared memories of its chief sufferers – their sons, notably between the ages of seven and eleven.' †

The model for Cedric was Burnett's second son Vivian: 'if there had not been Vivian, there would not have been Fauntleroy,' she told the writer Gertrude Brownell. The illustrations for the book, which probably did more even than the text to foster that sartorial craze, were based on an 1884 photograph of Vivian, aged seven, in a velvet suit. By the end of his life Reginald Birch regarded his association with the book as having ruined his subsequent career. Vivian entered the ranks of the children of children's writers whose lives were blighted by the connection.

More than half a century after the book came out a 'bald, square-cut' middle-aged man told a reporter plaintively: 'I was a perfectly normal boy – I got myself just as damn dirty as the other boys. I could write a book about what Fauntleroy has been to me. I try to

---

*   Thwaite, op. cit.

†   Irvin Cobb, *Goin' On Fourteen, Being Cross-sections Out of a Year in the Life of an Average Boy* (George H. Doran, 1924.

get away from it but I can't.' He lived with his mother on Long Island into adulthood,[*] managed her business affairs, and was to write a biography of her (*The Romantick Lady*, 1927) from which she emerges, as one critic put it, as 'aggressively domineering, offensively whimsical and abominably self-centred and conceited'.[†] When he died of a heart attack after coming to the rescue of a boating accident in 1937, his death was headlined: ORIGINAL 'FAUNTLEROY' DIES IN BOAT AFTER HELPING RESCUE 4 IN SOUND: 'Vivian Burnett, Author's Son who Devoted Life to Escaping "Sissified" Role, is Stricken at Helm – Manoeuvres Yawl to get 2 Men and 2 Women from Overturned Craft, Then Collapses.'[‡]

If Frances put Vivian into Fauntleroy, it was perhaps an imagined version of herself who appeared in *A Little Princess*. Its protagonist, Sara Crewe, is left in the care of Miss Minchin's school for girls in London while her doting father, a well-heeled widower, returns to work in India. To start with, the titular soubriquet is ironic: the other girls are jealous of Sara's lavish wardrobe and privileges. The obsequious and materialistic Miss Minchin ('large, cold, fishy eyes and a large, cold, fishy smile'; part Trunchbull, part Cruella) treats her with special regard because of her father's wealth. Sara – who graciously befriends the most hopeless and dim-witted of her classmates, Ermengarde, and Becky the scullery-maid – never puts on airs. But when news comes that Captain Crewe has died, and his riches have vanished after he invested in a friend's ill-fated diamond mine, her fortunes are reversed.

The little princess is now a penniless orphan. At once Miss Minchin takes her out of school, confines her to a freezing garret, and sets her to work as a drudge. Yet she maintains her aristocracy

---

[*] 'Names Make News', *People*, 15 May 1933.

[†] Marghanita Laski, *Mrs Ewing, Mrs Molesworth and Mrs Hodgson Burnett* (Arthur Barker, 1950).

[‡] *New York Times*, 26 July 1937.

of spirit: "'Whatever comes," she said, "cannot alter one thing. If I am a princess in rags and tatters, I can be a princess inside.'"

Accordingly, she is considerate, humble and solicitous whatever befalls her. Gandhi himself would be tempted to slap her, were he not to suspect that she'd get an intolerable degree of satisfaction from turning the other cheek. Like Cinderella, she makes friends with rats and sparrows. At a climactic moment in the story, hungry and cold, she finds a coin on the ground and goes to a bakery to buy six buns – before, her tender heart moved by the plight of a street-girl more wretched still than her, she gives five of them away. Of course, as the plot unwinds in strongly Dickensian style, it turns out that the diamond mines came good after all and that her father's guilt-stricken old pal has been searching for her all along. He is – drum roll – living *right next door*. As in *Fauntleroy*, Sara is spared the disagreeable necessity of virtue being its own reward in the long run: she's going to end up rich and happy, as are her humble pals, and Miss Minchin is going to spend the rest of her pinched little life regretting being such a meanie. It's a touching and well-made melodrama, and its resolution is as richly satisfying as it is ridiculous – but few children will see themselves faithfully represented in Sara.

So Cedric in *Little Lord Fauntleroy* and Sara in *A Little Princess* are paragons: children as turbocharged innocents; moral superheroes. They are designed above all to appeal to sentimental adults, and it was sentimental adults who drove the Fauntleroy cult. The child protagonists of *The Secret Garden* on the other hand are, at least at the outset, horrible.

Mary Lennox is ill-favoured in body and in temperament: 'everybody said she was the most disagreeable-looking child ever seen. It was true, too. She had a little thin face and a little thin body, thin light hair and a sour expression. Her hair was yellow, and her face was yellow because she had been born in India and had always been ill in one way or another'. She's lonely, neglected by her parents, accustomed to being waited on by native servants, and spoiled rotten. 'She was not an affectionate child and had never cared much for anyone.' She thinks nothing of calling her ayah 'Pig! Pig! Daughter of pigs!', 'because to call a native a pig is the worst insult of all'.*

Within the first few pages, both parents are dead and the whole passel of native servants have either been carried off by cholera or run for the hills. Discovered by chance, abandoned and forgotten, in her father's bungalow, she is packed off to live with her uncle in his vast manor house on the edge of the Yorkshire moors. She shows no enthusiasm for the project, and treats the servants assigned to look after her with the same absurd imperiousness she showed her ayah.

Even leaving aside Mary's brisk orphaning in the opening pages, this is a book deeply rooted in grief, and the trauma of grief. Misselthwaite Manor, as it turns out, is one great galumphing metaphor. Mary's widowed Uncle Archibald is seldom ever at home, and when he is he barely interacts with his niece or the servants who keep the place running. After the abrupt death of his beloved wife Lilias, he has checked out of ordinary existence. And as Mary learns, among the many walled gardens is the titular secret garden, the one that Lilias planted and tended and where she died in an accident a decade before. Mr Craven buried the key and forbade anyone ever to set foot in the garden again. Thanks to the borderline supernatural intervention of a robin, Mary finds the key – and then she finds the locked gate, hidden beneath a curtain of ivy...

The secret garden itself works in lots of ways. As metaphor, it's an Eden, one of those special Edens in children's writing that is (to the adult reader and writer) the lost good place of childhood itself. But it's also a living symbol of regrowth and replenishment, and a concrete example: it's a garden, as well as the idea of a garden. Its

---

* It's clear that abusing the help is disapproved of, here, though the undifferentiated 'dark' and 'ashy' faces of the servants – they're colonial set-dressing more than people – will mar the book's opening a little for the modern reader.

flora and fauna, its smells and sounds, are carefully and evocatively detailed. The robin* is just one of many avatars of the healing forces of nature in the book. The secret garden (where the robin lives) stands not just for forbidden knowledge, but for self-knowledge. The site of grief is also the site of rebirth.

> Mistress Mary went a step nearer to the robin and looked at him very hard. 'I'm lonely,' she said. She had not known before that this was one of the things which made her feel sour and cross. She seemed to find it out when the robin looked at her and she looked at the robin.

Another avatar of nature – we could think of him as a pre-school compost of Heathcliff, Mellors and St Francis of Assisi – is Dickon, the younger brother of Martha, the servant who is assigned to look after Mary. We hear a lot about Dickon before we see him. He's working class, uneducated, lives and breathes the Yorkshire moors and can tame and speak to all sorts of animals. And he's happy: he may not have pots of money, but he has affectionate siblings and a mother who loves him. Dickon befriends Mary and helps her bring the secret garden back to life – a friendship she hoped for but did not expect:

> 'He wouldn't like me,' said Mary in her stiff, cold little way. 'No one does.'
>
> Martha looked reflective again.
>
> 'How does tha' like thysel'?' she inquired, really quite as if she were curious to know. Mary hesitated a moment and thought it over.
>
> 'Not at all – really,' she answered. 'But I never thought of that before.'

---

*   An important character in his own right. Eccentrically, Burnett even writes a few pages of the story from his point of view. That might not have survived a modern editor.

When they first meet, Dickon's unaffected good nature – his identity with nature itself – instantly wins her.

The house has other secrets. Mary, alone in her room, hears crying at night from somewhere else in the house. She's told she's imagining it – until, exploring the empty corridors in the small hours, she chances into a room where she meets the other child in the book's triangular set-up, Colin: Archibald's neglected, sickly, bed-bound son – whom he can't bear to look at because he reminds him of his dead wife – is even more unpleasant than Mary. The adults around him have convinced him that he's going to develop a hunchback and die young, and the servants who tend him have been instructed to keep his very existence a deadly secret. They pander to his every whim for fear of worsening his condition, and in the process have created a monster of resentment, spite and self-pity.

The arc of the story is of these two children (thanks in part to the catalytic effect of their pet Green Man, Dickon) learning to heal each other, heal themselves, and in due course bring the wintry widower under whose roof they live back to life too. The miraculous return of Colin to health and vigour, and Mary growing fatter and prettier, is down to what they call the Magic.

The meaning of that Magic is at the heart of the meaning of the book. At a climactic moment, when the Doxology is recited in the garden, what seems to be a Christian gloss is put on this resurrection story[*] – and there are scriptural cadences here and there in the text. Colin's repeated assertion that 'I am going to live for ever and ever and ever' can't but evoke the New Testament's promise of eternal life. But the Magic of the book is pre-Christian, almost Lawrentian. When Dickon's mother Susan is first introduced to the garden, Colin asks her whether she believes in Magic.

---

[*]   There's even the possibility, far-fetched but not wholly implausible, that the passage in which Mr Craven hears the laughter of children in the locked garden may have been a source for T.S. Eliot's 'Burnt Norton'.

'That I do, lad,' she answered. 'I never knowed it by that name, but what does th' name matter?[…] Never thee stop believin' in th' Big Good Thing an' knowin' th' world's full of it – an' call it what tha' likes. Tha' wen singin' to it when I come into th' garden.'

There's a curious and very *fin-de-siècle* twin track of thinking in this book: a mystical appeal to nature sits alongside a burgeoning sense of the miraculous in science. Colin is determined to conduct a 'scientific experiment' on the Magic, and his stated ambition is to be a 'Scientific Discoverer' – rather than, say, a soldier or an explorer or a servant of empire. Few protagonists of children's stories in the previous century aspired to be scientists.

All that psychological acuity makes the book a profound step forward for Burnett. In this, just as in her previous books, it falls to children to show the way to adults. But these children aren't in a natural state of grace or of superhuman innocence. They have been built, morally, by their experiences – by the experience of being indulged, of being frightened, of being kept indoors; and above all by the experience of neglect. These aren't plaster saints: they are unsympathetic children, sympathetically understood. The formation of the International Psychoanalytical Association was four years in the future, but Burnett was thinking in a psychoanalytical way.

Indeed, in one remarkable passage she links an understanding of child psychology to a utopian sense, which in the early years of the twentieth century must have been easy to feel, that the world was marching ever faster forward:

In each century since the beginning of the world wonderful things have been discovered. In the last century more amazing things were found out than in any century before. In this new century hundreds of things still more astounding will be brought to light. […] One of the new things people began to find out in the last century was that thoughts – just mere thoughts – are as powerful

as electric batteries – as good for one as sunlight is, or as bad for
one as poison.

To flourish, children need food, and a connection to nature, and the
society of other children – and, no less than gardens need tending,
they need parental love. It was not enough, *The Secret Garden* says,
for adults (as Mary's parents had) to pursue their own pleasures and
leave their children to the servants. As one character remarks tartly:
'Perhaps if her mother had carried her pretty face and her pretty
manners oftener into the nursery, Mary might have learned some
pretty ways, too.' Dickon, speaking of Colin, says: 'he wishes he'd
never been born. Mother, she says that's th' worst thing on earth
for a child. Them as is not wanted scarce ever thrives.'

Burnett's own two children did not want for love. Indeed, she
perhaps channelled the love that was absent from her first marriage into coddling her two boys – and even into their teenage
years she spoke and wrote to them as if they were under ten. She
was always, like Cedric Errol's mother, 'Dearest'. Vivian Burnett
may have been scarred by having been the original of Little Lord
Fauntleroy – but he, at least, lived. The decisive trauma in Frances
Hodgson Burnett's life was the death from consumption of her
older son Lionel in 1890.

Lionel was only fifteen when it became clear that he was dying.
Frances's response was to drag him from their home in Washington
all over Europe in futile search of a cure, to 'wrap him in make-
believe' so that he would not know he was dying, and to divert his
attention with toys and games and gadgets. She wrote to a cousin
afterwards:

> He was ill nine months but I never allowed him to know that I
> was really anxious about him, I never let him know that he had
> consumption or that he was in danger – and when he died he
> passed away so softly and quickly that I know he wakened in the
> other world without knowing how he had left this one. I can thank

God for that… I shall never get over it. I suffered too much. But I kept it up to the last. The day before he died he slept softly all day and said he was quite comfortable, only so sleepy… The last words he spoke to me were, 'God bless Mammie', when we kissed each other good night.[*]

Neither her marriage to Swan Burnett nor her conventional Christian faith survived the loss of Lionel. She dabbled in theosophy and Christian Science in the early 1880s and led a separate life from her husband (they eventually divorced in 1898), making a disastrous marriage with her long-term protégé Stephen Townsend. The death of Lionel, I suspect, is what made the exploration of grief in *The Secret Garden* so much richer and more poignant. Colin's miraculous recovery from illness can be seen as a species of magical thinking: the wish-fulfilment version of Lionel's real-world decline and death.

---

[*]   Letter to Emma Daniels, quoted in Thwaite, *Beyond the Secret Garden*.

'Oh! my Daddy, my Daddy!'

E. NESBIT

The Story of the Treasure Seekers;
The Wouldbegoods; The New Treasure Seekers;
Five Children and It; The Phoenix and the
Carpet; The Story of the Amulet; The Railway
Children; Wings and the Child; The Magic City

EDITH NESBIT (1858–1924), DESCRIBED BY HER BIOG-
rapher Julia Briggs as 'the first modern writer for children', shared with Burnett that extraordinary ability to
remember what it was like to exist as a child. 'There is only one
way of understanding children,' she wrote in 1913 at the peak of
her success. 'They cannot be understood by imagination, by observation, nor even by love. They can only be understood by memory.
Only by remembering how you felt and thought when you yourself
were a child can you arrive at any understanding of the thoughts
and feelings of children.' Even in her youngest days, she said, she
had prayed 'fervently, tearfully, that when I should be grown up
I might never forget what I thought and felt and suffered then'.[*]

She might be forgiven for having wanted to forget. Edith Nesbit's
own childhood was one of griefs and terrors. Her oldest brother
(she was her parents' fifth child in as many years) died at the age

---

[*] E. Nesbit, 'My School Days: Memories of Childhood', *Girl's Own Paper*, October
1896.

of four a year before she was born. Her father died of consumption when she was three. And when she was only twelve years old her elder sister Mary, too, succumbed to consumption and died on the eve of her wedding.

Edith was raised, then, by a twice-widowed single mother (with a teenage daughter from her first marriage) in straitened circumstances in south London. She had a vivid imagination as a child and was terrified of the dark and haunted by the idea of the walking dead – a fear cemented by her encounter aged nine with the mummified bodies preserved in the church of St Michel in Bordeaux, which she called 'the crowning horror of my childish life'.

Those terrors fed into the horror stories she wrote as an adult and found their way in gently comic form into her children's fiction – in *The Phoenix and the Carpet*, Jane is terrified by her brother's talk of 'dungeons, and chains, and knobbly bare human bones' – but the worlds she creates in her writing for children are fundamentally deeply benign. She makes childhood anew – a version of childhood to which, as Noël Coward (who knew her a little at the end of her life) put it, she devoted 'her extraordinary power of describing hot summer days in England in the beginning years of the century'.

Nesbit's extraordinary career as a children's writer comes from the way she captured more acutely than anyone before her an authentic child's-eye view of the world, while making that world an essentially benevolent one. Her stories can contain magic wishing fairies, time travel, or *deus ex machina* Indian Uncles arriving laden with gifts, but the children in the stories are utterly realistic in their squabbling, messy, unworldly ways. They are, as she tells her readers in one of her novels: 'not particularly handsome, nor were they extra clever, nor extraordinarily good. But they were not bad sorts on the whole; in fact, they were rather like you.' But they are – as all child readers long to be – 'the sort of people that things DO happen to'.

Nesbit herself didn't have much luck in her adult life, either. Her husband, Hubert Bland, was an absolute rotter: six foot something of pompous, monocle-wearing male entitlement with a boxer's body and 'a voice like the scream of an eagle'. A family friend in later life described him as 'very hot-blooded… abnormally sexual, too much so for the tastes of his wife'. She was only nineteen when they met and she was seven months pregnant when, in the face of Bland's very voluble lack of enthusiasm for the institution, they married in a downbeat civil ceremony in 1880.

We can attribute it to bad luck, perhaps, that Hubert's brush-manufacturing business went down with all hands shortly after their marriage – his business partner, Hubert said, had run off with all the money, and he went as far as placing a letter in the paper appealing for information as to the man's whereabouts so he could receive the horsewhipping he was due. Other crackpot projects came to nothing and for much of their impoverished early marriage Edith was responsible for making ends meet. Lamenting the time it took from writing poetry, she sold stories piecemeal to magazines, like Albert-Next-Door's uncle in *The Treasure Seekers*, 'pegging away at the rotten novels he has to write to make a living', or Mother in *The Railway Children*:

> Mother, all the time, was very busy with her writing. She used to send off a good many long blue envelopes with stories in them – and large envelopes of different sizes and colours used to come to her. Sometimes she would sigh when she opened them and say: 'Another story come home to roost. O dear, O dear!' and then the children would be very sorry. But sometimes she would wave the envelope in the air and say: 'Hooray, hooray. Here's a sensible Editor.' Whenever an Editor was sensible, there were buns for tea.

What Edith didn't know then was that Hubert – who continued to live with his mother even after their marriage – had been carrying on with his mother's companion Maggie Doran and had got her pregnant around the time he and Edith met. That affair didn't end with their marriage. It was only after the birth of their second child

Mary that she happened to open a letter to Hubert from Maggie and discovered that her husband had been cheating on her and still was. It's a mark of her intense fair-mindedness that she didn't blame Maggie, who herself had no idea Hubert had a wife and two children and fondly imagined herself to be engaged to him. The times being what they were, Edith stayed with him.

Throughout their marriage, Hubert jumped into bed with anybody who would have him and Edith dealt with the humiliation as best she could. There was to be a lot of it – not least that Hubert started having an affair with her best friend Alice Hoatson. In 1886, Edith was wild with grief after she'd given birth to a stillborn child. Alice, who comforted her through it, was at that point pregnant with Hubert's daughter. When she gave birth, to protect her friend's reputation Edith agreed to have the baby girl christened Rosamund Edith Nesbit Bland and bring it up as her own. Six months later, though, it came out that Hubert was the father and Edith tried to throw mother and daughter out on the street, giving way only when Hubert threatened to go with them.

The unusual household settled into an uneasy stasis, Edith from time to time erupting in storms of rage (she was described as having a 'dramatic storm-and-brilliance quality'), which Hubert would expertly appease. One way and another, though, he got his way. Alice and Hubert continued their liaison – a second child, John, arrived in 1899, and again Edith raised it as her own – and though Edith seems to have flirted with other men throughout her life it's unclear whether she ever consummated those relationships.[*] Hubert wouldn't have taken it kindly if she did; despite his own philandering, he 'took a violently condemnatory tone in denouncing anyone who made any attempt at sexual freedom' – a case that, George Bernard Shaw remarked drily, was 'fundamentally a little weak'.

---

[*] George Bernard Shaw, who courted her ardently, complained to her: 'You had no right to write the preface if you weren't going to write the book.'

The family was unconventional and contradictory in other ways. Both Edith and Hubert (despite the latter's frock-coated conventionality and patriarchal, conservative and imperialist instincts) were prime movers in that very aristocratic group of socialists the Fabian Society. The Fabians prided themselves on doing 'our best to destroy the association between revolutionary literature and slovenly printing on paper that is nasty without being cheap'. They moved in the orbits of George Bernard Shaw, Beatrice and Sidney Webb and H.G. Wells. Edith cut her hair short and constantly had a fag on the go – descriptions of her always equip her with a long cigarette holder, Turkish slippers and armfuls of silver bangles (Hubert gave her a new bracelet every time she finished a book).

Did Edith suffer terribly? We cannot know. She depended on Hubert, and despite his sexual misbehaviour they seem to have had a deep bond and to have been intellectually *simpatico*. They wrote together under the pseudonym Fabian Bland (the name with which they later christened their third son), and Edith exorcised her resentment of his philandering in some of the poems and short stories she wrote for adults (in one, cheerful poem she imagines a wife murdering her unfaithful husband). Her maternal affection for Rosamund and John was at least outwardly as great as that towards her natural children. But there were darker undercurrents; when Rosamund was a young woman, H.G. Wells tried to elope with her – he claimed because he thought Hubert was paying her incestuous attention – and Hubert intercepted them at Paddington station and offered to punch the author of *The Time Machine*'s lights out.

Edith, oddly, wrote a scolding letter afterwards to Wells's wife Jane. Her political and personal radicalism didn't extend even to supporting women's suffrage (she refused to sign a petition in support of the 1910 Conciliation Bill, saying, 'I do not wish socialism to be endangered by an extension of the franchise to Conservative women'); Hubert, characteristically, took a less nuanced view: 'Votes for women? Votes for children! Votes for dogs!' Her writing for children tended to reinforce gender stereotypes rather than otherwise: girls 'have their nature, same as bull-dogs have, and it is this that makes them so useful in smoothing the pillows of the sick-bed and tending wounded heroes.' But in Edith's novel *The New Treasure Seekers* the narrator Oswald concedes that his sister makes a decent showing in a street fight:

> though Oswald cannot approve of my sister being in a street fight, he must own she was very quick and useful in pulling ears and twisting arms and slapping and pinching. But she had quite forgotten how to hit out from the shoulder like I have often shown her.

Edith's views on the relationships between the sexes – we can't know how much influenced by the patriarchal husband who had such a hold on her – seem in other words to have been mixed. At one time we find her affronting a radical audience by lecturing them on women's inferiority and the delicate 'flower of femininity'; at another, telling a fan: 'If you aren't a lady, don't try to be one; much better stay a free and happy bounder.'

Edith's Fabian politics also come through in the books with the fuzzy inconsistency of short-wave radio. In *The New Treasure Seekers* she affectionately sends up the poses of wealthy socialists in the excellently named Eustace Sandal: 'I do not know how to express his inside soul, but I have heard Father say he means well. He is a vegetarian and a Primitive Social Something, and an all-wooler, and things like that, and he is really as good as he can stick, only most awfully dull. I believe he eats bread and milk from choice.'*

The most naked entry of her politics into her fiction is the episode in her time-travel caper, *The Story of the Amulet*, when the

---

* This is harsh condemnation from Oswald. Nesbit is not alone among children's writers with a proper sense of children in noting how large food looms in their worlds: much of the trouble that her children get into comes in pursuit of more grub or despair at not getting any.

children travel into the future. They find a world in which littering is severely punished, nobody can walk on the grass or pick flowers, coal fires and horses are banned, nurseries are padded to prevent injury, Duties of Citizenship is a compulsory part of the curriculum, children all love school, property is held in common and even the pigeons are clean. A mother names her son Wells 'after the great reformer'. It's maybe unfortunate that this vision of the future has a slight smack to it of modern-day Singapore.

As I have said, the Fabians were a curious mix of radical and conservative, and Edith's books are shot through with both utopian ideas about social improvement and selflessness to other members of the community, and unquestioned ideas about class. She could chafe at the social structures of her own age in theory, but she found it hard to write herself clean out of them in practice. The vagaries of servants are frequently guyed. When the Bastable children cross the river to Millwall they might as well be on safari, amid the 'grey-brown streets with hardly any shops, and those only very small and common'. The street children they encounter there, like the hard-done-by baker's boy who Robert fights with in *Five Children and It*,* aren't presented as the protagonists' social equals. The less said about the portrayal of 'Chinamen', 'Red Indians', 'gypsies' and Jewish moneylenders in Nesbit – all of whom are stereotyped in a very of-their-time way – the better.

Where children's writing moves between poles of fantasy and realism, Nesbit somehow did both at once. One of her trilogies for children, the Psammead stories – *Five Children and It* (1902), *The Phoenix and the Carpet* (1904) and *The Story of the Amulet* (1906) – takes place in a universe in which you might find a sand-fairy with

---

* This blameless civilian is going about his lawful business when he's knocked off his bicycle and his cargo of loaves scattered on the ground. In the ensuing punch-up he blacks Robert's eye. Robert then wishes himself giant-sized, catches up with the baker's boy and strands him on top of a sixteen-foot haystack. The sympathies of most modern readers will be with the baker's boy.

the power to grant any wish buried in a quarry, where a junk-shop trinket can give you the power to travel to ancient Atlantis, or where you can accidentally get delivered a magic carpet with a phoenix egg wrapped in it from a 'poky little shop' on the Kentish Town Road. The Bastable books – *The Story of the Treasure Seekers* (1899), *The Wouldbegoods* (1901) and *The New Treasure Seekers* (1904) – don't contain so much as a whiff of the supernatural. Yet the broods of children in each series are recognisably kin to each other; they exist on the same level of reality.

Calling these trilogies 'novels', incidentally, is a loose way of putting it: they behave more like a string of independent episodes, which is consonant with the form in which they emerged. They were not always published in serial form in *The Strand* in the same order in which they appeared in book form. But they're given shape by a final chapter or two that resolves the basic situation in which they play out. The poverty of the Bastables is resolved; the holidays come to an end; the Psammead is released from harness; the Phoenix departs to regenerate; the quest for the amulet is over; or Daddy steps off the train.

Nesbit not only modelled in that extraordinary decade of productivity between 1899 and 1910 the type of children's writing that was to become general in the twentieth century, but cultivated the sort of personal relationship with her fans that later writers would perfect. Her friend F.E. Steele wrote in 1903: 'With the single exception of *The Jungle Book*, no children's book of recent years has had success to compare with that of *The Wouldbegoods*.' At the height of her success, she'd bash out three to five thousand words in a day. She received (and unfailingly answered) dozens of fan letters, as many as thirty in an evening. She even experimented – as Enid Blyton would go on to do – with publishing her own magazine, the *Neolith*.

The special genius of Nesbit's books is in their tone of voice. The reader is often (if not always) ahead of the characters and, in the Bastable books, as often as not ahead of the narrator. There's a constant play of ironic humour in them, sentence by sentence.

Her magical creatures have human failings. The Psammead is bad-tempered and resentful; the Phoenix wonderfully vain and suscep-tible to flattery. The adult reader, or the sophisticated child reader, will spot the children's malapropisms and misunderstandings and shake an indulgent head. Nesbit's deadpan is to be cherished, as in this exchange with the Psammead:

> '*Autres temps autres moeurs*,' said the creature.
> 'Is that the Ninevite language?' asked Anthea, who had learned no foreign language at school except French.

The narrative voice of the Bastable stories is a three-book running joke that never gets tired. Near the beginning of *The Story of the Treasure Seekers*, the narrator announces: 'It is one of us that tells this story – but I shall not tell you which: only at the very end per-haps I will. While the story is going on you may be trying to guess, only I bet you don't.' But, of course, you absolutely do guess. Even if the hint in the following sentence doesn't tip the author's hand ('It was Oswald who first thought of looking for treasure. Oswald often thinks of very interesting things.'), the narrator is forever making flattering reference to Oswald's resourcefulness and good character; and, so even child readers will get the joke, occasionally loses concentration and lapses into the first person.

Oswald (as Michael Moorcock later recognised in making a version of him the protagonist of a series of steampunk novels) is one of the immortals. At times his sentences have a flavour of P.G. Wodehouse: 'her voice was the kind that makes you look at each other when the grown-up has gone out, and you are silent, with your bread-and-butter half way to the next bite, or your teacup in mid flight to your lips. It was as we supposed. Albert's uncle did not come back for a long while. We did not keep the bread-and-butter on the wing all that time, of course, and we thought we might as well finish the raspberries and white currants. We kept some for Albert's uncle, of course, and they were the best ones too; but when

he came back he did not notice our thoughtful unselfishness.' Or:
'Denny quailed – though he said he did not – but then he doesn't
know what quailing is, and if Denny did not quail then Oswald
does not know what quailing is either.'

All Nesbit's books toy knowingly with their status as stories.
The books themselves are full of writing and writers – and the
imaginations of their child protagonists are visibly shaped by the
nursery bookshelf. Their minds are full of bandits, highwaymen,
pirates, knights of chivalry or disinherited princes of noble blood.
Fiction feeds into make-believe play, just as make-believe play
feeds into fiction. In *Five Children and It*, the place the children
are staying in the countryside strikes them as 'like an enchanted
city out of the *Arabian Nights*'. Mention is made in *The Story of the
Treasure Seekers* of the then-current theatrical production of *The
Water-Babies*, and in *The New Treasure Seekers* of *Shock-Headed
Peter* at the Garrick Theatre.

Long before Holden Caulfield spoke slightingly of 'all that David
Copperfield kind of crap', Oswald tells his readers:

> There are some things I must tell before I begin to tell about the
> treasure-seeking, because I have read books myself, and I know
> how beastly it is when a story begins, 'Alas!' said Hildegarde with
> a deep sigh, 'we must look our last on this ancestral home' – and
> then some one else says something – and you don't know for pages
> and pages where the home is, or who Hildegarde is, or anything
> about it. Our ancestral home is in the Lewisham Road.

The very premise of *The Treasure Seekers* is shaped by the children's apprehension of literary convention. In that book the adult
situation, only dimly apprehended, is that their widower father
is on the verge of bankruptcy as (like Hubert Bland) his business
partner has swindled him. That is delicately done: 'when he went
up to kiss the girls after they were in bed they said he had been
crying,' Oswald reports, 'though I'm sure that's not true. Because

only cowards and snivellers cry, and my Father is the bravest man in the world.'

The children know that finding treasure is how a noble family restores its fortunes in fiction, and they set about it in rather a literary way – whether digging for buried coins or seeking 'a Generous Benefactor, like in Miss Edgeworth'. 'Of course we have read Mr Sherlock Holmes,' we're told, and in *Five Children and It*, when another ill-conceived wish turns the house into a castle under siege, Robert tries to fill his conversation with the besieging knights with 'quothas' and 'beshrew me's' 'to make his talk sound like the talk of a boy in a historical romance'.

Kipling is everywhere in the stories: boisterous games of let's pretend are modelled on *The Jungle Book*; pranks are 'out of *Stalky*'. That testifies not only to Kipling's huge place in children's literary culture at the turn of the century but also to Nesbit's own devotion to him as a writer. In her middle years, in fact, they struck up an epistolary friendship, and Kipling's praise well expressed the power of her books over children. He described in a letter to her in March 1903 how his own children, then five and seven, 'never knew one magazine from another till it dawned upon Elsie that "a thing called the Strand", "with a blue cover and a cab" was where the Psammead tales lived. Since which as the advertisements say I knew no peace [...] I wish I could tell you what a joy it gave them and how they revelled in the fun of it. A kiddie laughing at a joke is one of the sweetest sights under Heaven and our nursery used to double up and rock with mirth. They were very indignant when the series came to an end.'[*] Their relationship only cooled when, in 1906, she became convinced that Kipling had plagiarised *The Story of the Amulet* in *Puck of Pook's Hill*.

So Nesbit both draws on the children's writing that came before her and gently, wonderfully, guys it. In *Five Children and It*, when

---

[*]   Eleanor Fitzsimons, *The Life and Loves of E. Nesbit*.

Robert returns from the Psammead to find the house under siege, here's how the leader of the besieging force is described:

> His armour and his weapons were all, I am almost sure, of quite different periods. The shield was thirteenth century, while the sword was of the pattern used in the Peninsular War. The cuirass was of the time of Charles I, and the helmet dated from the Second Crusade. The arms on the shield were very grand – three red running lions on a blue ground. The tents were of the latest brand approved of by our modern War Office, and the whole appearance of camp, army, and leader might have been a shock to some. But Robert was dumb with admiration, and it all seemed to him perfectly correct, because he knew no more of heraldry or archæology than the gifted artists who usually drew the pictures for the historical romances.

The juxtaposition between the children's romantic fantasies and the prosaic facts of the world about them – the 'ancestral home' is, after all, in the Lewisham Road – gives the stories their wit and poignancy. But the children aren't ever, quite, forced to leave their fantasy: the adults around them respond to it with indulgent kindness (Albert-Next-Door's uncle scatters coins for them to find as they excavate), and in the closing pages they really do find a Generous Benefactor in the Indian Uncle who whisks them all away to his mansion to live with him in luxury and plenty. The hair-raising destruction they wreak is always, somehow, undone or made good or forgiven. The sense here is that the children inhabit a slightly different moral order from their elders. Childhood is a sort of playpen – governed by child-to-child moral rules (don't sneak, keep your word, fight if you must but make up with 'Pax') that mirror but don't map onto the adult world. Adults who can connect with children on their level – such as Edith's proxy Mrs Bax in *The New Treasure Seekers* – shine; lofty Victorian disciplinarians such as Aunt Emma in *The Railway Children*, who 'believed in keeping children in their proper places', do not.

The children in Nesbit's books aren't just unformed: they are naughty. They set booby-traps. They defy injunctions. They get into scrapes. They threaten to cause, and often, in fact, cause, terrible harm. Kitchens are incinerated by experiments with fireworks; houses are flooded and barges full of coal upended; priceless antiques are given away to strangers. The second of the Bastable trilogy, *The Wouldbegoods*, describes a series of events in which, after forming the titular society for moral improvement, the children's best intentions go hilariously awry. *Five Children and It* tells the reader: be careful what you wish for.* Whether the children wish for beauty, money or adventure, one way or another the Psammead's magic comes round to bite them. 'The Sammyad's done us again,' says Cyril glumly at one point – an unimprovably concise precis of the book's theme. They try to be good, and fail, or try to make a wish that will do them good – but fail at that too.

Childhood happiness for Nesbit was linked with the countryside and being in nature. Her own happiest childhood years had been spent in Halstead Hall in Kent, where her mother Sarah retreated after Mary's death in 1871, and where she was to recall 'those dewy mornings – the resurrection of light and life in the woods and fields! Would that it were possible for all children to live in the country where they may drink in, consciously or unconsciously, the dear delights of green meadow and dappled woodland!'†

That expressly connects to freedom of action. In *Five Children and It*, she was to write that London (and by extension any city) is 'like prison for children'. The countryside was a place, in Nesbit's worldview, where children could – and should – run wild, and the arrival of the children in The White House is marked by rough and tumble:

---

* In Nesbit's words: 'And that, my dear children, is the moral of this chapter. I did not mean it to have a moral, but morals are nasty forward beings, and will keep putting in their oars where they are not wanted.'

† E. Nesbit, *Op. cit.*

When Robert had found the broken swing and tumbled out of it and got a bump on his head the size of an egg, and Cyril had nipped his finger in the door of a hutch that seemed made to keep rabbits in, if you ever had any, they had no longer any doubts whatever. The best part of it all was that there were no rules about not going to places and not doing things. In London almost everything is labelled 'You mustn't touch,' and though the label is invisible it's just as bad, because you know it's there, or if you don't you very soon get told.

In her 1913 book *Wings and the Child: Or, The Building of Magic Cities*, Nesbit lamented:

> The hideous disfigurement of lovely hills and dales with factories and mines and pot banks – coal, cinder, and slag; the defilement of bright rivers with the refuse of oil and dye works; the eating up of the green country by greedy, long, creeping yellow caterpillars of streets; the smoke and fog that veil the sun in heaven; the sordid enamelled iron advertisements that scar the fields of earth – all the torn paper and straw and dirt and disorder spring from one root. And from the same root spring pride, anger, cruelty and sycophancy, the mean subservience of the poor and the mean arrogance of the rich.

Here's the old Rousseauian anxiety about a prelapsarian identity with nature, linked with Nesbit's Fabian mistrust of commerce and industrialisation.

In her best-known work, *The Railway Children*, Nesbit's characteristic gleam of dramatic irony is put not so much to comic as to heartbreaking effect – because in this case the adult in the story knows more than the children, and the nearly grown-up daughter knows nearly as much as her mother does. The emotional heart of that story – a family broken and a mother desperate because the father has been framed and jailed on espionage charges (the book was being written in the aftermath of the Dreyfus affair) is just hidden from most of its child protagonists. The eldest daughter Bobbie first intuits and later (when she comes across a newspaper story) understands her mother's deep unhappiness – and, to protect her, pretends not to. The main action of the story takes place after, with father gone, the mother (a writer, like Nesbit), retreats with the children to a small cottage in the countryside.

Absent parents are a staple of Nesbit's work, as they are of so much children's writing before and since, and the longing for them suffuses this book, but it does so in complicated ways. The younger children – and this is surely true to child psychology – soon rebound from Father's absence. Like a finger pressed into rising dough, writes Nesbit, the sorrow at their new situation 'made a deep impression, but the impression did not last long. They soon got used to being without father…' The Bastable children's dead mother, too, is an emotional bruise that occasionally, but only occasionally, throbs.

Yet there's a plangent sense in *The Railway Children* that the pain of a lost parent is always there beneath the surface. It never, never goes away. In that book you can see the child-self shrouded in the anguished adult – in Mother as in Edith Nesbit – and a daughter learning, at some level, to parent her own mother.

'Are you fonder of us than Granny was of you when you were little?' Phyllis asked. Bobbie made signs to her to stop, but Phyllis never did see signs, no matter how plain they might be.

Mother did not answer for a minute. She got up to put more water in the teapot.

'No one,' she said at last, 'ever loved anyone more than my mother loved me.'

Then she was quiet again, and Bobbie kicked Phyllis hard under the table, because Bobbie understood a little bit the thoughts that were making Mother so quiet – the thoughts of the time when Mother was a little girl and was all the world to HER mother.

When she's ill with a fever,

> Mother talked to herself a good deal, but it did not seem to mean
> anything. And once she woke up suddenly and called out: 'Mamma,
> mamma!' and Bobbie knew she was calling for Granny, and that she
> had forgotten that it was no use calling, because Granny was dead.

After Mother has put on her best face for Bobbie's birthday, and
retreated to her room to continue writing, Bobbie looks in on her
on her way to bed.

> Mother was not writing, but leaning her head on her arms and
> her arms on the table. I think it was rather good of Bobbie to slip
> quietly away, saying over and over, 'She doesn't want me to know
> she's unhappy, and I won't know; I won't know.'

The book's climax sees Bobbie meet her father from the train – his
name, in another Nesbittian *deus ex machina*, cleared by the Old
Gentleman the children have happened to befriend as he passes
each day on the train.

> 'Oh! my Daddy, my Daddy!' That scream went like a knife into
> the heart of everyone in the train, and people put their heads out
> of the windows to see a tall pale man with lips set in a thin close
> line, and a little girl clinging to him with arms and legs, while his
> arms went tightly round her.

You could speculate, I think, that in this extraordinary book Edith
is both Mother and Bobbie; while she is also the narrator who so
tenderly watches Bobbie lead Father back to the cottage:

> now I see them crossing the field [...] Bobbie goes into the house,
> trying to keep her eyes from speaking before her lips have found
> the right words to 'tell Mother quite quietly' that the sorrow and

the struggle and the parting are over and done, and that Father has
come home. I see Father walking in the garden, waiting – waiting.
He is looking at the flowers, and each flower is a miracle…

What gave access to such a well of feeling in that book? The tragedy that so often seems to befall the real-life children of writers
for children fell heavily on the Bland household. In 1900, Edith
and Hubert's fifteen-year-old son Fabian – the model for Robert
in the Psammead stories – had been anaesthetised for a routine
operation and never woke up. Rosamund, two years younger, was
later to claim that she first learned that Edith was not her mother
after hearing her cry out: 'Why couldn't it have been Rosamund?'

In her 1907 story 'The Criminal', Edith wrote from the viewpoint of a bereaved mother.

My son; my little son, the house is very quiet, because all the other
children grew up long ago, and went out into the world. The lamp
has just been lighted, but the blinds are not drawn down now.
Outside the winter dusk is deepening the shadows in the garden
where, in the days when the sun shone, you used to shout and play.

The year before, In *The Railway Children*, Edith had made the
plainest possible statement of the recuperative hope of her fiction:

Peter's Mother put her arm round him suddenly, and hugged him
in silence for a minute. Then she said:–

'Don't you think it's rather nice to think that we're in a book
that God's writing? If I were writing the book, I might make
mistakes. But God knows how to make the story end just right –
in the way that's best for us.'

'Do you really believe that, Mother?' Peter asked quietly.

'Yes,' she said, 'I do believe it – almost always – except when
I'm so sad that I can't believe anything. But even when I can't
believe it, I know it's true – and I try to believe.'

'His Greatest Pretend'

J.M. BARRIE

The Little White Bird; Peter Pan in
Kensington Gardens; Peter and Wendy

T RYING TO BELIEVE WAS A PREOCCUPATION, TOO, OF A
writer whose key work passed so quickly into the territory of
myth that it's hard to see it as a single, stable text at all. Belief,
as everyone who has ever tried to keep Tinker Bell alive – 'clap your
hands if you believe in fairies!' – is the engine on which the strange
world of *Peter Pan* runs. That world was the creation of a sensitive,
singular Scottish writer called James Matthew Barrie (1860–1937).

The wickedly complicated publication history of the *Peter Pan*
stories – first as a series of chapters in a book for adults, then as a
stage play, then in various revisions as a book for children – shows
not only how much children's stories jumped between the page and
the stage at this point in history (we've already seen London productions of children's classics from the previous century appearing
in the background of E. Nesbit's novels, and *A Little Princess* started
life as a play just as *Little Lord Fauntleroy* turned into one). It also
shows how unstable the distinction between children's literature
and adult writing remained in the period.

Because Peter Pan entered the realm of the mythic from the
start – by which I mean it became available to retellings and rein-
terpretation even in the lifetime of its author – the original vanished quickly from sight. Humphrey Carpenter remarks: 'We are
dealing here with not just a piece of imaginative creation by one

man, but with a public phenomenon.'* On Barrie's death in 1937 this property of the story was already being remarked. The *Times Literary Supplement* said:

> [Barrie] was able not merely to instruct or entertain but to impregnate the collective mind of his audience. And if he did, indeed, possess this power, which is precisely the power of the great fairytales, criticism may as well throw its pen away, for then he is immortal by election.

Now, as with so many such children's properties, the Disney film version (Peter as fey as the principal boy in a pantomime; Tink pretty and pert) has overwritten in the collective consciousness a text that's much, much edgier than that. Barrie once said he hated sentimentality 'like a slave hates its master' – which, of course, implies a relationship to sentimentality but a very far from straightforward one. When the statue of Peter was erected in Kensington Gardens, Barrie didn't like it, he is said to have said, because 'It doesn't show the Devil in Peter'.†

What's so startling about the original Neverland‡ is how very violent it is. It's not so much a secret garden or an enchanted island as a perpetual Battle Royale:

> The lost boys were out looking for Peter, the pirates were out looking for the lost boys, the redskins were out looking for the

---

* Carpenter, op. cit.

† Leonee Ormond, *Scottish Writers: J.M. Barrie* (Mercat Press, 1987).

‡ Even the name is unstable. As a footnote to an Oxford University Press edition of the stories reports, the name may have originally been a reference to a district in Australia called 'Never, Never, Land'. The first draft of the play called Peter's island 'the Never, Never, Never Land', which became 'the Never, Never Land' in performance, 'the Never Land' in the published text of the play, and 'the Neverland' in *Peter and Wendy*. In *The Little White Bird*, by the way, there is no Neverland: Peter's island is in the middle of the Round Pond in Kensington Gardens.

pirates, and the beasts were out looking for the redskins. They were going round and round the island, but they did not meet because all were going at the same rate.

All wanted blood except the boys, who liked it as a rule, but tonight were out to greet their captain. The boys on the island vary, of course, in numbers, according as they get killed and so on; and when they seem to be growing up, which is against the rules, Peter thins them out; but at this time there were six of them, counting the Twins as two. Let us pretend to lie here among the sugar-cane and watch them as they steal by in single file, each with his hand on his dagger.

Pirates, redskins, lost boys and beasts stalk each other around the island in permanent readiness for ambush and battle – which, as in adventure stories and childhood games, exist in a blurred interstice between violence and play. To die, as Peter famously declares – in excited anticipation? in bravado? in ignorance? – will be 'an awfully big adventure'.

The story reconfirms, even as it mashes them up with cheerful absurdity, the place of pirates, bandits and 'Red Indians' in the childhood imaginary. And it shows how the make-believe that is as abundant here as in Nesbit and Burnett is shaped by children's writing itself. Captain Hook, it's said more than once, is 'the only man of whom Barbecue [Long John Silver's nickname in *Treasure Island*] was afraid'.

The theme of the story is not childhood innocence, but childhood carelessness – and it's underscored by the imaginary violence implied in many children's games. When the pirates fire their gun Long Tom, 'thus did the terrified three learn the difference between an island of make-believe and the same island come true'.

When the Darling children and Peter make what, in modern aviation, would be called their final approach to Neverland, there's a moment when they pause, just above the trees:

'There's a pirate asleep in the pampas just beneath us,' Peter told him. 'If you like, we'll go down and kill him.'

'I don't see him,' John said after a long pause.

'I do.'

'Suppose,' John said a little huskily, 'he were to wake up—'

Peter spoke indignantly. 'You don't think I would kill him while he was sleeping! I would wake him first, and then kill him. That's the way I always do.'

'I say! Do you kill many?'

'Tons.'

When we first meet him, in a disconcertingly self-referential moment, the narrator becomes complicit in a casual murder. The joke is that it's make-believe, because this is a book. But make-believe and pretending are unstable in Peter Pan's world:

Let us now kill a pirate, to show Hook's method. Skylights will do. As they pass, Skylights lurches clumsily against him, ruffling his lace collar; the hook shoots forth, there is a tearing sound and one screech, then the body is kicked aside, and the pirates pass on. He has not even taken the cigars* from his mouth.

It's not just goodies and baddies. No sooner do the Darlings arrive on the island than Tinker Bell, in a jealous rage, tries to trick the Lost Boys into killing Wendy – '"Peter wants you to shoot the Wendy [...] Quick, Tootles, quick." she screamed. "Peter will be so pleased."' – and it's only by pure luck that Wendy survives the attack. You could see Tink's murderous anger as adult ('she hated her with the fierce hatred of a very woman') or as an aspect of childishness that few would like to acknowledge – but its lack

---

* Captain Hook 'had a holder of his own contrivance which enabled him to smoke two cigars at once'.

of consequences belongs to the world of pretend. And look at the complex of emotions that strikes Tootles, whose bow launched the near-fatal arrow:

> Tootles' face was very white, but there was a dignity about him now that had never been there before.
>
> 'I did it,' he said, reflecting. 'When ladies used to come to me in dreams, I said, "Pretty mother, pretty mother." But when at last she really came, I shot her.'

'Begone from me for ever,' Peter tells Tink. By the end of the following paragraph he has commuted her sentence: 'Well, not for ever, but for a whole week.'

Peter Pan darts back and forth between make-believe and earnest. To adapt Marianne Moore's phrase about poetry – 'an imaginary garden with real toads' – you could call Neverland an imaginary island with real crocodiles. Childhood is, after all, a time when (like Frances Hodgson Burnett horrified at that 'Keep Off the Grass' sign) what later seem trivial things can be deadly serious, and what will later seem deadly serious – death, above all – is barely available to the imagination.

To leave childhood is to forget – just as in Barrie's stories babies, when they grow up, cease to speak the language of birds and forget how to fly. To reconnect with childhood, it has been suggested since Wordsworth on, is to access a deep primal knowledge. When the children first glimpse Neverland from the air, 'Strange to say, they all recognized it at once, and until fear fell upon them they hailed it, not as something long dreamt of and seen at last, but as a familiar friend to whom they were returning home for the holidays.'

Barrie said of childhood that 'children who were certainties in the old times have now become riddles'. That riddling gives the book its unsettling quality. The adults in the supposed real world are comically childlike. Mr Darling, for instance, faces off with

Michael when the latter refuses to take his medicine, boasting that as a child he used to take medicine without a squeak of complaint. He even boasts that he'd take his own 'much nastier' medicine right now as an example to his son, had he not lost the bottle. (Could Peter Pan have given us the expression 'lost his bottle?')* When Wendy, unhelpfully, produces the bottle he still tries to make excuses – 'it isn't fair!' – and squabbles with his son in playground style: 'Father's a cowardy custard.' 'So are you a cowardy custard.' 'I'm not frightened.' 'Neither am I frightened.'

Conversely, when Wendy is in Neverland, her make-believe is not about being perpetually childlike, but about being grown up. She is to be the Lost Boys' mother (Peter stands in as their father, though he disowns the role), and plays at domesticity. She tells them off for having damp feet, reads them fairy stories, soothes Peter when he has bad dreams and, just like a harassed Edwardian mother: 'Wendy's favourite time for sewing and darning was after they had all gone to bed. Then, as she expressed it, she had a breathing time for herself.' Psychoanalytic critics like to draw attention to the tiny house that the Lost Boys build around her to save her life: is it a pretty prison, or a protective shell? That, incidentally, is where we get the phrase 'Wendy House': replicas of the house from the stage play soon became popular with toy manufacturers, and have been a staple of middle-class gardens ever since.

The worm in the bud of *Peter Pan* – visible to its adult readers, but not to its child audience and certainly not to Peter himself – is sex. Peter simply cannot parse the feelings of Wendy, Tink and Tiger Lily for him, nor how it leads them to enmity: romantic love is dark matter in his cosmology. 'What are your exact feelings for me?' Wendy asks him. He responds: 'Those of a devoted

---

* Green's *Dictionary of Slang* follows the association of the phrase with Cockney rhyming slang ('bottle and glass' = 'arse') but its citations are all twentieth-century.

son, Wendy.' She sulks, and he is 'frankly puzzled', musing that
'Tiger Lily is just the same. There is something she wants to be
to me, but she says it is not my mother.' When Tink (having been
eavesdropping from her boudoir) is drawn into the exchange, Peter
muses that perhaps she wants to be his mother: 'You silly ass!'
she cries 'in a passion'. That blind spot is literalised in the bit of
business – a survival from Peter's exchange with Wendy's original, Maimie in *The Little White Bird* – with kisses and thimbles.
When Maimie offers to give Peter a kiss, he holds out his hand.
Embarrassed, she puts a thimble into it. Thereafter, the error is
never corrected: Peter believes a kiss is a thimble and a thimble
is a kiss.

So *Peter Pan* is as plural and as confounding a text, or set of
texts, as *Alice*. Its narrative voice is now knowing, now arch, now
plangent – a jagged compound of adult-in-child and child-in-adult,
just like its principal protagonists. In the stage production, the
actor who played Captain Hook would double as Mr Darling,
and Peter himself doubles his arch-nemesis when he imperson-
ates his voice from hiding, causing Hook to lose confidence in
his own identity: 'Against such fearful evidence it was not [the
crew's] belief in him that he needed, it was his own. He felt his
ego slipping from him. "Don't desert me, bully," he whispered
hoarsely to it.'

These doublings and echoes – Mr Darling and Hook and Peter,
Wendy and Tink and Tiger Lily, adults and children – are symp-
tomatic of doublings and echoes in Barrie's own life. The defining
episode of that life was the death in 1867, in an ice-skating accident,
of his older brother David. James Barrie was six; David was a day
off turning fourteen. Barrie's mother Margaret was broken by the
loss of her favourite child.

At first, they say, I was often jealous, stopping her fond memories
with the cry, 'Do you mind nothing about me?' but that did not
last; its place was taken by an intense desire... to become so like

him that even my mother should not see the difference ... Then I practised in secret.*

The younger boy tried to make it better not by competing with the boy who wouldn't grow up, but by becoming him: he imitated his brother's gait and whistle, wore his clothes. As he recalled, he once came into her room and she asked: 'Is that you?' 'I thought it was the dead boy she was speaking to,' he recalled. 'I said in a little lonely voice, "No, it's no' him, it's just me."'

But the story of *Peter Pan* is more complexly rooted even than that. Wendy the child-mother echoes Barrie's mother Margaret when she herself was a child. Their confiding relationship had made her own childhood – the death of her mother when she was eight had made her 'mistress of the house and mother to her little brother' – as vivid to the young Barrie as his own. He was to explain:

> The reason my books deal with the past instead of with the life
> I myself have known is simply this, that I soon grow tired of
> writing tales unless I can see a little girl, of whom my mother
> has told me, wandering confidently through the pages. Such
> a grip has her memory of her girlhood had upon me since I
> was a boy of six.

Barrie himself remained childless and childlike: he barely scraped 5'1" and didn't start shaving till his late teens. This tangle of emotions played, too, into his relationship with child-friends of his own. He met George and Jack Llewelyn Davies in 1897 while walking his dog in Kensington Gardens. They were then three and four, and their brother, born that same year, was called Peter. Barrie formed a friendship with their parents and became a childlike uncle to

---

* J.M. Barrie, *Margaret Ogilvy: Life is a Long Lesson in Humility* (Hodder & Stoughton, 1896).

the boys. The stories that were to form the basis of the Peter Pan mythos came out of stories he told those boys about their younger brother – among them the fantasy that all children had been birds before they were born and were able to fly as newborns because they forgot that they didn't have wings. As the children grew older, Barrie's stories started to expand into the tales of pirates and Red Indians that would provide the furniture of Neverland. *The Little White Bird* describes the paternal feelings of its bachelor narrator for 'David', a stand-in for George Llewelyn Davies. Here, just as in Neverland, is a fantasy of the child-parent.

Peter Pan's name has become journalistic shorthand for the desirability of eternal childhood – but Barrie's work is deeply ambivalent on the subject. He is, in Barrie's resonant but mysterious phrase, the 'tragic boy'. In the chapters in *The Little White Bird* that were to become the basis for the later stories, Peter's perpetual childhood is a form of exile. The emotional core of that story is Peter's return home to find the nursery window barred to him and his mother with another child sleeping in her arms.

> He went in a hurry in the end, because he had dreamt that his mother was crying, and he knew what was the great thing she cried for, and that a hug from her splendid Peter would quickly make her to smile. Oh! he felt sure of it, and so eager was he to be nestling in her arms that this time he flew straight to the window, which was always to be open for him.
>
> But the window was closed, and there were iron bars on it, and peering inside he saw his mother sleeping peacefully with her arm round another little boy.
>
> Peter called, 'Mother! mother!' but she heard him not; in vain he beat his little limbs against the iron bars. He had to fly back, sobbing, to the Gardens, and he never saw his dear again. What a glorious boy he had meant to be to her! Ah, Peter! we who have made the great mistake, how differently we should all act at the second chance. But Solomon was right – there is no second chance,

not for most of us. When we reach the window it is Lock-out
Time. The iron bars are up for life.

Peter isn't an eternal child because he chose to be: he's an eternal
child because he has made a mistake that he cannot ever recover
from. The same desolation attends the proposed departure of
Wendy from Neverland in *Peter Pan and Wendy*. Peter affects not
to mind her going, and to have very starchy feelings about mothers
in general, but of course he does.

> Not so much as a sorry-to-lose-you between them! If she did
> not mind the parting, he was going to show her, was Peter, that
> neither did he.
>
> But of course he cared very much; and he was so full of wrath
> against grown-ups, who, as usual, were spoiling everything, that as
> soon as he got inside his tree he breathed intentionally quick short
> breaths at the rate of about five to a second. He did this because
> there is a saying in the Neverland that every time you breathe, a
> grown-up dies; and Peter was killing them off vindictively as fast
> as possible.

There, in candidly murderous form, is the less well-remembered
flip side of clapping your hands if you believe in fairies. Worse,
Wendy then offers to take the Lost Boys back so that her parents
will adopt them too. As Barrie's narrator remarks bitterly of their
excited acceptance of the offer, 'They took it for granted that if
they went he [Peter] would go also, but really they scarcely cared.
Thus children are ever ready, when novelty knocks, to desert their
dearest ones.' Peter's response is, again, feigned indifference: 'To
show that her departure would leave him unmoved, he skipped up
and down the room, playing gaily on his heartless pipes.'

That phrase, that collocation of gay and heartless, is an important one. It appears, reconfigured, as the final sentence of the whole
book, when we learn that Wendy's female descendants will take it

in turns to be Peter's mother, and each in turn will grow old and forget him. Is it worse to be a human?

> When Margaret [Wendy's granddaughter] grows up she will have a daughter, who is to be Peter's mother in turn; and thus it will go on, so long as children are gay and innocent and heartless.

Children *are* heartless, and they do need to be loved. Becoming a 'common grown-up' means Wendy can never again fly, can never again return to Neverland. And meanwhile Peter's eternal youth doesn't save him from the pain of abandonment: it condemns him to have it re-enacted again and again for ever. Perhaps it's only by being gay and heartless that he can bear it.

> 'He does so need a mother,' Jane said. 'Yes, I know,' Wendy admitted rather forlornly; 'no one knows it so well as I.'

At the root of this complex of feeling was Barrie's own childhood. The *Peter Pan* stories are full of mothers broken with grief at their lost children, and the narrative voice oscillates between sympathy and contempt, just as Peter's attitude toward mothers in general oscillates between longing and dismissal.

In *The Little White Bird*, on Peter's first visit home he perches on the end of his mother's bed and watches her sleep: 'He was very glad she was such a pretty mother. But she looked sad, and he knew why she looked sad. One of her arms moved as if it wanted to go round something, and he knew what it wanted to go round.'

A version of that scene is reprised in *Peter Pan and Wendy*. The family, with its children gone, is broken. Mr Darling is in the dog-house (literally – that's where the idiom seems to originate: 'In the bitterness of his remorse he swore that he would never leave the kennel until his children came back'); Mrs Darling, 'the gaiety of her in the old days [...] all gone now just because she has lost her babes' (doesn't that single word 'just' complicate the emotional tenor of the passage?), waits in the night-nursery:

> If she was too fond of her rubbishy children she couldn't help it. Look at her in her chair, where she has fallen asleep. The corner of her mouth, where one looks first, is almost withered up. Her hand moves restlessly on her breast as if she had a pain there. Some like Peter best and some like Wendy best, but I like her best. Suppose, to make her happy, we whisper to her in her sleep that the brats are coming back. They are really within two miles of the window now, and flying strong, but all we need whisper is that they are on the way. Let's.
>
> It is a pity we did it, for she has started up, calling their names; and there is no one in the room but Nana.

The ambiguity in the story likely reflects Barrie's own knot of feelings – his love and sympathy for his mother, his buried anger at her grief; his envy of his brother, his longing to become him; his image of childhood as safety and his longing to escape it. Did he himself fully understand the story even as he wrote it? 'It is as if long after writing "P. Pan" its true meaning came to me,' he wrote in a notebook years later: 'Desperate attempt to grow up but can't.' A 1928 edition of the play included a stage direction following Peter's exclamation that 'I don't want to go to school and learn solemn things [...] I want always to be a little boy and have fun.' In brackets, underneath, is written: '(So perhaps he thinks, but it is only his greatest pretend.)'

'Poop! Poop!'

KENNETH GRAHAME

The Golden Age; Dream Days;
The Wind in the Willows

IN *THE WIND IN THE WILLOWS*, KENNETH GRAHAME
created another great pretend: one of the most hermetic worlds
of innocence in the whole history of children's literature. Its
idyllic quality is in proportion to the personal unhappiness from
which it arose. Grahame wasn't by any means the only writer for
whom the children's fantasy worlds they created offered an imaginative escape from adult life – but he was one in whom the need
is most starkly obvious. *The Wind in the Willows* is as notable for
what's not in it as for what is: there are no women; it is, as Grahame
put it to his admirer Theodore Roosevelt, 'clean of the clash of sex'.
It is a world of unbreakable male friendships, amiable idleness and
a pantheistic union with the natural world.

Grahame's infancy was spent in Scotland. An early memory
that stuck was of walking by the side of a loch with his father, the
man telling stories to the boy. Versions of the memory filter into
his work. In *The Wind in the Willows*, Mole goes along with Rat
'as one trots, when very small, by the side of a man who holds one
spellbound by exciting stories'; the frame story of 'The Reluctant
Dragon' exults in 'a walk with a real Man – why, that was a treat in
itself! […] 'Now then,' she said. 'tell us a story, please, won't you?'

Grahame was just five when his mother died of scarlet fever
(last words: 'It's all been so lovely') and his father, whose alcoholism

had just about been under control until then, collapsed altogether. The extended family moved decisively: the young Kenneth and his two siblings were packed off to the other end of the country to be raised by their chilly and formal maternal grandmother. At one point, the children were returned to their father in Edinburgh – a further wrench – but the experiment failed and Grahame senior left Kenneth's life permanently. ('Grown-up people really ought to be more careful,' he has the narrator say in his story 'The Magic Ring'.* 'Among themselves it may seem but a small thing to give their word and take back their word.')

Before he came to write for children, Grahame wrote extensively about childhood. By the time he published *The Wind in the Willows* in 1908, he was well known and widely admired as the author of two collections of vignettes of childhood published as *The Golden Age* (1895) and *Dream Days* (1898); fictions about a family of children who live in a large house, apparently without parents, and ministered to by a succession of remote aunts and uncles.

Adults are 'Olympians', their ways incomprehensible and remote: 'It was necessary, no doubt, that grown-up people should dress themselves up and go forth to pay calls. I don't mean that we saw any sense in the practice. It would have been so much more reasonable to stay at home in your old clothes and play.' Grahame elsewhere describes a rising consciousness 'like Caliban on Setebos' of the carelessness and 'stupidity' of adults: the 'vague sense of a ruling power, wilful and freakish', who 'having absolute licence to indulge in the pleasures of life [...] could get no good of it'. He writes, though: 'I can see now that to children with a proper equipment of parents these things would have worn a different aspect.' This is personal to him.

Dream Days ends with an account of the children sneaking out at night to bury their dolls and toys (they've outgrown them,

---

* Included in his 1898 collection *Dream Days*.

but can't bear for them to be given to the charity shop and they rescue the ones they can – including the beloved Rosa – from the box):

> Jerry and Esmeralda might shed their limbs and their stuffing, by slow or swift degrees, in uttermost parts and unguessed corners of the globe; but Rosa's book was finally closed, and no worse fate awaited her than natural dissolution almost within touch and hail of familiar faces and objects that had been friendly to her since first she opened her eyes on a world where she had never been treated as a stranger.

Grahame grew up into a formal, conservative, somewhat solitary man – broad in the beam, moustachioed and conventional. He rose high in the Bank of England, his writing career being a side-line, but was happiest as an adult rambling in nature; and he was happiest throughout his life in make-believe, what he came to call 'Cloudland', 'Elfland' or 'Poppyland'. Anywhere but here. 'Bitter it is,' his narrator exclaims in the short story 'Its Walls Were as of Jasper', when he's dragged from his imaginative immersion in a beautiful picture book, 'to stumble out of an opalescent dream into the cold daylight'.

As Grahame was to write sadly: 'The Olympians are all past and gone. Somehow the sun does not seem to shine so brightly as it used; the trackless meadows of old time have shrunk and dwindled away to a few poor acres. A saddening doubt, a dull suspicion, creeps over me. Et in Arcadia ego, – I certainly did once inhabit Arcady. Can it be I too have become an Olympian?'*

He had indeed, and nor could he get any good out of the 'pleasures of life'. 'The Magic Ring' describes a childhood visit to the circus in which two performers intoxicate the narrator with a previously

---

*   Kenneth Grahame, *The Golden Age* (Bodley Head, 1895).

unthinkable attraction to the female sex. Fair-complexioned Coralie stirs giddy romantic fantasies, but then comes dark-haired Zephyrine, who is sex itself: 'What was Coralie, with her pink silk, her golden hair and slender limbs, beside this magnificent, full-figured Cleopatra?' But such interest as Grahame had in sex and romance didn't survive its removal from the opalescent dream. (There's a school of thought that Grahame was a repressed homosexual.)

His marriage in late middle age to 37-year-old Elspeth Thomson in 1899 – made rather reluctantly in the wake of a hot-and-cold courtship conducted in letters full of horribly cutesy baby-talk – was a disaster from the off. She complained bitterly to friends about her romantic and sexual disappointment and wrote poems in which she reproached him for his lack of affection or fantasised about having him manhandle her like a doll. Elspeth, who hailed from a rather grand family and, as a child and young woman, had entertained Tennyson, Mark Twain and senior political figures, became withdrawn and increasingly eccentric. He retreated emotionally and physically from her, his study (filled, visitors noted, with children's toys) being his place of refuge.

We know that, however disastrously, Grahame and his wife did have sex at least once: they had a child. Born premature, sickly and blind in one eye, Alastair Grahame became the repository of his parents' thwarted hopes for themselves. They doted on him, insisting he was perfect, brilliant, destined for stardom – and yet abandoning him to a succession of nannies or governesses for long intervals. He turned, not that either of his parents would acknowledge it, into a conceited, spiteful and spoilt little brat. Here, in embryo, was Mr Toad. *The Wind in the Willows* had its origins in stories Kenneth told Mouse (the couple's nickname for Alastair), first orally and then in a succession of letters he sent the boy when they were separated. It was only when a visiting editor overheard Grahame reading them as bedtime stories – she had come to see Grahame in the hopes of soliciting more stories in the *Dream Days* mould for an American periodical, *Everybody's Magazine* – that she suggested he make them into a book.

Publishers, who were looking to him for stories of childhood rather than stories for children, and looking for stories about people rather than boat-bothering moles, took some convincing. Eventually Methuen reluctantly agreed to take a risk on it, publishing it first as *The Wind in the Reeds*. It looked initially like they were ill advised to do so. On first publication, Grahame's book was sniffily received. The *Times Literary Supplement*, in one of the great point-missing reviews of all time, complained that 'as a contribution to natural history, the work is negligible'. They were not, to be fair, wrong. In the course of the story we encounter juvenile hedgehogs breakfasting greedily on porridge and fried ham and Toad is, at one point, described parting his hair. As in Grahame's sort-of-predecessor Beatrix Potter, the world-building is a little vague. It's not always easy to get a steady sense even of what size these animals are.

The important ones seem to be human-sized, most of the time: Toad exchanges his clothes with a human washerwoman, for instance, and his caravan – which contains a caged bird – is drawn by a horse. But Mole's pantry contains sardines and Badger's contains hams and eggs – implying that a man-sized mole shares a universe with ordinary sized pigs and hens and fishes and songbirds. But, as the *TLS* noticed, this isn't a work of natural history – though it rhapsodically celebrates the natural world. Its animals are animal-like (migrating, becoming dozy in winter) in some respects, and not in others. Grahame sought 'by simply using the animal, to get away at once from weary sex problems & other problems, & just do jolly things without being suspected of preaching or teaching'.

It's a world of its own – one that must be taken all in all. A.A. Milne, who dramatised it in 1929 as *Toad of Toad Hall*, and the atmosphere of whose Hundred Acre Wood surely owes a debt to Grahame's riverbank, said that 'One can argue over the merits of most books [...] One does not argue about *The Wind in the Willows*. [...] The book is a test of character.'*

The main arc of the plot describes the adventures of the book's most morally compromised and, inevitably, most compelling character: Toad. Toad is a little warty Falstaff: conceited, wilful, faddish, larcenous and vainglorious. Where Mole, Rat and Badger inhabit a modest, bucolic world whose rhythms are those of the natural order, Toad – vulgar, boastful Toad – is fatally infatuated with modernity. As his friends wearily recognise, Toad is prone to being overcome by fads and manias, and the one that really does him down is the one for motoring. 'Poop poop!'

I wonder a little if Grahame's father's alcoholism, just by osmosis, seeps somehow into the book. Toad's behaviour looks from at least one angle very much like an account of the psychology of addiction. Give him a sniff of petrol, and Toad is overcome by craving. He lies, cheats and steals for his habit, and his behaviour nearly costs him his freedom, his home and his life. He swings between grandiosity and self-loathing. He hits bottom, swears off; and then relapses. Early on in the book, Badger and his friends even stage what would now be called an intervention, forcibly locking Toad in his bedroom in an effort to prevent him taking to the road again.

When we first meet him, Toad's romance with the open road takes the form of an enthusiasm for caravanning. That, it turns out, is a gateway drug. His pretty horse-drawn caravan having been run off the road by a motor car and almost destroyed, Toad feels not rage but the stirrings of love. Dazed, bruised, infatuated, he becomes a petrolhead. The obsession lands him in jail, and the story takes a consciously Odyssean turn as it follows his escape from prison and his trickster-hero tribulations as he attempts to return home.

---

* A.A. Milne, introduction to 1940 edition of *The Wind in the Willows*.

Toad lies, cheats and steals, and is proud of it. But the world of this powerful compensatory fantasy, even for the morally rudderless amphibian at the heart of it, is limitlessly forgiving. Exile from Toad Hall, exile from the affections of his friends, is only ever temporary. 'Home' is a word that resonates deeply in *The Wind in the Willows*. Here's a book written by a man who never truly felt secure in a home of his own: bereft of his mother, displaced and bewildered by his father's abandonment, desperately unhappy in his marriage. The story he wrote – initially for his own son – captures the sense of wishing to return to a childhood from which he was exiled before he ever properly dwelt in it.

Look at the feeling with which he evokes Mole's *hiraeth** as, passing his old burrow, he catches a whiff of his long-ago home:

> 'Please stop, Ratty!' pleaded the poor Mole, in anguish of heart. 'You don't understand! It's my home, my old home! I've just come across the smell of it, and it's close by here, really quite close. And I must go to it, I must, I must! Oh, come back, Ratty! Please, please come back!' The Rat was by this time very far ahead, too far to hear clearly what the Mole was calling, too far to catch the sharp note of painful appeal in his voice.

Rat, as often when he catches himself in an inadvertent cruelty, in due course catches on to Mole's distress, and berating himself – 'I see it all now! What a pig I have been!' – goes back with Mole to search for the burrow. When they find it, Mole is ashamed of its shabbiness. But Rat helps him to see it in the forgiving light of their friendship, helps him (if you like) to own his feelings. As the chapter ends:

> He saw clearly how plain and simple – how narrow, even – it all was, but clearly, too, how much it all meant to him, and the special

---

* Excellent Welsh word for the mournful longing for home.

value of some such anchorage in one's existence. He did not at all want to abandon the new life and its splendid spaces, to turn his back on sun and air and all they offered him and creep home and stay there; the upper world was all too strong, it called to him still, even down there, and he knew he must return to the larger stage. But it was good to think he had this to come back to, this place which was all his own, these things which were so glad to see him again and could always be counted upon for the same simple welcome.

But the book also contains two very strange chapters, written with an intensity that seems at odds with the droll humour of most of the story. 'The Piper at the Gates of Dawn', which was to give its name to Pink Floyd's first album, describes how Rat and Mole scull up the river in search of a missing baby otter. They are haunted, as they go, by an inexpressibly moving music – the wind in the willows of the title – and a journey upriver becomes something more like the journey into a dream.

'It's gone!' sighed the Rat, sinking back in his seat again. 'So beautiful and strange and new! Since it was to end so soon, I almost wish I had never heard it. For it has roused a longing in me that is pain, and nothing seems worthwhile but just to hear that sound once more and go on listening to it for ever. No! There it is again!' he cried, alert once more. Entranced, he was silent for a long space, spellbound.

'Now it passes on and I begin to lose it,' he said presently. 'Oh, Mole! the beauty of it! The merry bubble and joy, the thin, clear, happy call of the distant piping! Such music I never dreamed of, and the call in it is stronger even than the music is sweet! Row on, Mole, row! For the music and the call must be for us.'

The Mole, greatly wondering, obeyed. 'I hear nothing myself,' he said, 'but the wind playing in the reeds and rushes and osiers.'

The Rat never answered, if indeed he heard. Rapt, transported, trembling, he was possessed in all his senses by *this new divine thing*

that caught up his helpless soul and swung and dandled it, a powerless
but happy infant in a strong sustaining grasp [my italics].

The animals, here, are hypnotised (Rat speaks of a 'song-dream'
'as if in a trance') by a music that is the music of nature itself, and
which gives way to a vision of Pan – a sexless, nurturing Pan – at
whose feet the lost baby otter is curled, 'nestling between his very
hooves, sleeping soundly in entire peace and contentment'. The
language is of the numinous. Nature, here, is the divinity – and the
animals, rapt in awe, can only 'worship' before the deity gives his
gift of forgetfulness and they are returned, blinking and puzzled,
to sublunary reality. It's a truly bizarre interlude (most abridge-
ments and theatrical adaptations, starting with Milne's, quietly
omit it): like interrupting a Gilbert and Sullivan operetta with a
long acid-drenched number by Hawkwind – or, for that matter,
early Pink Floyd.

But as much as it's an odd chapter within the book, it's absolutely
in keeping with one of the buried themes of Edwardian children's
writing. The retreating sea of faith, with its melancholy long
withdrawing roar, did not leave a scoured beach in its wake but
a panoply of mysticisms. This was the era of theosophy, of spirit-
ualism, of William James's *The Varieties of Religious Experience:
A Study in Human Nature* (1902). The flavour of mysticism in the
author of *Pagan Papers* was one which spoke to the other anxieties
of the age: urbanisation, commerce, clock-time and the onward
push of modernity. Like Burnett's 'magic', here was a mysticism of
the natural world, of a rural England associated with an idealised
childhood untainted by all these things. It's a world in which the
dreary timetabled duties of adulthood need not impinge, a world
in which, per Peter Pan's impassioned outburst, you can 'always
[...] be a little boy and have fun'.

That mysticism coalesces in children's books, as it did in the
contemporary adult work of D.H. Lawrence, around the figure of
Pan. Barrie's perpetual child wears 'Pan' as a surname, and from his

earliest incarnation is seen playing a 'pipe of reeds'. Dickon, in *The Secret Garden*, is a clear incarnation of Pan. We meet him 'sitting under a tree, with his back against it, playing on a rough wooden pipe' and surrounded by animals 'as if they were all drawing near to watch him and listen to the strange little call his pipe seemed to make'. The animating spirit of Kipling's *Puck of Pook's Hill* (1906) is the titular Pan-like sprite, 'the oldest thing in England'.

The second odd-one-out chapter in *The Wind in the Willows* is 'Wayfarers All'. Ratty, 'restless, and he did not exactly know why', peevishly contemplates the fieldmice refusing to play with him because they are preparing for winter. He feels irritable at the 'feeling in the air of change and departure' as migratory birds slip away, and argues jealously with the swallows that they should stay. But as they talk of their migratory instincts, a 'new-born need' stirs in him. He starts to imagine, instead, passing beyond 'the great ring of Downs that barred his vision further southwards – his simple horizon hitherto'. He encounters a traveller passing through – a seafaring rat – and as they break bread together the traveller describes his adventures. Ratty, entranced by his descriptions of foreign exotica, falls into a 'waking dream'. He goes home and starts to pack for a voyage. He's on the way out of the door when he bumps into Mole,

> 'Why, where are you off to, Ratty?' asked the Mole in great surprise, grasping him by the arm.
>
> 'Going South, with the rest of them,' murmured the Rat in a dreamy monotone, never looking at him. 'Seawards first and then on shipboard, and so to the shores that are calling me!'

His eyes are 'glazed and set [...] not his friend's eyes, but the eyes of some other animal!' Mole restrains him, and after 'an hysterical fit of dry sobbing' overcomes him, Rat returns to his senses, barely able to put into words what he has just experienced. This chapter, in a book whimsically patterned on *The Odyssey*, corresponds to the passage about the temptations of the Lotus-Eaters. But here, the dangerous seduction is not (as it is in Homer) of sitting still, but of getting up and moving.

Grahame's world is an intensely conservative one. Be he never so roguish and silly, Toad's place is in Toad Hall. The invasion of the weasels and stoats and ferrets – which in our own age has an echo of Robert Mugabe's 'war veterans' taking over farms in Zimbabwe – represents a revolutionary inversion of the natural order. For the world to be made safe again, Toad Hall must be repossessed and the mustelids put back in their place.

This is a book where safety is always in the past. When the warm season is done, it's the practice of the woodland creatures to spend winter looking back on it: 'comparing notes on the past summer and all its doings'. Home and hearth and the familiar things mean safety – and the Wild Wood, let alone the Wide World, are places of threat and uncertainty. But Grahame inscribes within the book the sense of longing for them. Toad's manias – which are manias for travel and for the trappings of modernity – are as intoxicating as they are dangerous. His great refrain when a new fad takes him is one of regret for the past and longing for the future: 'all those wasted years that lie behind me, I never knew, I never even dreamt!' Just a year before Marinetti published his *Futurist Manifesto* (that intoxicated rhapsody to technological modernity), here is how Grahame describes the first glimpse of the fatal automobile: 'the magnificent motor car, immense, breath-snatching, passionate, with its pilot tense and hugging his wheel, possessed all earth and air for the fraction of a second'.

The book's two emotional poles – wanderlust and *hiraeth*, the longing to travel and the longing, the stronger, safer, longing, for home – seem to me to represent Grahame's very intense and conflicted feelings towards childhood itself. You are caught between a childhood happiness to which you can never return, and an adult world that is dangerous, hurtful and crude and will bring in time's inescapable revenges. The only escape is sideways, into a wonderland where every day is the same and there is nothing to do but mess about in boats. Compare, perhaps, the photographic present of *Alice*'s hidden garden, the arrested paradise of Hundred Acre Wood, or the freeze-framed Shire that is Bilbo Baggins's place of safety.

The future, the wide world, was fatal. It was fatal for poor Mouse, who in his first term at Oxford in 1920 killed himself by stepping in front of a train. It was May. Springtime. Grahame and his wife never recovered from his loss. His world dwindled still further. In 1910, Grahame had written: 'Granted that the average man may live for seventy years, it is a fallacy to assume that his life from sixty to seventy is more important than his life from five to fifteen.' His biographer Matthew Dennison glosses that remark as 'a restatement of the old familiar theme: that with the end of childhood comes death in life'. Such life in Graham as had survived the end of childhood – life enough to create an imaginary world in which childhood could be bottled – was now altogether extinct. He lived on another twelve years, but Dennison describes his final decade as having 'the quality of a recessional'.*

The future was fatal, too, to Mouse's whole generation. There is, to the modern reader, a prolepsis in *The Wind in the Willows* that sends a little shiver down the spine: Toad's song of triumph on his return to Toad Hall contains the quatrain:

The Army all saluted
As they marched along the road.
Was it the King? Or Kitchener?
No. It was Mr Toad.

In 1908, Kitchener was already a celebrity: commander in chief of British Forces in India. In 1914, with German soldiers digging in

---

* Matthew Dennison, *Eternal Boy*.

in Belgium and the Low Countries, he became secretary of state for war and posters all over the country showed his stern moustachioed face and pointing finger: 'Britons: [Lord Kitchener] Wants You!' That finger pointed at young men who would have laughed along to Toad's rhyme as children.

Nobody in that Edwardian idyll could have known what was coming. Tick, tick, tick, went the crocodile. The children who read these books – who flitted through Neverland with Peter or drifted through enchanted riverside afternoons with Mole and Ratty – were to end up, just a few years later, dying in their thousands on Flanders Fields.

In spring of 1915, the *New York Times* reported that J.M. Barrie's adopted son ('the original David of The Little White Bird') had been killed in action. He was twenty-one. Five months later, Rudyard Kipling's only son, too, went missing at the Battle of Loos. He was eighteen years old. It was a generation of boys who didn't grow up. They named their fortifications and redoubts for the reading of their childhoods: 'Hook Copse', 'Peter Pan Trench', 'Wendy Cottage'.*

---

* Sam Leith, 'Writing in Terms of Pleasure', interview with A.S. Byatt, *Guardian*, 25 April 2009.

VI

AN ENCHANTED PLACE

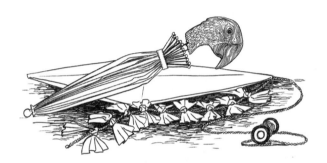

Hugh Lofting · A.A. Milne · W.E. Johns ·
Carolyn Keene · Franklin W. Dixon · Richmal Crompton ·
Arthur Ransome · P.L. Travers · Noel Streatfeild ·
J.R.R. Tolkien · T.H. White

BETWEEN THE WARS

I N JULIET NICOLSON'S SOCIAL HISTORY OF THE INTERWAR years, she writes that it was common to see East End pubs with a row of prams parked outside them, each filled with a wailing child.* Their mothers were out at work and their unemployable fathers, left holding the baby, drowned their sorrows inside. Hundreds of thousands of men had not returned from the war. Many of those who did make it home were physically crippled – the Savoy fixed nailbrushes to the wall in the gents' so one-armed veterans would be able to clean their nails – or were dealing with what we now call PTSD.

The distinguished journalist W.F. Deedes (1913–2007), whom I knew towards the end of his long life, once told me that the key to understanding the hectic gaiety of the Bright Young People in Evelyn Waugh's novels was trauma. 'What you have to understand about people at that time,' he said, 'was that they had suffered the most terrible grief. They were broken-hearted.'

How was children's literature to respond to such a world, to such a legacy of trauma? One way of dealing with it was to ignore it – or to seem to. That happened, at first. The striking thing about interwar literature is how little the experience of total war registered directly in the stories of the time. Indeed, if we remember that so much children's writing navigates, consciously or unconsciously,

---

* Juliet Nicolson, *The Great Silence*.

around the childhood not of its audience but of its author, that's to be expected. The generation of writers whose own childhoods were shaped by the war and its aftermath – who, like the poet Ted Hughes, grew up with a father who never quite left the trenches – was going to come into its own in the fifties and sixties rather than the twenties and thirties. Yet the mood music was inescapable.

The war had not just left heartbreak: it had accelerated a deeper shift in the social order. Women were taking a greater place in the world – the 1928 Representation of the People Act gave them the vote, and their wartime entry into the workplace was not reversed. Parents were taking a greater place in the lives of middle-class children. Homes staffed by cooks, housekeepers and nurses were less and less a middle-class given: by the late thirties there was talk of a 'servant crisis'.

All these changes were reflected (or tellingly avoided) in the children's writing of the time. The period saw the emergence of a huge number of enduring characters – who represented a confidence, freedom and sense of fun that can perhaps be read as a reaction to the drabness and fear of the war years.

Give Me Sunshine

HUGH LOFTING · A.A. MILNE

*The Story of Doctor Dolittle; The Voyages
of Doctor Dolittle; Doctor Dolittle's Post
Office; When We Were Very Young; Winnie-
the-Pooh; The House at Pooh Corner*

I T'S EXTRAORDINARY TO THINK THAT THE IRREPRESSIBLY
sunny *Doctor Dolittle* series, about an animal-loving country
doctor whose pet parrot teaches him the language of animals,
came directly out of the mud and despair of the Western Front.
Berkshire-born Hugh Lofting (1886–1947) had lived overseas
from the age of eighteen (he studied civil engineering at MIT and
travelled for work), but dutifully returned home to enlist in the
Irish Guards for the Great War. *The Story of Doctor Dolittle* (1920),[*]
was written in serial form in the letters Lofting sent home from
the trenches to his children.

'My children at home wanted letters from me – and they wanted
them with illustrations rather than without,' he later recalled.
'There seemed very little of interest to write to youngsters from
the Front; the news was either too horrible or too dull. And it was
all censored. One thing, however, that kept forcing itself on my
attention was the very considerable part the animals were playing

---

[*] Or to give it its full, whimsically eighteenth-century subtitle, *The Story of Doctor
Dolittle: Being the History of His Peculiar Life at Home and Astonishing Adventures in
Foreign Parts Never Before Printed*.

in the World War and that as time went on they, too, seemed to become Fatalists.'

The war, in Lofting's view of it, changed what children's literature should be. In a 1924 article for *The Nation*, he wrote:

> The boy may not have heard his father boasting of the glories of a crack regiment, but he has read a whole heap of so-called Children's Classics in which highly painted heroes galloped, glorious and victorious, across bloody battlefields. That kind of battlefield has gone for good – it is still bloody, but you don't gallop. And since that kind of battlefield has gone, that kind of book – for children – should go too.

It's as if, surrounded by death and the abuse of power on an international scale, Lofting set out to create a bounded space in his imagination on which none of that could possibly impinge. He succeeded. From this hellish early-twentieth-century landscape Lofting invented a collection of idyllic stories set in the early nineteenth century. Doctor Dolittle's character, and the world he inhabits, is one of shining benignity.

The language of the books is simple and direct and full of warm humour, and there's a pleasing childishness in the reduplicative names of his animal friends – Dab-Dab the duck, Too-Too the owl, Chee-Chee the monkey, Gub-Gub the pig, as well as Polynesia the parrot, Jip the dog and of course the courteous but shy Pushmi-Pullyu, an exotic creature with a head and a set of front legs at either end of its body. Here's a delightful and slightly surreal world in which porpoises can be dispatched to fetch a cargo of onions, a monarch uses a lollipop for a lorgnette, and Gub-Gub – feeling left out because he isn't getting any post – will send himself a whole series of letters full of banana skins.

The only note of sharpness in the books is a disappointment in humanity itself. As Polynesia the parrot remarks early on: 'I was thinking about people. People make me sick. They think they are so wonderful.' There's no human achievement – be it reading the seas, predicting the weather or carrying the post – that an animal can't do better, and do better without boasting about it either. Social prestige and worldly goods are nothing to the Doctor. In the third book, he fastidiously returns some priceless pearls to a spoonbill whose children are fond of using them as playthings. As he tells his sister, with childlike ingenuousness, when she complains that 'none of the best people will have you for a doctor' if he insists on keeping so many animals (there has been an unfortunate incident with a patient sitting on a hedgehog): 'But I like the animals better than the "best people".'

John Dolittle himself – 'this funny little man with the kind smiling face', equipped always with a shabby high hat and a black doctor's bag – is a sainted innocent. Such is his love for animals that, when we meet him in the first book, having started out as a universally respected doctor in the idyllic provincial town of Puddleby-on-the-Marsh, he is on the verge of destitution. He has filled the house with more and more pets and his patients have deserted him. He sells his piano (forcing the white mice who lived inside it to move to a bureau-drawer), then sells his good brown suit.

> And now, when he walked down the street in his high hat, people would say to one another: 'There goes John Dolittle, MD! There was a time when he was the best known doctor in the West Country – Look at him now – He hasn't any money and his stockings are full of holes!'
>
> But the dogs and the cats and the children still ran up and followed him through the town – the same as they had done when he was rich.

Migratory birds carry reports of his kindness worldwide. After Polynesia the parrot has taught our hero to speak to animals, the plot of the first book follows the Doctor's adventures as he crosses the seas in a borrowed boat to save the monkeys of Africa from a deadly pandemic. He puts in place a vaccination programme and all the animals, including the initially reluctant lion, muck in to help. Here is an account of the animal world from which even predation is almost wholly absent, or only very briefly mentioned. The lion really does lie down with the lamb.

A crocodile whose toothache the Doctor cures sleeps in the fishpond at the bottom of the garden, having 'promised not to eat the fish', and remains 'gentle as a kitten'. When a shark politely volunteers to eat some pirates whom Dr Dolittle and his crew have bested, the Doctor declines. The pirates are instead condemned to live out their days as birdseed-farmers. An island thought to be populated by terrible dragons is, in fact, full of amiable vegetarians who blow mist from their noses to frighten off human visitors. 'We are,' confesses one of these beasts, 'really more harmless than sheep.'

Not only do the books present a cosy vision of the natural world, they offer a cosy vision of Englishness. For all its implied mild snobbery, Puddleby remains an English idyll no less than Tolkien's Shire or Kenneth Grahame's riverbank. The Doctor takes his Englishness, in his high hat, wherever he goes. At the floating post office he establishes for the King of the African microstate of Fantippo (headquarters of an international Swallow Mail, staffed by birds, whose European hub is Puddleby) 'tea was served to everybody – the clerks and the customers as well – regularly at four o'clock every afternoon, with cucumber sandwiches on Sundays'.

The swallows pine for 'solid English buildings' to build their nests in. When Cheapside the cockney sparrow arrives in Fantippo he reports, like some avian Rupert Brooke, on the state of the garden back home. Puddleby is the secure hearth from which the Doctor and his friends are regularly exiled in their adventures (which take them, eventually, as far as the moon). It was an Englishness seen from abroad for the author, too. After being nearly killed at the front and invalided out of the army, he emigrated with his young family to Connecticut in 1919. He lived the rest of his life in the States, dying in California in 1947.

Doctor Dolittle himself is not a child, but he is childlike (short and round of body, short on hair, oversized of head), and he speaks to children on the level. Tommy Stubbins, the narrator of the second book (*The Voyages of Dr Dolittle*, 1922), is taken on by the Doctor as an apprentice, and even on first meeting (Stubbins is barely ten) the boy is struck by the way he 'called me "Stubbins" instead of "Tommy" or "little lad" (I did so hate to be called "little lad"!) This man seemed to begin right away treating me as though I were a grown-up friend of his.'

Many of the Doctor's attitudes are progressive for the 1920s, let alone the 1830s when the stories are set. Unsurprisingly, he's ahead of his time on animal rights. 'A bullfight is a stupid, cruel, disgusting business,' he says, before tricking the people of a Spanish town into abolishing the practice altogether. 'If I had my way, Stubbins,' he tells his disciple at another point, 'there wouldn't be a single lion or tiger in captivity anywhere in the world. They never take to it. They're never happy [...] You can see it in their eyes, dreaming – dreaming always of the great open spaces where they were born.' A fish reporting on his life in an aquarium describes crowds 'looking in at us through the glass – with their mouths open, like half-witted flounders. We got so sick of it that we used to open our mouths back at them; and this they seemed to think highly comical.'

Lofting is also hip to the way human greed, in the form of extractive capitalism, ruins the environment. The Doctor discovered the North Pole in 1809 but kept his discovery secret on the request of the polar bears, who 'told me there was a great deal of coal there, buried beneath the snow. [...] So would I please keep it a secret. Because once people began coming up there to start coal-mines, their beautiful white country would be spoiled.'

When he is, very reluctantly, made the King of Spider-Monkey Island, he essentially invents a bicycling monarchy: 'if he must be a king he meant to be a thoroughly democratic one, that is a king who is chummy and friendly with his subjects and doesn't put on airs. And when he drew up the plans for the city of New Popsipetel he had no palace shown of any kind. A little cottage in a back street was all that he had provided for himself.'

The worldview of the books, then, leans against chauvinism and exploitation. Lofting even seems to have imperialism's number. The King of the Jolliginki doesn't lock the Doctor and his companions in his prison because he's a cannibal or a savage, but because bitter experience has warned him to mistrust the white man:

> 'You may not travel through my lands,' said the King. 'Many years ago a white man came to these shores; and I was very kind to him. But after he had dug holes in the ground to get the gold, and killed all the elephants to get their ivory tusks, he went away secretly in his ship – without so much as saying "Thank you." Never again shall a white man travel through the lands of Jolliginki.'

The Doctor avers that 'these Indians were ignorant of many of the things that quite small white children know – though it is also true that they knew a lot that white grown-ups never dreamed of'. The greatest naturalist in the world, he says, is not Charles Darwin but the Red Indian Long Arrow, and when he meets Long Arrow he greets him as a peer.

Yet Lofting does include racial stereotypes of a sort that are now problematic. The native characters, in his illustrations, are thick-lipped darky caricatures, and phrases of the sort that would have been unremarkable in Lofting's age and milieu – 'We'll have to work like niggers', for instance, or allusions to pawning 'gew-gaws at that Jew's shop' – have not aged well. Nor, notoriously, has the Doctor's second escape from the Jolliginki in the first book.

The king's son Prince Bumpo, reading a book of fairytales, sighs aloud: 'If only I were a *white* prince!' The Doctor arranges to dye him white in exchange for his freedom: 'The Prince's face had turned as white as snow, and his eyes, which had been mud-coloured, were a manly gray!' As the Dolittle party makes their escape, the Doctor admits: 'I feel sorry about Bumpo. I'm afraid the medicine I used will never last. Most likely he will be as black as ever when he wakes up in the morning...' Without any great fuss, and without any great loss to the reader, modern reissues of the books have tended to quietly excise this subplot and other racial slurs. That seems to me a sensible solution.

Lofting, in his writing for children, retreated from and repudiated the world that had shaped his young manhood. So did another veteran of the Great War, Alan Alexander Milne (1882–1956). The youngest son of a provincial schoolmaster, and already a rising literary star when he went to fight, Milne served as a signals officer on the Somme in 1916. Invalided home with what was described as 'trench fever', he wrote in his autobiography: 'I should like to put asterisks here, and then write: "It was in 1919 that I found myself once again a civilian." For it makes me almost physically sick to think of that nightmare of mental and moral degradation, the war.'*

Just a few years after Doctor Dolittle set out on his voyages, Milne created, in *Winnie-the-Pooh* (1926), a world even more fantastical and unthreatening, more resistant to modernity, than Puddleby-on-the-Marsh. In literary terms, and in terms of his conception of childhood, Milne is more like a Victorian writer than an interwar one.

His first poetry collection for children, *When We Were Very Young* (1924), privileges sound over sense in the confounding and delighting manner of Edward Lear. Its poems are set in a weightless world of kings and queens, nannies and nurses and dairymaids, top-hatted doctors and sailing ships, that belong halfway between a fairytale or nursery rhyme and Milne's own Victorian childhood.

It was a colossal hit right away. Two months after publication, there were more than 40,000 copies in print, and more than a quarter of a million copies were sold in the three years that followed. Even Rudyard Kipling – still a towering figure in children's writing – wrote Milne a fan letter; to which Milne responded: 'If you can

---

*   A.A. Milne, *It's Too Late Now*.

remember what you once said to Tennyson, you will know what your letter makes me want to say to you. I am proud that you like the verses.' (Kipling had told Tennyson that 'When a private is praised by his General he does not presume to thank him, but fights the better afterwards'.)

Writing in the 1950s, the critic Geoffrey Grigson, who deplored its niceness and what he saw as its cosy middle-class milieu, nevertheless touched on an aspect of its appeal to the people who bought it to read to their children:

> Children, in my experience, of every generation since and including the Twenties, have found the poems nauseating, and fascinating. In fact, they were poems by a parent for other parents, and for vice-parental nannies – for parents with a war to forget, a social (and literary) revolution to ignore, a childhood to recover.*

This misses, I think, the observed truth of the children in the poems: they chafe at constraint, they are wilful and whimsical, and they live in the moment. When in 'Vespers' Christopher Robin is saying his prayers, he's always getting distracted and getting it wrong. The speaker of 'Politeness' dutifully parrots the formulae of good manners but admits how wearisome he finds them. Undoubtedly, though, 'a war to forget' and 'a childhood to recover' will have been powerful selling-points to the book's first readers-aloud.

Any peril in these poems – the bears waiting to pounce on children who step on pavement-cracks, for instance – is of the mild variety. And the childhood it idealises is a space held apart from materialism. In 'Puppy And I', the speaker of the poem meets a series of characters on errands to the village to pick up food and is invited to accompany them. He turns them all down until he meets a puppy headed for the hills on no greater errand than 'to roll and

---

* Quoted in Thwaite, *A.A. Milne: His Life*.

play'. In 'Market Square', the speaker finds his pockets filling with money as the stanzas go by, but none of the stalls is selling a rabbit, which is what he actually wants to buy. When finally, pockets empty, he strolls onto the 'old-gold common', he sees rabbits in abundance.

Even if some of the more whimsical poems do cross the line into cutesy, it's a work of extraordinary technical command. 'James, James, Morrison, Morrison, Weatherby George Dupree' survives in part because of the comic way that it inverts the child–adult relationship: the child sternly scolding his mother for going down to the end of the town unaccompanied, the archetypal childish fear of abandonment turned reassuringly on its head. But what really makes it work is its metrical virtuosity. The humbling of Sir Brian Botany – which, *pace* Grigson, was very much in keeping with Milne's egalitarian politics – is another extraordinary feat of metrical precision.

Milne himself made no bones about this. A well-established comic writer and assistant editor of *Punch* even before the war, he was a sophisticated and urbane figure whose acquaintances included H.G. Wells and J.M. Barrie, and who locked horns with T.S. Eliot and Graham Greene. *When We Were Very Young*, he wrote, 'is not the work of a poet becoming playful, nor of a lover of children expressing his love, nor of a prose-writer knocking together a few jingles for the little ones, it is the work of a light-verse writer taking his job seriously, even though he is taking it into the nursery.' Nevertheless, he was to come to regret the way in which the success of his children's writing overshadowed his other work.

Overshadow it, though, it did. Edward Bear and Christopher Robin make their first appearances in *When We Were Very Young*, but they were to reach their most perfect expression in the two books of stories that followed. The world of *Winnie-the-Pooh* and its sequel is even more remote from our own than that of *When We Were Very Young*, which at least contains houses and streets and people with jobs. It's a perfectly sealed-off universe. Only Christopher Robin can ever leave it, and the poignancy is that, in the end, he must.

What actually happens in the stories is the least of them. A bear and a piglet go in search of a woozle and don't find it. A bear falls into his own heffalump trap. A depressed donkey gets an empty pot and a burst balloon for his birthday. A baby kangaroo falls in the water and is fished out. A donkey falls in the water and is fished out. A wooden lean-to moves from one side of a field to another. A bouncy creature discovers that it likes extract of malt. Pooh, apparently discovering the concept of object-permanence, invents a new game. Tone of voice, dialogue and the surface play of language are all.

Winnie-the-Pooh and *The House at Pooh Corner* are the most obvious descendants of Lewis Carroll's *Alice* books, and arguably the only direct ones, in the canon. Like *Alice*, there are layers to the fiction: the telling of the story is inscribed in the story itself. The opening pages of *Winnie-the-Pooh* introduce Edward Bear, also known as Winnie-the-Pooh ('He's Winnie-ther-Pooh. Don't you know what 'ther' means?'), and who inexplicably lives 'under the name of Sanders', coming down the stairs 'bump, bump, bump' behind Christopher Robin.

The narrator, at Christopher Robin's request, starts to tell Pooh a story about himself. A few sentences in, Pooh himself (or, perhaps, Christopher Robin speaking in 'a growly voice'), interrupts the narrator. The narrator goes on, embarking on the story of Pooh's abortive attempt to steal honey from bees by ascending under a balloon disguised as a small cloud.

> He crawled out of the gorse-bush, brushed the prickles from his nose, and began to think again. And the first person he thought of was Christopher Robin.
>
> ('*Was that me?' said Christopher Robin in an awed voice, hardly daring to believe it.*
>
> '*That was you.' Christopher Robin said nothing, but his eyes got larger and larger, and his face got pinker and pinker.*)
>
> So Winnie-the-Pooh went round to his friend Christopher Robin, who lived behind a green door in another part of the forest.

'Good morning, Christopher Robin,' he said.
'Good morning, Winnie-the-Pooh,' said you.

And we're off, plunged into an enclosed world that is the figure for an idealised childhood – one in which Pooh and his friends have absolute freedom of action and nothing important to do. Like the world of P.G. Wodehouse's fiction, Milne's forest is a place of complete safety, shadowed only dimly by the awareness that there's a larger world outside it. It's so funny, and so inventive, and so self-contained, that earnestly applying the tools of literary criticism to it risks, as was said of Wodehouse, taking a spade to a soufflé.

Inasmuch as it records a response rather than an analysis, then, Dorothy Parker's famous verdict on *The House at Pooh Corner* – 'Tonstant Weader fwowed up' – avoids this hazard. It's also a little unfair. The stories are sentimental, but they are not quite saccharine. Eeyore's sulphurously passive-aggressive outlook, and the characters' small vanities and self-deceptions, shade the whole thing with irony. The different animals are psychological types (we all know an Eeyore or a Tigger), but they also manage to be winningly and memorably particular.*

The connection to *Alice* – a spikier and wilder text, but a kindred spirit – can be seen especially in the absurdist wordplay. There's a lot of thinking that goes on in the Pooh books, but almost none of it results in anything that resembles a thought; and there's a lot of talking, but almost nothing meaningful is ever said. Words are unmoored from things. Meanings are turned on their heads. Sentences deconstruct themselves on the go: 'Everybody said "How-do-you-do" to Eeyore, and Eeyore said that he didn't, not to notice, and then they sat down.' 'Tigger kept disappearing, and then when

---

*   The creatures of the forest are a bit of a Rorschach blot. One (anachronistic) theory sees the toys as representing different mental health conditions – Eeyore as a depressive, Piglet as suffering anxiety, Tigger as having ADHD and so on. The writer Nicola Shulman identifies them with Romantic poets.

you thought he wasn't there, there he was again, saying, "I say, come on," and before you could say anything, there he wasn't.'; 'The more he looked inside, the more Piglet wasn't there.'

In the Snark and Jabberwock tradition, searches are undertaken for non-existent creatures: 'It is either Two Woozles and one, as it might be, Wizzle, or Two, as it might be, Wizzles and one, if so it is, Woozle.' Traps are laid for Heffalumps and Backsons are at large:

'Have you seen a Backson anywhere about in the Forest lately?'

'I don't know,' said Rabbit. 'That's what I came to ask you. What are they like?'

'Well,' said Owl, 'the Spotted or Herbaceous Backson is just a—'

'At least,' he said, 'it's really more of a—'

'Of course,' he said, 'it depends on the—'

'Well,' said Owl, 'the fact is,' he said, 'I don't know what they're like,' said Owl frankly.

'Thank you,' said Rabbit.

It's easy enough to see why philosophers of a whimsical cast have found material in the apparently simple adventures of Christopher Robin and his brigade of stuffed animals — most notoriously in Benjamin Hoff's 1982 *The Tao of Pooh*. The great divide between doing and being is a constant presence in the books, and Pooh, like a little bodhisattva, has a head blissfully empty of self-consciousness.

When they are perfectly in tune, Christopher Robin shares Pooh's ability to empty the world of conscious meaning. As the book closes, he's in an in-between space where he can still access the world of the forest and feel 'all sunny and careless, and just as if twice nineteen didn't matter a bit, as it didn't on such a happy afternoon'. The sort of 'knowledge' that doesn't require you to know anything is available to him: 'he thought that if he stood on the bottom rail of the bridge, and leant over, and watched the river slipping slowly away beneath him, then he would suddenly know everything that there was to be known, and he would be able to tell Pooh, who wasn't quite sure about some of it.'

The world of the forest is that world in which, in its purest form, it's possible to live without thinking: to exist as yourself is total knowledge. But, of course, Christopher Robin grows up and stuffed toys don't. He's going to school, where twice nineteen will matter, and going nowhere and doing nothing will dwindle into memory.

There's an echo of Carroll's envoi – the White Knight's melancholy farewell to Alice in *Through the Looking-Glass* – in the closing pages of *The House at Pooh Corner*. Christopher Robin knights Pooh:

> Then he began to think of all the things Christopher Robin would want to tell him when he came back from wherever he was going to, and how muddling it would be for a Bear of Very Little Brain to try and get them right in his mind. 'So, perhaps,' he said sadly to himself, 'Christopher Robin won't tell me any more,' and he wondered if being a Faithful Knight meant that you just went on being faithful without being told things.

The notoriously tear-jerking pay-off – 'So they went off together. But wherever they go, and whatever happens to them on the way, in that enchanted place on the top of the Forest a little boy and his Bear will always be playing.' – repeats Carroll's fantasy of capturing childhood, with its irrecoverable set of loving relationships, in a frozen bubble of time. That's the 'golden afternoon', the space in which Alice will always be 'moving under skies / Never seen by waking eyes.' Here, though, the patient abandoned knight is not the adult helplessly watching a child un-selve as she grows up; it's the child, or inner child, losing a parent who is also a friend and a peer.

Like the beautiful garden Alice glimpses, Hundred Acre Wood is a metaphor; but, unlike that garden, it's also a real place. You can stand there. In fact, a commemorative plaque *does* stand in Ashdown Forest, which inspired the landscape of the Pooh stories;

Milne first visited the forest as a child, and he lived and wrote the Pooh books at Cotchford Farm nearby. As he was later to say, it was 'Gill's Lap that inspired Galleon's Lap, the group of pine trees on the other side of the main road that became the Six Pine Trees, the bridge over the river at Posingford that became Pooh-sticks Bridge.' The bachelor inhabitants of the forest, with the exception of Owl and Rabbit, were based on Christopher's stuffed animals – Pooh, Eeyore and Piglet were all toys he owned, and Roo, Kanga and Tigger, as in the books, were latecomers.

With his own happy childhood, Milne was not, unlike so many children's writers, writing from a wound; but he did, like so many children's writers, create one. Even though Christopher Robin isn't the central figure in the Pooh stories – he most often swoops in at the end of an adventure to sort things out with an exclamation of 'How I love you, Pooh!' or 'Silly old bear!' – Milne's only child Christopher became a celebrity 'original' no less than Vivian Burnett. In 1934 an American magazine named him in a list of the most famous children in the world, alongside Yehudi Menuhin, Crown Prince Michael of Romania and Princess Elizabeth. As Christopher was to recall, he 'was beginning to be what he was later to become, a sore place that looked as if it would never heal up'. The fame of his father's books caused him to be badly bullied at school, and he described the 'toe-curling, fist-clenching, lip-biting embarrassment' that 'Vespers' – describing the boy saying his prayers with syrupy mock-reverence – caused him.

'It seemed to me,' he wrote in his autobiography, 'almost that my father had got to where he was by climbing upon my infant shoulders, that he had filched from me my good name and had left me with the empty fame of being his son.'* It was not just his accidental celebrity that shaped his reaction. Christopher speculated later, looking back on a family holiday after the early death

---

*   Christopher Milne, *The Enchanted Places*.

of Alan's closest brother, Kenneth, that his father, 'I now suspect, saw me as a sort of twin brother, perhaps a sort of reincarnation of Ken… He needed me to escape from being fifty.'

Estranged from both his parents as a young adult, Christopher Milne was only able to make peace with his legacy by taking control of his own story in his 1974 memoir *The Enchanted Places*, which served 'to lift me from under the shadow of my father and of Christopher Robin, and to my surprise and pleasure I found myself standing beside them in the sunshine able to look them both in the eye'.* Even in the most effervescently innocent of children's stories, then, there's something at stake. An adult, writing towards childhood, is always in some sense serving an adult need, and that can come at a psychic cost. As the literary historian Peter Hunt puts it, the 'collision between adult writer and child reader [is] the central conundrum of children's literature'.†

---

* Christopher Milne, *The Path Through the Trees* (McLellan and Stuart, 1979).

† Hunt, op. cit.

Opening a Franchise

W.E. JOHNS · CAROLYN KEENE ·
FRANKLIN W. DIXON · RICHMAL CROMPTON ·
ARTHUR RANSOME

The Camels Are Coming; Biggles Defies the Swastika;
Biggles of the Special Air Police; Biggles Does Some
Homework; The Secret of the Old Clock; The Tower
Treasure; Just William; More William; William Again;
Still William; William the Outlaw; Just William's
Luck; William the Dictator; William and Air Raid
Precautions; William and the Evacuees; William and
the Moon Rocket; Swallows and Amazons; We Didn't
Mean to Go to Sea; The Picts and the Martyrs

THERE WAS ONE NOTABLE EXCEPTION TO THE TEN-
dency of writers of the interwar period to turn away
from the horrors of the First World War: Biggles. The
ground war, as Lofting saw, was too horrific, too grinding, too static
and boring to make its way into children's stories directly. But the
romance of early aviation could, perhaps, be something around
which a mythology of sorts could be built.

Nevertheless, the flyer we first meet in 'The White Fokker' (a
short story published in *Popular Flying* in 1932 and later collected
that same year in the first Biggles book *The Camels Are Coming*) is
not the carefree character he later became. He is described waiting
on the ground at an airfield, in unspoken anxiety, awaiting the
return of a patrol:

His deep-set hazel eyes were never still and held a glint of yellow fire that somehow seemed out of place in a pale face upon which the strain of war, and sight of sudden death, had already graven little lines. His hands, small and delicate as a girl's, fidgeted continually with the tunic fastening at his throat. He had killed a man not six hours before. He had killed six men during the past month – or was it a year? – he had forgotten.

The story follows Biggles's attempt to take out a white Fokker that has been ambushing British patrols as they limp home, and death, the fear of it and the feeling of responsibility for it, are strong presences in the story. When his first attempt to down the enemy plane fails, it costs lives and Biggles's shot nerves send him close to the edge of reason.

'I've lost Swayne and Maddison,' he said grimly, as the others joined him. 'I've lost Swayne and Maddison,' he repeated. 'I've lost Swayne and Maddison, can't you hear me?' he said yet again. 'What the hell are you looking at me like that for?'

Aerial warfare was exceptionally dangerous, and the author W.E. Johns (1893–1968) – who served as an infantryman in Gallipoli and Macedonia before transferring to the Royal Flying Corps in the last year of the war – had personal experience of it, though he didn't spend more than a few months in the air. Johns didn't enjoy his hero's virtuosity or luck. He is reported to have lost three planes in as many days to technical malfunctions and went on to lose two more by shooting off his own propellor. During a bombing mission over Germany in September 1918 he was shot down and taken prisoner.

As Johns was to write in an author's note prefacing the first edition, 'One could not exaggerate the stunning horror of seeing two machines collide head-on a few yards away, and words have yet to be coined to express that tightening of the heart-strings that comes of seeing one of your own side roaring down in a sheet of flame.'

Biggles's flight path, over the decades that followed, was to take him a long way from there. It describes a trajectory away from a quasi-realistic portrayal of First World War aerial combat aimed at adults and older adolescent readers, towards the child-friendly series that endures in popular memory. Notoriously, a case of whisky was quietly swapped out for lemonade when one story was reprinted in the 1953 collection *Biggles of the Special Air Police*.

Biggles's creator Captain W.E. Johns wasn't actually a captain, but then Colonel Sanders wasn't actually a colonel. You could compare their productions. There's not much to Biggles nutritionally speaking, but there's plenty of it: a vast series of highly disposable adventure stories set in a homosocial world of old-time pluck and gallantry. Biggles is on one level a superhero-cum-knight-errant. But with its nicknames, the absence of sex and its institutional codes and hierarchies, the world he inhabits might as well belong to the tradition of boarding school stories. Biggles, Ginger and Algy are the Stalky, Beetle and M'Turk of the Royal Air Force – though they are far less anarchic than their predecessors.

By the time we reach *Biggles Defies the Swastika* – which sees Biggles operating behind enemy lines after the Nazi invasion of Norway – there's any amount of shooting and bombing and biffing, but nobody dies as it were on screen. Biggles's nerves speak more of bitten nails, these days, than borderline PTSD. '"Okay," agreed Ginger, "but I'm bound to say it sounds a sticky business to me," he added glumly. "All war is sticky business," Biggles reminded him.'

Johns's writing is never more than workmanlike, as witness this contemplative moment for example: 'The sun went down. Purple twilight, ever darkening, hung for a little while over the silent waters, and then gave way to night. Stars appeared, twinkling. Biggles munched a biscuit thoughtfully.' Reports are to be found 'ringing' in ears, thoughts 'flash' through minds, and when someone is shaken it's apt to be 'to his very core'. But the pacing is on point, the plotting is engagingly hectic as scrape succeeds scrape, and the chivalric code within which Biggles operates belongs as much to the games field as to the airfield.

Like any respectable superhero Biggles has an arch-enemy, in Erich von Stalhein, a monocle-wearing German intelligence officer who, oddly enough, at one point in the series goes over to the Soviets. Getting Biggles trumps ideology every time. Johns published around a hundred *Biggles* books, full of the cherishable squawks of surprise their detractors like to mock: 'By thunder!' 'By jingo!' 'Holy smoke!' 'Suffering rattlesnakes!' He was still cranking them out when he dropped dead in 1968. The unfinished *Biggles Does Some Homework* was published posthumously in 1998. Touchingly, it describes the ageless aviator preparing for retirement.

As the longevity of Biggles indicates, something else was going on in this period. Children's publishing – the idea of a distinct children's literature and a stable and sizeable market for it – was now fully established. By 1939 nearly half of Britain's public libraries had a dedicated children's section. Boys' magazines like the *Gem* and the *Magnet*, and girls' journals like *School Friend* and *Schoolgirls' Weekly*, commanded readerships in the hundreds of thousands, churning out formulaic school stories and tales of adventure. In December 1922, a whole new medium for children's storytelling – which would go on to become a competitor – launched in the shape of the first BBC *Children's Hour*.

The ripple effects of mass literacy were being felt. In the sphere of children's literature, that meant that you started to see not only many more children's books, but the emergence of definite franchises. Fiction was turning into an industry, and children's fiction was no exception. In the States that was taken even further. The Hardy Boys made their first appearance in 1927, in *The Tower Treasure*. 1930 saw the publication there of *The Secret of the Old Clock* – the first Nancy Drew mystery, in a series that would go on to encompass nearly two hundred novels right up into the twenty-first century. The publication history of these two teen mystery franchises – with their changes of publishers and endless reboots – is almost impossibly tangled: they really were industrial products. They were still selling strongly in my 1980s childhood, and I grew a long shelf of the primrose-coloured Armada editions.

I was besotted with the plucky, red-haired girl detective. I would have no truck with *The Hardy Boys*, which I considered an inferior literary product: Franklin W. Dixon, author of the latter, was not a shred of the writer that Carolyn Keene, creator of Nancy Drew, was. What I did not know then, and learned only very much later, is that neither Keene nor Dixon existed. They were both pen-names adopted by the Edward Stratemeyer writing syndicate. The same group of hacks was turning out both book series, the differentiation being a marketing proposition. Mildred Wirt Benson (1905–2002), a journalist who lived in Toledo, Ohio, turned out all but seven of the first thirty books in the original *Nancy Drew* series and was paid a flat fee of between $125 and $250 per book. Dozens of others, also uncredited, would go on to write the stories.

The UK didn't have writing syndicates in the same way, but the idea of writing for profit – of publishing into this growing market for fiction – was taking hold of the middle-class imagination. 'Everyone Can Write,' claimed the strapline for one of the countless writing classes and correspondence courses that burgeoned in the first half of the twentieth century. The young Enid Blyton grew out of this soil. The author of the *William* books, Richmal Crompton (1890–1969), like Blyton, had her start in 1922 and continued well into the second half of the twentieth century; but her defining volumes belong to these interwar years. Crompton was a lifelong spinster who taught classics at a girls' school until she contracted polio in her early thirties and, invalided out of her profession, turned to full-time writing. She was at work on the 359th *William* story at the time of her death in 1969. She wrote dozens of novels for adults, but none of them is now remembered in the way the *William* books are. She called him 'my Frankenstein monster': 'I've tried to get rid of him, but he's quite impossible to get rid of.'*

The *Just William* books (all but one – 1948's *Just William's Luck* is a novel) are collections of short stories about the adventures of a middle-class boy of eleven called William Brown. If ever there were a final rebuke to the late-Victorian ideal of children as paragons of virtue, William is it. You could see him in a tradition looking backwards towards the unruly parlour-arsonists of E. Nesbit (or even further back towards Beatrix Potter's Tom Kitten) and forwards towards the catapult-wielding likes of Dennis the Menace.

William is extremely interested in: food (of all sorts, but especially sweets), animals (rats, mice and dogs to train; lizards to drop down the necks of enemies), get-rich-quick schemes and property damage. He is extremely hostile to: schoolwork, washing his face and hands, girls – except for his next-door neighbour Joan, an honorary Outlaw – and sitting still. 'To William,' Crompton writes, 'the fascination of any game consisted mainly in the danger to life and limb involved.'

William may be well-meaning, at least sometimes, but he's not so much naughty or unruly as borderline criminal. His gang of friends call themselves 'The Outlaws', and his fantasy life principally consists of being a robber-chief or a pirate. The first book includes a paragraph sketching a typical morning's activities:

> They had engaged in mortal combat with one another, they had cooked strange ingredients over a smoking and reluctant flame with a fine disregard of culinary conventions, they had tracked each other over the countryside, they had even turned their attention to kidnapping (without any striking success), and these occupations had palled.

---

* BBC radio interview, 1968.

William is appealing because of his good heart, his cockney-style idiolect (he never says 'and' when he can say 'an')[*] and his unbowed determination to overcome whatever footling obstacles – be they parental prohibitions or social conventions – the world puts in the way of his doing exactly as he damn well pleases. He's an agent of chaos, and the books' charm consists in quite how chaotic and how mortifying his antics are to the adults around him. The butler in a grand house into which William is mistakenly introduced as a new servant has his number: "'Eatin' an' destroyin' of 'is clothes," he said gloomily, returning to the kitchen. "It's all boys ever do – eatin' an destroyin' of their clothes.'"

The series is remembered not just for its protagonist but for William's most celebrated antagonist – the spoilt and lisping Violet Elizabeth Bott, introduced in the fifth book *Still William* (1925) as the daughter of a family of nouveau-riche manufacturers. She's a pre-teen Madeline Bassett crossed with Veruca Salt. Here she is, as first introduced:

> Violet Elizabeth's small pink and white face shone with cleanliness. Violet Elizabeth was so treasured and guarded and surrounded with every care that her small pink and white face had never been known to do anything else except shine with cleanliness. But the pièce de résistance about Violet Elizabeth's appearance was her skirts. Violet Elizabeth was dressed in a white lace-trimmed dress with a blue waistband and beneath the miniature blue waistband, her skirts stood out like a tiny ballet dancer's in a filmy froth

---

[*] He joins a long line of children's books in which the imperfect or malapropic speech of the child protagonists is reproduced phonetically for the benefit of adult readers. Before the twentieth century this tended to be for sentimental reasons, as in the work of Mary Louisa Molesworth (1839–1921); latterly, more often for comic effect. It goes on to this day – see, for instance, Lauren Child's Charlie and Lola series (first instalment: *I Will Not Ever Never Eat a Tomato,* Orchard Books, 2000), which in turn seems to take its cue from Kay Thompson's *Eloise* books.

of lace-trimmed petticoats. From this cascade emerged Violet Elizabeth's bare legs, to disappear ultimately into white silk socks and white buckskin shoes. William gazed at this engaging apparition in horror.

'Even at that tender age,' we're told, 'she possessed the art, so indispensable to her sex, of making her blue eyes swim with tears at will.' Her catchphrase, which she uses to bully William into including her in his games or going along with his plans, has passed into the stock of common phrases: "F you don' play houth with me, I'll thcream 'n' thcream till I'm thick.' For all his subversive behaviour, the William stories tend to bolster the patriarchy. The worldview of *Just William* is characteristic of its age: little girls are made of sugar and spice, and little boys are made of slugs and snails and puppy dogs' tails.

The Browns are a respectable Home Counties household equipped, at least in the early books, with a maid and a cook, but his parents – pointing, perhaps, to a social shift – are a presence in William's life, and he in theirs. Indeed, instead of William trying to escape their influence, they are frequently trying to escape his. A standard set-piece has William chasing his older sister Ethel or his long-suffering father from room to room with pestering questions:

'Father, what was the date of the Armada?'

'Good Heavens! How should I know? I wasn't there.'

William sighed.

'Well, I'm tryin' to write about it and why it failed an' – why did it fail?'

Mr Brown groaned, gathered up his paper, and retired to the dining-room.

'Impossible to get rid of', indeed. Here he is, for instance, in the middle of a typical school day:

He brightened, however, on remembering a lizard he had caught on the way to school, and drew it from its hiding place in his pocket. But the lizard had abandoned the unequal struggle for existence among the stones, top, penknife, bits of putty, and other small objects that inhabited William's pocket. The housing problem had been too much for it… Finally the lizard was dropped down the neck of an inveterate enemy of William's in the next row, and was extracted only with the help of obliging friends. Threats of vengeance followed, couched in blood-curdling terms, and written on blotting paper. Meanwhile Miss Drew explained Simple Practice to a small but earnest coterie of admirers in the front row.

That dry joke about the 'housing problem', and the poised archness of 'earnest coterie of admirers', indicate the key to Crompton's mastery of tone in the books. You root for William, but you also see him with the jaundiced eye of the adults who have to deal with him. Child readers will relish the escapades of a child who goes much further than they would dare; adult readers will relish the mock-heroic framing: 'Fate was against him in every way.' Or, when he's told to read a book: 'William walked across the room with an expression of intense suffering, took out a book at random, and sat down in an attitude of aloof dignity, holding the book upside down.' They are, at their best, extremely funny.

The books also gently guy the adult pretensions of the age. William is, above all, a disrupter – sometimes witting, sometimes accidental – of the orderly world of grown-ups. Here's a secular descendant of the sentimental notion from the previous century that childhood innocence is a rebuke to the worldly and fallen world of the adult. A small boy won't show your sinfulness up for what it is, Fauntleroy-style, but he will embarrass you in front of the neighbours. He is a creature of base and candid appetites, oblivious to the social niceties of civilisation. He's a little id in a scuffed cap.

Every long-running series of this kind has to make an accommodation with the passing of time. The *William* stories went on to take in the events of the Second World War (*William the Dictator, William and Air Raid Precautions, William and the Evacuees*) and the space race (*William and the Moon Rocket*). A television quietly appears in the Browns' house, and the servants quietly disappear. But William remains eleven years old. There's something rather winning, too, in the way Crompton never sweats the small stuff. The age of William's comely older sister Ethel (whose suitors William tends to exploit or thwart) fluctuates, the physical appearances of recurring characters alter at random and William's neighbour Joan goes through three different second names over the course of the series. I read that not as sloppiness, but as a sign of the lightness, the offhandedness, in which this long-running and charming *jeu d'esprit* was conceived.

Arthur Ransome's (1884–1967) *Swallows and Amazons* (1930) – about the adventures of the four Walker children, Titty, John, Susan and Roger, who spend their Lake District holidays messing around in boats – was the first volume of a franchise that ran to twelve books and remains one of the most popular children's stories of all time. Its opening pages describe the arrival of the celebrated telegram – sent by their absent father – giving them permission to take the boat *Swallow* out on the lake: 'BETTER DROWNED THAN DUFFERS IF NOT DUFFERS WONT DROWN.' ('"What does it mean?" asked Susan. "It means Yes," said Titty.')

There, straight away, is the set-up: *'Yes.'* Here are four children between the ages of seven and twelve given freedom of action with an edge (a very slight, comical edge) of jeopardy. The children use this freedom to explore and make camp on Wild Cat Island in the middle of the lake, and they form an initially rivalrous friendship with the local Blackett girls, Nancy and Peggy, whose own dinghy is called *Amazon*. It is an adventure story, but it's an adventure story that has been thoroughly domesticated.

Where many previous children's stories, once the parents have been tidied out of the way, plunge children into quasi-adult perils, *Swallows and Amazons* does the opposite. Their freedom is the freedom of imaginative play. The geography of the real lake and its inhabitants becomes a palimpsest over which a fantasy world borrowed from children's literature itself – *Treasure Island* and *Robinson Crusoe* above all – is inscribed. The grumpy gentleman in a houseboat – first an antagonist, then an ally – is a retired pirate, 'Captain Flint'; the children's mother and their servants are 'natives'; ginger beer is 'grog'. A lakeside town is 'Rio', and a high promontory is 'Darien', so christened because Titty 'had heard the sonnet read aloud at school, and forgotten everything in it except the picture of the explorers looking at the Pacific Ocean for the first time'. The book's grown-ups – outstandingly Captain Flint, the stand-in for Ransome himself – connive willingly in the fantasy. It's not a book about children exploring the adult world so much as about adults entering the world of children.

> 'Hullo, Man Friday,' said Titty joyfully.
> 'Hullo, Robinson Crusoe,' said Mother. That was the best of Mother. She was different from other natives. You could always count on her to know things like that.
> Robinson Crusoe and Man Friday then kissed each other as if they were pretending to be Titty and Mother.

As Ransome's biographer Roland Chambers argues, the war – which had claimed Ransome's younger brother Geoffrey – is present in its absence no less than it is in the warm fantasy of *Doctor Dolittle*:

> For those who had lived through the war, it was the promise Ransome made to himself that appealed most deeply: the promise of a world in which the rules had not been broken; in which parents loved and trusted their children; in which children, secure in that knowledge and in the excellent character of their guardians, set out on their own to discover new lands, engage in mock battles, and when the excitement was over, to return to warm beds, roaring fires, familiar faces and the prospect of repeating the adventure

year after year, without fear of interruption or irretrievable tragedy, as though the real war had not been fought at all. *Swallows and Amazons* was a book about recovery...*

It's a very wholesome, very reassuringly bounded world that the stories inhabit. It's bounded in space by the shores of the lake (though later books in the series explore the Norfolk Broads), and it's bounded in time by the school holidays; the flip side, perhaps, of the boarding school stories whose action is likewise bracketed by term dates but takes place on the other side of the brackets. The vigour of both those traditions indicates how defining, by the early twentieth century, the experience of school had become of childhood itself.

There's a great delight in food (isn't there always?): 'The captain, mate, and the crew of the *Swallow* squatted round the frying-pan, and began eating as soon as the scrambled eggs, which were very hot, would let them. Mate Susan had already cut four huge slices of brown bread and butter to eat with the eggs. Then she poured out four mugs of tea, and filled them up with milk from a bottle [...] Then there was a big rice pudding [...] Then there were four big slabs of seed-cake. Then there were apples all round.'

There's a great delight, too, in practical knowledge. The story was shaped by Ransome's spending the summer of 1928 in the Lake District teaching the children of his friends Dora and Ernest Altounyan to sail. Their boat *Swallow* found its way into the story and three of the children (Titty, Roger and Susan) gave their names to the Walkers. The technical vocabulary of sailing is lovingly reproduced – all sheets and painters and reef points. And though John, the oldest, captains *Swallow*, Ransome is admirably even-handed when it comes to gender roles: the girls are at least as resourceful as the boys, and it is Titty who single-handedly captures *Amazon* when the two crews are in competition.

---

* Roland Chambers, *The Last Englishman*.

The idyllic quality of Ransome's Lake District, and its intense Englishness, is given special emotional force by counterpoint. In a 1958 note, he wrote that the book had its origins in the summer holidays he and his siblings spent 'on a farm at the south end of Coniston': 'Going away from it, we were half drowned in tears. While away from it, as children and as grown-ups, we dreamt about it. No matter where I was, wandering about the world, I used at night to look for the North Star and, in my mind's eye, could see the beloved skyline of great hills beneath it. *Swallows and Amazons* grew out of those old memories.'

Ransome, in adult life, did plenty of wandering about the world. As a young journalist he reported on the Russian Revolution and the formation of the Comintern and – dismayingly – became one of its most enthusiastic Western cheerleaders. In fact, there's very strong evidence that he may have been a Soviet spy: he met Trotsky and Lenin, became close friends with the latter's propaganda chief Karl Radek, and at one point smuggled thousands of roubles worth of diamonds out of the country for them. MI6, after much pestering by Ransome, signed him up – but it's hard to make out whether he was spying on the Russians for the Brits, the Brits for the Russians, or a bit of both.

He was a weak, prickly and unhappy man. IF NOT DUFFERS WONT DROWN will have had a slightly sour resonance for a writer who recalled in his autobiography his father's attempt to teach him to swim by throwing him off a boat (sink or swim? Arthur sank). 'I was a disappointment to my father in many ways,' he wrote.* That disappointment calcified when Professor Ransome died when his eldest son was just thirteen. Commander Walker – trusting, authoritative, absent – became an idealised version of his father, just as the capable and manly John became an idealised version of the younger Ransome himself, who had

---

* Rupert Hart-Davis (ed.), *The Autobiography of Arthur Ransome*.

been homesick, short-sighted, academically inept and much bullied at school.

In young manhood, Ransome was an ardent but scattergun suitor – he proposed to practically every girl he knew until one, seemingly much to his surprise, said yes. His marriage in 1909, blessed on April Fool's Day, appears in the chapter of his autobiography titled 'Disasters'; his wife, Ivy, was highly strung and his mother-in-law, whom he ungallantly described as a 'blowfly' leaving 'poison germs wherever she set her foot', was even worse. The man who, in Ian Jack's words, 'gave England its jolliest idea of Utopia'*, fled his marriage into an affair with Leon Trotsky's secretary Evgenia Shelepina – who only after a protracted and painful divorce became his second wife.

Evgenia treated him better than Ivy, but she was a bossy soul and nicknamed him 'Charlie' because he walked like Charlie Chaplin when his haemorrhoids were bad. She's thought by some, indeed, to have been responsible for the premature end of his career, when she gave him some rather direct feedback on the eleventh book in the series, *The Picts and the Martyrs* (1943): 'I finished reading your book and I think it is hopeless […] the book as a whole is dead […] pale imitations of something that happened many times before […] imitation and rehash […] even your faithful readers […] would find it dull'. Her complaint was that 'if the Swallows were not allowed to grow up, if they are put into the same background with the same means of enjoying themselves as they have done holidays after holidays – they can't help repeating themselves.'† Which is, of course, exactly to miss the point. Like Carroll and so many others before him, Ransome was seeking to capture something out of time. That jolly utopia was a refuge from adult life, not a stepping-stone towards it.

---

* Cover quote for Roland Chambers, *The Last Englishman: The Double Life of Arthur Ransome* (Faber & Faber, 2009).

† Letter to Ransome, August 1942, quoted in Chambers, *The Last Englishman*.

Ladies First

P.L. TRAVERS · NOEL STREATFEILD

Mary Poppins; Mary Poppins Comes Back;
Mary Poppins Opens the Door; Mary Poppins
in the Park; Ballet Shoes; Tennis Shoes

F OR MOST OF BRITISH HISTORY, MIDDLE-CLASS CHIL-
dren were both the protagonists and the audience for
children's stories – and for most of British history, the experience of childhood was mediated by servants: nannies, governesses,
nurses or, for colonial children, ayahs. The relationships between
middle-class parents and their children would be remoter than the
day-to-day interactions with Nurse or Nanny (and, not long after,
with teachers at boarding schools). That is reflected in the stories.

Even when families find themselves in radically straitened circumstances – as at the beginning of *The Railway Children* – they
still have *help*. Even the hapless Darlings, in *Peter Pan*, have a
nanny, though it's a giant dog rather than a human. One way of
solving the old problem of getting the parents out of the way was
not to have them in the way in the first place. P.L. Travers's *Mary
Poppins* stories are, depending on how you read them, either the
high-water mark or the last gasp of a tradition in which the help
play an outsize role in the childhoods of their protagonists.

Here's yet another indictment to add to the charge sheet of
children's classics that have been rendered by Walt Disney. I use
'rendered' in the architectural sense: their original facades have been
slathered in something like a pink concrete meringue, which needs

chipping off before we can see them properly. Even the author, in this case, objected to Disney's 1964 musical comedy treatment so strenuously that it took decades, and much cautious wooing, before she allowed Cameron Mackintosh to turn it into a stage musical. She only gave permission in the first place because she was short of cash and Walt Disney very much wasn't. She loathed the use of animation sequences (it's reported that at the after-party for the premiere she said: 'Well. The first thing that has to go is the animation sequence,' and Walt answered: 'Pamela, the ship has sailed'), and she disapproved of the soft-centred and twinkly version of her otherworldly protagonist.

The Mary Poppins of the books may be a good fairy, but she's no Julie Andrews. She is neither warm nor maternal, nor in any obvious way obliging. She's comically vain, shockingly snobbish, and in a permanent bad temper. That adds a sweet-sour savour to the magical adventures in which she embroils her charges. One of the running jokes is that she can't pass a shop window without stopping to admire herself, and when she passes a tobacconist whose frontage is so angled as to afford three reflections at once she's positively made up:

Mary Poppins sighed with pleasure, however, when she saw three of herself, each wearing a blue coat with silver buttons and a blue hat to match. She thought it was such a lovely sight that she wished there had been a dozen of her or even thirty. The more Mary Poppinses the better.

And the gaslighting. My god, the gaslighting! The formula for the books is that each chapter recounts a self-contained episode – the children will attend a circus performance for the heavenly constellations, mingle with whales and starfish at an undersea drinks party, whoosh round the world with a magic compass, fly through the air tethered to magic balloons or riding giant peppermint candy-cane horses, spend an afternoon eating a cream tea upside-down on the ceiling, or some such random nonsense. At bedtime, the children will make some reference to their fantastical adventure, and Mary will outright deny it happened, and do so with considerable indignation.

When Michael innocently mentions her arrival on a kite-string near the beginning of the second in the trilogy, *Mary Poppins Comes Back* (1935), her reaction is typical:

> Mary Poppins stared at him. He could not tell if she was more astonished than angry, but she looked as if she was both. And her voice when she spoke was worse than her look. 'Did I understand you to say that—' she repeated the words slowly, between her teeth – 'that I came down from somewhere on the end of a string?' 'But you did!' faltered Michael. 'Today. Out of a cloud. We saw you!' 'On the end of a string. Like a Monkey or a Spinning-Top? Me, Michael Banks?' Mary Poppins, in her fury, seemed to have grown to twice her usual size. She hovered over him in her nightgown, huge and angry, waiting for him to reply.

She is the cause of episodes of great joy and excitement – 'Oh! Oh! Oh! What a *delicious* feeling!' – but she utterly refuses to acknowledge as much. Hers is a very peculiar, very closeted and oblique form of love and affection; and, indeed, it's sometimes hard to see why everyone professes to adore her. She's a guide, though, to something that looks a bit like a multiverse: an austere and capricious god with a parrot-handled brolly.

The stereotypical Englishness of the setting was itself part of the fantasy. P.L. Travers (1899–1996) was born Helen Lyndon Goff and grew up in Australia, not coming to London (where she was to live the rest of her life) until she was twenty-five. She was born into middle-class affluence, but her Irish-born father's alcoholism sent the family fortunes in a series of decreasing circles. Lyndon (as she was known; nobody ever called her Helen) adored him, but was terrified by his drunken rages. He was a bank clerk who failed downward and died when Lyndon was just seven, leaving her mother and baby sister all but destitute.

The young Lyndon was an eccentric little thing. She coped with loneliness, as her biographer reports, by pretending to be a chicken: 'For most of her childhood, Lyndon was absorbed by the experience of being a bird, brooding, busy, purposeful. She sat for hours, her arms clasped tightly around her body. "She can't come in, she's laying," her family and friends would say.'*

That loneliness, that desire to be someone (or something) other, stayed with her. She romanticised her father and his Irish background, protesting that she was only Australian by accident. As a young woman she initially embarked on a career as an actress, a career of pretending, though her greatest transformation was into a writer, another alter ego. The pen-name Lyndon chose, Pamela Lyndon Travers, took her father's Christian name as the surname. Under that name she was to dream up – in George Banks – a fictional father who was stable, reliable, and unfailing in his kindness. Into Mary Poppins went a mix of her mother's sayings and of the character of her forceful and eccentric Great-Aunt Ellie, with whom the young Lyndon had frequently been sent to stay.

Speaking to an interviewer in 1965, she said that her fantastical stories had sadness at their root: 'the cup of sorrow is always full. For a grown-up it's a flagon, for the child, it's a thimble, but it's never less than full [...] We are all looking for magic. We all need to feel we are under a spell and one day a wand will be waved and the princes that we truly feel ourselves to be will start forth at last from the tattered shapeless smocks.'† Her fears and hopes never left her. As an adult she was cautious about money, intensely private, anxious and hypochondriacal. Magical thinking – she was in adult

---

*   Valerie Lawson, *Mary Poppins, She Wrote*.
†   Interview with Boston radio station, quoted in Lawson, *Mary Poppins, She Wrote*.

life a disciple of Jung and Gurdjieff – goes through the children's books she wrote with a special plangency. Mary Poppins may have been stern, but she was undoubtedly a guardian angel of the sort that Helen Lyndon Goff never had.

The eponymous first book was published in 1934, and the final *Mary Poppins* stories came out more than half a century later, in 1988. Mary does not move with the times, though. Indeed, it's an open question how with the times she was even on first publication. Its incidental cast of match-sellers and sooty-handed chimney-sweeps, its courtly world of umbrellas and perambulators, will have been starting to date even by the mid-thirties. The vibe is Edwardian – which is when the film version was set – or even late Victorian. The *Mary Poppins* stories take place in a world in which the Great War has not happened.

Mary Poppins comes to 17 Cherry Tree Lane three times, each visit being described by one of the books in the original trilogy, *Mary Poppins* (1934), *Mary Poppins Comes Back* (1935) and *Mary Poppins Opens the Door* (1943). The subsequent volumes of stories all describe previously untold episodes from her three visits because, as Travers wrote in a preface to *Mary Poppins in the Park* (1952): 'She cannot for ever arrive and depart. And, apart from that, it should be remembered that three is a lucky number.' There's a mythological integrity to be respected – and the books do return to the monitory theme that nothing, and especially not childhood, lasts for ever.

Each time her arrival is unexpected and her departure unheralded. Each time she has her parrot-handled umbrella tucked neatly under her arm, produces her personal effects from an empty carpet bag, and takes over the running of everything. Her origins and her inner life are as unknowable as those of the gods of myth. She is a unique figure – 'A wonder. An Absolute, Marvellous, Wonderful Wonder!'; 'different… the Great Exception' – and she is recognised and respected by the whole of creation, up to and including the sun, the wind, the quasi-biblical figures who bring spring about by painting the trees, and the houses on the street (which are also intermittently seen to be conscious).

There's more going on here than just a wildly scattershot magical cosmology. Travers seems to me to dramatise the social anxiety of an interwar period in which – class barriers having been eroded in the trenches and traditional gender roles too having been disrupted, with men away at war – traditional structures are feared to be crumbling.

Mary Poppins (she's almost always given her full name in the stories) turns the employer–servant relationship upside down. She arrives when she wants to (blown up to the front door by the wind, in the first book; later descending from the heavens at the end of a kite-string or out of the spark from a firework) and chides Mrs Banks for her gaucheness in asking for a reference. When Mrs Banks tells her she'll get every third Thursday off from two till five, she replies sternly:

> 'The best people, ma'am,' she said, 'give every second Thursday, and one till six. And those I shall take or–' Mary Poppins paused, and Mrs Banks knew what the pause meant. It meant that if she didn't get what she wanted Mary Poppins would not stay. 'Very well, very well,' said Mrs Banks hurriedly, though she wished Mary Poppins did not know so very much more about the best people than she did herself.

She leaves, too, without notice, when she damn well pleases. She does the family good – in fact, it's the collapse of order in the household that brings her back each time – but she knows better than her employers what's needed as well as what's socially respectable. She never asks permission and never explains herself. And her effect on the family is not, to put it mildly, to reassure:

> 'She makes me feel small and silly, as though I were a little girl again. And I'm not!' Mrs Banks tossed her head and flicked a

speck of dust from the Spotted Cow on the mantelpiece. 'I'm a very important person and the Mother of five children. She forgets that!' And she went on with her work, thinking out all the things she would like to say to Mary Poppins, but knowing all the time that she would never dare.

There's an obvious debt to J.M. Barrie in *Mary Poppins*. Like that of Barrie's Darlings, here is a shabby-genteel London household in which the adults aren't very good at being adults, and everything is prone to going to hell in a handcart without outside help. The breadwinner is Mr Banks:

> Now, the City was a place where Mr Banks went every day – except Sundays, of course, and Bank Holidays – and while he was there he sat on a large chair in front of a large desk and made money. All day long he worked, cutting out pennies and shillings and half-crowns and threepenny-bits.

But as we discover he still lives in mortal fear of his childhood governess Miss Andrew ('the Holy Terror'), he's frequently threatening to run away from his own life to sail the high seas or emigrate, and when the idle and hopeless manservant Robertson Ay absent-mindedly boot-blacks his hat, or gives him one black shoe and one brown, he huffs and puffs about it but doesn't have the backbone to complain, still less carry through his threat of sacking the man. Just as Mrs Banks is bullied by Mary Poppins, the family's social insecurities are pointed up by Miss Andrew, who on arrival tut-tuts about the peeling paint, the untidy garden, the dirty front door and smudged steps: 'Mrs Banks bit her lip. Miss Andrew was turning her lovely, comfortable house into something mean and shabby, and it made her feel very unhappy.'

Mary Poppins's battle with Miss Andrew has something of the character of a turf-war, then, rather than a simple goodie-versus-baddie face-off. Miss Andrew – in whom, I fancy, we can detect a prototype of Roald Dahl's Trunchbull – is the wrong sort of bossy and bad-tempered nanny, and Mary Poppins is the right sort.

If P.L. Travers sought in some sense to avert our eyes from the crumbling certainties of interwar society, Noel Streatfeild's unusual *Ballet Shoes: A Story of Three Children on the Stage* (1936) looked at them more directly. *Ballet Shoes* is about a household without men. It's about an unconventional, non-nuclear, blended family. Its three girl protagonists Pauline, Petrova and Posy are orphans, acquired in a series of unlikely circumstances and sent home in the opening pages by the eccentric, one-legged Great-Uncle Matthew to be brought up in his roomy house in the Cromwell Road by his adult great-niece Sylvia, also orphaned, and her old nurse Nana. The sort-of-paterfamilias, 'Gum' (as Great-Uncle Matthew is known) is absent for the main part of the book, roaming the world on fossil-hunting expeditions (his mania for palaeontology is reflected in the girls' elective surname, Fossil) and returning only as a final-act *deus ex machina*. Gum is, like Mr Banks, a child-adult.

This set-up is suggestive. It allows the book to be directed squarely at a female readership, and to foreground the three girls' agency in the world. But, written as it was by an author who was twenty when the Great War broke out, it also perhaps has an echo of the real experience for many households of the post-war shortage of men. The Fossils' existence is precarious. 'Garnie' – as the girls' guardian Sylvia is known – has to take in lodgers, who become mentors to the girls. As the story progresses and, with the money running out, Gum shows no signs of returning from his travels, she even contemplates selling the house. The same social anxieties present in *Mary Poppins* are present here. Even as money grows tighter, there are a cook and a nurse at Cromwell Road – and Nana, though without quite the hauteur of Mary Poppins, bosses her employer, insisting from time to time that Gum get rid of some of his fossils, and getting her way.

The three girls attend stage school. Pauline (the pretty one) starts to flourish as an actor and the youngest, Posy, becomes a prodigious ballet dancer; while dark, tomboyish Petrova – even as she takes acting roles in her sister's shadow – moonlights as a car mechanic and dreams of becoming a pilot. There's a wan line of humour, drawn you'd have to think from experience, about the indignities of a second-rank acting career:

> That Christmas, Pauline was engaged for the Fairy Godmother in a pantomime of 'Cinderella', and Petrova was one of twenty-four jumping beans, who were to do speciality dances in 'Jack and the Beanstalk' in a theatre in the suburbs.

Far from being a weightless fantasy of artistic fulfilment, *Ballet Shoes* is deeply interested in the nitty-gritty of theatrical practice (Streatfeild herself worked for a decade as an actress), and it's deeply interested in money: how it's saved, how it's spent, how it's managed.

These aren't girls living out a Ballerina Barbie dream. Even as their sisterly affection and occasional bickering is traced with a keen psychological touch, they are adolescents with careers: jostling for roles, helping to support the household, even pawning possessions to pay for audition frocks. Here, amid the pertly surreal comedy of Great-Uncle Matthew's unworldliness and monomania (Gum seems to be a cross between Doctor Dolittle and Susan Cooper's Merriman Lyon), is a streak of realism and a documentary view of the hazy border between childhood and adulthood.

When Pauline is engaged for a role before the age of majority (a child was allowed on the stage from her twelfth birthday), she has to get a licence from the council to perform. The provisions of the Children Act are starting to trickle, visibly, into the literature of childhood:

> Sylvia obtained from the Education Officer's department of the County Hall a copy of the London County Council's rules for

children employed in the entertainment industries. They were all good, and framed to look after the employed child's health and well-being.

The law demands that parents or guardians lodge a proportion of child actors' take-home pay in a Post Office savings account but, when at the age of fourteen Pauline decides that she wants to keep more to help the family, she wins the argument:

'I'm not putting any more in the post office.'

Sylvia, Petrova, and Posy stared at her.

'A child,' Posy recited, 'has-to-put-at-least-one-third-of-its-earnings-in-the-savings-bank, or-as-much-more-as-may-be-directed-by-its-parents-or-guardian. This-is-the-law. I learnt that in French with Madame Moulin, I forget what the French was, but that was what it meant in English.'

Pauline looked braver than she felt. 'It's quite right. That is the law; but I'm not a child. I've just had my fourteenth birthday. The law lets me work; I don't need a licence, and I can do what I like with my own money.'

The three girls have more than just survival in mind, though. From their early years, they are in the habit of swearing a solemn vow together every time one of them has a birthday:

'We three Fossils vow to try and put our name into History books because it's our very own and nobody can say it's because of our Grandfathers.'

The Fossil girls are presented as female role-models; not princesses, not appendages or helpmeets to boys. That's made explicit in the closing words of the book: '"I wonder" – Petrova looked up – "if other girls had to be one of us, which of us they'd choose to be?"' So it was to continue in Streatfeild's many subsequent books. *Ballet*

Shoes was followed up by *Tennis Shoes* (1937) – which also, bizarrely, includes a one-legged father figure – and their successors followed in a podiatric groove: *Theatre Shoes*, *Party Shoes*, *Dancing Shoes*, *Skating Shoes*, *Family Shoes*, *Traveling Shoes*. Here was a writer asking girls who they'd choose; or, you might say, in whose shoes they'd prefer to be.

In the Ruin of the Year

J.R.R. TOLKIEN ·
T.H. WHITE

The Hobbit; The Sword in the Stone;
The Queen of Air and Darkness;
The Ill-Made Knight;
The Candle in the Wind

I F THE BOOKS OF THE 1920S AND EARLY 1930S HAD over them the long shadow of a terrible war past, those that came towards the end of the 1930s slipped into the shadow of a war to come. It's widely noted that the experience of the Second World War lays its footprint firmly on the Middle-earth of *The Lord of the Rings* (1954–5), much of whose composition took place during the war years. *The Lord of the Rings* is tricky to fit into the story of children's literature, though: it both belongs, and it doesn't. Though it drew knowingly on a whole range of mythological predecessors, it did more than any other single book to create the magical fantasy genre as it now stands. Wizards, dragons, dwarves, elves and goblins: every children's book that contains them owes a debt to Tolkien. At the same time, with its thousand-plus-page heft and its intricately fastidious linguistic and political and mythological world-building, it is more likely to be found on the student than on the nursery bookshelf.

But that book's predecessor, *The Hobbit, or There and Back Again* (1937), is squarely a children's book – both simpler in language, lighter in theme and brisker in tone than what was to come.* It's also a book that insistently looks backwards. If the general movement of children's writing through the previous decades had been, at least on the surface of things, away from fairytales, Tolkien very knowingly set out to write a story that went back to those roots. It was a mythological quest narrative, with magical helpers and medieval military politics, monsters and mazes and dark, dark woods.

C.S. Lewis's stepson Douglas Gresham, talking about the Narnia stories, described the exchange between Lewis and his great friend Tolkien:

> They seem to have talked about the children's literature of the late 1940s and early 1950s with dismay, finding nothing that they would have enjoyed as children or even could enjoy as adults. The literature that children were being expected to read and enjoy at that time seemed to teach them things that sensible parents would rather their children did not learn – all about 'issues' and 'complexes' and such. High Adventure, Chivalry, Personal Responsibility, Personal Commitment, Duty, Honor, Courtesy, and Honesty all seemed to have been dismissed as out of date or passé. Jack and Tolkien both agreed that such qualities and virtues were essential to human civilization and decided that they themselves had better have a try at writing about them. So they did. [†]

---

* *The Hobbit* has a slightly complicated publication history. Rather than *The Lord of the Rings* being a sequel to *The Hobbit*, the first book was revised in later editions to become a prequel to *The Lord of the Rings*. Originally, the invisibility ring Bilbo filches from Gollum is just one more magical MacGuffin, and the story's most important treasure is the Arkenstone, the dwarven gem the adventurers retrieve from the dragon's hoard. Only in 1938, while embarking on what was to become *The Fellowship of the Ring*, did Tolkien realise what a big deal the One Ring needed to be in his novel-sequence. He went on to retcon Bilbo's encounter with Gollum to reflect its corrupting power: 'Thief! Thief, Thief, Baggins! We hates it, we hates it, we hates it forever!'
† In 'A Conversation with Douglas Gresham', in C.S. Lewis, *The Chronicles of Narnia* (HarperCollins, 1998).

Lewis had his try, as Gresham indicates, in the early 1950s, but for Tolkien the project began much earlier.

His starting point was the sentence that begins the book: 'In a hole in the ground there lived a hobbit.' Hobbits were an original contribution to fantasy literature's mythological bestiary* and described as follows:

> They are inclined to be fat in the stomach; they dress in bright colours (chiefly green and yellow); wear no shoes, because their feet grow natural leathery soles and thick warm brown hair like the stuff on their heads (which is curly); have long clever brown fingers, good-natured faces, and laugh deep fruity laughs (especially after dinner, which they have twice a day when they can get it).

In the story Tolkien tells, he gives his bestiary loving attention, filling it with wargs and spiders, dwarves and elves, talking eagles, shapeshifters and trolls. Goblins, for instance, nasty grabby little creatures, are evoked with a run of epistrophe – 'there were all the baggages and packages lying broken open, and being rummaged by goblins, and smelt by goblins, and fingered by goblins, and quarrelled over by goblins.' When they're annoyed, Tolkien relishes a Dr. Seuss burst of sound-effects: 'The yells and yammering, croaking, jibbering and jabbering; howls, growls and curses; shrieking and skriking, that followed were beyond description.' The narrative voice of *The Hobbit*, throughout, is tuned to be read aloud, full of such sound-effects and rhetorical patternings and peppered with conversational turns ('Now, you know enough to go on with. As I was saying...') or exclamations: 'Gandalf! If you had heard only a quarter of what I have heard about him...'

---

* The creators of the fantasy role-playing game *Dungeons & Dragons*, who ripped off all manner of Tolkieniana, including Ents and Balrogs, included hobbits in their universe as 'halflings' for legal reasons, but they are clearly hobbits.

Tolkien here, as seldom in *The Lord of the Rings*, doesn't mind being funny. Gandalf is described as having 'long bushy eyebrows that stuck out further than the brim of his shady hat', and the description of Bilbo's fright when Thorin blithely mentions that he expects some or all of the party 'may never return' is pure Looney Tunes: 'At *may never return* he began to feel a shriek coming up inside, and very soon it burst out like the whistle of an engine coming out of a tunnel.'

There are certain unexpected parallels, when you strip away their very different set-dressings, between *The Hobbit* and *The Wind in the Willows* (the Shire is another avatar of the Riverbank; while Mirkwood and the Wild Wood share an atmosphere of unknown perils) – above all, in their most characteristic tension, which is that between wanderlust and the call of the hearth. Bilbo Baggins is a hobbit divided, and the divide is in his very blood. As a Baggins, Bilbo is a pillar of the caricaturally conservative community of the Shire: 'people considered them very respectable, not only because most of them were rich, but also because they never had any adventures or did anything unexpected.' But, since *The Hobbit* is the story of how he 'had an adventure' and 'lost the neighbours' respect', there's a tearaway side to him too, which descends through his mother 'the famous Belladonna Took'. She hails from a branch of the tribe considered 'not entirely hobbitlike': 'once in a while members of the Took-clan would go and have adventures. They discreetly disappeared, and the family hushed it up.'

Much of the comedy of the early part of the book (it's quite some time before Bilbo embarks on his adventure) is in how the boisterous crowd of dwarves disturb the bourgeois proprieties of his home. 'Chip the glasses and crack the plates! Blunt the knives and bend the forks! That's what Bilbo Baggins hates – Smash the bottles and burn the corks!' they sing cheerily as they do the washing-up. Bilbo tries to be polite, but he is, in modern idiom, more than a bit triggered. There's an echo here, to my mind, of Beatrix Potter's home-invasion fantasy *The Tale of Mrs Tittlemouse*.

Yet as the story goes on, Took and Baggins wrestle for control of Bilbo's soul. He is, after all, expressly recruited to the adventuring party as a 'burglar' – anathema to law-abiding hobbit orthodoxy (and, we can notice, echo of the pretend-criminal games of pirates and bandits that are such a staple of the playground). When he later hears the dwarves singing, in this case about quests and treasure and their ancient homes rather than about washing-up,

> something Tookish woke up inside him, and he wished to go and see the great mountains, and hear the pine-trees and the waterfalls, and explore the caves, and wear a sword instead of a walking-stick.

As he approaches the end of his quest, 'I am afraid [Bilbo] was not thinking much of the job, but of what lay beyond the blue distance, the quiet Western Land and the Hill and his hobbit-hole under it.' With the hurly-burly done and the battle lost and won, 'The Tookish part was getting very tired, and the Baggins was daily getting stronger. "I wish now only to be in my own armchair!" he said.'

Doesn't that tension speak to one of the profoundest contradictions in childhood itself? Children want to grow up, and they want to remain children for ever. It's the paradox encapsulated in the fractal narrative of J.M. Barrie's 'tragic boy'. Children yearn to have independent agency in the world, to be brave and consequential and grown-up, to see excitements and novelties, and their literature offers them fantasies of doing so; but at the same time they are deeply conservative. They long for the familiar, the safe, the comprehensible: to return home triumphant and to find, like Max in *Where the Wild Things Are*, that 'his supper was waiting for him, and it was still hot'.

That journey, and the twin impulses that send its hero on it, is the matter of *The Hobbit*. Bilbo, like every mythological quest hero, travels out into the big world, undergoes trials and tests, meets helpers, acquires magical objects (the dagger Sting and the Ring), discovers qualities in himself that the instigator of his quest saw but he did not, and returns to the safety of home transformed. The journey he makes consists of a string of set-piece encounters and is full of folkloric motifs.

The party's very first encounter is with three trolls in a wood. With the dwarves captured, the trolls fall to arguing 'whether they should roast them slowly, or mince them fine and boil them, or just sit on them one by one and squash them into jelly'. Bilbo plays a Rumpelstiltskin-like riddle-game with Gollum for the ring. There are magical prohibitions. In Mirkwood, like so many places of magical peril, our heroes are warned not to leave the path; and when staying with the were-bear Beorn, they are told, 'you must not stray outside until the sun is up, at your peril'. Visions of three magical feasts, each bigger than the last, are what lure the travellers into danger. There's a black river of forgetting, which places one of the dwarves into a magical coma like a lotus-eater. Smaug, with a gap in his jewel-armoured belly under 'the hollow of the left breast', has an Achilles armpit.

Tolkien's evocation of the creatures and their environments is first rate – from the dank underground labyrinth of the goblins where he first encounters Gollum, via the hallucinatory menace of Mirkwood with its predatory spiders, to the echoing halls of the abandoned Dwarvish stronghold under the Lonely Mountain. The dreamlike quality of the progress through Mirkwood (in a story full of dreams and dreamlike states) is especially effective. When Bilbo stabs a giant spider: 'Then it went mad and leaped and danced and flung out its legs in horrible jerks, until he killed it with another stroke; and then he fell down and remembered nothing more for a long while.'

As the story progresses, the convivial narrative register of the opening sections starts to take on graver accents. 'There was little grass, and before long there was neither bush nor tree, and only broken and blackened stumps to speak of ones long vanished. They were come to the Desolation of the Dragon, and they were come at the waning of the year.' Tolkien is dipping, here, into the ornate registers of the Old Norse and Anglo-Saxon sagas that he draws on: 'A whirring noise was heard. A red light touched the points of standing rocks. The dragon came.'; 'The others remained with Dain, for Dain dealt his treasure well.'

Smaug with his pile of ancient treasure is a straight lift from *Beowulf* – and the third part of *Beowulf*, at that; the autumnal phase of the story when Beowulf is an old man and his heroic vigour is in eclipse. *The Hobbit* has a very Anglo-Saxon worldview – one in which the heroic age is already passing into legend and modern-day man (or hobbit) is left to walk in awe around its ruins. Gandalf explains that he discounted a full-frontal attack on the dragon:

> 'That would be no good,' said the wizard, 'not without a mighty Warrior, even a Hero. I tried to find one; but warriors are busy fighting one another in distant lands, and in this neighbourhood heroes are scarce, or simply not to be found. Swords in these parts are mostly blunt, and axes are used for trees, and shields as cradles or dish-covers; and dragons are comfortably far-off (and therefore legendary)...'

The epic register in *The Hobbit*, though present, is kept in balance with its hobbit-scale humour. Gandalf is as much twinkly surrogate grandparent as he is powerful arch-mage. Even Thorin's deathbed speech – in contrast to the grave sonorities of the Grey Havens chapter in *The Lord of the Rings* – is touchingly brisk and matter-of-fact.

> 'There is more in you of good than you know, child of the kindly West. Some courage and some wisdom, blended in measure. If more of us valued food and cheer and song above hoarded gold, it would be a merrier world. But sad or merry, I must leave it now. Farewell!' Then Bilbo turned away, and he went by himself, and sat alone wrapped in a blanket, and, whether you believe it or not, he wept until his eyes were red and his voice was hoarse. He was a kindly little soul.

That kindly little soul is returned, at last, to his hole in the ground with a reminder from Gandalf that he is marked out by no special providence. You could say that it's the acceptance of his non-heroism – the realisation that even if he's brave and good, he's not the centre of the story – that makes Bilbo an adult:

> 'You don't really suppose, do you, that all your adventures and escapes were managed by mere luck, just for your sole benefit? You are a very fine person, Mr. Baggins, and I am very fond of you; but you are only quite a little fellow in a wide world after all!'
>
> 'Thank goodness!' said Bilbo laughing, and handed him the tobacco-jar.

The very next year, 1938, saw another landmark in fantasy writing with the direct reworking of another ancient myth – one which gave it a pointedly contemporary resonance. T.H. White's *The Sword in the Stone* (1938) was the first in a four-book reimagining of Malory's medieval *Morte d'Arthur*, published in collected form in 1958 as *The Once and Future King*.* It's a quite dazzling tetralogy, and it does what myth does so well – adapts in the retelling to the times in which it's told. Its influence on subsequent fantasy writing has been huge. Ursula K. Le Guin said in a jacket blurb for a later edition: 'I have laughed at White's great Arthurian novel and cried over it and loved it all my life.'

It's a rich and eccentric piece of work: worldly, witty, wise, joyous, mournful, serious and flippant. It's a fairytale penetrated by intense psychological realism – indeed, by psychoanalytic insight. The first book, *The Sword in the Stone* (1938), narrates the story of Wart, an orphaned boy brought up at the Castle Sauvage in the affectionate care of Sir Ector and under the tuition of the magician

---

* A fifth book, *The Book of Merlyn*, written in 1941 but posthumously published in 1977, is often appended to the series.

Merlyn. Wart is destined to be squire to his adoptive brother Kay when the latter is a knight – but, of course, he is in fact the son of King Uther Pendragon and his destiny is to become King Arthur.* The book closes with his honouring the prophecy by drawing the titular sword from the stone, demonstrating his rightful claim to the throne.

White locates his Arthurian legends not in the Dark Ages but in a medieval version of England he calls 'Gramarye', in which Uther Pendragon led the Norman Conquest.† In a through-the-looking-glass piece of whimsy, the historical English kings are frequently referred to: in this universe they are mythological figures. The chronological setting is fudged a bit. An arch but moving meta-fictional touch at the end of the fourth book has the elderly King Arthur talk to a young pageboy called Tom, from Newbold Revel in Warwickshire. He charges him with keeping the candleflame of his story alive. Tom is of course, by implication, Thomas Malory.‡

On the face of it, *The Once and Future King* doesn't look much like a children's book at all. It contains incest, rape, adultery, mat-ricide, depression, mass murder, extremes of cruelty and violence, a handful of smutty jokes and a good deal of political and moral theory, and it's preoccupied for most of its course with the com-promises and regrets of age. Its author himself wrote to a friend in

---

*   Freud described the archetypal 'family romance', in which a child fantasises that he or she will turn out to be born to different, higher-status parents. Here, in outline, is a plot that runs through countless children's stories.

†   This is maybe a nod to the metafictional gleam of the novels: 'gramarye' is a medieval word meaning book-learning.

‡   In fact, Malory's identity remains obscure. The Newbold Revel man is only one of several candidates. In any case, this would place the action of White's story in the early fifteenth century; but elsewhere the narrator airily places the story 'in the twelfth century, or whenever it was', and at least on the face of it we're just a generation on from the Norman Conquest. So, as I say, a fudge. White was quite knowing about this, noting in a letter to a friend that Malory dressed the past in the armour of his own age and that 'We [i.e. White and Malory] care very little for exact dates.'

1938 (of the first book): 'It seems impossible to determine whether it is for grown-ups or children. It is more or less a kind of wish-fulfilment of things I should like to have happened to me when I was a boy.'[*]

That's shrewd. Terence Hanbury White (1906–1964) is both Wart and, in an idealised fantasy form of the schoolmaster he was when he wrote the book, Merlyn. Wart may be fatherless and motherless, but he has the sort of sublimely happy childhood that Tim White (he was christened Terence but his undergraduate nickname, after a chain of chemists called Timothy White, stuck) emphatically did not. We glimpse him and his adoptive brother Kay, at one point, chasing autumn leaves: 'For the mere sport of catching them, of shouting and laughing and feeling giddy as they looked up, and of darting about to trap the creatures, which were certainly alive in the cunning with which they slipped away, the two boys were prancing about like young fauns in the ruin of the year.'

Wart is loved. After he spends a night lost in the forest in the first book, trying to catch a goshawk that Kay has allowed to escape its rein, 'Sir Ector came bustling out with his greaves on back to front, and kissed the Wart on both cheeks. "Well, well, well," he exclaimed moistly. "Here we are again, hey? What the devil have we been doin', hey? Settin' the whole household upside down." But inside himself he was proud of the Wart for staying out after a hawk, and prouder still to see that he had got it'. At the end of that book, when the sword has been pulled from the stone and Wart's grand destiny becomes clear, there's a piercing moment when he sees Sir Ector.

> He saw that his dear guardian was looking quite old and powerless, and that he was kneeling down with difficulty on a gouty knee.

---

[*]　Letter to L.J. Potts, 14 January 1938, quoted in Sylvia Townsend Warner, *T.H. White: A Biography*.

'Sir,' said Sir Ector, without looking up, although he was speaking to his own boy.

'Please do not do this, father,' said the Wart, kneeling down also. 'Let me help you up, Sir Ector, because you are making me unhappy.'

Tim White had no Sir Ector. His father was an alcoholic and his mother was selfish, capricious, and glacially unfeeling towards the little boy. So White is Lancelot, too, a character when introducing whom he writes: 'It is fatally easy to make young children believe they are horrible.' The marriage broke up, acrimoniously, in White's adolescence: 'My parents loathed each other and were separated; divorced, when I was about fourteen or so,' he said flatly in a lecture in later life. 'This meant that my home and education collapsed around my ears, and ever since I have been arming myself against disaster.'*

That unloving mother appears barely transformed in the books as the Orcadian witch-queen Morgause, the mother of Wart/ Arthur's nemesis, his illegitimate son Mordred. Morgause doesn't get much screen-time, but she is a memorable monster. She does not love her boys, except capriciously – and they are twisted by their yearning for her approval. In one set-piece they kill a unicorn and profane its beauty in the vain hope of pleasing her: '[Gawaine] hated it for being dead, for having been beautiful, for making him feel a beast. He had loved it and helped to trap it, so now there was nothing to be done except to vent his shame and hatred of himself upon the corpse.'

White wrote of his mother in a diary entry after her death: 'Either there were the dreadful parental quarrels and spankings of me when I was tiny or there were excessive scenes of affection

---

* 'The Pleasure of Learning', lecture delivered in Troy, New York, 1963, quoted in Townsend Warner, *T.H. White: A Biography*.

during which she wooed me to love her – not her to love me. It was my love that she extracted, not hers that she gave.'* In *The Candle in the Wind,* White talks about Mordred's evil:

> It is the mother's not the lover's lust that rots the mind. It is that which condemns the tragic character to his walking death. It is Jocasta, not Juliet, who dwells in the inner chamber. It is Gertrude, not the silly Ophelia, who sends Hamlet to his madness.

White in adult life was a contradictory, fugitive, hard-to-know man. He tried on identities. His very sympathetic biographer Sylvia Townsend Warner wrote that 'every single person who talked to me about White had known a different White. I had a thousand incompatible Whites to put together.'† The abrupt swerves and shifts in his great work reflected the abrupt swerves and shifts in its author. He thirsted for practical knowledge – falconry, aviation, carpentry, painting, medieval Latin shorthand – and he wrote (in *The Sword in the Stone*): '"The best thing for being sad," replied Merlyn, beginning to puff and blow, "is to learn something. That is the only thing that never fails."'

White poured love into the natural world – especially his dog, Brownie. Under 'Recreations' in his *Who's Who* entry he wrote simply: 'Animals.' He struggled with drink, with his acknowledged but not acted-upon homosexuality,‡ and with deep sadomasochistic impulses that he attributed to being beaten at school. (There's

---

* Diary entry quoted in Townsend Warner, *T.H. White: A Biography.*

† Ibid.

‡ I should be less categorical. White considered himself homosexual and thought that doomed him to unhappiness. He tried and failed to court women, and in later life he was unrequitedly and secretly tormented by love for a boy his diaries called Zed. His agent and friend David Higham, though, thought Townsend Warner painted him as a tormented closet-case to fit her own agenda, going so far as to claim he had put her in touch with a female lover of White's whose evidence she ignored. Let's just leave it with the traditional 'he never married'.

a flick of this in the villainous Sir Turquine, who 'has sixty-four knights in prison, whom he has captured in single combat, and he spends the time beating them with thorns. If he captures you, he will beat you too, all naked.' Lancelot responds: 'He sounds an exciting man to fight.')

Townsend Warner concluded that he was driven by fear:

Fear of being afraid, of being a failure, of being trapped. He was afraid of death, afraid of the dark. He was afraid of his own proclivities which might be called vices: drink, boys, a latent sadism. Notably free from fearing God, he was basically afraid of the human race. His life was a running battle with these fears, which he fought with courage, levity, sardonic wit, and industry.[*]

Fear is there in the books, too. But it sneaks up slowly. *The Sword in the Stone*, the first one, is overwhelmingly a comic novel. The material it deals with doesn't come from Malory, and White has fantastic fun sending up chivalric convention. It contains some remarkable tonal switchbacks. White's easy lyricism is on show when, lost in the Forest Sauvage, Wart comes upon a knight errant:

There was a clearing in the forest, a wide sward of moonlit grass, and the white rays shone full upon the tree trunks on the opposite side. These trees were beeches, whose trunks are always more beautiful in a pearly light, and among the beeches there was the smallest movement and a silvery clink. Before the clink there were just the beeches, but immediately afterwards there was a knight in full armour, standing still and silent and unearthly, among the majestic trunks. [...] All was moonlit, all silver, too beautiful to describe.

---

[*]   Prologue to *The Book of Merlyn* (University of Texas Press, 1977).

But then when he addresses Sir Pellinore (for it is he), that is mer-
cilessly undercut:

> The ghost lifted up its visor, revealing two enormous eyes frosted
> like ice; exclaimed in an anxious voice, 'What, what?'; took off its
> eyes – which turned out to be horn-rimmed spectacles, fogged by
> being inside the helmet; tried to wipe them on the horse's mane –
> which only made them worse; lifted both hands above its head and
> tried to wipe them on its plume; dropped its lance; dropped the
> spectacles; got off the horse to search for them – the visor shutting
> in the process; lifted its visor; bent down for the spectacles; stood
> up again as the visor shut once more, and exclaimed in a plaintive
> voice, 'Oh, dear!'

Sir Pellinore is an absurd figure, in permanent unsuccessful search
for the 'Beast Glatisant' (a chimerical monster from Malory with
a leopard's body, snake's head, lion's legs, stag's feet and a tummy
that rumbles like the yapping of hounds in pursuit), as is his
family's destiny, but dreaming of a nice night in a feather bed.
When Sir Pellinore duels with another knight, in a roistering
comic set-piece, the tone is Tweedledum and Tweedledee by way
of Monty Python.

Wart's adventures in the first book – his education largely
consists of Merlyn changing him temporarily into an animal – are
broadly comic but the alterity of an animal view of the world is
breathtakingly well imagined. Here he is as an owl on the wing:

> It was curious, but he was not taking life seriously. He felt the castle
> walls streaking past him, and the ground and the moat swimming
> up. He kicked with his wings, and the ground sank again, like
> water in a leaking well. In a second that kick of his wings had lost
> its effect, and the ground was welling up. He kicked again. It was
> strange, going forward with the earth ebbing and flowing beneath
> him, in the utter silence of his down-fringed feathers.

Extraordinary that such passages can coexist with the knocka-bout comedy of Sir Pellinore (and, indeed, that Sir Pellinore can become a figure of such pathos in the later books). Those tonal variations, often paragraph by paragraph, are present throughout the tetralogy. In the second book* two knights try to cheer up the lovesick Sir Pellinore by disguising themselves as the Beast Glatisant, pantomime-horse-style, only for the real beast to show up and take an amorous fancy to them in the dark: 'Somethin' keeps bumpin' me behind.'

But the register describes a wider, slower arc towards seriousness. My sense is that White, having started the books as a mocking *jeu d'esprit* of urbane cynicism, got caught up in the stately tragedy of his source material. We follow the rise and collapse of Arthur's court and of his ideals, and trace the exquisitely tortured triangular relationship between Arthur, Lancelot and Guenever.

The final book, *The Candle in the Wind*, sees the Round Table in ruins, and Arthur set against his best friend and his beloved wife not by personal enmity but by the laws that he takes kingship too seriously to ignore.

Arthur is, in that resonant phrase, the once and future king; and his childhood tutor Merlyn is a time-traveller of sorts. 'I unfortu-nately was born at the wrong end of Time,' he tells his protégé on their first meeting, 'and I have to live backwards from in front, while surrounded by a lot of people living forwards from behind. Some people call it having second sight.' The books, too, have a very strange relationship with time. Merlyn frequently refers to nineteenth- and twentieth-century figures. His collection of junk includes 'a complete set of cigarette cards depicting wild fowl by Peter Scott', and at one point he accidentally wizards a top hat out of thin air before crossly returning it. The book's similes gleefully

---

* Originally *The Witch in The Wood* (1939), but substantially revised and retitled as *The Queen of Air and Darkness* in the 1958 collected edition.

jump through time. Lancelot is 'a sort of Bradman, top of the batting averages'; two jousting knights clang together 'like a motor omnibus in collision with a smithy'; ducks fly through the air 'looking like champagne bottles balanced on a nimbus of wings'.

The books' implied audience, the contract between speaker and hearer, is absolutely fixed in the early twentieth century. That isn't just an engine of their humour. That they were published in the run-up to and during the first years of the Second World War inflects them deeply. The large political preoccupation of Arthur's kingship is how you deal with the human impulse to violence. In the early years of his reign, Arthur discards the established rules to wage 'total war' – 'Arthur began with an atrocity and continued with other atrocities' – in order to establish peace. This strategy's resonance, with the Great War still in recent memory, will not have escaped White's early readers. But Arthur comes to think 'the whole thing was a mistake [...] It was a mistake because the Table itself was founded on force. Right must be established by right: it can't be established by Force Majeure.'

It's Arthur's heroic attempt to codify an abstract system of justice, and the way that conflicts with his human loyalties, which shapes his personal tragedy. 'The King likes Lancelot so much that he is forced to be unfair to him – for fear of being unfair to other people.' As he's to discover, the letter killeth while the spirit giveth life. The book's political and human themes dovetail quite marvellously.

Merlyn's second sight means the story's relevance to the European situation at the time of its writing doesn't even have to rest on the level of allegory. Merlyn at one point refers darkly to 'an Austrian who invented a new way of life and convinced himself that he was the chap to make it work. He tried to impose his reformation by the sword, and plunged the civilized world into misery and chaos.' When Arthur's bitter bastard son Mordred rises to power leading a 'popular party' in the final book he does so as a Nazi in all but name, his black-uniformed followers calling themselves Thrashers and bearing the emblem of 'a scarlet fist clenching a whip'.

As Arthur heads towards his final encounter with Mordred – the novel leaves him on the eve of that encounter – he is beset by doubts. The whole edifice of his project is built on the idea that man is innately good. What if he isn't? A passage that comes to resonate through the whole novel is one from the first book, in which Wart (as he then is) spends time transformed into an ant and witnesses the ants going to war against a neighbouring colony:

Later in the afternoon a scouting ant wandered across the rush bridge which Merlyn had commanded him to make. It was an ant of exactly the same species, but it came from the other nest. It was met by one of the scavenging ants and murdered.

The broadcasts changed after this news had been reported – or rather, they changed as soon as it had been discovered by spies that the other nest had a good store of seeds.

Mammy – mammy – mammy gave place to *Antland, Antland Over All*, and the stream of orders were discontinued in favour of lectures about war, patriotism or the economic situation. The fruity voice said that their beloved country was being encircled by a horde of filthy Other-nesters – at which the wireless chorus sang:

When other blood spurts from the knife,
Then everything is fine.

White himself, when war came, sat it out in Ireland writing his book. A diary entry from September 1939 opened: 'I suspect that this war may be the end of such civilization as I am accustomed to. I don't mind much.'

VII

LASHINGS AND LASHINGS

Enid Blyton · Alison Uttley ·
Philippa Pearce · Lucy M. Boston · C.S. Lewis ·
Tove Jansson · Astrid Lindgren

POST-WAR WRITERS

I F THE GREAT WAR SCARRED THE NATIONAL PSYCHE — with the countless young men who never came home or came home irrevocably damaged – the Second World War too left its marks. More than the first war, it marked not just the adults but the children who lived through it. The experience of aerial bombardment, and the realistic fear of invasion, meant that the violence wasn't over there, but over here. Families had lived through blackouts, become familiar with the close confines of Anderson shelters, jostled with strangers as they sheltered in tube stations from the bombs. In ruined cities, children made improvised playgrounds of bomb craters.

The evacuation of children to the countryside began on the day Germany invaded Poland in 1939. One and a half million children were displaced in three days. They called it 'Operation Pied Piper.' (Did nobody remember that in Robert Browning's poem the piper was leading children into danger, not out of it?) Families were separated. New connections formed where the evacuee children were taken in by strangers, and new worlds opened up to the evacuees: town mice found themselves amid country mice, and the children of the poor fell, often, on the charity of the more prosperous.

But there was also mistrust, misunderstanding, homesickness and the pain of separation. When the feared bombing raids didn't at first materialise, around half that first wave of evacuees were brought home by their anxious parents just a few months after leaving, in the face of government advice to leave them where they were. Further waves of evacuations followed in 1940 when the bombing raids started and when there were fears of a German naval invasion.

It need scarcely be said that as the war came to an end, and the liberating armies crossing Europe discovered the death camps, there came a general reappraisal in the adult world of what modern civilisation meant, if anything. The Holocaust doesn't make its way into children's stories directly – hard to see how it could – though Anne Frank's *The Diary of a Young Girl*, published in the original Dutch in 1947, went into English in 1952. It shadows, you could say, the children's stories of the era.

The post-war years were far from triumphal. Rationing in the UK went on till 1954: fresh eggs, meat and dairy were scarce. In his memoir *Miracles of Life* (2008), the writer J.G. Ballard described arriving in the UK from China in 1946:

> Looking at the English people around me, it was impossible to believe that they had won the war. They behaved like a defeated population. I wrote in *The Kindness of Women* that the English talked as if they had won the war, but acted as if they had lost it. They were clearly exhausted by the war, and expected little of the future. Everything was rationed – food, clothing, petrol – or simply unobtainable. […] More importantly, hope itself was rationed, and people's spirits were bent low.

The post-war decades saw the places in which children lived starting to change, too.* A million new houses, many of them prefabs, were built between 1945 and 1955. The 1946 New Towns Act paved the way for the birth of a whole series of new developments – Stevenage,

---

* I think it's in this context – make-do-and-mend, a sense of the instability of home – that we can consider the pint-sized Proudhonists of *The Borrowers* (1952), the first in Mary Norton's series about a family of tiny people who live in the walls of Victorian houses and 'borrow' from humans what they need to survive.

Crawley, Harlow, Welwyn Garden City, Cumbernauld in the mid-fifties and, in the late sixties, the gigantic Milton Keynes. Slum clearances and relocations were coming, and high-rises started to spring up. The divide between the propertied aristocracy and upper middle classes, and the urban or rural poor, was shifting. More and more people were living in places without a history. The grand country houses that had symbolised pre-war privilege and stability – and for which Evelyn Waugh's *Brideshead Revisited* (1945) articulated an elegiac longing – had been requisitioned during the war and were now handed back to their impoverished owners in a dilapidated state. The wrecking ball was coming for Toad Hall.

This long post-war rupture produced new forms and new story-telling possibilities – as well as new audiences. But it also produced a longing, if an equivocal longing, for connection with the past, with older forms of storytelling, and with something that would embed childhood in a history from which it must have felt like it had come unmoored.

An Englishman's Home

ENID BLYTON · ALISON UTTLEY · PHILIPPA
PEARCE · LUCY M. BOSTON

Child Whispers; The Famous Five;
The Secret Seven; Noddy; Malory Towers;
The Magic Faraway Tree; The Five Find-Outers;
The Naughtiest Girl in the School; The Secret
Island; The Little Black Doll; The Story of
My Life; Little Grey Rabbit; Tom's Midnight
Garden; The Children of Green Knowe

'WOULD YOU LIKE TO COME WITH ME AND VISIT A village so small that you will tower over the houses?' Enid Blyton asked her readers in 1950. 'Would you like to know what it would be like if you visited Fairyland, and felt like a giant, because everything was so tiny, and the people hardly came up to your ankles? Well, I live quite near to a little village like this – it is so close I can see it from my bedroom window. Shall I take you there?'

That is the promise of Enid Blyton's work – and it is a promise that made her the era-shaping figure of mid-century children's fiction. It's the promise of something entirely safe: a pretty little world, like a doll's house, where everything is under control. Not the haunted wood of folktale, but a carefully tended suburban garden. 'All my life I have loved a garden,' she wrote. 'It is said that one of the most characteristic things about the British people is their love of a garden, no matter how tiny, and we are supposed to have the loveliest gardens in all the world, small or large.'

There was a real model village, too. Blyton's home in Beaconsfield, where she lived for the last thirty years of her life, was right next door to the Model Village at Bekonscot, which had sprung up, aptly enough, in the back garden of an accountant in the late 1920s. It stands there to this day – a network of seven tiny villages, an acre and a half of 'immaculate gardens' and nearly ten miles of railway lines reproduced at a scale of one inch to one foot. 'Stuck in a 1930s time warp,' its website boasts today. 'See England how it used to be, and discover a wonderful little world tucked away from the hustle and bustle of everyday life.'* The future Queen Elizabeth II visited Bekonscot in 1934, when she was eight years old.

Though her first book, *Child Whispers*, was published in 1922 (the same year as *Ulysses* and *The Waste Land*), it was in the years during and after the Second World War that Blyton really got going – the point at which, you could say, her model-village view of the world answered a thirst in a population for the illusion of order and a triumphal view of Englishness. Her earliest work was full of elves and pixies and brownies, coasting in the last of the slipstream of the post-*Peter Pan* vogue for fairies. The notorious Cottingley Fairies – in 1917 two little girls claimed to have photo-graphed fairies dancing on flowers at the bottom of their garden, and Arthur Conan Doyle was only one of those who swallowed the hoax whole – were still in memory.

But she worked, furiously, towards what was to make her suc-cessful. The first in her *Naughtiest Girl* series, *The Naughtiest Girl in the School*, was published in 1940. The first in her *St Clare's* school series was 1941. The first *Famous Five* book appeared in 1942. (1941 had seen the lesser-known squib *The Adventurous Four*, a try-out that fizzled.) *The Magic Faraway Tree* came in 1943, as did the first of her *Five Find-Outers* stories. 1946 was the first *Malory Towers*. The *Secret Seven* series got going in 1949 as, to the eternal regret of

---

* https://www.bekonscot.co.uk.

many readers, did the wretched *Noddy* books – about the adventures in Toyland (itself modelled on Bekonscot) of the eponymous bell-hatted buffoon and his asinine best friend Big Ears.

Perhaps the funniest passage in Sue Townsend's *The Secret Diary of Adrian Mole Aged 13¾* (1982) is also a telling one as to Enid Blyton's place in the culture even a decade and a half after her death. Townsend's young protagonist hopes to signal his passage to moody adolescence by slapping black paint over the Noddy wallpaper in his childhood bedroom. No matter how many times he paints over them, the bright yellow bell on Noddy's hat still shows through: 'Went over hat bells with black felt-tip pen, did 69 tonight, only 124 to go.'*

Blyton was voracious. She tried everything. As early as 1924, she confided to her workbook after meeting one publisher: 'It's definitely decided I'm to do 36 books for them!' She created franchise after franchise. She was the first children's writer who, during her own lifetime, was a brand. The bibliography of her works numbers well over 700 volumes, and in her 1950s heyday she was banging out several dozen books a year. She has sold more than 600 million books, at the last count. She described her creative process as something like automatic writing: 'The story comes out complete and whole from beginning to end. I do not have to stop and think for one moment.' You don't so much analyse Enid Blyton's work as weigh it.

The forgotten ones seem to tell the story of her popularity as much as do those that remain in print. There were great series of *Enid Blyton Annuals*, *Enid Blyton's Bedside Books*, *The Enid Blyton Holiday Book*, *Enid Blyton's Jolly Story Book*, *Enid Blyton's Sunny Stories*, *Enid Blyton's Treasury*, *My First Enid Blyton Book*, *My Second Enid Blyton Book*, and so on. She even edited – which points to her

---

* Sue Townsend, *The Secret Diary of Adrian Mole, Aged 13¾* (Methuen, 1982).

status as the metropolitan power in middle-class children's writing – a series of *Daily Mail* annuals for children. She marked her territory with self-branded versions of established stories, retelling the Brer Rabbit story and La Fontaine's fables, and producing *Tales of the Ancient Greeks and Persians*, *Tales of the Romans*, *The Knights of the Round Table*, *Tales from the Arabian Nights*, *The Adventures of Odysseus*... even, which some will think a bit of a cheek, *Enid Blyton Bible Stories*.

She treated her writing as an industry, consciously adapting popular genres in adult fiction to juvenile audiences: the *Famous Five* stories were thrillers for kids; *The Secret Seven* and the *Find-Outers* were essentially golden-age crime capers. Here too were animal stories after Potter or Sewell, circus stories, desert-island Robinsonades (*The Secret Island*), myths and fairytales, fantasy quests, and school-hols adventures after the pattern of Arthur Ransome. When Blyton embarked on her *Malory Towers* series about high-spirited boarding-school girls, for instance, she was adding the merest dribble to a great torrent of popular children's literature in the boarding-school genre; catching it, as it happens, as post-war social change saw its popularity start to fade away. Originality wasn't the point: and why, in a literary tradition that recycles and adapts ceaselessly, does it need to be?

Blyton didn't just take advantage of the panoply of children's periodicals that offered publishing outlets: from 1953 onwards she published her own, *Enid Blyton's Magazine*. Throughout her life, she was attentive to her relationship with her child readers, answering fan-mail, encouraging them to join clubs (the Famous Five Club had 30,000 members within a year of its inception) and cultivating her family of what she called in the dedication to her memoir 'my friends, the children, everywhere' – as we'll see, somewhat to the exclusion of her own real-life children. She was at the peak of her powers just as children's publishing – the post-war baby-boom having produced a welcome bump in new readers – was coming into its own maturity.

In 1962 a publishers' association called the Children's Book Circle was founded (it survives to this day), and by the 1970s every mainstream publisher in the UK had a children's division. The expansion of children's publishing in the decades after the war wasn't a steady rise so much as an explosion. The influential editor Kaye Webb (1914–1996), who helmed Penguin's Puffin imprint from 1961 to 1979, deserves mention here as its presiding genius. She increased Puffin's list more than twenty-fold in under a decade, introduced the promotional Puffin Club in 1967 and edited its quarterly newsletter *Puffin Post*.

Blyton wasn't an ambitious stylist, or a stylist at all. She dismissed 'highbrow culture' early on, with excellent high-handedness, as 'doleful, morbid or sad': 'I'm young and normal, and I prefer something more wholesome.' Her main stylistic distinction is the excitable use of exclamation marks and a weakness for bolt-on adverbial qualifiers: 'said her aunt, laughing'; 'said George, going rather red'; '"Woof," said Tim, in his deep voice.' She insists, sometimes in the narrative itself, and sometimes in the dialogue, on reminding the reader that something exciting has happened, noting that something exciting is happening, or preparing the reader for something exciting to happen.

> The girls laughed. They felt happy and excited. Holidays were fun. Going back to Kirrin was lovely. Tomorrow the boys would come – and then Christmas would be there!

But as much as that may seem bland or annoying to the adult reader, it was absolutely part of Blyton's design. Unlike so many of the more sophisticated children's stories we've touched on in previous chapters – books that are at least half designed to enchant the grown-ups – Blyton was interested in speaking very directly, and in very simple language, to children themselves. Short sentences, words of one or two syllables, excitable prose, snappy pacing and fast-moving plots were all. The adult gatekeepers, meanwhile, would be satisfied by the certain knowledge that there was nothing in these books to challenge or disturb. Blyton was safe; there wasn't a hint of sex and violence in her books.

Nevertheless, even in her lifetime her work attracted the disapproval of high-minded librarians who imagined that its simplicity and its popularity were rotting young minds. Her literary agent, George Greenfield, observed in 1970 that 'It is easy to sneer at the Enid Blyton stories with their soft padded bourgeois backgrounds and their simple vocabulary'*. The counter-argument – that she 'got children reading' – is the same one we see mounted today against those who affect to disapprove of the success of J.K. Rowling.

She wasn't, despite what her critics thought, writing for children just as entertainment: she came at her work from a background in education. Her first successes as she started to build her career in the 1920s were while she was working as a teacher in Surbiton, and she was trained in the 'Froebel system' – which emphasised play, and time in nature, as 'the highest expression of human development in childhood'. At the time there were a number of periodicals, called things like the *Teacher's Times* and the *Schoolmistress*, which carried articles about the latest ideas in education and pedagogy alongside poems and stories for children, intended for classroom use.

In 1923, having contributed occasional pieces to *Teacher's World*, Enid snagged a regular column, which ran for four years. In 1926, *Teacher's World* sent her to interview A.A. Milne and (of course) Christopher Robin. She presented Christopher Robin with a copy of her *Book of Bunnies*. Her presence in *Teacher's World* was a networking opportunity, a chance to hone her craft, a chance to think in public about education and childhood – and a venue for self-invention.

---

* George Greenfield, 'Enid Blyton: Phenomenon or South Sea Bubble? Phenomenon', *Books 2*, Winter 1970.

Blyton went on in her writing to present a model-village version of England: one in which the wartime and post-war privations that afflicted almost every child in the country were absent, in which poverty and urban decay were invisible, and good health and high spirits came as standard. For much if not most of her audience, that was not the world they saw around them. Blyton, then, set out – as if her name itself was a hopeful play on words – to reinvent Blighty.

The world of her most successful books is a world of peppy, white, middle-class children roaming an idealised Home Counties countryside in endless school holidays or getting up to hijinks in boarding schools during term-time. The feasts and picnics and cream teas for which she is now so mocked, with their 'lashings and lashings of ginger beer', were a potent fantasy. Hers is a world in which everything turns out all right in the end. Blyton has become a byword for a particular rosy vision of post-war English childhood – one that existed more in the imagination than in reality. And it's a very partial, very insular, very little-England world. Over the years the overtly racist and xenophobic aspects of her work – the wicked golliwogs in Noddy; the 'ugly black face' of the doll in *The Little Black Doll* (1937) – have been noted and, in modern editions, expunged.

Hers was a deeply conservative vision. The Second World War had shaken Britain's social order and its secure sense of its own place and its own destiny in the world. Blyton's work sought to reassure. Its child protagonists had freedom of action, and sometimes they would be 'naughty', but they did so in a secure and orderly social framework. Blyton herself used the bully-pulpit of her celebrity, in the post-war years, to speak out against what she saw as the corruption of childhood and the degradation of society. She hopped on, and whipped up, moral panics against bad mothers, juvenile delinquents, the popularity of comic books and the wickedness of socialism.

In this context, incidentally, it seems a stretch to claim George, in the *Famous Five* books, as an *avant-la-lettre* trans character. 'I shall only answer if you call me George,' she says in the first book (and repeats with minor variations in the ones that follow), 'I hate being a girl. I won't be.' George may be what we'd now call gender-non-conforming, and Blyton would certainly have called a 'tomboy', but it seems highly unlikely, not to say anachronistic, to suppose that Blyton would have seen her as male. George's tomboyishness, as a defining character trait, quietly reinforces rather than subverts the normative world of the books.

Blyton herself worked to embody the stereotype of suburban middle-class respectability: first in 'Old Thatch', in the commuter town of Bourne End which was the model for the setting of her *Find-Outers* stories; and then as chatelaine, from 1938, of an eight-bedroom mock-Tudor mansion in Beaconsfield (named 'Green Hedges', after Blyton asked her child readers to vote on the name when she moved in). Her recreations were housewifely: playing golf and bridge, arranging flowers and planning menus. To produce books at the extraordinary rate she did, though, she had – as few of her readers now would – teams of servants to help. Her personal life, like her brand, was aggressively curated. She wasn't as innocent, or as conventional, as all that.

The real Enid Blyton was born in 1897 in a flat above a shop in East Dulwich, and not long after her birth the family moved to the lower-middle-class area of Beckenham, 'where their neighbours were a mixture of clerks, builders, cab drivers and fishmongers'.* They were a family on the rise: by the time of the 1911 census they were in a fancier street and had a live-in servant. By all accounts Enid adored her father Thomas, who kindled in her a love of reading and walks in nature. The thunderbolt came when Enid was just thirteen: Thomas abruptly abandoned his family to take up with another woman. Rather than sympathising with her unimaginative mother Theresa – whose preoccupations were housework and

---

*   Andrew Maunder, *Enid Blyton: A Literary Life*.

respectability, and who was so mortified by Thomas's departure she insisted that he was 'away on business' – Enid, angry and ambitious, took out her rage on her and withdrew emotionally. She left home at eighteen, lodging with a friend's aunt she called 'Mums' and determining to make her own way in the world. Her father died of a heart attack in 1920. The rift with her mother never healed. When Theresa died in 1950, Enid didn't bother going to the funeral.

Enid later expunged from the record, too, her first marriage – to a blue-eyed young publisher called Hugh Pollock, whom she met in January 1924 and whom she likened on first acquaintance to the Prince of Wales, telling her diary: 'I want him for mine.' She got him. Pollock, who was already married with two children, divorced his wife and the pair were married that summer. Theirs was a professional as well as a romantic partnership. Pollock's position at the publisher Newnes, where he also published Noel Streatfeild, is credited with helping Enid's career along – not least in launching her as the editor of (and sole contributor to) a new weekly publication, *Sunny Stories for Little Folks*. Their daughters Gillian and Imogen were born in 1931 and 1935.

That relationship foundered during the Second World War. Hugh, perhaps still carrying the trauma of the First World War service that had earned him a DSO, was sinking into alcoholism. Enid, by now thoroughly launched on the world, started an affair (not her first; at least one account of her life includes a lesbian fling with one of the children's nannies) in 1941 with a surgeon – a rather dull, squeaky-voiced fellow called Kenneth Darrell Waters. When Hugh learned of the affair, he threatened to divorce her. Enid persuaded him to let her initiate the divorce so that her adultery didn't enter the public record and contaminate her reputation. She married Waters in 1943, and wrote Pollock out of her history altogether, making no mention of him in her autobiography *The Story of My Life* (1952) and cutting off his contact with their children. In later life she allowed it to be assumed that Waters was the father of her daughters. Pollock survives in the Blyton myth only in the pen-name Mary Pollock, under which she wrote some of her early work.

She was a bit ruthless, in other words. She was near-neighbours in Beaconsfield with another very successful, though not *as* successful, children's writer of the era, Alison Uttley (1884–1976) – author of the Beatrix-Potter-inflected *Little Grey Rabbit* books. They did not make friends. Uttley was jealous of the woman she called 'the Blyton'. In 1941 Uttley sent a friend to the Beaconsfield branch of WHSmith to try to persuade the manager to stock her work. She was furious to hear that the manager had said there was no demand for them: 'Now, if it was Miss Enid Blyton's books! They sell marvellously!' The manager, calling Enid a 'charming woman', even produced a photograph: 'the awful picture,' judged Uttley, 'of a vulgar, curled woman.'

Well-meaning neighbours once brought them together for lunch, assuming the two children's writers would have much in common. Uttley affected not to have any idea who Enid was: 'I know the book you wrote about a horse,' she said, 'but what else have you written?' Enid – and this, given the previous incident, must have hit more of a nerve even than she realised – retorted: 'Smith's window is *full* of my books. You can see a few titles if you care to look.' Uttley later told another guest, in feigned mortification: 'I had mixed her up with Enid Bagnold and *National Velvet*.' Uttley herself was a cookie full of arsenic, incidentally: she described her lifelong illustrator Margaret Tempest to her diaries as 'absolutely awful' and 'a humourless bore', and was described by the editor of those diaries as 'a singularly controlling and dominating person'. Some of that spilled through into her work. Cosy though the world of Little Grey Rabbit and Fuzzypeg the Hedgehog may have seemed, the first book in the series does end with Little Grey Rabbit bartering her own tail to an owl for gardening advice and roasting a weasel alive. But I digress.

The wholesome, motherly creature Enid constructed for public consumption was not, at least according to her real-life daughter, anything like the real story. Enid's ambition, and the policing of her image, left little room for Imogen, who in *A Childhood at Green Hedges* (1989) recalled 'the confusing mixture of beatings and pocket money handed out by "the woman with dark curly hair and brown eyes" who worked on a typewriter downstairs'.[*] In Imogen's account she realised only quite belatedly that the 'absolute ruler of our household' was 'also my mother'. 'The truth is,' wrote Imogen, 'Enid Blyton was arrogant, insecure, pretentious, very skilled at putting difficult or unpleasant things out of her mind, and without a trace of maternal instinct. As a child, I viewed her as a rather strict authority. As an adult, I did not hate her. I pitied her.'

Another famous children's writer as a parent; another child on whom, like Christopher Milne, or Vivian Burnett, or Alastair Grahame, the psychic fallout of that writing was to settle. Many of the greatest children's writers, it seems, are so profoundly preoccupied with creating an ideal childhood in their work, to heal the wounds of their own childhood selves, that they don't have room in their moral imaginations for their flesh-and-blood offspring. It's an occupational hazard: too busy imagining children to be a parent.

After Blyton's death in 1968, Green Hedges was demolished to make way for a new housing development. In 1997, on the centenary of her birth, a replica of Green Hedges was installed in Bekonscot model village, at a scale of one inch to a foot. Enid's older daughter Gillian unveiled it.

If Blyton sought to remedy a rupture with the past by, effectively, ignoring it, two other writers who were to follow – Philippa Pearce and Lucy M. Boston – took a subtler and more elegiac approach. The former's Carnegie-winning timeslip novel *Tom's Midnight Garden* (1958) sees its protagonist travelling between the world of the Golden Age stories and the bleak and shabby post-war reality.

---

[*]   Ibid.

As it opens, Tom's brother Peter has been quarantined with measles, and Tom is sent away from the family house in London to stay with his childless uncle and aunt in the fens:

> They drove on through Ely and the Fens, and then through Castleford and beyond, to where the Kitsons lived, in a big house now converted into flats. The house was crowded round with newer, smaller houses that beat up to its very confines in a broken sea of bay-windows and gable-ends and pinnacles. It was the only big house among them: oblong, plain, grave.

'Converted into flats' is not a phrase I've noticed in any pre-war children's stories. The high-ceilinged, servant-tenanted west London townhouses inhabited by E. Nesbit's characters were disappearing into the past. Tom is billeted in a poky room – space has been carved out of it with a thin wall to make a bathroom – whose barred window is the only indication that it was once a Victorian nursery. The MacGuffin – the pivot around which the story's time-travelling plot revolves, the contact between present and past, the anchor in time – is an ancient grandfather clock in the hallway on the ground floor, the screws that hold it to the wall rusted and immovable.

Tom discovers that when the malfunctioning clock strikes thirteen, in the unreal extra hour after midnight, the house slips in time: he is able to sneak out of the back door and in place of the scrubby backyard – a creosote-smelling 'strip of pavement where dustbins were kept' – he finds the titular midnight garden. The hallway becomes as it once was – broad, luxurious, peopled by uniformed housemaids and glass cases of stuffed birds – and the garden outside is a vast and well-tended collation of alcoves, archways and 'beetle-browed yews'.

Night after night, Tom slips out into the garden, where – mostly invisible to the human inhabitants, except for an unhappy young girl, Hatty, whom he befriends – he explores and pieces together the house's past. He thinks Hatty is a ghost; Hatty thinks he is a ghost. They argue fiercely about it. (It doesn't occur to either of them, thankfully for the story's delicious sense of mystery and wistfulness, to ask the other what year it is.) Time, here, is hinky: Tom can spend hours in the past and return to the present moments after he has left; but when he returns to the midnight garden months or maybe years will have passed. Hatty, unlike a ghost, is growing up (at their last encounter, she is a young woman); Tom, like a ghost, is not. Tom thins and disappears; he passes, in the past, through solid objects; his footsteps leave no trace on the grass. In some sense Tom is a ghost of the twentieth century haunting the nineteenth.

The midnight garden represents a refuge from Tom's loneliness, and a refuge from modernity itself. From the garden wall, Tom is able to look out

> beyond the garden and the house, to a lane, down which a horse and cart were plodding. Beyond the lane was a meadow, and then a meandering line that he knew must be the river.

But in the tawdry present, when he walks with Aunt Gwen down to the same river, it is polluted:

> 'I know it means that the river isn't pure and healthy any more,' said Aunt Gwen. 'It's something to do with all the houses that have been built, and the factories. Dreadful stuff gets into rivers from factories, I believe.'
> Tom looked at the river-water: it did not look foul, but he saw that the weeds below the surface of the water, instead of being slim and green and shining, were clothed in a kind of dingy, brown fur.

As Tom's stay with his uncle and aunt nears an end, he becomes distraught at the thought of losing his access to the midnight garden. Every moment that passes brings him closer to the moment when he can step out into timelessness; and every moment that passes brings him closer to the day he must go home to the city and be shut out of timelessness for good:

> As they came in through the front-door of the big house, the first thing Tom heard was the ticking of the grandfather clock. It would tick on to bedtime, and in that way Time was Tom's friend; but, after that, it would tick on to Saturday, and in that way Time was Tom's enemy.

It's a powerful way of giving life to the experience of childhood itself. The book's denouement has Tom discover that Hatty is still alive – that, as an old woman, she's living in the very same house (she's the elderly landlady), and that she *remembers* him – is a masterly and moving *coup de théâtre*. It's also a reminder, strange to think of now, that there would have been some people who read the then-new *Alice's Adventures in Wonderland* as children still, just about, alive at the end of the Second World War. Hatty, aka Mrs Bartholomew, isn't quite that old – she is, as she says, 'a late Victorian' – but she has been living, quietly, through all the years across which Tom steps by magic.

> 'We had two children – boys. They were both killed in the Great War – the First World War they call it now.' Mrs Bartholomew did not cry, because she had done all her crying for that so long ago. 'Then, many years later, Barty died, and I was left quite alone. That was when I came here; and I've lived here ever since.'

We all, *Tom's Midnight Garden* tells its readers, travel through time. The child lives on in the adult. Lonely childhood, in this story, is able to call to lonely childhood and share the experience in a dream, or a fantasy – or in a story.

> He had longed for someone to play with and for somewhere to play; and that great longing, beating about unhappily in the big

house, must have made its entry into Mrs Bartholomew's dreaming mind and had brought back to her the little Hatty of long ago. Mrs Bartholomew had gone back in Time to when she was a girl, wanting to play in the garden; and Tom had been able to go back with her, to that same garden.

The closing words of the book are a proper three-hanky tear-jerker.

'Good-bye, Mrs Bartholomew,' said Tom, shaking hands with stiff politeness; 'and thank you very much for having me.'

'I shall look forward to our meeting again,' said Mrs Bartholomew, equally primly.

Tom went slowly down the attic stairs. Then, at the bottom, he hesitated: he turned impulsively and ran up again – two at a time – to where Hatty Bartholomew still stood …

Afterwards, Aunt Gwen tried to describe to her husband that second parting between them. 'He ran up to her, and they hugged each other as if they had known each other for years and years, instead of only having met for the first time this morning. There was something else, too, Alan, although I know you'll say it sounds even more absurd … Of course, Mrs Bartholomew's such a shrunken little old woman, she's hardly bigger than Tom, anyway: but, you know, he put his arms right round her and he hugged her good-bye as if she were a little girl.'

Timeslip stories satisfy a very particular yearning. That same spooky yet consoling sense of how a house can travel through time was present in Lucy M. Boston's *The Children of Green Knowe* (1958), the first in a series of six books about an ancient manor house, dating back to the Norman Conquest, which turns out to be extremely haunted. Again, the protagonist is a lonely boy.

When we first meet Toseland Oldknow, he is sitting in a railway carriage, 'looking out at the rain, which was splashing against the windows and blotching downward in an ugly, dirty way. He was not the only person in the carriage, but the others were strangers to him. He was alone as usual.' His mother is dead. His father is away, and he is 'miserably shy' of his stepmother. He's on his way to Green Knowe to stay for the school holidays with his great-grandmother, Linnet. When he arrives he finds a house literally cut off from the outside world by flooding. He makes the last stage of his journey by dinghy.

When he greets his great-grandmother, her first words to him are:

> 'So you've come back!' she said, smiling, as he came forward, and he found himself leaning against her shoulder as if he knew her quite well. 'Why do you say "come back"?' he asked, not at all shy. 'I wondered whose face it would be of all the faces I knew,' she said. 'They always come back.'

That is a little unnerving – 'they always come back', in another context, could be a horror-movie line – yet it's tempered by the instant connection: 'he found himself leaning against her shoulder as if he knew her quite well'.

As Tolly (the nickname his great-grandmother gives him) comes to discover, Green Knowe has been inhabited by generations of his ancestors – a whole series of Toselands and Linnets, whose groundskeepers are a whole series of Boggises – and it still is. Tolly tunes in, as it were, to three children who lived and died in the seventeenth century. They are shadows and glimpses at first: an image in a mirror, a sense of being watched, a shadow that's the wrong shape, the whinnying of a long-dead horse in a stall. But bit by bit, the past and present come together.

The house and its grounds are a sort of temporal palimpsest. Time is behaving strangely here, too. Granny (as Tolly calls her – what's a generation when time past and time present coexist?) lives among the ghosts. The house reduplicates itself: 'Everything is twice here,' exclaims Tolly, not knowing how true he speaks. A painting of the three children with their mother contains objects still in the house. His room has a doll's house in it:

> He opened the front of the doll's house. 'Why, it's this house!' he said. 'Look, here's the Knight's Hall, and here's the stairs, and here's my room! Here's the rocking-horse and here's the red box, and here's the tiny bird-cage! But it's got four beds in it. Are there sometimes other children here?'
>
> Mrs Oldknow looked at him as if she would like to know everything about him before she answered. 'Yes,' she said, 'sometimes.'

Green Knowe is a place apart from the twentieth century. Ancestral objects come to light and Tolly takes possession of them. Linnet tells him stories within the story. He comes to be able to speak to and interact with the ghosts. It is magnificently spooky, but also, oddly, comforting. Green Knowe's ghosts – or, at least, some of them – are benign. This lonely boy finds companionship with this old woman, and with children dead three centuries before. He is, at last, not-alone.

But there's an exorcism, of sorts, in the pipe: the house's name is a corruption of 'Green Noah', the name given to the great cursed yew-tree that, in a terrifying denouement, comes alive and seems to be stalking Tolly through the dark garden. With its sense of generational return, its enchanted objects and meaningful animals, and its part-menacing, part-healing magic deeply rooted in geographical place, the *Green Knowe* series seems to me to be a natural predecessor to the stories of Alan Garner and Susan Cooper.

Always Winter and Never Christmas

C.S. LEWIS

The Lion, the Witch and the Wardrobe; Prince Caspian; The Voyage of the Dawn Treader; The Silver Chair; The Horse and His Boy; The Magician's Nephew; The Last Battle

'SOMETHING COLD AND SOFT WAS FALLING ON HER. A moment later she found that she was standing in the middle of a wood at night-time with snow under her feet and snow-flakes falling through the air. Lucy felt a little frightened, but she felt very inquisitive and excited as well.' This passage from *The Lion, the Witch and the Wardrobe* describes the moment after Lucy Pevensie takes her first steps through the back of the wardrobe into the magical kingdom of Narnia. A little frightened, but very inquisitive and excited as well. Could there be a better and more concise expression of what it's like, as a receptive child reader, to step into a story?

The seven-book sequence we know as *The Chronicles of Narnia* was cooked up by a scruffy, beery, tweedy old geezer who reeked of pipe-smoke (in between pipes he managed sixty cigarettes a day) and had no children of his own. But they were the creation, you could say, of the child he had been rather than the adult he became. Born the son of a solicitor in Belfast at the very tail end of the nineteenth century, Clive Staples Lewis (1898–1963) – known lifelong as 'Jack' – had an anxious, frequently sickly childhood. His mother died when he was nine years old. Within a fortnight of her death, he had been dispatched along with his older brother Warren to a small boarding school in Hertfordshire, Wynyard, which he was to describe in his autobiography* as resembling a 'concentration camp'.

It was his imaginative life, as he moved from school to school, that nourished him. He came to adore the Greco-Roman and, especially, the Norse myths – and, finding his way into academia (he went up to Oxford as an undergraduate in 1917, though his studies were suspended while he fought in the Great War), he made a career of them, spending thirty years teaching English Literature at Oxford University and his last decade as a professor of Medieval and Renaissance literature at Cambridge. He renounced religion at fifteen, 'angry with God' and, with much resistance, came back to it in middle age.

His love life was tormented and unsatisfactory. His first major relationship with a woman was with Janie Moore, the divorced mother of a friend he'd made in army training who was killed in the war. She was forty-five and he was eighteen, and she visited him in hospital after he was wounded in action; his father did not. He called her 'Mother'; though more than one Lewis biographer believes they were lovers. Whether or not the relationship was sexual, she was a kind of wife.

They lived together for half of Lewis's life until her death in 1951. Jack's brother Warren, who lived with them for a time, came to see Janie as a tyrant who 'interfered constantly with [Jack's] work, and imposed upon him a heavy burden of minor domestic tasks',† and that his whole life was 'subordinated to hers – financially, socially, recreationally: the pity of it is that on his selflessness her selfishness fattens'.‡ Certainly, the strain of looking

---

*   C.S. Lewis, *Surprised By Joy: The Shape of My Early Life* (Geoffrey Bles, 1955).
†   Warren H. Lewis, 'Memoir of C.S. Lewis' in *Letters of C.S. Lewis* (Geoffrey Bles, 1966).
‡   Warren H. Lewis, *Brothers and Friends: The Diaries of Major Walter Hamilton Lewis* (HarperCollins, 1982).

after her as she declined into what A.N. Wilson calls 'malign senility' (not helped, it should be said, by the difficulty of coping with Warren's alcoholism) saw him break down.* He went on to marry Joy Davidman – an American divorcee with two young sons – in 1956, only to see her die of cancer four years later, as his own mother had. (That experience went into his 1961 book for grown-ups about the experience of mourning, *A Grief Observed*.)

Lewis's *Narnia* stories – which encode his own anxieties and fantasies of redemption and comfort and escape, and into which he poured all his knowledge of mythology as a scholar and feeling as a man – remain one of the great monuments of twentieth-century children's fantasy. There's no getting around them. Though readers and writers can and have taken issue with their theology, their cultural politics, their racial stereotyping and their attitudes towards women and sex, Lewis builds their universe with extraordinary originality and imaginative power. Every fantasy novelist to follow owes them a debt.

The war had just finished when Lewis started writing the books, and the war supplied a new means for a children's author to get the parents out of the way. The Pevensie children, in that first book, are evacuees to the country to escape the Blitz, and it's in the large country house – another one – of Professor Digory Kirke that Lucy stumbles across the wardrobe that opens a portal to Narnia: that enchanted fantasy land of talking animals which, when we first meet it, is famously shrouded in cold – always winter and never Christmas.

The first book was originally conceived as a stand-alone volume, and it is perfectly self-contained, but over Lewis's (and his characters') serial visits to Narnia that resonant story built out into something more like a mythos. The crucifixion story – Aslan sacrifices himself to redeem Edmund, and then returns to life – is present

---

*   A.N. Wilson, *C.S. Lewis: A Biography*.

there, just as an account of the creation is to be found in its prequel *The Magician's Nephew* and something like the Book of Revelation in the series' final book, *The Last Battle*.

The *Narnia* books just about hang together as a series, though they weren't written that way. Like Tolkien tweaking *The Hobbit* to make it a prequel to *The Lord of the Rings*, Lewis retconned the world of Narnia as he went on. The first in chronological sequence – *The Magician's Nephew* – was the penultimate to be written and published; and it has the effect of reframing the rest of the sequence, placing it in a larger and more complex universe. It also anchors the story, for the first time, in Lewis's own Edwardian childhood: 'In those days Mr. Sherlock Holmes was still living in Baker Street and the Bastables were looking for treasure in the Lewisham Road.'

When we meet that book's protagonist Digory, he is crying. Like so many children we've encountered in late Victorian and Edwardian stories, his father is away in India. His mother is ill, apparently dying, and he has been parked with an unsympathetic Uncle Andrew. Andrew's Faustian experiments are soon to lead Digory and his friend Polly into great peril. He gives them magic rings whose workings he has only half-understood himself: he imagines they will send them into another world, but in fact they transport their users into an in-between place, the Wood Between the Worlds, a 'rich place; rich as plum-cake', each of whose moss-fringed pools is a gateway to another universe.

Stepping into one of them, they find themselves in the dead world of Charn – and they accidentally free that world's only living inhabitant, Jadis, from a state of suspended animation. Jadis – who in due course will become the White Witch – has destroyed her own world by speaking the 'Deplorable Word' of forbidden magic (it's not 'Avada Kedavra', but we can guess where J.K. Rowling got the hint). Now, she rampages into 1900s London, where she proposes to take over our world, creating a scene of comical chaos that draws heavily on E. Nesbit's description in *The Story of the Amulet* of the riotous time-travelling visit to London of the Queen of Babylon.

The Magician's Nephew is an origin story: it lets us see the creation of Narnia itself, and stitches that fantasy realm into a vast cosmic scheme that includes our own universe. And it solves some of the mysteries of the previous books. Why is there a lamppost in the middle of a forest in Narnia? Because when Jadis throws a chunk of London ironmongery at Aslan, it lands in the ground as he is singing Narnia into being and grows like a tree. Why does the elderly professor, in *The Lion, the Witch and the Wardrobe*, believe Lucy about Narnia? Because that elderly professor was Digory, the first human being to set foot there.

It's also a warning. At least by the mid-fifties, when that book was published, Narnia had become more than just a fantastical alternative to our own world. When they're discussing the way that Jadis laid waste to her home world of Charn with the 'Deplorable Word', Aslan makes a bald reference to the dangerous knowledge of nuclear war:

> 'It is not certain that some wicked one of your race will not find out a secret as evil as the Deplorable Word and use it to destroy all living things. And soon, very soon, before you are an old man and an old woman, great nations in your world will be ruled by tyrants who care no more for joy and justice and mercy than the Empress Jadis. Let your world beware.'

Yet Narnia was also religiously didactic in a way that allied it to the children's writing of a previous era. Like Tolkien, Lewis was unsatisfied by the direction that the children's stories of his own time were taking. A number of subsequent writers have objected to what A.S. Byatt once described to me as the 'Christian arm-twist-ing'* of the Narnia books. There's not much getting round that

---

* Sam Leith, 'C.S. Lewis's Literary Legacy: "Dodgy and unpleasant" or "exceptionally good"?', *Guardian*, 19 November 2013.

arm-twisting. The religious message of the books isn't a regrettable add-on: it is the substance of them. Lewis was a Christian convert – a reluctant one, in his account of it. When in 1929, in part under the influence of his friend and colleague, the devoutly Catholic Tolkien, he finally 'gave in, and admitted that God was God, and knelt and prayed', he was, he later wrote 'the most dejected and reluctant convert in all England'.

These books are instinct with theological argument. There are at least two versions of the temptation of Adam – Digory's encounter with Jadis in the (unnamed) Garden of Eden being the most obvious one, but his ringing the magic bell in Charn being another. There's a Mosaic baby in a basket: the protagonist of *The Horse and His Boy*, Shasta, is a foundling, washed up in an empty boat, and turns out to be a child of destiny. There's sin and redemption – Edmund and Eustace are both turned into heroes, having started as selfish and spoilt brats. The journey of *The Horse and His Boy* shows, 'Footprints-in-the-Sand'-style, the operation of grace:

> 'I was the lion.' And as Shasta gaped with open mouth and said nothing, the voice continued. 'I was the lion who forced you to join with Aravis. I was the cat who comforted you among the houses of the dead. [...] I was the lion you do not remember who pushed the boat in which you lay, a child near death, so that it came to shore where a man sat, wakeful at midnight, to receive you.'

But the Narnia stories are doing something rather different from, and more interesting than, offering an allegory of the Christian story. Lewis himself – and as an academic expert on medieval literature, he could be expected to know – rejected the term 'allegory' for what he was doing. He called the stories 'suppositional'. They were addressed to the question: 'What might Christ become like, if there really were a world like Narnia and He chose to be incarnate and die and rise again in that world as He actually has done in ours?' That's the sort of question that fiction is equipped to answer in a way that theology is not. 'What might it be like?' is a novelist's question. Lewis thought, as he wrote in a letter to a friend, 'You can get into children's heads a good deal which is quite beyond the Bishop of Woolwich.'*

The *Narnia* books offer an embodied theology. Narnia is a world in which the divine is experienced directly, and through the senses. Aslan is a physical, not just a spiritual presence: blood, fur, breath and roar. His double nature is that he is both gentle and terrifying. 'Though its soft pads made no noise, you could feel the earth shake beneath their weight.' When the girls romp with him 'whether it was more like playing with a thunderstorm or playing with a kitten Lucy could never make up her mind'.

Lewis seems to me entirely successful in making him something more than just a character in the story. He's a lion – a real, actual, warm-blooded lion – and a creature of unimaginable power and presence, which is, of course, the imaginative reality of the incarnation. The phrase 'Aslan is on the move' can still raise hairs on necks.

Aslan, like God in Lewis's apprehension of Him, resonates with each child's created nature (treacherous Edmund gets 'mysterious horror') and does so even before the hearer has any conscious understanding of his nature. He's just there, underpinning everything: a bass-note under creation, waiting to be heard. You may or may not buy the theology, but Lewis brings it off as storytelling. Aslan really does acquire a special gravity in these stories.

Much as they are full of biblical tropes and episodes, the *Narnia* stories also seem to contain hints of the new physics. The books posit a multiverse of linked worlds perpetually coming into being and dying, and there's a strange and resonant sort of relativity. Time dilates. The human protagonists who come and go between

---

* Letter to Nancy Warner, 26 October 1963, in Walter Hooper (ed.), *The Collected Letters of C.S. Lewis, Volume III: Narnia, Cambridge and Joy 1950–1963* (HarperCollins, 2007).

Narnia and our world age and grow and learn in Narnia – as kings and queens in Narnia, the protagonists of the first book live most of a lifetime in the seat of the Narnian monarchy, Cair Paravel – but return to our own world as children, not a moment later than they departed.

They are children, but also adults: '"Ah, but we were sort of grown-up then," said Peter. "We reigned for years and years and learned to do things. Aren't we just back at our proper ages again now?"' When they return, first in *Prince Caspian* and later in *The Last Battle*, they have themselves become mythological figures in Narnia – once and future kings. Narnia itself forgets. In *Prince Caspian*, the usurper Miraz upbraids his nephew: 'There never were those Kings and Queens. […] And there's no such person as Aslan. […] And there never was a time when animals could talk. Do you hear?'

Our world is shadowed by Narnia, and Narnia itself, as revealed in *The Last Battle*, is itself an imperfect shadow of the 'true Narnia', into which the characters finally come after the judgement of Aslan. There's always a layer further back. The White Witch's hubris, and her imperfect knowledge – like Uncle Andrew's – mean that she knows about the Deep Magic from the Dawn of Time but doesn't imagine there's a Deeper Magic from Before the Dawn of Time. Aslan is God, but Aslan's father, the Emperor-Beyond-The-Sea, is more powerful and more ancient still.

To lay out Lewis's cosmic scheme, though, is to flatten what makes the books work. It's the quiddity of the individual stories, of the characters and situations, that makes these stories live (and that has set any number of child readers to hopefully prodding the backs of the wardrobes at home). They are not schematic. There are mysteries and oddities. Why is it that only Sons of Adam and Daughters of Eve – i.e. humans – can rule Narnia? We know that Jadis is an incomer from another world – but where does the serpentine 'Lady with the Green Kirtle', antagonist of *The Silver Chair*, come from? *The Voyage of the Dawn Treader* – which takes the characters to the very edge of the world – is as trippy as *The Odyssey* remade as a 1970s concept album.

But that Christian arm-twisting, for child readers, is part of what gives these books their grandeur. They don't just let you imagine what it's like to be plucked from the platform of a railway station and plonked into a world full of talking animals and deadly Turkish delight: they let you imagine what it would be to have that happen as part of a vast providential scheme, crossing hundreds of years, and that is thrilling. These are real children, but they are also mythological heroes.

As Lewis's biographer A.N. Wilson puts it, Lewis's writings were 'self-consciously and deliberately at variance with the twentieth century'.[*] Lewis's deep conservatism is everywhere in evidence. There's a heavy-handed running joke about the progressive school where Eustace Scrubb (protagonist of *The Voyage of the Dawn Treader*) is a pupil. Experiment House is co-educational, doesn't have corporal punishment, has a headmistress rather than a headmaster and 'girls are not taught how to curtsey' there. In Lewis's eyes this makes it ripe for mockery.

Eustace's bumptious and arrogant character, we're invited to speculate, may be down to his parents and his schooling: 'He didn't call his father and mother "Father" and "Mother", but Harold and Alberta. They were very up-to-date and advanced people. They were vegetarians, non-smokers and teetotallers, and wore a special kind of underclothes.' Eustace is a self-proclaimed pacifist and a republican, and grumbles that giving Lucy a better cabin than him on the *Dawn Treader* is 'really lowering [i.e. patronising] girls'. Eustace must be transformed into a dragon and back before he starts to get with the Narnian programme.

There are other ways in which Lewis now looks problematic. The southern race of the Calormen are coded as Arab Muslims – all

---

[*]   Wilson, *C.S. Lewis: A Biography*.

curved scimitars and florid *Arabian-Nights*-style diction – and
are slavers, idolaters and your basic treacherous infidels. Heavy-
handed comedy is made of their language: 'My son, by all means
desist from kicking the venerable and enlightened Vizier: for as a
costly jewel retains its value even if hidden in a dung-hill, so old
age and discretion are to be respected even in the vile persons of
our subjects.' In *The Horse and His Boy* a Calormene noble plots
to abduct and marry (i.e. rape) Queen Susan, and the plot turns
on its hero Shasta's ride to warn the people of Archenland of a
treacherous surprise attack.

Another serious charge against Lewis, in these books, is that
of misogyny. He has slighting things to say about 'dumpy, prim
girls with fat legs', and much ink has been spilled about the way
in which the older Pevensie child, Susan, can never return to
Narnia. In *Prince Caspian*, their exile is foreshadowed when Aslan
takes her and Peter aside: '"There were things he wanted to say to
Su and me because we're not coming back to Narnia." "Never?"
cried Edmund and Lucy in dismay. "Oh, you two are," answered
Peter. "At least, from what he said, I'm pretty sure he means you
to get back some day. But not Su and me. He says we're getting
too old."'

In *The Last Battle*, though, Peter does return to Narnia. Susan
doesn't. She is 'no longer a friend of Narnia', remembering her
siblings' visits there only as 'playground games'. As Jill says,
'She's interested in nothing nowadays except nylons and lipstick
and invitations. She always was a jolly sight too keen on being
grown-up.'

Is it that interest in 'nylons and lipstick and invitations' – the
stuff of a burgeoning sexuality – that condemns her to apparently
permanent exile in the 'real world'? I think the most we can say is
that it's ambiguous. What does for Susan's connection to Narnia,
and it is primarily about her age rather than her sexual self, is her
refusal to believe in it any more: she is 'grown-up'. But Narnia is an
apparently childish world in which grown-up things are at stake.

As Lewis warns: 'Even in this world, of course, it is the stupidest children who are the most childish and the stupidest grown-ups who are the most grown-up.'

To me, what really sticks out about the ending of the *Narnia* books is not that Susan doesn't get to go back to Narnia: it's that Susan *lives*. The 'happy ending' of which she's deprived – which Lewis saw as a way of giving imaginative body to the experience of heaven – requires the children to die. None of them returns to Digory's country house, or to school after the holidays, or to Experiment House. They are killed in a train crash. Their spirits are safe and unchanging in the ultimate secret garden, Aslan's country. They never find their way back out of the haunted wood. Like Barrie's 'tragic boy', they will never grow up.

Our Friends in the North

TOVE JANSSON · ASTRID LINDGREN

*The Moomins and the Great Flood; Comet in
Moominland; Finn Family Moomintroll; Pippi
Longstocking; Karlsson on the Roof; Karlsson
Flies Again; The World's Best Karlsson; The
Bullerby Children; The Children on Troublemaker
Street; Lotta's Bike; Never Violence*

HALF A CENTURY BEFORE ADULT BOOKSHOPS WERE
hit by the vogue for Scandi crime, Nordic children's stories were establishing themselves in the English nursery
canon. That was down to two writers, both of whom started arriving in English in the middle of the century: the Finn Tove Jansson
(1914–2001) and the Swede Astrid Lindgren (1907–2002). These
were both writers whose stories went worldwide and whose characters, as was said of Barrie's *Peter Pan*, 'impregnate the collective
mind of [their] audience [...] are immortal by election'.

Jansson's *Moomin* stories are among those cultural artefacts
where the iconic characters have escaped from the stories in which
they first appeared. Every late-twentieth-century child knew what a
Moomin looked like even if they had never heard of Tove Jansson:
you'd have had a Moomin pencil case, Moomin pyjamas or a
Moomin lunchbox, or watched your parents remove a pie from
the oven with Moomin oven gloves.

Jansson was described, accurately, by one critic as 'an artist with
two native languages': words and pictures. The vibe of her world,

its physical oddity, is primarily conveyed by the images with which she accompanied the texts (and, indeed, she turned the Moomins into comic-strips with considerable success – syndicated to 120 newspapers and reaching twelve million readers). Moominvalley, accompanied by Jansson's own illustrations, offered a vast menagerie of benign oddities: that famous soft, hippo-like family of trolls and their friends and associates in what you might see as a psychedelic Nordic version of Hundred Acre Wood.

Jansson – who had started her career, and still thought of herself, as a serious painter and artist – said later that the characters had come to her 'when I was feeling depressed and scared of the bombing and wanted to get away from my gloomy thoughts to something else entirely… I crept into an unbelievable world where everything was natural and benign – and possible.'* The series brought her fame and fortune but she came to resent the way it eclipsed her other artistic work: 'Those damn Moomins,' she wrote privately. 'I don't want to hear about them any more. I could vomit on the Moomintrolls.'†

Jansson had grown up in an artistic household – her Finnish father was a sculptor and her Swedish mother an illustrator – and had drawn from a very young age. She studied art, as a young woman, in Stockholm, Helsinki and Paris. But the war, which came when she was twenty-nine – the Soviet Union invaded the country in 1939 – was a rupture. Her brother Per Olov was away fighting, and she lived with the constant anxiety that he might not return.

But as much as her books aimed to present a world, like Milne's, quite apart from and a refuge from our own, Jansson didn't quite manage it. Moominvalley was more freighted with real-world anxieties than you'd suppose. The first two books – *The Moomins and*

---

* Letter to Eva Konikoff, 23 February 1950, in *Letters From Tove*, Boel Westin and Helen Svensson (eds), Sarah Death (trans), (Sort of Books, 2019).
† Private note, quoted in Mark Bosworth, 'Tove Jansson: Love, War and the Moomins', *BBC Magazine*, 2014: https://www.bbc.com/news/magazine-26529309.

the Great Flood and *Comet in Moominland* – deal with apocalyptic disasters and picture their characters fleeing through a scary forest as refugees or anticipating the wipe-out of everything they know. Her friend Boel Westin said: 'The war had a great effect on Tove and her family [...] Tove's anxiety and grief are embedded in the first two books.'*

The third – which was the first to go into English, as *Finn Family Moomintroll*, in 1950 – can be peculiarly dark in tone too. The treasures Moomintroll and Snork Maiden gather in a cheerful afternoon's beachcombing – among them a lifejacket and a ship's figurehead – are plainly the flotsam of a shipwreck. Terror is a near-constant: 'Sniff lay under his blanket and screamed'; 'Moomintroll stared into the darkness [...] Moomintroll was terrified and woke Snufkin'. There's a nightmarish encounter with a blind and deaf species of ambulant grey-white mushroom creatures called Hattifatteners:

> And between the trees came still more Hattifatteners, with their staring eyes and silent tread. 'Go away!' screamed the Hemulen: 'Shoo! Shoo!' But still they came silently nearer. Then the Hemulen picked up his skirts and began to climb up the pole. It was nasty and slippery, but terror gave him un-Hemulenish strength...

If Moominvalley can be said to be dreamlike, let us admit that it's often a cheese-dream. The magical Hobgoblin's Hat they find by chance transforms eggshells into lovely, bouncing clouds and river water into raspberry juice; but it also causes a poisonous plant to grow though the Moomins' home like a jungle; and it transforms Moomintroll into an unrecognisable parody of himself with all his fat parts grown thin and vice versa. He thinks the others are playing a game when they don't recognise him, and that tips

---

*   Ibid.

over into panic – the spell is only broken at the last minute by a mother's love:

> 'Isn't there anyone who believes me?' Moomintroll pleaded. 'Look carefully at me, mother. You must know your own Moomintroll.'
>
> Moominmamma looked carefully. She looked into his frightened eyes for a very long time, and then she said quietly: 'Yes, you are my Moomintroll.'
>
> And at the same moment he began to change. His ears, eyes, and tail began to shrink, and his nose and tummy grew, until at last he was his old self again.
>
> 'It's all right now, my dear,' said Moominmamma. 'You see, I shall always know you whatever happens.'

The characters, too, are prone to more in the way of adult existential anxiety than you normally associate with the inhabitants of a children's fantasy (Jansson's first drawing of what became Moomintroll was made after an argument with one of her brothers about the philosopher Immanuel Kant). There's Snufkin, with his 'night wandering'. When we first meet the studious Hemulen he is 'in despair' at having completed his stamp collection – 'It's finished. There isn't a stamp or an error that I haven't collected. Not one. What shall I do now?' The philosophical Muskrat longs to 'retire to a deserted spot and live a life of loneliness and peace, giving up everything'.

Jansson herself, in later life, ambivalent about the success of her most famous creations, did something not dissimilar – she retreated with her life-partner Tuulikki Pietilä to a tiny house they built on an uninhabited island in the Gulf of Finland. She had male lovers in her youth, but went to what she called 'the ghost side' in the early 1950s – around the time the Moomins were really taking off. She said of her lesbianism, then still illegal in Finland, 'I'm finally experiencing myself as a woman where love is concerned, it's bringing me peace and ecstasy for the first time.'

—

Astrid Lindgren – who started her career as a local newspaper journalist and secretary (and whose first child was born, scandalously, out of wedlock after an affair with her editor), ended it as one of the most celebrated Swedes on the face of the planet. Her funeral in 2002 was attended by the king and the prime minister, and she gives her name to what's still the most well-remunerated prize for children's literature anywhere in the world. They put her portrait on banknotes.

Lindgren wrote books for all ages and in several genres, and is one of the most translated authors ever, with tens of millions of books sold. *The Bullerby Children* was a realist depiction of family life in rural Sweden, and *The Children on Troublemaker Street*, relating the adventures of a wilful toddler called Lotta and her older siblings, included both chapter books and picture books (*Lotta's Bike* is a classic of velocipedal peril). It's her more surreal work that really made her reputation in the UK, though.

The *Pippi Longstocking* series, the first of which was published in 1945, describes a little girl whose exuberantly anarchic adventures offer a vision of female agency – and female agency on its own defiant terms. Pippi is nine years old and lives all by herself in the dilapidated Villa Villekulla on the outskirts of a tiny little town. 'She had no mother or father, which was actually quite nice, because it meant that no one could tell her that she had to go to bed just when she was having most fun. And no one could make her take cod liver oil when she would rather eat sweets.'

Pippi lives from the off outside any family structure, and outside the frame of social convention – and, unlike Peter Pan, she uncomplicatedly loves it. She imagines her mother, who died when she was young, looking down on her from heaven ('Pippi would often wave to her and say, "Don't worry! I can always look after myself!"') and believes that her beloved father, who fell overboard while they were travelling the seas, has washed ashore on a desert island and become 'King of the Natives'. Until such time as her dad comes back, Pippi is more than happy alone.

Pippi is rich: she has a great bag of gold coins. Pippi has super-powers: she's strong enough to lift a horse. Pippi owns, as well as a horse, a pet monkey called Mr Nilsson. And she can do exactly what she likes, always. She has a home-made patchwork dress, long ginger plaits, odd stockings and oversized shoes. She walks backwards, tells eye-stretching fibs about her foreign travels, sleeps with her feet on the pillow and her head under the covers, doesn't mind looking weird or making a mess, and with her huge strength makes short work of bullies, policemen, burglars, circus strongmen and representatives of the social services.

She represents, in other words, a fantasy of absolute freedom of action and freedom from convention; and she befriends and entrances her next-door neighbours Tommy and Annika, who are 'two very nice, well-mannered and obedient children'. When the children encourage Pippi to attend school, or one of their mother's coffee mornings (where the women gossip and moan about the inadequacies of their servants), she causes chaos. The child reader is able to look at Pippi from Tommy and Annika's viewpoint, but also to fantasise about being her. Lindgren, who invented the character to amuse her own daughter Karin when she was ill, said Pippi 'represents my own childish longing for a person who has power but does not abuse it'.

Marginally less well known now, but even more original, is another of Lindgren's series. *Karlsson on the Roof* (1958) and its sequels *Karlsson Flies Again* (1977) and *The World's Best Karlsson* (1980) – another story of a conventional child whose world is enlarged and disrupted by a magical friendship. In this case it's with a fat little man who lives outside Smidge's bedroom window and has a propellor on his back, which is activated when he turns a winder on his tummy. You could see Karlsson as a wickedly ungainly male fairy godmother; an imaginary friend who isn't imaginary. Karlsson doesn't so much enter seven-year-old Smidge's world as elbow his way in, and the comedy of his adventures is in Karlsson's bumptious and boastful personality. Like Pippi, he brings a touch of anarchy into the 'very ordinary apartment building on a very ordinary street' in Stockholm where his child friend lives. Like Pippi, he's kind-hearted; unlike Pippi, he is a childlike character with the pomposity of an adult.

The stories serve very directly and openly that ancient fantasy: for a child to discover that he or she is, after all, special. Smidge first meets Karlsson towards the end of 'one of those difficult days when it wasn't the least fun being Smidge': a day when he's told off for making holes in his trousers, for dawdling home late from school, for meeting a dog and wishing he had a dog but knowing that it was another little boy who would be petting that dog at another home that evening.

Retreating to his room in a sulk, with the grandiose self-pity the parent of any cosseted seven-year-old will recognise, Smidge hears a buzzing noise and soon he sees a 'fat little man' flying slowly past his window. After a couple of passes, Karlsson hovers outside the window ledge and greets Smidge with the first of his several catchphrases: 'Heysan hopsan.'

By the end of that first meeting, Karlsson has described himself as 'the world's best stunt flyer', 'the world's best steam engine driver' and 'the world's best motor mechanic' (see also: 'the world's best cockerel painter', 'the world's best meatball fetcher', 'the world's best jiggery-poker', *et passim*); and, in the course of airily trying to prove the second thing by activating the model steam engine that Smidge is never supposed to use without parental supervision, he has burned the varnish on the bookcase and blown the steam engine to smithereens. Another catchphrase: 'A mere trifle!'

As we'll discover, Karlsson's *amour propre* is invincible. He's a fat, clumsy little thing, and causes catastrophe with everything he puts his hand to, but describes himself unfailingly (with only very slight variations over the course of the books) as 'a handsome, highly intelligent, reasonably stout man in my prime'. So Karlsson is a very attractive figure – he promises unusual adventures (another catchphrase: 'It has to go bang and it has to be fun, otherwise count me out.'); he's an adult who is a fun special friend; and he's also someone the child reader can laugh at and even somewhat patronise. Smidge is the sensitive, favoured younger child; too old, as Lindgren says, to sit on his mother's lap but always longing to. If you were of a psychoanalytic cast of mind, you could see Karlsson – with his readiness to fib, his selfishness, his boastfulness, his passive-aggression and greed (he's always extorting toffees out of Smidge) – as externalising the childlike qualities and appetites that the well-behaved Smidge would be reluctant to admit to.

Karlsson is a secret, at least until the closing pages of the first book: Smidge's parents believe him to be an imaginary friend; they are understandably sceptical of the idea that there's an actual stout man with a propellor on his back living in a tiny house next to the chimney-pot on the roof of their Stockholm townhouse. More fool them.

Lindgren also has an extra-literary place in the annals of child-hood. For most of their history, children's stories have contained beatings and spankings and canings and slipperings and clips round the ear as matters of unremarkable course; children take these on the chin (or the backside) as part of the order of things. Even Pippi Longstocking jokingly alludes to it, when Tommy and Annika ask her 'who tells you to go to bed at night' when she has no parents: 'I do. First I tell myself once, very nicely, and if I don't obey, then I tell myself again, very sternly, and if I still don't obey, then it's time for a spanking, of course.' There's a moment in *Karlsson Flies Again* in which Smidge, put under the temporary care of a formidable housekeeper (his mother is away convalescing, his father is away on business and his siblings have scarlet fever), gets a clip round the ear: 'Smidge's eyes had glazed over. He was on the verge of tears. He had never had a clip round the ear before, and he didn't like it.'

Lindgren didn't like it either – and she leveraged her fame as an author to end corporal punishment in her native Sweden. Receiving the Peace Prize of the German Book Trade in 1978, she made a speech that has come to be known as 'Never Violence'. In it, she argued that the violence of adults was inculcated in childhood – and that the non-violent raising of children was the first step to eliminating the violence and bloodshed that plagues the wider world.

In it, she told a personal story:

When I was about twenty years old, I met an old pastor's wife who told me that when she was young and had her first child, she didn't believe in striking children, although spanking kids with a switch pulled from a tree was standard punishment at the time. But one day when her son was four or five, he did something that she felt warranted a spanking – the first of his life. And she told him that he would have to go outside and find a switch for her to hit him with. The boy was gone a long time. And when he came back in, he was crying. He said to her, 'Mama, I couldn't find a switch, but here's a rock that you can throw at me.'

All of a sudden the mother understood how the situation felt from the child's point of view: that if my mother wants to hurt me, then it makes no difference what she does it with; she might as well do it with a stone. And the mother took the boy onto her lap and they both cried. Then she laid the rock on a shelf in the kitchen to remind herself for ever: never violence. And that is something I think everyone should keep in mind. Because violence begins in the nursery – one can raise children into violence.*

She felt strongly about this. When she submitted her speech ahead of the ceremony, the organisers asked her not to give it on the grounds it would be too controversial; she refused to accept the award unless she was allowed to make the speech. It was published that year in book form in Germany and Sweden, and the following

---

* Speech by Astrid Lindgren to the German Book Trade, 27 October 1978.

year, as a direct result, corporal punishment of children was banned in Sweden – the first such law anywhere in the world.

What came out of the war years, and the decade or two that followed, wasn't just nostalgia for a lost connection with the past. There were also the first stirrings of a literature that sought not to flee from the post-war world but, in some sense, to re-enchant it. The 1960s were to see the arrival of a cohort of fantasy and genre writers who sought to bring the magic and terror of fairytales, and the real lives of children in a world they would recognise, closer together than ever before.

VIII

A CRACK IN THE TEACUP

Alan Garner · Susan Cooper · Diana Wynne Jones ·
Ursula K. Le Guin · Madeleine L'Engle ·
Nicholas Fisk · Robert Westall

SIXTIES AND SEVENTIES
FANTASY AND SCIENCE FICTION

T HE SIXTIES AND SEVENTIES SAW A FLOURISHING OF genre-writing. The broad sort of magic-and-monsters fantasy, descending from folktale but given its modern shape by Lewis and Tolkien, was taken on and developed by a new generation of writers. A lurid seam of science fiction and even horror material started to enter the mainstream, too. Children's writing was entering one of its long slaloming swerves between high fantasy and something like realism.

Folk memory has the sixties as the age of sex and drugs and rock 'n' roll – all things we think of as adult or late adolescent preoccupations. But it was an era of change for children, too. Post-war make-do-and-mend was giving way to what became known as the consumer society. Supermarkets colonised the high streets, mail-order shopping became the rage, and after the Conservative victory in the 1959 election a cartoon in the *Daily Mail* pictured Harold Macmillan sitting in peaceable conference with a whole array of consumer durables.

Children were also becoming consumers. Pocket-money was a concept originally popularised in the work of the parenting guru Sidonie Gruenberg (1881–1974), who argued in 1912 that a regular allowance would help children learn how to manage money.[*] It

---

[*] Sidonie Gruenberg, *Your Child Today and Tomorrow* (Lippincott, 1912).

had been establishing itself, for better or worse, throughout the first half of the twentieth century. A 1943 survey reported disapprovingly that 'school children in the poorer districts had far more pocket-money than those of the better class,' and that they were spending it on sweets, comics and ice-cream.* The historian Hugh Cunningham notes that in the US the 1960s 'the balance in the purchasing of toys switched more decisively towards children.'† There's every reason to suppose that the same change took place across the Atlantic.

More than that, there was a cultural transformation under way that made a few popinjays in feather boas on Carnaby Street look like a sideshow: television had become general. Mary Poppins had been replaced by the one-eyed childminder.

---

*   Women's Group on Public Welfare, *Our Towns* (Oxford, 1943).
†   Cunningham, op. cit.

The Idiot Box

A CHORUS SUNG BY THE OOMPA LOOMPAS IN *Charlie and the Chocolate Factory*, shortly after Mike Teavee meets his Waterloo, gives voice to a suspicion of the medium that has been with us since its very arrival. It isn't a very good song, but it does let you know (via his midget proxies) what Dahl thinks. He warns that parents should never let their children watch television and, ideally, should not install 'the idiotic thing' in the first place. The song goes on to warn in unbroken block capitals that television rots the sense, kills the imagination, clutters the mind and makes children 'dull' and unable to appreciate 'fantasy' or 'fairyland'.

Dahl's message, back in the early sixties, was not just that the then infant technology would make children stupid: it was that it existed in a zero-sum war against children's literature. He enjoined parents to throw their TV sets away and install instead 'a lovely bookshelf'. Dahl might as well have been spitting into a hurricane for all the effect such an injunction would have on the course of cultural history. Also, he was wrong.

The relationship between television and children's fiction is a complicated one – and not as simply antagonistic as Dahl suggests. What is undoubtedly the case is that the narrative worlds of children were changing, and that television, as the dominant cultural medium, had a huge part in that. It would become quite normal for children to come home from school and settle down in front of the TV with a packet of Wotsits and a carton of Um Bongo. But it hasn't shown any sign of wiping out children's literature, any more than videogames (the moral panic of our own day) have seen off television.

Television came to be freighted with the same anxieties as, two centuries before, fairy stories had been. In her memoir Jacqueline Wilson, born in 1945, remembers the early days of television – her family, like many, acquired their first set in 1953 to watch the coronation – when children's programmes lasted 'for one hour, from five to six. That was your lot,' and the offering included the inane antics of *Muffin the Mule*.

She remembers, too, parental disdain for the medium: 'ITV started up when I was about eight but Biddy [her mother] fought not to have it. She said it was common.' All the children at school were talking about the cowboy show *Wagon Train*, but, even when the family did acquire a new set that could receive ITV, 'I still wasn't able to join in the *Wagon Train* discussions at school. We watched one episode and Biddy poured scorn on it.' Each generation panics that a new and powerful medium will corrupt or stultify its audience – and especially its impressionable child audience. Programmes adored by children made adults nervous. *Doctor Who* was too frightening; *Grange Hill* was too vulgar and too realistic (it was enough that children at struggling comprehensives should swear, bully each other and take drugs; must they also watch fictional versions of themselves doing so on telly?).

As early as 1954 academic work was being produced into the effects of television on children. The Himmelweit Report was commissioned by the Nuffield Foundation on behalf of the BBC's Audience Research department. As the Nuffield Foundation's chair Hector Hetherington framed it in his foreword:

A good deal of concern was felt about the effect of this new medium on children and especially on very young children. Some maintained that television was on balance bad, that young children were intent on the screen when they should be out at play, that older children spent on it time that should have gone to their homework, and that adolescents were diverted from their youth clubs and their games. Some stressed the dangers arising from the passive character of television viewing, fearing that it would make young people mentally lazy. Some, on the other hand, thought that viewing could help young children, make their homes more attractive, expand their horizons, stimulate new interests, and provide a new basis of contact between the generations. These were the questions which the BBC had in mind.[*]

At that point there were televisions in only one in five houses in the UK. The concern was, in effect, to make a scientific inquiry while there even existed a control group. The study sought to investigate not only the question of how television reshaped the average child's leisure time, but also the trickier question of how its content reshaped their view of the world. They studied nearly 4,000 children in four English cities – pairing off television-watchers with counterparts in the control group of similar age, sex, intelligence and social background – as well as a 'before-and-after study' where they observed the same children in Norwich before and after the arrival of that city's first television antenna.

They found, no doubt to the alarm of Jacqueline Wilson's mum, that

> Three-quarters of the votes for the most favoured programme went to adult programmes, particularly to crime thrillers and, to a lesser extent, to comedies, variety programmes, and family serials. Westerns were much favoured by the younger children. Other types of programme – such as puppets, nature and animal programmes, and how-to-make programmes – were not especially popular. Only among the 8–10-year-olds did children's television programmes or *Watch with Mother* appear among the top five favourites.[†]

---

[*] Hilde T. Himmelweit, *Television and the Child: An empirical study of the effect of television on the young* (Oxford University Press, 1958).
[†] Ibid.

But they found no strong correlation between the content consumed – especially on-screen violence – and the real-world behaviour of the children.* And on the question of what was being
neglected to make way for the two hours a day of television, they
had a surprise for Roald Dahl:

> At first, television decreased the proportion of books to comics
> read. But as children got used to viewing they gradually reverted
> to books; so that after a few years the viewers were once again
> reading as many books as the controls, and the duller children
> had even increased their share. Ultimately, therefore, television
> favours book- rather than comic-reading. Book-reading comes into
> its own, not despite television but rather because of it. Television
> stimulated interest in reading, through its serial dramatisation of
> books; it also aroused the child's interest and curiosity so that he
> became interested in a wider range of books than before, including
> non-fiction. Television may reduce children's reading skill at first,
> but not in the long run.†

As it turned out, what really suffered when the one-eyed babysitter
joined the family was radio. If kids had a telly, they stopped listening
to the wireless. Video really did kill the radio star.

Children's broadcasting and children's literature, then, fed off
one another as much as they were in competition. *Jackanory*, which
ran on the BBC for more than three decades from 1965, invited
guest actors to sit in an armchair and read children's stories aloud:
a bedtime story through the television. (*Listen With Mother*, the
nearest radio equivalent, ran from 1950 to 1982.) As Himmelweit's
even-handed assessment had it: 'many children cut down their book
-reading as a result of the time they gave to television, but […] at the

---

* Subsequent studies, it should be said, have found correlations between exposure
to on-screen violence and increased aggression in children.
† Himmelweit, op. cit.

same time they were stimulated to read some of the books which had been dramatized on television.'* Indeed, the report found that television could actively 'broaden and stimulate children's interests' in reading.†

In some ways, the trajectory of children's television follows the trajectory of children's books: adult anxiety, the attempt to tame its unruly appeal for moral or educational purposes; and the countervailing tendency of children to vote with their feet for what gave them pleasure and excitement. More than that, television picked up the baton from theatre when it came to dramatising children's stories. The second half of the twentieth century saw countless children's books adapted for the small screen – just as, from Lewis Carroll and J.M. Barrie right through to Enid Blyton, characters and stories jumped from the stage to the page and back again.

This seems to me a crucial point. Children's stories have *always* existed, where they get the chance, in more than one medium, and spilled between them. Playground games draw on things that children have read about in books – remember the Bastables playing *The Jungle Book* on the lawn? – and children's stories in turn draw on or feature playground games and children's books. Children's stories themselves depict children consuming children's stories and using children's stories to make more children's stories. In this respect, these properties have something of the quality I've remarked on in myth: a blurriness, an availability to be reinvented, and even an orality, in the way that the spoken performances of the playground remix the mythos each time. The boundaries of children's writing, of children's storytelling, are as indistinct as the boundaries of the haunted wood itself. They never stay between the covers of a book.

Indeed, as the television age advanced, the traffic started to go in other directions. Popular TV shows gave rise to novelisations –

---

* Himmelweit, op. cit.
† Ibid.

Terrance Dicks's *Doctor Who* novels being only one of the more prominent cases in point. 'Annuals' – the *Wombles, Crackerjack, Blue Peter, Sooty, Playschool* – and collectible sticker-books proliferated. Popular TV shows and films gave rise to toys; and by the 1980s toys were starting to give rise to TV shows. G.I. Joe was a toy, originally launched in 1962, that became a comics and later film franchise. *Teenage Mutant Ninja Turtles* jumped from a (rather sophisticated) underground comic book in 1984 to a range of action figures, and thence to the small and big screens. *Transformers* was a TV cartoon that began life (in 1984) as a marketing exercise for a range of toys, and spawned a multimedia franchise incorporating feature films, videogames, comic books and novelisations.

In our own age there are probably more videogames that have become TV series than there are videogames made *of* TV series. Lego, which started off appropriating established characters and *mises en scene* (the own-brand 'Space Lego' of the 1980s is now Star Wars Lego), has become something like a whole new medium of its own. You don't just have Batman Lego: you have a Lego Batman videogame and a big-screen Lego Batman movie.

From the top-down point of view, this is no more than the free market doing what it does: finding ever more abstruse ways to suck profit from intellectual property on every platform in which, as marketing folk might say, brand recognition can be leveraged. But from the bottom-up, child's-eye perspective, it's completely natural: stories spill over. When you're playing with an action figure, you're writing a story. Children are omnivorous: they see a natural continuity between the books, the comics, the videogames, the TV show, the feature film, the action figures, the dressing-up costume.

Television, in other words, like theatre and radio before it and like role-playing games and the choose-your-own-adventure books that had a vogue in the seventies and eighties, took its place in a storytelling ecosystem that was, and continues to be, roomy enough to accommodate potentially endless diversity.

Genius Loci

ALAN GARNER · SUSAN COOPER ·
DIANA WYNNE JONES

*The Weirdstone of Brisingamen; The Moon
of Gomrath; Elidor; The Owl Service; Red
Shift; Over Sea, Under Stone; The Dark
Is Rising; Greenwitch; The Grey King;
Silver on the Tree; Charmed Life*

L IKE ALL THE FANTASY WRITERS OF HIS GENERATION,
Alan Garner's path to eminence was paved by Tolkien
and Lewis. His first novel, *The Weirdstone of Brisingamen*
(1960), was plucked from a publisher's slush pile by an editor
still smarting over having turned Tolkien down. Garner, looking back, was to describe that first novel as 'a fairly bad book'
– and, if only by his own later standards, he wasn't wrong. He
had to get out from under Tolkien before he could become
himself.

The story follows two children, Susan and Colin, as they seek
to prevent the titular magic rock from falling into the hands of a
Sauron figure called Nastrond. Most of it is an interminable chase
sequence interspersed with stock fantasy figures speaking gibberish.
There are noble dwarves, ethereal elves and Gollum-like goblins.
Wizards say things like: 'Long years ago, beyond the memory or
books of men, Nastrond, the Great Spirit of Darkness, rode forth in
war upon the plain. But there came against him a mighty king...'
Dwarves say things like: 'Durathror, son of Gondemar am I; Prince

of the Huldrafolk, and friend to the lios-alfar. We have not time for gossip: come.'

But in a crucial way, and one he was to take much further, it marked a departure from its predecessors. Tolkien offered his readers a magical alternative world; Lewis invented a magical alternative world to which you could travel from this one. Garner and the fantasy writers of the sixties and seventies, though, offered a magical alternative world that existed at the same time and in the same place as the world in which we live. They re-enchanted the ordinary, so that the rabbit-hole was always all around us and, in Auden's words, a crack in the teacup opened a lane to the land of the dead.

Garner created a syncretic mythology from a pick-n-mix of names and motifs from Norse, Welsh, Irish and Anglo-Saxon myths; and then rooted that patchwork mythos in a real landscape: Alderley Edge, in Cheshire, where he grew up. Where his great predecessor invented a magical Middle-earth that might fleetingly echo our own, Garner invented one that coexisted with our world: a palimpsest in which the magical and the mundane share space. As Neil Gaiman puts it, in Garner's work 'real English places emerged from the shadows of folklore, and [...] people found themselves walking, living and battling their way through the dreams and patterns of myth'.*

From the point of view of a child reader, it became thrillingly imaginable that you, like his protagonists, might find yourself the central figure in a drama of cosmic importance taking place in a landscape as familiar to you as home. Garner describes himself as writing 'under the discipline of Ordnance Survey grid references: you may not believe that this happened – but I can show you where it didn't.'

---

* 'Praise for Garner' in *The Weirdstone of Brisingamen (50th Anniversary Edition)* (HarperCollins, 2010).

There's a fine comic example of this in *Weirdstone*, when the protagonists have a rendezvous with the wizard 'on the summit of Shuttlingslow yonder at dawn on the morning of the fourth day from this'. The excellently sensible farmer's wife Bess – she's ironing one of the dwarves' tunics at the time – injects a welcome pragmatism into proceedings:

'You say as you've to get our Bridestone to the top of Shuttlingslow by Friday morning? Well, that wunner be difficult. You two con stay here, if you've a mind to, and catch a bus from Macclesfield to Wildboarclough, and then all you'll have to do is climb up the hill and meet your wizard.'

'We must take no chances,' said Fenodyree. 'That would be a dangerous course; we shall go on foot.'

'Well, I don't see it, myself,' sniffed Bess.

The later books are often thick with authentic Cheshire dialect but have none of that Giblet-Son-Of-Gimlet nonsense. From *Weirdstone*'s sequel *The Moon of Gomrath* (1963) onwards, there starts to creep a register that feels closer kin to Browning's 'Childe Roland' than to *The Hobbit*. 'Colin [...] grabbed at the hand. But though it looked like a hand, it felt like a hoof.' Or: 'The bridge itself was the worst part. It was low, and the air stank of slime, and Susan fell against things that moved away from her in the darkness.'

Two things in particular seem to me to shape Garner's work. The first is biographical. Born in 1934, he was of the first generation who benefited from the selective grammar-school education provided for by the 1944 Education Act. Winning a free place at Manchester Grammar School and going on to Oxford to study classics, Garner was the first of his family to receive a higher education, and, much as it launched him into the world, it also made him a 'pariah'.[*]

---

[*] Interview with author, 2022.

School was 'the only place I could be myself'; but being himself meant alienation from his origins.

His experience tracks a deep shift in the experience of growing up in the middle of the twentieth century in Britain. The hierarchical, geographically limited pre-war society was fissuring yet further. Cleverness, success in the eleven-plus, could send you to grammar school, then to university, and into a world that would have been unavailable, and often incomprehensible, to your parents and grandparents. Garner's own grandfather was an unlettered blacksmith, and it was sitting with him in the darkness of the forge that the seven-year-old Garner first heard the local legends – among them the idea that a wizard guarded a magical army of sleeping knights under the hill – that would feed his fiction.

That gives a special poignancy to the stories that Garner has woven and continues to weave around Alderley Edge. The here and now, and the land of lost content, are one and the same thing. The Garner who has lived his whole long life in the place he grew up was also exiled from that place by his education. His mythologising of the Edge is at once an act of lament and of reparation. It became Garner's version of the beautiful garden Alice glimpses down the rabbit-hole.

The second stream that fed Garner's creative project was neither literary nor mythological, but scientific: his growing interest in theoretical physics. The mind-bending discoveries of the first years of the century were trickling out into the wider world in the post-war period. Werner Heisenberg talked in the 1950s about the 'Copenhagen Interpretation', and Hugh Everett's many-worlds theory was first published (though it was widely ignored or ridiculed at first) in 1957. Scientists were telling us that reality was far stranger and more magical than it appeared.

For something to be there and not there at the same time, for the universe to contain many avatars of the same character in various worlds, quantum superposition, spooky action at a distance, the many-worlds hypothesis, and the discoveries physicists have made about the extraordinarily peculiar nature of time itself: all of these were grist to Garner's mill.

In a haunting biographical detail, as a young man Garner befriended a figure who stood on the boundary between the old world and the new: Alan Turing. An outstanding schoolboy runner in the early 1950s, Garner trained for competition by pounding the country paths around his home and found himself falling into step, and into conversation, with another runner. His new friend was a 'delightful, funny, immature mathematician [with] a high-pitched, aristocratic voice [...] who could run the socks off me because he was a marathon runner'.

For nearly two years, they would meet by arrangement to run and talk together. Turing, though Garner would not know until years later, was at the time going through the hell of chemical castration after his 1952 conviction for indecency (homosexuality remained illegal till 1967). Garner would go on to imagine strange physics, science twining with magic. Turing had been among the brilliant minds at Bletchley Park who changed the course of the Second World War, and was the father of artificial intelligence and the digital age. Both were in a process of transformation. Neither was fully known by the other.

Their friendship came to an end abruptly when Garner was visited by the police, who issued him with a formal warning to have no further association with his friend. 'No explanation given,' Garner said, seventy years later. 'It almost destroyed me. It took me decades to get over.' Shortly afterwards Garner went to do national service. While he was away Turing killed himself. In imitation of his favourite fairy story, 'Snow White', Turing ate an apple poisoned with cyanide.

Alan Garner still lives in a house in Cheshire 'on top of a Bronze Age burial mound on a site which has been occupied without a break culturally since the end of the last ice age'. It's right next door to Jodrell Bank Observatory. The Lovell Telescope first started to take readings from the universe in the year he moved in. 'We've been in step for sixty-five years,' he said.

Science made a steadily greater showing in the work as time went on. By the time he wrote *Elidor* (1967) Garner was starting to see how the world of myth and the world that realist literature describes can be brought electrifyingly together. On the face of it, *Elidor* takes its cue from C.S. Lewis: four siblings, wandering through a broken-down backstreet in Manchester, stumble through a portal into a magical realm that is under threat from an encroaching evil. They are tasked to retrieve from a tumulus four magical objects – a sword, a chalice, a spear and a keystone – that will in some unspecified way save the kingdom of Elidor.

But the otherworldly quest stops abruptly. The rest of the story takes place in our world, where the magical objects appear as bits of junk (though, like that foot that feels like a hoof, they feel in the hand like swords and spears). The story is not about human children trying to save a magical world, but about the menacing possibility of incursions from that world into our one. The proximity of magical objects, which exist in both worlds at once, affects electric razors and stand mixers. The antagonists triangulate their power, like radio signals. And instead of the default fantasy trope of omniscient magical beings spouting mysterious prophecies, the magical creatures are just as baffled by the prophecies as their human counterparts.

The Elidorian Malebron says that the mystical 'The Lay of the Starved Fool' was originally read in Elidor 'only for its nonsense' – but that when parts of it started to come true he saw in it 'a waking memory of what was to be' and started to work to make sense of it. 'I knew nothing,' he confesses to the children, 'of what I have just told you about our two worlds. I have had to find out that for myself by trial and thought, by asking all the time: how is this true, and if it is true, how can it be?' Elidor, too, has its folklorists, its scholars of myth, its experimental scientists. As the fantasy novelist Jonathan Stroud put it in his introduction to a later edition of the book, 'Novels like *Elidor* are themselves a boundary, set like standing stones between earlier tales of movement between worlds and recent books (so common now) that mingle magic with the day-to-day.'

In the books that followed, Garner turned into quite another writer than the wizard-and-goblin merchant of his earliest work. *The Owl Service* (1967) was a bewitchingly sinister contemporary retelling of a folktale from the Mabinogion as a drama of family breakdown and sexual anxiety, its characters inescapably re-enacting the trauma of the deep past. 'Nothing's safe any more. I don't know where I am. "Yesterday", "today", "tomorrow" – they don't mean anything. I feel they're here at the same time: waiting.' Physics is there, too: the crockery of the book's title, plates whose patterns can be interpreted as a floral motif or as one of owls, are likened to batteries, storing the power of the myth.

1973's *Red Shift* – the title is taken from a term used to describe the Doppler effect on the wavelength of light, which allows scientists to demonstrate that the universe is expanding – took three time periods from English history and juxtaposed them. Entirely gone, in that book, is any trace of *Weirdstone*'s fey archaism: Garner's Roman soldiers speak, in fact, like US marines, and the My Lai massacre (then fresh in the news) finds an extraordinarily savage echo in the dirty warfare of pre-modern Britain.

Garner, incidentally, has never accepted the label 'children's writer': 'I'm writing for anybody who cares to read, after I have written for myself.' That is more, I think, than just a writer demanding his due. Garner is in the myth business – and myths, back at their roots, were never for children. He seems to me, too, to offer a suggestive metaphor. In fantasy writing like Garner's, the portals between worlds go both ways. The story puts an adult writer on the threshold of the world of childhood, a world vibrating with enchantment; and it puts children on the threshold of a world of adult agency, of adult responsibility, of adult peril.

In *Elidor* the children are chased down an ordinary suburban street by dimension-hopping warriors. When they call out for help, curtains twitch closed and they hear bolts sliding shut. Here's a classic children's fantasy moment: adults won't understand and can't help. It sits on the shivery/thrilling borderline between a fantasy of being alone in a vital responsibility and the terrifying reality of being, well, alone in a vital responsibility. Does it not also, perhaps, reflect a growing anxiety about the fraying of communities in the here and now? The organic unity of the pre-modern village has given way to a society of suburbanites, safe behind their curtains, not caring to put their noses in the business of their neighbours.

Following hard on Garner's heels and startlingly close in approach to his early work was another gifted writer, Susan Cooper. Her *Dark is Rising* series began in 1965 with *Over Sea, Under Stone*, and concluded with 1977's *Silver on the Tree*. The first book even shared Garner's Enid Blyton-ish set-up (children staying in a strange old house on a countryside holiday; in Cornwall, in Cooper's case, rather than Cheshire) and finding themselves drawn into a mythological quest. The magical milieu of Cooper's books also draws on existing mythologies associated with the geographies of their settings: in her case Cornwall, North Wales and the Thames Valley. She and Garner both mined the Mabinogion. And Cooper even manages a Black Rider, which can't but be a hat-tip to Tolkien.

The mythologies and even some of the story beats cross over. *The Moon of Gomrath* and *The Dark Is Rising* both include a version of the Wild Hunt, a motif that appears all over Northern European folklore, as Jacob Grimm observed more than a century before. A malevolent magical winter has a pivotal place in both sequences, as do evil parliaments of rooks. In both, the antagonists at various points take the shape of formless clouds of darkness. In both, keeping to ancient pathways offers protection from evil magic.

Above all, like Garner, Cooper offers a sense of the way that deep time and old magic are buried just beneath the surface of our own world. The eschatological scheme jostles with the ordinary furniture of modernity: Garner imagines that mundane bus route to the endpoint of the quest; Cooper describes how the Dark's uncanny blizzard affects what later generations will come to call the Muggle world, with 'British Rail [...] fighting numerous electrical failures and minor derailments caused by the snow'. Both succumb from time to time to the reactionary nostalgia endemic to children's writing: we're invited to wince a little at the way the ancient purity of their landscapes is despoiled by hikers, litter and tourists.

In the building of Cooper's sequence the connective tissue is the mythology itself – an immemorial struggle between the Light and the Dark that takes place behind history. The only character shared between the first book and the second, for instance, is the enigmatic white-haired Merriman Lyon, whose real identity is hinted at in a wonderfully spine-tingling moment in the closing pages of *Over Sea, Under Stone* – '"Merriman Lyon," he said softly to himself. "Merry Lyon... Merlion... Merlin."'

Cooper's story follows several protagonists as they struggle to find (and protect from the Dark) a series of ancient magical objects, guided by riddling old songs. In book one, the three Drew children are engaged in a Dan-Brown-style pursuit of the Grail, complete with ancient maps, secret chambers and geographical puzzle clues. In book two, which deepens the resonance and scope of the story, the seventh son of a seventh son, Will Stanton, discovers his destiny (his birthday surprise is finding out he's the last of the Old Ones) and searches through time for the six Signs that, united, will give the Light the power to push back the rising Dark.

That second book – published eight years after the first, and considerably more ambitious and grandiose – takes the series out of harbour. From *Greenwitch* (1974) onwards, the stories link: the Drew children from *Over Sea, Under Stone* and Will come together to follow the breadcrumb-trail after the Things of Power and a fifth player, a pale-skinned Welsh foundling called Bran, is introduced in *The Grey King* (1975). The whole sequence is uneven – its high

points are books three and four, which are lean as elvers, grounded
in their landscapes and electrically connected to their myths – and
the final book, though it contains some of Cooper's best writing, is
confused and overlong. But the whole sequence is thrilling to read
and full of unexpected and haunting moments and ideas.

As in Garner's work, there's more than one layer to the mythology: the magical struggle between good and evil sits atop a still older
set of powers (the equivalent of Garner's 'Old Magic' is Cooper's
'Wild Magic') that precede good and evil itself.* As that contrast
develops – the children both in and out of a magical world or
slipping through time – the moral scope of the stories broadens.
In Cooper's jumbled but resonant cosmology, the millenarian
struggle between Light and Dark sometimes steamrollers frail
human feeling.

Among the most poignant and troubling figures in the book is
Hawkin – an ordinary man plucked from his home in the thirteenth
century to serve the Light. He realises that his master Merriman is
quite prepared to sacrifice his life if circumstances require it, and
he is cursed to spend centuries tramping the earth as 'the Walker',
a human *poste restante* waiting for the Sign-Seeker to be born so he
can hand over a package. The betrayal shocks him into going over
to the other side. Being a pawn of destiny, in Cooper, isn't always
fun. The magical objects in *Greenwitch* and *Silver on the Tree* are
guarded by creatures who seem, above all, *depressed* by their place
in the eschatological scheme: a sacrificial totem, racked with a
childlike loneliness; a catatonically sad king immured in a tower
in the Lost Land. As Merriman puts it: 'This is a cold battle we are
in, and we must sometimes do cold things.'

---

*   If I were a Freudian, I might speculate that this structure has a psychological
truth to it: that, even as these stories draw their child readers into the world of moral
conflict that is part of growing up, they remind them that, down in the basement
of all our existences, there's an ancient, collective, amoral id that precedes morality
and language itself.

Robert Macfarlane, who in 2022 adapted the second book for the radio, wrote ahead of broadcast: 'Though it's structured around a Manichean opposition of Light and Dark, Cooper's novel refuses to cleave into neat binaries. I think of it, in fact, as a cold war novel, first published in 1973 and kindred in its moral complexities to early le Carré; describing a conflict fought in the shadows, in which no one is clean.'*

Once again, the adult world shades that of even the most fantastical children's story. Macfarlane's framing the book as a Cold War novel accounts for the darker shades in its moral tapestry. There is, which seems to me a subtle lesson for a children's story, a ruthlessness to those dedicated to a higher purpose, or working on a timescale measured in millennia rather than decades.

> Those men who know anything at all about the Light also know that there is a fierceness to its power, like the bare sword of the law, or the white burning of the sun [...] At the very heart, that is. Other things, like humanity, and mercy, and charity, that most good men hold more precious than all else, they do not come first for the Light [...] in the very long run the concern of you people is with the absolute good, ahead of all else.

The sequence closes with the Dark routed and the Light – in the form of the Old Ones, King Arthur and the gang – retiring on a magic longship to Cooper's equivalent of the Grey Havens. What's left is the human, the here and now – something prefigured in what otherwise seems an uncharacteristic intrusion of contemporary politics into the sequence early in the final book when the Drew children interrupt the racist bullying of a Sikh schoolboy.

---

* Robert Macfarlane, 'Midwinter magic: Robert Macfarlane on the enduring power of *The Dark Is Rising*', *Guardian*, 3 December 2022.

A series of books that put England in dialogue with its deep Celtic/Nordic mythic past now also, glancingly, noticed the multiracial society into which they were published. Though children's writing would take another generation to really come to grips with that change – preferring to treat black or brown characters as comical or peculiar, and helpers rather than protagonists – it was making itself known. In 1977, when *Silver on the Tree* was published, the dark was rising in the real world. The UK's fascist National Front was at the height of its popularity, and skinheads in Birmingham, Leicester and London launched unprovoked assaults on Asian people, what they called 'Paki-bashing'. 1976 saw the formation of Rock Against Racism; 1977 the forming of the Anti-Nazi League. There really was a fight going on in the world into which its readers were growing up.

In valediction, Merriman tells the children: 'remember that it is altogether your world now. You and all the rest. We have delivered you from evil, but the evil that is inside men is at last a matter for men to control. The responsibility and the hope and the promise are in your hands – your hands and the hands of the children of all men on this earth.' That sounds a lot, in the context of a fantasy novel, like growing up. The last words of the book – echoing Kent in *King Lear* – are spoken by Will: 'I think it's time we were starting out. We have a long journey to go.'

Garner and Cooper were of a generation, as was Diana Wynne Jones (born in 1934, a few months before Garner and less than a year before Cooper) – third in the great triumvirate of British post-Tolkien writers of fantasy for children. Her star has now been somewhat eclipsed. Not all viewers of the Studio Ghibli hit *Howl's Moving Castle* (2004) will at first have realised it was based on the work of a British writer – though its popularity among the anime-loving Generation Z gave her a whole new audience in the late noughties. Wynne Jones's work has been influential on what followed, though. Her series of seven *Chrestomanci* novels are a fantasy in which a state bureaucracy regulates the control of magic and, in the first, 1977's *Charmed Life,* two orphans are trained in the use of magic in Chrestomanci Castle. It includes a multiverse in which our own universe figures (the trainee witch Gwendolen swaps places with the version of herself that exists in our magic-free world) and contains, in the eponymous Chrestomanci, a 'You Know Who' that characters are fearful of naming aloud. Her work is an acknowledged touchstone for both Philip Pullman and J.K. Rowling's work.

Pushing the Boundaries

URSULA K. LE GUIN · MADELEINE L'ENGLE

A Wizard of Earthsea; The Tombs of
Atuan; Tehanu; A Wrinkle in Time

A CROSS THE ATLANTIC, MEANWHILE, WERE TWO writers – Ursula K. Le Guin (1929–2018) and Madeleine L'Engle (1918–2007) – who sought with varying success to put a tweak on the white male inheritance of mainstream science fiction and fantasy. The first novel in Le Guin's *Earthsea* trilogy, *A Wizard of Earthsea*, came out in 1968, capping off the decade that saw Garner and Cooper get their starts. She was no less important a writer, but she was in some respects a very different one.

Le Guin's fantasy setting was not a hidden palimpsest of our own: there is no portal to Earthsea in Berkeley, California; there is no Object of Power hidden somewhere in Portland, Oregon. Her imaginary world came with politics and detailed local mythologies and, satisfyingly, with maps – she said that when the idea for the book came to her 'the first thing I did was sit down and draw a map [...] on a very large sheet, probably butcher paper, which I had rolls of for my kids to draw on.'* Its connection with our real world was psychological and mythopoeic.

The protagonist of *A Wizard of Earthsea*, Ged, is a trainee magician in a world in which enchantment is a widespread technology

---

* Author's Introduction to *The Books of Earthsea* (Gollancz, 2018).

and (in keeping with so many accounts of magic) the mastery of objects and forces comes through the knowledge of their occult true names. Her starting point was that 'Back then, in 1967, wizards were all, more or less, Merlin and Gandalf. Old men, peaked hats, white beards. But this was to be a book for young people. Well, Merlin and Gandalf must have been young once, right?'*

So it's a book about growing up. Ged's powers are considerable, but uncontrolled – and it's when he casts a forbidden spell, and it goes wrong, that he brings into being his principal antagonist, a 'shadow-creature' of horrible and unceasingly shifting forms whose first attack scars him. For the first part of its existence the shadow implacably chases Ged; then, realising he must confront it, Ged chases the shadow. Their final confrontation takes place in a tenebrous space beyond the bounds of the known world where Ged overcomes the shadow by speaking its name aloud. The name is his own:

> Ged spoke the shadow's name and in the same moment the shadow spoke without lips or tongue, saying the same word: 'Ged.' And the two voices were one voice. Ged reached out his hands, dropping his staff, and took hold of his shadow, of the black self that reached out to him. Light and darkness met, and joined, and were one.

Ged finds victory in a sort of defeat; defeat in a sort of victory: 'Ged had neither lost nor won but, naming the shadow of his death with his own name, had made himself whole: a man: who, knowing his whole true self, cannot be used or possessed by any power other than himself, and whose life therefore is lived for life's sake and never in the service of ruin, or pain, or hatred, or the dark.'

The book's themes are the seductions of power, the perils of pride and the way in which evil is not something external to us – as it is in

---

* Author's Afterword, ibid.

so many simpler children's stories – but a part of every individual soul. Astonishingly, given how deeply the book resonates even at the level of vocabulary ('the shadow') with Jungian thought, Le Guin claimed not to have read Jung when she wrote *A Wizard of Earthsea*.

Le Guin further pushed the normative assumptions of the genre by making Ged brown-skinned and his friend Vetch black. Not that her publishers always noticed. As she complained, she had to contend for years with cover designers whitewashing her creation: 'Earthsea was bathed in bleach.'* The second and fourth books (*The Tombs of Atuan*, 1971 and *Tehanu,* 1990) both had a female protagonist.†

Even so Le Guin, looking back, believed that the eighteen-year gap between the third and fourth books in the series was because 'an increasing sense of something missing in my own writing, which I could not identify, had begun to paralyze my storytelling ability. Without the feminist writers and thinkers of the 1970s and '80s, I don't know if I ever could have identified this absence as the absence of women at the center. Why was I, a woman, writing almost entirely about what men did?'‡

She wrote passionately, too, against the association of fantasy writing with childishness.

> The conventionality of the story, and its originality, reflect its existence within and partial subversion of an accepted, recognized tradition, one I grew up with. That is the tradition of fantastic tales and hero stories, which comes down to us like a great river from sources high in the mountains of Myth – a confluence of folk and fairytale, classical epic, medieval and Renaissance and Eastern romance, romantic ballad, Victorian imaginative tale,

---

* Author's Introduction, ibid.
† *Tehanu* was originally subtitled 'The Last Book of Earthsea', though it wasn't – Earthsea turned out to have other ideas.
‡ Author's Introduction, ibid.

and twentieth-century books of fantastic adventure such as T.H. White's Arthurian cycle and Tolkien's great book.

Most of this marvellous flood of literature was written for adults, but modernist literary ideology shunted it all to children. And kids could and did swim in it happily as in their native element, at least until some teacher or professor told them they had to come out, dry off, and breathe modernism ever after.*

By the time the series concluded, she said: 'I [...] abandoned any attempt to suit my vision of Earthsea to a publisher's category or a critic's prejudice. The notion that fantasy is only for the immature rises from an obstinate misunderstanding of both maturity and the imagination.' Or as she also put it: 'Despite what some adults seem to think, teenagers are fully human. And some of them read as intensely and keenly as if their life depended on it. Sometimes maybe it does.'†

Madeleine L'Engle's Newbery award-winning *A Wrinkle in Time* (1962) freely mashed up fairytale and mythic elements with hard science fiction, sending its protagonists Meg Murry and her younger brother Charles Wallace Murry on an adventure across distant planets in search of their missing scientist father. Here's another writer for whom the poetic resonances of post-Newtonian physics offered possibilities. Meg and Charles's means of travel is 'tessering' through wormholes when spacetime is folded (the tesseract is the name given to a five-dimensional cube); yet her fictive universe also includes a trio of ancient and eccentric creatures called Mrs Who, Mrs Which and Mrs Whatsit, who are something between benevolent witches and guardian angels. Charles Wallace – bullied by his classmates as a 'moron' – seems to be what we'd now call neurodivergent; he has savant-like linguistic abilities and, for the

---

*   Author's Afterword, ibid.

†   Ibid.

purposes of the book, an ability to 'read' other people and predict their behaviour that borders on telepathy.

Like C.S. Lewis, L'Engle drew explicitly on her Christian faith for her *Time Quintet* (*A Wrinkle in Time* had four sequels). The principal antagonist is a 'Black Thing' – evil reified, essentially – that is swallowing planets and which, only from a very great distance, can be seen threatening our own world. When the children find their way to the planet of Camazotz, where it holds absolute sway, they find a world of unbroken uniformity and obedience, plus some hellacious bureaucracy. The Black Thing is metaphysical, but it's also totalitarian. It is temporarily seen off – and its hypnotic grip on Charles Wallace broken – only by the application of the one thing antithetical to it: love.

L'Engle celebrates parental and sibling love, and childhood difference – Meg is worried about being plain, and impatient, and aggressive and 'an odd man out'; her friend Calvin lacks love in the home and finds it with the Murry family; Charles Wallace is special in a way that the world cannot understand. The world didn't understand Madeleine L'Engle either. Her celebration of nonconformity was too nonconformist for most publishers, and *A Wrinkle in Time* was rejected (in L'Engle's account) by something between twenty-six and forty of them before finally finding its way into print. Her diagnosis, which has the ring of truth about it, and which tells us something about how siloed children's publishing was even then, is that publishers just weren't prepared to countenance a science-fiction novel with a female protagonist. Children's writers were starting to push the boundaries – but the boundaries, at this stage, were still prone to pushing back.

Wars of the Worlds

NICHOLAS FISK · ROBERT WESTALL

Grinny; Starstormers; Trillions; Monster Maker;
A Rag, A Bone and a Hank of Hair; Pig Ignorant;
The Machine Gunners; Fathom Five; Futuretrack 5;
Children of the Blitz; The Making of Me

I T'S ODD TO THINK THAT SCIENCE FICTION AND HORROR or ghost stories don't really become visible in modern children's writing until the second half of the twentieth century. They're present in the deep past, and they're present, here and there, in the nineteenth century. But for the first half of the twentieth century, they were thin on the ground.

Jules Verne's prototypical science fiction undoubtedly had child readers. *Flash Gordon* and *Buck Rogers* had been presences in American comics since the 1930s, and Dan Dare appeared on the cover of the first issue of the *Eagle* in 1950. Boys' short-story periodicals such as *The Boys' Friend* kept up a plentiful supply of speculative tales from the end of the nineteenth century – from pre-steampunk airship adventures to tales of imperial defence. But it was only after about 1960 that science fiction took serious hold in published books rather than ephemera. In part, as often, the burgeoning of a genre in children's writing accompanies or trails a vogue in adult writing. The great age of literary science fiction arrived in the mid-century – its booster rockets being the atom bomb and the moon landings – and bled across into children's and young adult writing.

Then there's horror, spooks, and things that go bump in the night. Ghosts and murderers have long played an outsized part in children's ghoulish imaginations, and in adult anxieties about children. The oral tradition is full of them. Children formed a vast segment of the audience for the 'penny-blood' publishing craze that reached its peak in the mid-nineteenth century – cheaply printed serial pamphlets about crime and violence distributed to the working classes at a fraction of the prices at which 'respectable' novels were circulated. The great moral panic in the US that led to the introduction of the 1954 Comics Code saw William Gaines, the publisher of EC horror comics, testify before a senate subcommittee on Juvenile Delinquency.

Where did all that fear go? To be a child, in any generation, is to be afraid: of the dark, of strangers, of being lost, of the unknown. Fairytales, which lie at the back of the whole canon of children's writing, are substantially about the frightening and inexplicable: monsters, magic and transformation. Growing up is a process of getting your fears under control, or at least swapping them for different fears. Adult fear (or the type adults will admit to) is, by and large, rational. Childhood fear – where the world is still an unknown quantity, and the border territory between fantasy and reality is still contested – is peculiarly intense. You don't know, as adults do, that monsters don't exist.

In his fine book *Danse Macabre* (1981), Stephen King writes about how his storytelling imagination was fuelled by a 1950s provincial American childhood filled with campfire stories, EC comics, urban legends, B-movie horror flicks. (King, if it's not a paradox to say so, seems to me to be someone you could think of as writing children's books for grown-ups.) The fantasy writer Neil Gaiman, author of the matchless *Coraline*, told *Desert Island Discs* in 2021 that childhood terrors fed his adult imagination, too. What was he scared of? 'You name it, definitely the dark, shadows, witches, anything that really did exist and anything that didn't... I couldn't switch that off and I thought of that as my big weakness.

I didn't realise that one day I would grow up and that would be my superpower.'*

Nicholas Fisk (the pen-name for David Higginbottom, 1923–2016) shared that superpower. By now a largely forgotten writer of science fiction and fantasy for children, he was a major figure in the genre in the late twentieth century, producing a book or two a year between the mid-sixties and the mid-nineties. He was described in D.L. Kirkpatrick's *Twentieth-century Children's Writers* (1995) as 'the Huxley-Wyndham-Golding of children's literature'. Fisk's books are marred by the odd of-its-time racial crassness (you'll find 'Jap' used casually) and by a sexism that is wearisome when it isn't mildly alarming. But as a storyteller he has a lasting power, and a visceral ability to inhabit the worldview of a child.

His work, which explores human cloning, alien intelligence and time travel, has a disconcerting strangeness to it. The otherwise average *Starstormers* series, which describes the adventures of children who escape from boarding school in a home-made spaceship and take to the stars in the hope of joining their parents off-planet, has as its principal antagonist a planet of animate dust (does he prefigure Philip Pullman here?); and *Trillions* describes the panicky human response to an alien hive-mind whose moral status is almost indecipherable.

Aliens, in Fisk, really are alien. The traumatised astronaut Blythe tells one of the protagonists in that book that space is:

'Alone, Apart, Foreign. Unlike anything known to man. Alien.'
   'Alien good, or alien bad?'
   It took a long time for Blythe to reply. At last he said, 'That's the puzzle. That's the mystery. How can you tell? How can you begin to understand something completely alien? Good, bad, I don't know. All I know is – alien.'

---

*   *Desert Island Discs*: Neil Gaiman, BBC Radio 4, 3 December 2021.

Space, for Fisk, is the haunted wood. His key work – and certainly, the one that made the strongest impression on this reader – is his 1973 novel *Grinny*, which brings the science fiction and horror genres together to startling effect. Its narrator is eleven-year-old Timothy Carpenter, who lives an ordinary suburban existence with his father and mother and seven-year-old sister Beth. In the very first paragraph, the doorbell rings and he answers it. On the step, 'with two gi-normous trunks', is a little old lady. '"I'm your Great Aunt Emma," she says. "You must be Tim."'

> She is rather a queer old party. Very short, with a hat with a veil, and gloves, and a way of smiling vaguely. Her teeth are very good (false?) and she is very neat. Her shoes hardly have creases in them over the instep, as if she never walked, yet she is quite spry considering her age and soon she and Mum were chattering away about the journey and so on.

The thing is that, while Tim and Beth are disconcerted by this unexpected arrival, whose name has never been mentioned in the family, their parents take her in immediately. One moment, Tim's mother is asking: '*Who?* Great Aunt who?' Then the queer old party says: 'You remember me, Millie!' At once, Millie exclaims: 'Great Aunt Emma! Oh do come in, you must be freezing. Tim, help with the luggage.' Great Aunt Emma, in the manner of her arrival and in the immediate power she has over the hopeless adults, is the nightmare Mary Poppins.

Great Aunt Emma – or GAE as she is abbreviated in Tim's diary – is billeted in the spare bedroom. Without discussion or warning, and with no end in sight, she is part of the family. And it soon becomes clear that there is something very strange about her indeed. But even as Tim and Beth come, bit by bit, to first notice and then (though only ever partly) to understand her strangeness, their parents remain completely oblivious. Even now, as Tim writes in his retrospective introduction, 'Of course, I can never talk to my father and mother about Aunt Emma – they quite literally *would not hear me.*'

As Tim's introduction explains, the diary entries that make up the main body of the text have been published at his urging by his writer friend Nicholas Fisk. Tim, now the book has been published, is fifteen: 'I was too young to have done anything about Aunt Emma when she was with us because I was never sure what it all meant and even when everything got frightening and sinister I could neither have proved anything nor gone to someone for help.' What we're reading, then, is the literary equivalent of 'found footage' horror: a story unfolding in contemporary documents in real time. There's no reassuring sense of an author making it up or shaping the story to make it make sense.

The diaries of this eleven-year-old boy – pretentious, loquacious, slangy, telegraphic – read like the diaries of an eleven-year-old boy. Any reader with a sibling will recognise Tim's bickering and competitive relationship with Beth, and his scorn at the way his friend Mac likes to ingratiate himself with her. So the gathering horror of the situation jars with the tone, which at times has a flavour of Molesworth. 'Taking the bull by the horns,' he says, 'Well, cough cough, that's enough swimming for me, hum hum, I think I will get out now.' 'Got Beth over hogging black cherry jam – none left for breakfast. Kid stuff, but A Man Must Do What A Man Must Do.' The pages are filled with memos-to-self, rhetorical questions in parenthesis, daily trivia, multiple exclamation marks, tags like 'Etc., etc.,' and abbreviations.

So *Grinny* isn't full of the foreshadowing and foreboding that make lesser horror stories scream, paragraph by paragraph, that they are horror stories. GAE's oddities are, at first, just that: oddities. Why does she seem to be nervous around electricity? How can she smoke untipped Gauloise after untipped Gauloise? Is that connected to Beth's observation that – under the fag smoke – she doesn't smell of anything at all? How come – such a sinister detail, because so unexpected and incidental and unexplained – the tops

of her shoes are uncreased? Beth nicknames her 'Grinny' because
of her incessant smiling.

Grinny asks odd questions. Is she being funny when, after the
children mention a championship-winning 'cast-iron conker', she
seems to expect it to be made, literally, of iron? She doesn't seem to
know how humans reproduce: Beth, whose teasing of her becomes
ever more pointed and probing, tells her that she won't be able to
have a baby until she's 'nine, or even ten', and Emma answers, 'Yes,
of course.' When she comes in on the family bathing naked in the
swimming pool they nickname 'Muscle Beach', she stares, oblivious
to the idea that they might be embarrassed at being seen undressed.

Then, the reveal. Grinny slips on ice and breaks her wrist. Tim
records Beth's horrified witness to the incident:

> *'The skin was gashed open but there was no blood. The bones stuck out
> but they were not made of real bone – they were made of shiny steel!'*
>
> [...] She said there was no blood, no blood at all, the skin was
> just split open. I asked her what colour the skin was and she said
> the same colour outside as in. I said, well, there must have been
> meaty stuff where the bones were, but she said no. There was noth-
> ing but the steel ribs and that the skin was just a thick layer 'like
> the fat on a mutton chop before it is cooked', but with a tear in it.

As the children come to realise with deepening terror, Grinny is
the scout for an alien invasion. Flying saucers appear. At one point
Tim goes into Grinny's room at night:

> Grinny was lying flat on her back on the bed, with her arms by
> her side above the covers. She was rigid and still, like a corpse or
> an Egyptian mummy. But she was luminous. There was even a
> faint glow through the bedclothes.
>
> I went closer – I wasn't frightened yet – and saw another thing:
> her eyes were wide open. She was staring at the ceiling, staring at
> nothing. And her eyes were lit up from inside. Like water when

you put the lens of a lit torch in it. Her mouth was open. She was grinning. I don't mean she was making the movement of smiling, I mean her mouth was set in a grin. And from her open mouth I thought I heard a slight fluttering, twittering sound. But it might have been my own pulses. I think it was the reflection of her luminosity on her teeth that made me give a sort of scream.

Isn't that lit torch/water image virtuosic? And that fluttering, twittering sound – which in my imagination resembles the unworldly blips and squawks of a tape drive or a dial-up modem – is the language that the children come to call 'Grinnish'.

What makes *Grinny* so effective is its extreme oddness and the specificity of that oddness. We are in the territory of what Freud called the *unheimlich*. The root of that word – *heimlich* literally translates as homely – points to why it is so disturbing in this context. The call is coming from inside the house: Grinny is inside the home, inside the place that in most children's literature is the locus of comfort and security, and which children leave to have their adventures and return to at the end.

Perhaps it's no coincidence that the anxiety that underpins two of the most enduring genres in horror, vampires and zombies, is that of home invasion; think of the threshold festooned with bulbs of garlic, or grazed survivors frantically nailing planks over windows while green-grey hands plunge and clutch through the gaps. The adults, who in most children's literature are the guarantors of the home's comfort and security, are no use at all. Grinny has them hypnotised. Did you ever have one of those recurring dreams where you were running from monsters, and you reached the safety of your mother and father – and then they reached down to their chins, and slowly pulled off their masks...? (No? Just me, then...)

The novel gives so deep and memorable a scare because so little is explained. We know Grinny is a threat, an existential threat – not only to the planet but, more viscerally, to the safe order of childhood experience itself. We have a series of irreducible nightmare images – a bloodless wound; a sheaf of steel spokes; a watery light in the eyes; luminous teeth; uncreased shoes; and in the climax a dull metal 'torch thing' 'as busy and unstoppable as a rat, never pausing from its nibblings and humped-up scurryings and lunges and tugs'.

It's possible to wonder whether the steady rise in science fiction and dark fantasy or horror material was kick-started, in part, by the experience of real-life horror: that it in some way refracted the experiences of a generation of writers who had been through the war in their own youth or childhood. That generation produced a body of work not of consolation or wish-fulfilment, but of anxiety: of the everyday butting up, just as in *Grinny*, against the alien and the unknown.

Nicholas Fisk was born in 1923. He was of a generation of writers who were too young to have experienced the first war, and old enough to have experienced the second not as a disruption in their adult lives but as the defining grounds of it. If you accept the premise that children's writing most often sees writers mining their own childhoods – writing both from, and often to, the children that they themselves were – you'd expect the traumatising experience of war to inflect not the children's writing of wartime or the immediate post-war period but two or three decades afterwards.* That is what we see here.

In a short memoir published as part of Walker Books's Teenage Memoirs series, *Pig Ignorant* (1992), Fisk described his adolescence and young manhood in the run-up to the Second World War. It has as its epigraph a line from Victoria Wood: 'I believe we all have a

---

* Ian Serraillier (1912–1994) was one of only a tiny handful of writers to address the Second World War soon after it had happened. His *The Silver Sword* (1956) was set amid the refugee crisis and told the story of three children roaming Europe in search of their parents. But as a book written by someone who had been an adult (and a non-combatant) during the war years, that fine book occupies a slightly different category.

certain time in our lives that we're good at. I wasn't good at being a child.' Much of that short book narrates his attempt to leave his childhood and find a secure identity as a young adult: 'For Nick, school is over! He's free! He's his real self at last!'

But the child is never quite left behind. Fisk's narrator self introduces us to his adolescent self as 'a walking, talking, breathing solid ghost. Not the ghost of someone dead. I am still alive. His flesh is my flesh, his heartbeat is my heartbeat. Because he is me. But so long ago...' This Nick – tall, gawky, pink-faced – both is and is not the boy jeered at by bullies as 'muvver's darling' (like the protagonist of *Monster Maker*). But the furniture of his identity is unstable. He affects to smoke a pipe because a girl he fancies (*Pig Ignorant* seethes with remembered lust) doesn't like men who smoke cigarettes. He gets a job as a receptionist and typist to a theatrical agent. He finds his shy, faltering way into the jazz clubs where he would come to moonlight as a guitarist – and witnesses frightening eruptions of a world still alien to him: a fight with a cut-throat razor, sex, gin.

But over all this hangs the war. One image from the aftermath of an air raid, of Fisk and a warden finding someone half-buried in the rubble, chimes with that horrible scene in *Grinny*:

> It is an elderly man, very thin, wearing a sort of striped waistcoat. The ghastly face is masked in plastic dust. A butler? 'There you are, mate, coming along nicely, soon have you out, you're all right.'
>
> But the man is not all right. There is only the upper half of him left... Shiny wet tubing...

In another of Fisk's works, the remarkable *A Rag, A Bone and a Hank of Hair* (1980), the pre-war world of that memoir is given science-fictional framing. Its protagonist Brin lives in a dystopian near future in which the birth rate has plummeted globally after a nuclear catastrophe. Its ruling gerontocracy hopes to save humanity by cloning 'reborns' from the genetic material of people who died before the disaster, and whose fertility will be unimpaired. Brin is set the task of testing the reactions of some of these reborns in a *Matrix*-like 'scenario': two children and a housekeeper live the same day over and over in a two-room stage-set designed to replicate the downstairs of a house in 1940. Brin is to share this space with them.

The unreal 1940 is, of course, far more real-feeling than the antiseptic science-fictional furniture of the 'real' world outside. Brin is startled by the rawness and appetite, even the violence, of his new housemates. The boy, Brian, 'seemed big, raw and animal. His knees were grey with dirt, red with a cut, white where the skin had been scraped.' In Brin's world everyone wears implants that make aggression not just impossible but barely thinkable. Yet this animal world has its comforts – not least the discovery that it contains toast and Marmite cut into soldiers; the way to a child reader was ever through his or her stomach. It has a degree of linguistic living colour, too, that the story's 'present' entirely lacks. The scientists supervising the experiment marvel at the catchphrases the reborns spout: '*Barmy. Nuts. Super. Gosh. I say. Soppy. Ridic. Nark it. Gertcher.*'

Why 1940? Among other things, it's because children then were frightened; because they were less entitled; because they were less likely to try to leave the house and discover that the world they thought they were living in was an illusion; in 1940 'you were stuck in your home, once darkness fell, because there was no point in going out'. When Brin wonders why the experiment couldn't have been done for 1960, he's told: 'By 1960 or 1980, children wanted all kinds of things – and got what they wanted! They expected freedoms and possessions and excitements. So later children wouldn't have done for us.'

Here's a writer reflecting on the shift in the experience of childhood between the age in which he grew up and that in which his readers have grown up. What's more, Fisk recasts his own childhood as a provisional, threatened, illusory world, charged with uncertain meaning, whose inhabitants barely understand their own reality. Brin discovers, as the novel goes on, that he doesn't understand his own. Again, home is not a safe place; and, again, there's a reality behind the surface of things that is far stranger than we can imagine.

———

A writer who gave a more direct voice to wartime childhood was Robert Westall (1929–1993). His novel *The Machine Gunners* (1975), which won the Carnegie Medal, drew on his own experiences under German aerial bombardment in Tynemouth, where he grew up. The area, renamed Garmouth in the book, is recognisably the shipbuilding working-class north-east of England.

Originally, Westall had no thoughts of publication. He wrote it longhand, in school exercise books, in the autumn of 1973. 'It was written solely for my son, Christopher, when he was twelve, to show him how things had been for me when I was twelve, in the war.'[*] That is as direct as possible a statement of how so much children's writing comes from one child to another. As his partner Lindy McKinnel was to write suggestively after his death: 'He wanted to share childhoods with his son.'[†] *The Machine Gunners* is a tremendously exciting, tough-minded and subtle piece of writing that describes not war itself, but the way in which war presses in on childhood – and the way that children, resiliently, bravely, naively, absorb it into the permanent scheme of their worldview.

When we first encounter its protagonist Chas McGill, he's waking in an air-raid shelter in the grey of dawn, and the narrative relays what could have been remarkable and frightening with the matter-of-factness of ordinary life: 'Everything was just the same:

---

[*] 'About *The Machine Gunners*', in *The Machine Gunners* (Macmillan Children's Books, 1975).

[†] 'The Life of Robert Westall 1929–1993', in *The Machine Gunners* (Macmillan Children's Books, 2015).

same whistling milkman, same cart-horse. But there was too much milk on the cart and that was bad. Every extra bottle meant some family bombed-out during the night.'

He witnesses, again matter-of-factly, adult trauma:

'You remember that lass in the greengrocer's?'

'The ginger-haired one?' said his mother, still bending over the stove.

'Aye. A direct hit. They found half of her in the front garden and the other half right across the house.'

But for Chas, the war is more like a treasure-hunt. It doesn't mean terror and loss. It is made sense of through the prism of schoolboy one-upmanship.

Chas had the second-best collection of war souvenirs in Garmouth. It was all a matter of knowing where to look. Silly kids looked on the pavements or in the gutters; as if anything there wasn't picked up straight away. The best places to look were where no one else would dream, like in the dry soil under privet hedges. You often found machine-gun bullets there, turned into little metal mushrooms as they hit the ground. Fools thought nothing could fall through a hedge. As he walked, Chas's eyes were everywhere. At the corner of Marston Road, the pavement was burnt into a white patch a yard across. Incendiary bomb! The tailfin would be somewhere near – they normally bounced off hard when the bomb hit.

Chas is looking for those 'little metal mushrooms' in the same way Tom Brown shins up a tree in search of birds' eggs. And isn't 'normally' – in the context of sheared-off tail-fins and strikes from incendiary bombs – a masterful psychological touch?

The novel's action centres on the discovery of the ultimate war souvenir. In a thickly overgrown copse, Chas discovers the tail-fin of a downed bomber. In it, still hanging from the straps, is the body of a German gunner and, half wrenched from its mounting but intact, the plane's tail gun. Secretly enlisting the help of his friend Cem, he sneaks up and saws the machine gun off with his father's hacksaw, then squirrels it away in an old sewage pipe in a disused builders' yard. When the authorities realise that this dangerous piece of equipment has gone missing, they hunt for it. These very adult children confound and deceive them like veteran spies in enemy territory.

In due course Chas, Cem and a couple of other children play soldiers for real. They establish the precious machine gun in a dugout facing over the cliffs in the direction from which the bombers come in the air raids, hoping to shoot down a German plane. They don't, quite – but they have a part in the string of events that leads to a German gunner baling from his plane and ending up their prisoner in the dugout.

Child's play and real danger mingle. This is, if that makes sense, a profoundly realistic book about fantasy. The climactic episode of the book is a German invasion that never happens. That is a fantasy: an adult fantasy. In fact, the children in the book are in some respects closer to the reality of the war – harbouring as they do the downed flyer Rudi and coming to know him as a human being – than the adults whom they at every turn outwit. The war has turned the relationships between adults and children upside down. Chas plays the child at various points, but strategically. And his friend Clogger – a Glaswegian boy from a broken home – lives outside the nuclear family altogether.

Sexual awakening, or sexual anxiety, runs as a thread through the book, as does Chas's introduction to real violence, real fear, real danger: 'Chas felt very strange. He had prickles up and down his spine. He felt bigger and stronger than ever before, and yet more frightened at the same time.'

As ever, it does to pay attention to the food. It looms so large in childhood, as in the writing about childhood (think, for instance, of the unspeakable porridge in Orwell's *Such, Such Were the Joys*), and the memory of wartime cuisine clearly stayed with Westall no less than with the toast-loving Fisk: 'Chas cheered up. Two whole slices of fried bread and a roll of pale pink sausage-meat. It tasted queer, not at all like sausage before the war. But he was starting to like the queerness.'; 'School dinner was a kind of self-discipline: the potatoes and the thin translucent custard tasted so queer that they required an effort of will to eat.'

Here's one of the funny things about children's writing: there is a sort of generational lag in the way that it processes the material of history. An adult, writing for adult contemporaries, will take the stuff of his or her own personal or historical experience and turn it into fiction to be consumed by an audience that will often share that experience. But an adult who writes for children from his or her own childhood is writing for a generation who won't have had the first-hand experience: those readers don't compare it to the fiction; they experience it *through* the fiction.

Westall was writing for an audience for whom *The Machine Gunners* and the books that came after shaped a mythology of wartime Britain. He tried, too, to share as many childhoods as he could, anthologising in 1985's *Children of the Blitz* the letters and stories that had been sent to him by readers of *The Machine Gunners* about their own wartime childhoods.

Westall's own life was marked by tragedy. His only son Christopher, for whom he had written the book that started him on his career, died in the summer holidays of 1978, at the age of eighteen, in a motorcycle accident. In the mid-1980s, Westall lost both his parents in short succession and following a breakdown took early retirement from his work as a teacher. His wife Jean, who had suffered serious mental and physical illness, was heavily medicated and hospitalised at various points, and by 1987 their marriage had ended. Jean took her own life in 1990 and Westall himself died from viral pneumonia in 1993. He was only sixty-three. But he left behind a canon of work consisting of dozens of novels for children: many of war, in the realistic mode of *The Machine Gunners*, including its sequel, *Fathom Five* (1979), but also tales of the supernatural, and science fiction, such as *Futuretrack 5* (1983). A posthumous memoir, *The Making of Me*, was published in 2006.

Westall's service to children's literature doesn't begin and end with his books. After his death his partner Lindy McKinnel donated £100,000 from his estate to what was to become the UK's only dedicated centre to children's writing, Seven Stories in Newcastle upon Tyne, not ten miles from Westall's own birthplace.

Seven Stories is a place where the value of the written word is affirmed in the age of television. In its collections you can see what the writers of this period demonstrated once again: that it's possible to take archetypal story-shapes and give them new life; that the fantastical or magical can exist just a breath away from the workaday world; and that the childhoods of the past and the childhoods of the present, in a story, can touch hands.

IX

HARSH REALITIES

S.E. Hinton · Robert Cormier ·
Judy Blume · Richard Adams · Roald Dahl

THE DARKER SIDE OF
CHILDREN (AND RABBITS)

CIENCE FICTION'S SPECULATIVE FUTURES TELL US about the present. Fantasy is about the real world. Ghost stories are always about our own fears. It is primarily through those genres that children's literature has obliquely dealt with, where it has not outright avoided, the disturbances and terrors of the middle of the twentieth century. Perhaps because of that, and because of the association of magic with fairy stories, it has been half-assumed that these genres belonged to children's literature. Even grown-up fantasy and science-fiction writing sometimes struggles to be taken seriously, to be seen as quite grown up. There's a certain amnesia in that, as I hope I've made clear: the earliest stories were fantasies and fables and myths, and they only latterly came to be relegated to the nursery.

But even as these stories were flourishing, something else started to happen in the late 1960s and early 1970s: another swerve in the temper of the times, the waking of a greater appetite for a form of realism in children's writing. I don't just mean realism strictly as a literary-critical term. In the sense that the *Famous Five* and the *Secret Seven* contained no elements of the supernatural, you could call them realist fiction; yet they were representing a version of reality no less fantastical, in its way, than the *Narnia* stories. The realism that started to creep into children's fiction in the last quarter of the twentieth century was one that was interested in representing children to

411

themselves not as they (or adults) might dream of them being, but as they were.

That is, they would start to represent children who weren't middle-class, who didn't have two parents, who didn't enjoy bucolic summer-hols adventures, and above all who might experience violence and the stirrings of sexuality. As the 1970s dawned, that sort of realism was budding – perhaps surprisingly, as the defining image of the time came to be flower-festooned hippies wafting around San Francisco – in the United States. The works of Robert Cormier, S.E. Hinton and Judy Blume brought a hard edge of recognisably real-world adolescent sexuality, violence and cruelty into mainstream fiction for young readers. And all of them, accordingly, activated adult outrage to the extent that all have been paid the dubious compliment of appearing multiple times in the American Library Association's lists of 'Most Challenged Books' – i.e. the ones that have been targeted for removal from libraries or school curricula.

The stage had been set as early as 1944, when the phrase 'young adult' first appeared in the title of an annual newsletter about books for young people sent from the New York Public Library to schools and libraries across the States. A publishing niche – one that covered the transition from children's books to grown-up reading material – had been identified. The idea of adolescence as a distinct phase of life (the term 'teenager' came into general use in the 1940s) was taking hold on both sides of the Atlantic. The emergence of this category, a step away from the putative innocence of childhood, but adrift from the orderly world of adulthood, both fascinated and unsettled adult onlookers.

Stories about rebellious or dangerous teens filtered into some of the defining imaginative works of the 1950s, such as *The Catcher in the Rye* (1951), *Lord of the Flies* (1954), *Rebel Without a Cause* (1955) and *West Side Story* (1957). The perennial moral panic about 'juvenile delinquency' – which can be found in most ages through history in one form or another – surged afresh. Teens had new clout as consumers, greater social freedoms, and a distinctive set of tribal identities in the emergent pop and rock 'n' roll culture, even as the post-war baby boom reshaped Western demographics in the direction of the young.

In 1952 Enid Blyton, a leading voice of social conservatism in post-war English fiction, published a poem called 'The Little Thug' in *The Sunday Times*:

> So you had a gang and you swore and you spat,
> But you're not yet thirteen years old?
> Poor little sallow, undersized brat,
> You strutted so brave and so bold.

That little thug is voiceless in Blyton's poem: fiction aimed at adolescents didn't yet seek to inhabit the points of view of those teens who looked troubled, alienated or socially unacceptable. That was to change.

Bad Teens

S.E. HINTON · ROBERT CORMIER

The Outsiders; The Chocolate War;
I Am the Cheese; Beyond the Chocolate
War; After The First Death

I WROTE IN THE INTRODUCTION THAT CHILDREN'S BOOKS are not written by children. A notable exception was a book that reshaped the very idea of the young adult genre: S.E. Hinton's *The Outsiders* (1967). Susan Eloise Hinton (1948–) was a high-school senior in Tulsa, Oklahoma, when she wrote her remarkable first novel, one arguably more grown up than its near-namesake by Albert Camus. Raised in a poor district of North Tulsa, she turned the violent rivalry she observed at Will Rogers High School between two youth gangs – the working-class 'Greasers' and the privileged 'Socs' (pronounced *So*-shes, for 'social') – into fiction. 'I'd wanted to read books that showed teenagers outside the life of "Mary Jane went to the prom",' she later said. 'When I couldn't find any, I decided to write one myself. I created a world with no adult authority figures, where kids lived by their own rules.'

Its settings – real-world places like the Admiral Twin drive-in and the Jasper Street Park – are the settings in which she herself grew up, the daughter of what she described in a rare interview as an 'extremely cold' father and a 'physically and emotionally abusive mother'*.

---

* Dinitia Smith, 'An Outsider, Out of the Shadows', *New York Times*, 7 September 2005.

It was while the former was dying of a brain tumour (Hinton was fifteen) that she threw herself into writing the novel. It found a publisher after the encouragement of a friend whose mother wrote children's books. Hinton sent the manuscript to her agent, and Viking bought the rights for $1,000. They initially published it as a paperback aimed at adults and, as Hinton has said, it 'died on the vine'.* But Viking realised that it was selling to schools – teachers were giving it to their students – and they remarketed it for younger readers. It was published in the UK in 1970 and has since sold more than fourteen million copies.

As the title suggests, Hinton's story presents the world from the point of view of what the straight world would consider a juvenile delinquent. The little thug had got a voice at last. The book's protagonist is fourteen-year-old Ponyboy Curtis, a Greaser whose hair is 'longer than a lot of boys wear theirs' but who is no sort of hippie. He smokes furiously, and is the junior member of a gang for whom violence, drunkenness ('in our neighbourhood it's rare to find a kid who doesn't drink once in a while') and petty criminality are the stuff of daily life. 'I can understand why Sodapop and Steve get into drag races and fights so much,' Ponyboy reflects: 'both of them have too much energy, too much feeling, with no way to blow it off.'

Ponyboy's family is precarious and unconventional but, as the book movingly shows, is no less a family for it. Both his parents have been killed in a car crash. He is raised by his older brothers, Darry and Sodapop, in the shadow of the care system or the reformatory: 'The three of us get to stay together only as long as we behave.' Soda – an amiable and energetic high-school dropout – goofs around; Darry, muscular and no-nonsense, is Ponyboy's austere and sometimes resented father figure.

They also have a wider family, in the shape of their gang. It's a story about a child who, you could say, has grown up too soon;

---

* Jon Michaud, 'S.E. Hinton and the YA Debate', *The New Yorker*, 14 October 2014.

and it describes his growing up yet further. Ponyboy and his friend Johnny are ambushed in the park by some Socs (there's a beef over a girl), and in the ensuing scuffle Johnny – who has been traumatised after being beaten half to death by the Socs before – stabs one of their attackers to death. The boys go on the run with the help of an older, harder boy who gives them a gun and directions to a hideout, before a compelling if improbable series of events brings them home (semi-)safely. When he's reunited with Darry and Soda, Ponyboy at last recognises what's going on in the family:

> I let go of Soda and stood there for a minute. Darry didn't like me... he had driven me away that night... he had hit me... Darry hollered at me all the time... he didn't give a hang about me... Suddenly I realised, horrified, that Darry was crying. He didn't make a sound, but tears were running down his cheeks. [...] In that second what Soda and Dally and Two-Bit had been trying to tell me came through. Darry did care about me, maybe as much as he cared about Soda, and because he cared he was trying to make something of me [...] This was his silent fear then – of losing another person he loved [...] I listened to his heart pounding through his T-shirt and knew everything was going to be okay now. I had taken the long way around. I was finally home to stay.

Hinton tells the story, then, through a child-narrator whose understanding grows and broadens in the course of the novel. The Greaser/Soc divide, for instance, is made blurrier by Ponyboy's prickly friendship with Cherry, the girlfriend of the Soc who Johnny kills.

> 'Hey,' I said suddenly, 'can you see the sunset real good from the West Side?'
> She blinked, startled, then smiled. 'Real good.'
> 'You can see it from the East Side, too,' I said quietly.

'Thanks, Ponyboy.' She smiled through her tears. 'You dig okay.'
She had green eyes. I went on, walking home slowly.

The restraint and offhandedness of those last two sentences seem
to me remarkable; Hemingwayesque, almost.

But Hinton also gives voice to the sheer exuberance of her
young protagonists in a way that an adult writer – for whom these
characters would traditionally have been objects of disapproval or
pity – would likely not. Here, for instance, are the boys leaving the
house all suited and booted for the climactic 'rumble', an organised
fight against the Socs:

> Two-Bit stuck his head in the door just as Darry went flying out of
> it. Leaping as he went off the steps, Darry turned a somersault in
> mid-air, hit the ground, and bounced up before Soda could catch
> him. 'Welup,' Two-Bit said cheerfully, cocking an eyebrow, 'I
> see we are in prime condition for a rumble. Is everybody happy?'
> 'Yeah!' screamed Soda as he too did a flying somersault off
> the steps. He flipped up to walk on his hands and then did a
> no-hands cartwheel across the yard to beat Darry's performance.
> The excitement was catching. Screeching like an Indian, Steve
> went running across the lawn in flying leaps, stopped suddenly
> and flipped backward.

Ponyboy, despite his outsider status, is a reader; as his brothers
and social peers are, for the most part, not. And in more than just
Hinton's fully formed prose style, *The Outsiders* is a deeply literary
book. A retrospective metafictional framing device casts Ponyboy's
first-person narration as an assignment delivered for his school
English class. Ponyboy dreams of doing exactly what Hinton's
book sought to do, to speak to:

> hundreds and hundreds of boys living on the wrong sides of cities,
> boys with black eyes who jumped at their own shadows [...] I

could see boys going down under street lights because they were
mean and tough and hated the world, and it was too late to tell
them that there was still good in it, and they wouldn't believe you
if you did. [...] Someone should tell their side of the story, and
maybe people would understand then and wouldn't be so quick
to judge a boy by the amount of hair oil that he wore.

As the critic Dale Peck noted in a retrospective essay on the book,
this explicit statement of the moral value of fiction is backed by a
slew of echoes and references in Hinton's text.* Pony and Johnny
discuss the Robert Frost poem 'Nothing Gold Can Stay' ('that
poem, that guy that wrote it, he means you're gold when you're a
kid, like green. When you're a kid everything's new, dawn.') and
the doomed antihero Dally is understood through the gallantry of
Confederate soldiers in *Gone with the Wind*. Peck finds echoes of, or
references to, Salinger and Shirley Jackson, *The Great Gatsby* and
Moby-Dick. The vaunted realism of the story is a very literary sort
of realism. Ponyboy is a very bookish sort of juvenile delinquent.

Where Hinton led, others followed. One such was Robert
Cormier (1925–2000), whose novels for young adults explored the
darker side of the freedoms that the imaginative spaces of children's
writing offered to their readers. Cormier, like Hinton, came from a
working-class background (in his case Leominster, Massachusetts,
still in the backwash of the Great Depression) and started young.
His first published work was a poem that his professor submitted
to a magazine while he was still an undergraduate. He never left
his hometown, and worked as a journalist for three decades before
the success of his novels freed him to write full time.

S.E. Hinton's precarious and violent world can be said to be
redeemed by a poetic, almost a romantic, sensibility. There's no
poetry in Cormier. His breakthrough work, *The Chocolate War*

---

* Dale Peck, '*The Outsiders*: 40 Years Later', *New York Times*, 23 September 2007.

(1974), set in a private Catholic boys' school, reads like *Stalky & Co.* rewritten by Bret Easton Ellis. In its bristling tension and the crisp viciousness of its prose, there's no room for sentimentality at all. Even the football pitch, on the opening page, is a site of warfare: 'They murdered him. As he turned his head to take the ball, a dam burst against the side of his head and a hand grenade shattered his stomach.' Cormier's books spooked traditionalists with their candour about violence and masturbation, but his real subject is cruelty.

Cormier's protagonist Jerry Renault is caught between the two poles of power in the school: the creepy acting headmaster Brother Leon, and the Vigils, a secret society of senior boys who hold absolute sway over the student body. School stories had usually drawn their tension from the benign but stuffy authority of teachers being subverted by the ingenuity and naughtiness of the students. In *The Chocolate War* the reader is presented, rather, with a cruel and arbitrary despot in formal authority over the school – and a still crueller and more arbitrary, while more organised, student authority. The two are in uneasy alliance.

The titular chocolate war is a struggle of wills over a school fundraiser. Leon enlists the pupils to sell boxes of chocolates, twice as many and at twice the price as the previous year. Openly, he exhorts them with peer pressure, public shaming and an appeal to 'school spirit'; covertly, as he knows he needs to, he enlists the help of the Vigils, via their arrogant leader Archie. It's clear where the power really lies. When Leon first approaches Archie for help, the latter takes in the 'moustache of moistness' on his upper lip and his watery eyes and realises that this virtuosic classroom sadist is 'riddled with cracks and crevices': 'the proof of what he'd always suspected, not only of Brother Leon but most grownups, most adults: they were vulnerable, running scared, open to invasion.'

The Vigils help Leon, but only so far. They give Jerry an 'assignment' – the penalty for refusing an assignment is never stated but nobody ever refuses – to decline to sell the chocolate. This he does, formally, day after day, at roll-call – a challenge to Leon's authority that enrages the teacher. But when the assignment is over, Jerry for reasons that he can't quite articulate continues his mulish refusal: which adds up to the greater risk of challenging the Vigils themselves. Jerry's refusal to bow the head to either authority – like Melville's Bartleby, the Scrivener, his act of existential heroism is to say no – is savagely punished. There's no sort of happy ending here: just a bruising beating on the darkness of the school football field, and Jerry's realisation that resistance is futile. You can read Cormier backwards to *Lord of the Flies*, and forward to Morton Rhue's *The Wave* (1981), a parable of the disturbingly frictionless rise of a fascist organisation in an ordinary high school. By the time *The Chocolate War* was published in the UK, the idea of school as a space of innocence had already been disrupted: Lindsay Anderson's film *If* (1968), a violent satire of English boarding school life, and *Oz* magazine's 'School Kids' issue (1970), which was written *by* teenagers and contained luridly sexual material *épater la bourgeoisie*, were both recent memories.

Cormier's is a vision of adolescence not as a hopeful or even a melancholy transition to adult life, but as a wasteland giving onto another wasteland. Ponyboy, in *The Outsiders*, is enjoined to 'stay golden', to retain the freshness of youth. Cormier's characters fear growing up too, but they also have every reason to fear staying as they are. Jerry's single moment of emotional connection with his austere, disappointed father is a helpless hug at his mother's funeral. He sees his father's face reflected in his features in the mirror and 'the thought made him cringe'.

> Was this all there was to life after all? You finished school, found an occupation, got married, became a father, watched your wife die, and then lived through days and nights that seemed to have no sunrises, no dawns and no dusks, nothing but a grey drabness.

The grown-up world looks to these adolescents like death-in-life:

> Paul felt sorry for older people, stuck in their houses and tenements with kids to take care of and housework to do. He thought of his own parents and their useless lives – his father collapsing into his nap every night after supper and his mother looking tired and dragged-out all the time. What the hell were they living for?

And those 1970s flower children I mentioned, who might stand in for an alternative and freer model of adulthood? They are present in Cormier – but they are the incomprehensible other: temptation and rebuke. As he waits for his bus in his mandatory shirt and tie, Jerry watches them as they mill around the Common. He is looking across the divide from one world into another. He is confronted by a straggly nineteen-year-old longhair who catches him watching: 'Hey, man, you think we're in a zoo? [...] You know who's subhuman, man? You. You are. Going to school every day. And back home on the bus. And do your homework. Square boy. Middle aged at fourteen, fifteen, already caught in a routine. Go get on your bus, Square boy. Don't miss that bus, boy. You're missing a lot of things in this world, better not miss that bus.'

As that sneering hippie warns, the boys at Trinity are halfway to their parents' condition already. Lustful, frightened, thwarted, for Jerry 'the one devastating sorrow he carried within him was the fear that he would die before holding a girl's breast in his hand'. Instead of love, reliable friendship or hope for the future, what these boys have in their stifling closed society is bullying, conformity and the naked will to power. Cormier's despairing protagonists find themselves marooned between a brutally amoral adolescent world and a stultifying adult one. Cormier's subsequent novels for young adults were scarcely less bleak. *I Am the Cheese* (1977) and *After the First Death* (1979) both had traumatised protagonists in mental hospitals, and the sequel *Beyond the Chocolate War* (1985) contains an attempted rape. He was formally experimental, too: *I Am the Cheese* is a riddling work in which an account of a long bicycle ride taken by the protagonist alternates with the transcripts of an interview with a psychiatrist. Fragments of a sinister back-story fall into place piecemeal. We're a long way, with Cormier, from Hundred Acre Wood.

Ralph Comes Out to Play

JUDY BLUME

*Are You There God? It's Me, Margaret; Then
Again, Maybe I Won't; Deenie; Blubber;
It's Not the End of the World; Forever*

I F CORMIER BROUGHT A TRANSGRESSIVE PSYCHOLOGICAL
realism to young adult writing for boys, it was Judy Blume
(1938–) who more than anybody else did the same for female
readers (though her books were by no means confined to that audience; the protagonist of *Then Again, Maybe I Won't* (1971) is a newly
pubescent boy experiencing wet dreams and crushes). Like Cormier
and Hinton, she found an audience on both sides of the Atlantic,
and like Cormier and Hinton she was subject to ferocious pushback
from the moral majority. 'Shallow', 'pandering', 'salacious' and
'trashy' were just four of the representative compliments paid to
an author whose work at the time of writing has sold more than
ninety million copies in thirty-two languages. If she's pandering,
she's certainly getting it right.

Blume's books aren't just works of psychological realism either.
There are no dramatic adventures and double-crosses, no lives at
stake, no portals to other worlds. The basic milieu of a Judy Blume
novel is the humdrum, everyday life of the young teenagers who
are both her protagonists and her readers. Blume sought to inhabit
the experience of late childhood and adolescence from inside. The
narrator-protagonists of her novels have complex and sometimes
contradictory inner lives – there's a lot going on with them at

once – and those inner lives jostle with the social conventions in which they find themselves immured.

These are not books of wish-fulfilment or escapist fantasy, and they are not straightforwardly didactic. She's not telling teenagers about alternative lives they might thrill to imagine leading: she's telling them about the aspects of their own lives that may be mysterious to them, the aspects (principally sexual ones) that in the 1970s would often go undiscussed, and in the process seeking to help them feel less alone. As a librarian, Pat Scales, expressed it in the documentary *Judy Blume Forever*, 'The realism that was available prior to Judy was not realistic at all.'*

Looked at from one angle, Blume's young adult books are issue novels – bullying in *Blubber* (1974), disability and inclusion in *Deenie* (1973), sexual exploration in *Forever* (1975), anxieties around puberty in *Are You There God? It's Me, Margaret* (1970), the impact on children of divorce in *It's Not the End of the World* (1972) and so on. But she's deft enough, and her worlds complex enough, that they don't read like single-issue books. *Deenie* – whose protagonist's pushy and immature mother is determined that she become a model, even though she's not particularly interested in being one – is also a book about the pressure of parental expectation. *Are You There God?* is also about family tensions and religious affiliation – its protagonist is negotiating her relationship with God and organised religion even as she undergoes the transition to adolescence.

Blume's own childhood was the crucible of her work. She described herself as having 'absolute recall... I can put myself back there. I know how I felt.'† Bloom was born and raised in suburban New Jersey as the Second World War began, and her childhood proper was one of airless post-war conformity. She recalled a sense

---

* Amazon Prime Original, 2023.
† In *Judy Blume Forever*.

that 'adults kept secrets from kids… I *hated* those secrets'; the first
spark to her imagination was an attempt to imagine what those
secrets might be. In the fifties, she said, 'so much was about pretend'.
The young Judy pretended to be a good girl.

Her father was the nurturer in the family, and her mother was
anxious, chilly and inaccessible: 'We couldn't talk about anything.
I knew never to ask her personal questions.' Like her future protagonist Margaret, Blume bargained with God, terrified that her
father (like his siblings) would die young. She recalled the 'burden'
of feeling she was responsible for keeping him safe, the impossibility
of 'confiding the things that were deep down inside'.

Her writing life, not just the fact of it but the form it would take,
was determined by that repressed childhood and a conventional
young womanhood. Her prayers for her father were not answered.
He died abruptly, when she was twenty-one, five weeks before her
wedding, and – still grieving – she plunged into an entirely conventional marriage in which she found herself marooned and frustrated
as a suburban homemaker. 'I went from being my parents' little
girl to John's little wife – and I was lost.' She wrote – picture books,
unsuccessfully, at first – as a refuge. Her husband took no interest
in her work. (They divorced when Blume was thirty-seven. Her
adult novel *Wifey* (1978) gave fictional voice to the frustrations of
the sort of marriage she was escaping, becoming itself a *succès de
scandale*.)

Her breakthrough came when she poured her experience of
early adolescence into her third book, a novel rather than a picture
book: *Are You There God? It's Me, Margaret*. During its composition
she wrote to her editor Dick Jackson: 'I am having the best time
writing this book! […] It is terribly controversial I think […] It deals
with sixth-grade girls, religion, menstruation, bras, boys and other
goodies!'* Its child protagonist agonises over the onset of puberty,

---

*   Ibid.

praying not to be the last of her friendship group to get her period (another girl lies about having started, as Blume herself did in the sixth grade), longing to get a bust, looking with envy and occasional spite on more precocious girls. In an era when most novels targeted at teenage girls were chaste romances of the sort S.E. Hinton derided, this was groundbreaking. Its success was immediate.

Blume went on to attack more taboos: but perhaps her greatest achievement was to do so in a way that integrated the breaking of those taboos unshowily into a story of relatable normality. *Deenie*, for instance, is notorious for its casual references to female mastur-bation – but these really are casual references. Here, for instance, is how Deenie introduces the subject.

> As soon as I got into bed I started touching myself. I have this spe-cial place and when I rub it I get a very nice feeling. I don't know what it's called or if anyone else has it but when I have trouble falling asleep, touching my special place helps a lot.

The main theme of the book is Deenie's discovery that she has scoliosis, and the way that that changes her experience of going through the world as an able-bodied person. She has to wear a body-brace, which not only puts paid to her mother's ambition for her to pursue a modelling career but also forces her to deal with the feeling of difference and the many humiliations her condition entails (she gets her period when she's strapped into the brace and has to enlist her sister's help to fetch sanitary products: 'She looked at me. I felt like a freak').

Blume is alive not only to the anxieties of childhood but – like Cormier and Hinton – to its cruelties. *Blubber* describes with savage precision the viciousness of a gang of bullies:

> The girls in the back started their song again. Blubbery blubber… blub, blub, blub, blub… The bus driver yelled, 'Shut up or I'll put you all off!' Nobody paid any attention. Linda picked the spit balls

out of her hair but she still didn't say anything. She just sat there, looking out the window.

[…]

'You're going to turn into a real whale if you keep eating like that,' Wendy told her.

'Just shut up,' Linda said, more to her sandwich than to Wendy.

'Well, listen to that!' I said. 'Blubber told Wendy to shut up. Can you imagine!'

'Some people don't know how to talk nice,' Caroline said.

'Didn't your mother teach you any manners, Blubber?' Wendy asked.

'I don't think so,' I said. 'Otherwise Blubber wouldn't chew with her mouth open.'

Bullies have appeared in children's fiction, of course, for years – *Tom Brown's School Days* gave us Flashman – but Blume's story doesn't offer a pat moral resolution. The book's narrator Jill is an enthusiastic participant in the bullying of Linda; and when she finally stands up to the head of her clique she becomes the object of bullying herself, bullying in which Linda fully and enthusiastically participates. The story concludes with an uneasy peace – a muted reshuffling of the class's alliance, rather than a moment of revelation or moral resolution.

The most notoriously frank of Blume's books was 1975's *Forever*. Its inspiration, she said in *Judy Blume Forever*, came from her then teenage daughter Randy:

When my girl was fourteen, Randy was still reading books where if a girl succumbed and did this terrible thing with a boy, which was never really spelled out in the book, the girl was punished; her life was ruined, and this would lead to banishment or illegal abortion. And the girl would die. Randy said to me, Mommy, could you write a book about two nice kids, and they fall in love, and they do it, and nobody has to die? And I thought: yes! Yes! I should write that book.

The book was initially marketed as 'her first novel for adults' –
which Blume said in the same documentary 'made me crazy –
because it wasn't meant for adult readers'. Here was a book about
teenage sex, that sought to speak directly and frankly on the subject
to teenagers themselves. It didn't punish its protagonists for their
transgression; but nor did it sugar-coat the experience by implying
that first love would last for ever. The novel ends with the couple
splitting up, and their awkward leave-taking:

> I wanted to tell him that I will never be sorry for loving him.
> That in a way I still do – that maybe I always will. I'll never
> regret one single thing we did together because what we had
> was very special. Maybe if we were ten years older it would have
> worked out differently. Maybe. I think it's just that I'm not ready
> for forever.
>
> I hope that Michael knew what I was thinking. I hope that my
> eyes got the message through to him, because all I could manage to
> say was, 'See you around…' 'Yeah,' he answered, 'see you around.'

Naturally, it was passed furtively from hand to hand in schools
everywhere it was published. It was true to life because it was awkward and fumbling rather than pornographic. A whole generation
of readers, for instance, will remember with a snigger the funny/
absurd appearance of 'Ralph'.

> 'Don't,' he said, wiggling out of his pajama bottoms. He led my
> hand to his penis. 'Katherine… I'd like you to meet Ralph… Ralph,
> this is Katherine. She's a very good friend of mine.'
>
> 'Does every penis have a name?'
>
> 'I can only speak for my own.'
>
> In books penises are always described as hot and throbbing but
> Ralph felt like ordinary skin. Just his shape was different – that
> and the fact that he wasn't smooth, exactly – as if there was a lot
> going on under the skin. I don't know why I'd been so nervous

about touching Michael. Once I got over being scared I let my hands go everywhere. I wanted to feel every part of him.

It's hard to overestimate the impact of Blume's work on her child readers – or on the shape of the culture. At the height of her popularity in the 1980s she got between one and two thousand letters from children a month. The New York *Daily News* described her as being 'Miss Lonelyhearts, Mister Rogers and Dr Ruth rolled into one'.[*] Here was an author in the role of something like a therapist or guru.

The pushback against Blume's work indicates how profoundly, still, adults continue to fear the influence of children's writing on young minds and young behaviours. It was felt less in the UK than in her native United States, where it caught a political wave after the election of Ronald Reagan in 1980. 'After the presidential election of 1980,' Blume has said, 'overnight the censors came out of the woodwork.'[†] The so-called Moral Majority, an alliance of Christian conservatives who campaigned for the Republican Party, took fiercely against Blume's work. Conservative school boards campaigned to remove her work from libraries, and she found herself debating Pat Buchanan on CNN's political talk show *Crossfire*. '*Deenie* is not a book about masturbation,' she found herself saying in exasperation. 'It's about a girl with scoliosis […] Are you hung up about masturbation? It's one scene in one book!'[‡]

The UK has never had a Moral Majority of comparable political clout, so the fights over Blume's work were less dramatic and less public in this country. But confiscations and furtive sharing were, for many at least of my generation, the norm: books that spoke to children of things that adults find difficult and embarrassing have always been hot potatoes.

---

[*] 'Dear Judy: My mother doesn't understand me…' New York *Daily News*, 13 May 1986.

[†] In *Judy Blume Forever.*

[‡] Ibid.

Rabbit, Rabbit, Rabbit

RICHARD ADAMS

Watership Down

RICHARD ADAMS'S *WATERSHIP DOWN* (1972), AT FIRST glance, might look like a counterexample to the current of psychological and social realism I've described as taking hold in the 1970s. To state the obvious: it's about rabbits – and what's more, it's about *psychic* rabbits. But it's also a work of considerable literary and psychological subtlety, a work that speaks to young adult readers without any compromise of tone or hint of condescension. It doesn't in any straightforward way stand in the tradition of animal stories for children. Hazel, Fiver and Bigwig are much closer kin to Ponyboy Curtis and Jerry Renault than they are to Peter Rabbit or Mole from *The Wind in the Willows*. And it's aggressively realistic: it's realistic *about rabbits*. (Extrasensory perception aside, that is.)

The story had its origins, as so many children's stories have, in oral tales improvised by the author for his own children. Richard Adams (1920–2016) beguiled long car journeys by telling his daughters Juliet and Rosamond an adventure story about rabbits, and it was at their insistent urging that he eventually came to write the story down. It's another book, though, that sits on the borderline between adult literature and children's writing. Despite its origins, Adams himself didn't think of it as a children's book, and it was first published in an adult imprint. It is a very, very strange work. Its first publisher Rex Collings, who took it on after most of the major

London publishers had turned it down flat, wrote to a friend: 'I've just taken on a novel about rabbits, one of them with extra-sensory perception. Do you think I'm mad?'*

He was not mad. This very singular book tells a hugely exciting story, and an archetypal one: about a group of outcast rabbits who (after Fiver senses danger) leave the safety of their familiar warren to strike out in search of a new home, the titular Watership Down; who arrive there after a series of false starts and terrible dangers; and who are then forced to defend their new home when a gang of rabbit fascists turn up in the hopes of seeing them off.

I said it was realistic about rabbits, and it is: often solemnly so. Its principal source, credited frankly not only several times in the text but also in Adams's original acknowledgements, is a natural history book about bunnies.

> I am indebted, for a knowledge of rabbits and their ways, to Mr R.M. Lockley's remarkable book, *The Private Life of the Rabbit*. Anyone who wishes to know more about the migrations of year-lings, about pressing chin glands, chewing pellets, the effects of over-crowding in warrens, the phenomenon of re-absorption of fertilized embryos, the capacity of buck rabbits to fight stoats, or any other features of Lapine life, should refer to that definitive work.

Female rabbits reabsorbing embryos into the linings of their wombs is only one of the gruesome biological details from life that feature in the plot. Adams set his story, too, in a real place – Nuthanger Farm and its surrounding fields are real places in Hampshire. Like Alan Garner, Adams wrote 'under the discipline of Ordnance Survey grid references'.

---

* Quoted by Isabel Quigly (recipient of the letter) in 'Obituary: Rex Collings', *Independent*, 8 June 1996.

Yet at the same time, Adams gives these true-to-life bunnies a mythic grandeur, and shapes his narrative according to the precepts of classical epic. Adams was familiar with Joseph Campbell's work on comparative mythology. *Watership Down* has echoes of the biblical Exodus, with Hazel as Moses. It has been described by the novelist Madeline Miller as 'a sort of Lapine retelling of the *Aeneid*... mixed with a few other famous mythological episodes, including the kidnapping of the Sabine Women and the Land of the Lotus-Eaters'; she notes debts, too, to Homer, Shakespeare and Livy. Chapter epigraphs come from Aeschylus, Xenophon, Yeats and Browning at their more vatic, Bunyan and the Bible.

It is further layered by the series of stories-within-stories, often told by Dandelion, about the rabbits' own mythology: tales of the adventures of El-ahrairah, the trickster hero and rabbit ancestor, alternatively favoured and punished by the creator god Frith. And in its wire-tight accounts of patrol, siege and ambush – both strategy and close combat – it adds in what cannot but be versions of its author's experiences as a lieutenant in the Second World War. His daughter Juliet Johnson, announcing his death in 2016, said that his wartime experiences had informed his fiction: 'He missed terribly his friends who were killed in the war.'

The disparity between the small lives of its bunny heroes and the weight of the mythic motifs they bear is what makes the book so moving and effective. It rolls the dice on something that shouldn't come off at all – but, such is Adams's conviction and skill in inhabiting his characters' worldview, it does. These rabbits are human, in the sense that their emotions and interactions are recognisable to the reader; but they are rabbits, too.

Adams never loses sight of how short a rabbit's life is, nor how dangerous. These rabbits, even the lionhearted Bigwig, are physically exhausted after travelling just a few hundred yards; and they are terrified, debilitatingly terrified, almost all the time:

Rabbits above ground, unless they are in proved, familiar sur-
roundings close to their holes, live in continual fear. If it grows
intense enough they can become glazed and paralysed by it – *tharn*,
to use their own word.

Adams has imagined his way into a non-human worldview, even
down to the different way they negotiate the landscape:

> A man walks upright. For him it is strenuous to climb a steep hill,
> because he has to keep pushing his own vertical mass upwards and
> cannot gain any momentum. The rabbit is better off. His forelegs
> support his horizontal body and the great back legs do the work…
> On the other hand the man is five or six feet above the hillside and
> can see all round. To him the ground may be steep and rough but
> on the whole it is even; and he can pick his direction easily from
> the top of his moving, six-foot tower. The rabbits' anxieties and
> strain in climbing the down were different, therefore, from those
> which you, reader, will experience if you go there.

In several sections, where the rabbits attempt to grasp something
for which their rabbit-hood does not equip them (they can't count
past four, for instance), the literary comparison that springs to mind
is William Golding's *The Inheritors* (1955).* Here's Holly, surviving
witness to the destruction of the original warren by gas:

---

*   Here's Golding's exquisitely disorienting account from a Neanderthal's
uncomprehending point of view of having an arrow shot at him: 'Suddenly Lok
understood that the man was holding the stick out to him but neither he nor Lok
could reach across the river. He would have laughed if it were not for the echo of the
screaming in his head. The stick began to grow shorter at both ends. Then it shot out
to full length again. The dead tree by Lok's ear acquired a voice. "Clop!" His ears
twitched and he turned to the tree. By his face there had grown a twig: a twig that
smelt of other, and of goose, and of the bitter berries that Lok's stomach told him he
must not eat. This twig had a white bone at the end. There were hooks in the bone and
sticky brown stuff hung in the crooks. His nose examined this stuff and did not like it.'

'Then another of the men fetched some long, thin, bending things. I haven't got words for all these men-things, but they were some-thing like lengths of very thick bramble. Each of the men took one and put it on one of the heavy things. There was a kind of hissing noise and – and – well, I know you must find this difficult to understand, but the air began to turn bad.'

The worldview of these rabbits, even though it invites the reader's human sympathy, is not human. Rabbits live too short a time to be sentimental. They have strong emotions but short memories:

They have a certain quality which it would not be accurate to describe as callousness or indifference. It is, rather, a blessedly circumscribed imagination and an intuitive feeling that Life is Now. A foraging wild creature, intent above all upon survival, is as strong as the grass.

Adams compares them to 'primitive humans'. They are also, you could say, a little like children. Nor does Adams fudge or humanise the pragmatic morality of the rabbit world; there's nothing very progressive about their attitude to women. Does, in their Darwinian world, are a resource.

'Right,' said Bigwig. 'By the way, what are the rules about mating?'
'Mating?' said Chervil. 'Well, if you want a doe you have one – any doe in the Mark, that is. We're not officers for noth-ing, are we? The does are under orders and none of the bucks can stop you.'

The apocalyptic conflict between the Watership Down rabbits and the Efrafan minions of General Woundwort is set off by the former having set out in search of female rabbits: they know that an all-male warren will die out in a generation (not to mention that does, rather than bucks, are the great excavators of the rabbit world). This is a war that starts because a bunch of bunny-rabbits have blue balls. Silly, perhaps, but no less silly than *The Iliad*.

The terrifying General Woundwort – grizzled, scarred, ferocious, a cotton-tailed Voldemort – is, we learn, three years old. A year is a long time in rabbits. The sketch we get of his early life is one of unrelenting violence and trauma: his 'happy-go-lucky and reckless buck' of a father is ambushed in a potato patch and shot; their warren is dug out; a weasel kills his mother before his eyes.

A 'kind old schoolmaster from Overton' picks the kitten Woundwort up and nurses him to health, feeding him milk from a dropper – but he can't mend the rabbit's mind: Woundwort 'grew up very wild, and like Cowper's hare, would bite when he could'. The rabbit turns his trauma into aggression. His rabbit nature itself has been crumpled. As Bigwig notes, 'He's not like a rabbit at all [...] Flight's the last thing he ever thinks of.'

The shortness of rabbit generations, and the contrast with their epic striving, is what gives the book not only its pathos but one of its most magnificent literary effects. As it closes, and we look back on the events of the main narrative from the future, we come to realise that the adventures of Hazel and Fiver, which we have watched close up, have already themselves become myths. Hazel creeps up on a doe, Vilthuril, telling her children a story:

'So after they had swum the river,' said Vilthuril, 'El-ahrairah led his people on in the dark, through a wild, lonely place. Some of them were afraid, but he knew the way and in the morning he brought them safely to some green fields, very beautiful, with good, sweet grass. [...] But Frith came to Rabscuttle in a dream and warned him that the warren was enchanted. And he dug into the ground to find where the spell was buried. Deep he dug, and hard was the search, but at last he found that wicked spell and dragged it out. So they all fled from it, but it turned into a great rat and flew at El-ahrairah. Then El-ahrairah fought the rat, up and down, and at last he held it, pinned under his claws, and it turned into a great, white bird which spoke to him and blessed him.'

'I seem to know this story,' whispered Hazel, 'but I can't remember where I've heard it.'

Hazel lives long – for a rabbit: 'He saw more young rabbits than he could remember. And sometimes, when they told tales on a sunny evening by the beech trees, he could not clearly recall whether they were about himself or about some other rabbit hero of days gone by.' Bigwig is a King Arthur figure: 'a great and solitary rabbit, a giant who drove the elil like mice and sometimes went to silflay in the sky. If ever great danger arose, he would come back to fight for those who honoured his name.' General Woundwort has become a bogeyman to scare kittens with: 'first cousin to the Black Rabbit himself'.

And when Hazel finally departs this world, invited by El-ahrairah himself to join his Owsla, Adams has abundantly earned the sense that we're seeing the hinge between one great era and the next. He brings the story in to land just beautifully:

> The sun was shining and in spite of the cold there were a few bucks and does at silflay, keeping out of the wind as they nibbled the shoots of spring grass. It seemed to Hazel that he would not be needing his body any more, so he left it lying on the edge of the ditch, but stopped for a moment to watch his rabbits and to try to get used to the extraordinary feeling that strength and speed were flowing inexhaustibly out of him into their sleek young bodies and healthy senses.
>
> 'You needn't worry about them,' said his companion. 'They'll be all right – and thousands like them. If you'll come along, I'll show you what I mean.'
>
> He reached the top of the bank in a single, powerful leap. Hazel followed; and together they slipped away, running easily down through the wood, where the first primroses were beginning to bloom.

Little Horrors

ROALD DAHL

*James and the Giant Peach; Charlie and the
Chocolate Factory; Charlie and the Great Glass
Elevator; The Witches; The BFG; The Giraffe
and the Pelly and Me; Danny, the Champion
of the World; Matilda; George's Marvellous
Medicine; The Twits; Fantastic Mr Fox; The
Enormous Crocodile; Revolting Rhymes; Boy*

MID THE CONTINUING DRIFT TOWARDS SOME VERSION
of realism, then, how are we to place the dominant writer
of children's fiction of his age? Roald Dahl couldn't, on
the face of it, have cared less about representing the real lives of
children back to them. He succeeded, instead, in nourishing their
imaginative lives by piling magic on fantasy on absurdism. Here
were window-cleaning giraffes, potions that caused disagreeable
old women (and blameless chickens) to swell to many times their
ordinary size, toeless witches, seafaring peaches, magic fingers and
glass elevators that shoot into outer space. Between, roughly, the
publication of *Charlie and the Chocolate Factory* (1964) and *Matilda*
(1988), Dahl enjoyed a quarter of a century of ascendency. By
1968 *Charlie* alone had earned Dahl more than a million dollars
in royalties.

Like so many children's writers, Dahl mined his own childhood – be it greed for sweeties, tobacco-stinking Scandinavian
grandparents or the 'mean and loathsome' old sweetshop owner

who inspired *Matilda's* Miss Trunchbull. There is a demonic energy to Dahl's work, a directness of address and a linguistic fizz that instantly captivates its intended audience. The voice of the books is almost anti-literary: it's a storyteller's voice, an oral performance on the page. The reader is a disciple or a co-conspirator.

He was clear about what children liked: 'They love being spooked. They love suspense. They love action. They love ghosts. They love the finding of treasure. They love chocolates and toys and money. They love magic.' (He might have added: they love practical jokes and fart gags and violence.) Dahl had an unerring sense of the basic and extravagant appetites of children, perhaps because his own inner child was so near the surface. He loved inventions and ingenuity and silliness. And he empathised intensely with children chafing under the authority of lazy, cruel, thwarting or inconsiderate adults, their agency limited, and wanting *more*. The most basic form of this is appetite for food. Can there have been a more feelingly written passage in all his works than the one in which he describes how Charlie Bucket eats the chocolate bar he gets once a year?

Only once a year, on his birthday, did Charlie Bucket ever get to taste a bit of chocolate. The whole family saved up their money for that special occasion, and when the great day arrived, Charlie was always presented with one small chocolate bar to eat all by himself. And each time he received it, on those marvellous birthday mornings, he would place it carefully in a small wooden box that he owned, and treasure it as though it were a bar of solid gold; and for the next few days, he would allow himself only to look at it, but never to touch it. Then at last, when he could stand it no longer, he would peel back a *tiny* bit of the paper wrapping at one corner to expose a *tiny* bit of chocolate, and then he would take a *tiny* nibble – just enough to allow the lovely sweet taste to spread out slowly over his tongue. The next day, he would take another tiny nibble, and so on, and so on. And in this way, Charlie would make his sixpenny bar of birthday chocolate last him for more than a month.

Here is a child's-eye view, an intensity of sensual focus, that reminds me of Steven Spielberg's trick of shooting *E.T.: The Extra-Terrestrial* (1982) with the camera at the height of an eight-year-old. The passage not only sets up Charlie's archetypal child's yearning to become less powerless, to have access to treats that are ordinarily out of his reach – but it wraps the meaning of the chocolate bar in a penumbra of familial love. The whole family saves up their money so that, once a year, Charlie can get a taste of chocolate.

As his life story shows, Dahl himself was prey to strong appetites – for fantasy, for adventure and intrigue, for food (especially chocolate), for power over others and the freedom to act, for the affirming love of family and (which did not come out in his children's books but was a theme of his bawdy novels and short stories for adults) for sex. The critic Kathryn Hughes talked of his 'grandiosity, dishonesty and spite'. His first wife, Patricia Neal, talked of his conviction that 'although life was a two-way street, he had right of way'. That he was not an especially nice guy, and the ways in which he was not an especially nice guy, may have been part and parcel of what made him so effective a writer for children. He had a child's id.

He was a vain, bullying, entitled man – though one of hugely impressive productive energies; in a speech at his daughter's wedding he declared, oddly for a writer, 'action is always better than words' – and he was a spoilt boy. His older sister Astri and his father Harald died in close succession when Dahl was a little boy, leaving him the adored only son in a household of women. He was nicknamed 'Apple' for the position he held in his mother Sofie Magdalene's eye. He didn't get in much trouble, as a child, when he was caught tying pillows round his baby sister and shooting at her with an air rifle. His relationship with his mother seems to

have been the most sustained and respectful relationship he ever
had with a member of the opposite sex.

'Boy' (as he titled one of his two memoirs) hated and never
forgot the attempt to curtail his freedoms that his schooldays at
Repton represented. Authority figures were viciously caricatured –
one master was, he wrote to his mother, 'a short man with a face
like a field elderberry'* – and even libelled: he was to claim that
a future Archbishop of Canterbury, Geoffrey Fisher, had given a
savage beating to Dahl's best friend for no good reason.[†] He bri-
dled at the proprieties of the expat set when he worked for Shell
in what was then called Tanganyika as a young man. He wrote
one hostess off as 'a frightful old hag who weighs 19½ stone (and
is proud of it) and looks like a suet dumpling covered in lipstick
and powder'.[‡]

The high point of his life, as he looked back on it, was the action
he saw serving in the Second World War. Dogfighting – he had
five confirmed kills in action over Palestine and Greece – was, he
later said, 'in a way the most exhilarating time I have ever had in
my life'.[§] He suffered lifelong pain from injuries sustained when
he crashed a plane into the Egyptian desert in 1940. Typically, he
mythologised the incident. He ditched through inexperience and
overconfidence, and likely only survived thanks to another pilot
coming to his rescue. But at various times he claimed to have been
shot down, and nowhere in his accounts of the incident did the
other pilot get a mention.

He came to writing for children late – and in part out of frustration that his career in adult fiction had somewhat stalled. He'd

---

* Sturrock (ed), *Love from Boy*.
† This was badly wrong. The boy in question was beaten after Fisher had left
the school; and it was for sexually molesting a younger child. When the mistake
was pointed out, Dahl refused to correct the passage in later editions of the book.
‡ Sturrock, op. cit.
§ Dahl, *Going Solo*.

had early success in post-war Washington (he was seconded from the air force as an assistant air-attaché to the British embassy) with a whimsical 7,000-word fable about the 'gremlins' that sabotaged RAF planes. He was courted by Walt Disney for the film rights, invited to a lot of fancy parties, and – having secured his golden ticket to American high society – spent his energies on committing adultery with rich women he didn't much like, and espionage.

Indeed, he was in his mid-forties by the time his first children's book appeared in print, and in a letter while he was expecting his first child he offered a sneering view of the genre: 'I can see it all. Nursery books for Knopf. Once upon a time there was a dear little bunny…' Dear little bunnies appeared nowhere in his work. Indeed, looking at the arc of publishing history, you could see Dahl's success as having put a severe dent in the dear-little-bunny market.

Nevertheless, if their set-dressing is gaudier and nastier than that of their predecessors, the structure of the stories is in some respect the same. The books conform to the time-honoured pattern of taking their child protagonists out of one world and putting them into another, secret, magical world. They travel behind the gates of the chocolate factory, or to the land of the BFG (an uncommonly sunny entry in his oeuvre), or above the clouds on a peach carried by seagulls, or enter the demented school environment of Crunchem Hall. Or they discover a secret world behind this one, the subterranean world of *Fantastic Mr Fox* or the differently subterranean world of the poacher in *Danny, the Champion of the World*. These are all worlds in which the children can be the centres of their own stories, in which they can *act* – as Danny does in the thrilling night-time drive towards the end of that latter book.

Adults in Dahl's books, with very few exceptions (Danny's father, the grandmother in *The Witches*, Miss Honey in *Matilda*) are not just distant or irrelevant: they are untrustworthy, foolish or vicious. The writer Michael Rosen has argued that this was by design: 'Dahl knew what he was doing, remarking that we both love and hate our parents, even if we don't admit it to ourselves.'*

Even leaving aside the vicious tang of Dahl's personal anti-semitism – 'Even a stinker like Hitler,' he wrote, 'didn't just pick on them for no reason' – his work, more than that of many other writers for children, has made adults uneasy. Critics and librarians have frequently thought it vicious or vulgar. Ursula K. Le Guin complained that exposure to *Charlie and the Chocolate Factory* had made her daughter 'quite nasty'. Even the NAACP took a dim view of that book's racial stereotyping of Oompa Loompas; though that is to ignore the startling fact that its protagonist was, in an early conception, to have been Black.

Humphrey Carpenter, in a glancing mention in *Secret Gardens*, calls Dahl's work 'amoral' – which seems to me to get it almost exactly wrong. Dahl's work is fiercely moral; but it is moral in a way that would horrify milquetoast Anglicans or herbivorous liberals. There's not a bit in it of turning the other cheek. It is an Old Testament morality – or, perhaps, a Calvinist one – which divides the world into goodies and baddies and takes a limitless and openly sadistic relish in the physical punishment of the wicked. As Dahl put it: 'I'm afraid I like strong contrasts. I like villains to be terrible and good people to be very good.'

That is surely exactly what makes children find Dahl so attractive: his morality is as capricious and self-serving as the worldview of a child. There's not a lot of turning the other cheek in the average eight-year-old. Children love revenge. Dahl's writing provides a fantasy world in which their imaginative proxies have the power to take it, and permission to revel in it. Instead of preaching to children, as 'improving' children's writing has from time to time been anxious to do, or even expanding their sympathies by introducing

---

* Michael Rosen, 'Roald Dahl: my hero', *Guardian*, 31 August 2012.

a literary sense of moral shading, Dahl's books gleefully pander to those very atavistic instincts.

That is not the only way in which Dahl's work seems to look backwards rather than forwards. Tonally, there's a distinct flavour of Hilaire Belloc's macabre *Cautionary Tales* (1907) or Heinrich Hoffmann's *Struwwelpeter* – two gleefully arch send-ups of moralising work for children. Dahl himself had memorised by heart the whole of *Cautionary Tales* by the age of nine. He's on record as having disdained *Swallows and Amazons* as 'too soft'. And couldn't his whangdoodles and hornswogglers and snozzwangers – or his encyclopaedic explanations of the physical characteristics and social behaviour of witches or flesh-eating giants – be refugees from the wilder corners of Pliny the Elder's *Natural History*? A child's inner map of his or her environment, after all, is always bordered with misty patches across which might be inscribed: 'here be dragons'.

His breakthrough work, *Charlie and the Chocolate Factory*, resembles nothing so much as a medieval morality play or a Restoration comedy of humours, in which each of the child visitors to Willy Wonka's chocolate factory embodies a particular vice. Some of these vices are traditional Christian ones – gluttony in Augustus Gloop, covetousness in Veruca Salt – and some spring from the canon of Dahl's own disgust at modernity; vulgar, gum-chewing Violet Beauregarde, or the square-eyed Mike Teavee.

Each of them, in Dantean style, receives a punishment appropriate to their crime – and each such episode is crowned by a choric interlude in which the Oompa Loompas sing a song commemorating, without much regret, their fate ('Veruca Salt, the little brute, / Has just gone down the rubbish chute'). The children are retrieved and restored before being sent home – but that has a cursory feel to it. Nobody – not the reader, not Willy Wonka, not Roald Dahl, probably not even the too-saintly Charlie Bucket – shows any sign of much caring if Augustus drowns in chocolate or Violet spends the rest of her life as a human blueberry.

Nobody mourns the cruel aunts Spiker and Sponge, flattened by the giant peach as it makes its escape from their hilltop garden. Nobody thinks twice about the genocidal programme set out in the closing pages of *The Witches*. And young readers positively cheer when – in the immortal few lines from *Revolting Rhymes* (1982) – Red Riding Hood does for the wolf: 'The small girl smiles. One eyelid flickers. / She whips a pistol from her knickers. / She aims it at the creature's head / And bang bang bang, she shoots him dead.'

Goodies are goodies, in Dahl, and baddies are baddies. It's very medieval. Physical deformity goes hand in hand with moral deformity. Witches are bald and toeless. Miss Trunchbull snorts and radiates heat and marches about like a stormtrooper. Mr and Mrs Twit are grotesque *because* they are unpleasant: 'If a person has ugly thoughts, it begins to show on the face. And when that person has ugly thoughts every day, every week, every year, the face gets uglier and uglier until you can hardly bear to look at it.' Being fat – to which Aunt Sponge, Augustus Gloop and Farmer Boggis in *Fantastic Mr Fox* among many others bear witness – is also a sure sign of moral failure in Dahl. When in 2023 it emerged that Puffin had reissued Dahl's works in a new edition combed by 'sensitivity readers' to remove racist, sexist, ableist and fat-shaming language there was the predictable culture-wars ding-dong; but little remarked was the larger problem, which is that if you take the nastiness out of Roald Dahl you're removing something absolutely fundamental to the success of the stories.

The anarchy and grotesquerie evoked by Dahl's prose found a perfect expression in the electrically expressive lines of the illustrator Quentin Blake. Blake and Dahl join the partnerships of Tenniel and Carroll or Rackham and Barrie in the pantheon of the English nursery bookshelf.* It's easy to forget, so closely is their

---

* That David Walliams has had many of his children's books illustrated by Quentin Blake seems to me to be a very naked declaration of his publishers' intent to position him as an heir to Dahl.

work associated, that Dahl was halfway through his career before he started his relationship with the illustrator. The two men were brought together in the late 1970s, when Dahl's publisher Tom Maschler asked Blake to supply illustrations for the picture book *The Enormous Crocodile* (1978).

Their working partnership continued until Dahl's death in 1990, and he ended up also illustrating editions of all the works that preceded their meeting. The standard edition of any Dahl book, these days, will come with Quentin Blake illustrations (even, and perhaps incongruously, Dahl's single foray into something like realism, *Danny, the Champion of the World*). Blake's vision of the BFG – with his saucer-like hairy ears, wrinkled face, vast hands and gigantic Norwegian sandals (Dahl sent Blake one of his own as a model) – is at least as important to the character's iconicity as any of the author's words.

Dahl's success is, I think, a rebuke to the idea that children's books must be nice. Children, he insisted after a century of conventional wisdom framing them as innocents in a world of adult wickedness, are not nice. He saw the potential for cruelty in children – not just teenage delinquents – and he spoke to it. In that, he has more in common with the dirty realists across the pond than it might at first seem.

X

REPRESENTING

Malorie Blackman · Jacqueline Wilson

HOW CHILDREN'S STORIES
BECAME DIVERSE

T HE ATTENTIVE READER MAY HAVE NOTICED SOME absences in the story up to this point – the story, that is, from prehistory up to the second half of the twentieth century. Most of the children who have peopled the best-known works of children's literature have been middle- or upper-middle-class. And almost all of them, especially the protagonists, have been white. That had been true, at least partly, of the audience as well as of the material presented to them. Britain, before the middle of the twentieth century, was a far more racially homogenous and class-bound place than it is today. But that had been undergoing a sea-change since the end of the war. In the work of two writers of the early 1990s, whose breakthrough books came just a year apart, you can see that sea-change finally receiving full expression in the literature of childhood. Not only was the readership of children's literature continuing to expand across racial and class barriers; so were its authors.

Cross-Currents

MALORIE BLACKMAN

Noughts & Crosses; Knife Edge; Checkmate;
Double Cross; Crossfire; Endgame;
Hacker; Boys Don't Cry; Just Sayin'

T HE BREAK-UP OF THE EMPIRE, AND ESPECIALLY
Indian independence in 1947, precipitated a wave of
non-white immigration, with people arriving from
what became India, Pakistan and later Bangladesh in the wake
of Partition. In 1948, the arrival of the *Empire Windrush* brought
the first substantial influx of West Indian migrants to the UK,
and the many Afro-Caribbean arrivals that followed are still
known as the Windrush Generation. The 1962 Commonwealth
Immigrants Act gave the right of residence to all citizens of the
British Empire's successor formation the Commonwealth – and in
its wake we saw people arriving from all over the former Empire.
In 1972, the Ugandan dictator Idi Amin expelled his country's
South Asian minority, and 30,000 of them settled in the UK. They
made their homes, for the most part, in urban areas and became
nurses, hospital porters, textile workers, food workers and small
shopkeepers.

As society changed, its literature – the way in which it represented
itself to itself – changed too, but it changed slowly. We've seen how
Victorian children's writing tended to other or orientalise people
of colour (as did the Eurocentric worldview from which it arose),

and you could easily draw up a hitlist of low points that were to follow. Some cast the peoples of what we now call the global south as exotic stereotypes – part of the unfamiliar furniture of 'over there'; others patronised them; a few promulgated something closer to outright white supremacism. It seems futile or redundant to go back scolding the long-dead writers of out-of-print books one by one, but it's striking for how long these books remained common currency.

Some of them were very far from marginal. *The Story of Little Black Sambo* (1899) – with its picaninny-style illustrations – was popular well into the middle of the twentieth century; its hero, apparently Tamil rather than a Black African, is resourceful enough to outwit four hungry tigers (he tricks them into chasing each other round a tree until they melt into ghee) and end up with a stack of pancakes for his breakfast, but these days there's no getting round the title and the shock-haired, rubber-lipped images of the protagonist. Later editions detoxified the story by giving the protagonist a different name and re-illustrating it, but I remember reading an original edition in what must have been the late 1970s.

Hergé's *Tintin in the Congo* (1931) remains notorious for its bone-through-nose-style images of African natives no less than for its increasingly eyebrow-raising enthusiasm for big game hunting. It presents the natives of a country whose Belgian colonial regime was vicious even by the high standards of colonial regimes as amiable simpletons in need of the civilising hand of white Europeans. They say things (in the 1991 English translation) like 'White mister! You come save us! King lion, him getting very angry!' Hergé in any case had form. He gave us hook-nosed and scheming Jewish characters in *The Shooting Star* (1961 in English, but first published in Belgium under the Nazi occupation), warbonnet-adorned 'redskins' in *Tintin in America* (1931; in English in 1973) and vicious, bucktoothed Japanese caricatures in *The Blue Lotus* (1935; in English in 1983). Hergé later explained: 'The fact is that while I was growing up, I was being fed the prejudices of the bourgeois society that surrounded me.'*

It's fair to note that the six decades between the French-language publication of *Tintin in the Congo* and the appearance of an English translation, or the various alterations to *Little Black Sambo*, indicate that publishers and audiences were aware that all this stuff might raise some issues. But sensitivity to them was much, much lower. And the golliwog – created by Florence Upton for the 1895 children's book *The Adventures of Two Dutch Dolls and a Golliwogg*, and with its origins in America's blackface minstrelsy – had an afterlife that reached well into the second half of the twentieth century, not least thanks to Enid Blyton's taking the figure up in her *Noddy* books.

You can see versions of the same tropes in Willard Price that you can see in G.A. Henty; and, even rereading the children's writing of the 1970s and 1980s, you will find yourself wincing at the wrong notes – in Robert Westall's 1983 *Futuretrack 5*, for instance, we encounter 'an old Negress [lying] on a torn settee'. The issue was barely noticed in the publishing industry.

Ursula K. Le Guin later recalled that, when she wrote her first Earthsea novel, *A Wizard of Earthsea*:

> A great many white readers in 1967 were not ready to accept a brown-skinned hero. But they weren't expecting one. I didn't make an issue of it, and you have to be well into the book before you realize that Ged, like most of the characters, isn't white. [...] Ged is copper-brown and his friend Vetch is black. I was bucking the racist tradition, 'making a statement' – but I made it quietly, and it went almost unnoticed. Alas, I had no power, at that time, to combat the flat refusal of many cover departments to put people of color on a book jacket. So, through many later, lily-white Geds,

---

* 1983 interview, quoted in 'Tintin's Racist Past', *Forbes*, 23 July 2007.

Ruth Robbins's painting for the first edition – the fine, strong profile of a young man with copper-brown skin – was, to me, the book's one true cover.[*]

Where the issue bears most interestingly on the history of children's literature, it seems to me, is the question not of racism, broadly defined, but of representation. As recently as 2018, a report found that of more than 9,000 children's books published in the UK the previous year just four per cent featured ethnic minority characters and only one in a hundred had a main character of colour.[†] This minority of books was also narrow in genre: more than half the brown children in these books featured in stories labelled as 'contemporary realism'. Fantasy and comedy, not so much. Since around a third of schoolchildren in the UK at that point were non-white, this represented an extraordinary failure of stereotyping and representation.

Nikesh Shukla, himself a successful YA author, was on the steering committee that oversaw the publication of the report. He said:

> When you're figuring out the world, being able to see yourself in books, as well as people who don't look like you, is really important. It means you see your story as valid, and it can contribute to who you imagine yourself to be – and a kid should be able to imagine themselves as anyone in the world. These mirrors are so important.[‡]

The central point about diversity in children's writing, as Shukla argues, is a simple one: how are you to fully engage in the pleasure

---

[*]   Author's Afterword to *The Earthsea Quartet* (Penguin Books, 2012).

[†]   *Reflecting Realities: Survey of Ethnic Representation Within UK Children's Literature 2017*, produced by the Centre for Literacy in Primary Education.

[‡]   Quoted in Alison Flood, 'Only 1% of children's books have BAME main characters – UK study', *Guardian*, 17 July 2018.

of a children's story if you can't see yourself, or some version of the world you recognise, represented in it?*

Sophisticated critics of adult literary fiction tend to be sniffy about identification. They will take a certain pleasure in rolling their eyes if you say you didn't enjoy *L'Etranger* or *Crime and Punishment* because the protagonists are so unlikeable. But there's no question that in most popular fiction, and in pretty much all children's writing, there's a character the reader is supposed to root for. It's an observation that was clearly made as long ago as Kenneth Grahame's memoir of childhood, *Dream Days*, where he recalls of the picture books on the nursery bookshelf that his sisters preferred *The Pilgrim's Progress* 'where women had a fair show, and there were generally enough of 'em to go round': 'We were all best pleased with a picture wherein the characters just fitted us, in number, sex, and qualifications; and this, to us, stood for artistic merit.'

That's not to say that a boy can't identify with a female protagonist, or vice versa. My pre-teen Nancy Drew binges are personal testament to that. Nor is it to say that the success of a story can be indexed by how closely its protagonist happens to resemble its reader. That's why fiction is fiction; art, as George Eliot argued, has its moral value in the extent to which it enlarges the reader's sympathies. All fiction is an exercise, to some extent, in imagining what it might be like to be somebody else. But, that said, if you were a Black kid growing up in the UK in the 1960s, and every single book in the children's section of the library had a white kid on the cover, you might feel a bit left out. You might feel a bit

---

* The situation has improved since then. In November 2023 a longlist was drawn up for the inaugural £30,000 Inclusive Books for Children Award in two categories – picture books for ages 3–7 and fiction for children aged 5–9 – seeking to reward work whose excellence included representation of racialised minority, disabled, neurodivergent or LGBTQIA+ protagonists, with the first award in 2024. The awards are run by a charity set up in 2022 by Sarah and Marcus Satha.

invisible, a bit less worthy of representation. You might even feel a bit cheesed off.

That, certainly, was the experience of Malorie Blackman – who came to be the breakout Black writer of children's fiction in the UK. Blackman was born in 1962 to first-generation Bajan immigrant parents. Her father was a carpenter and her mother was a factory machinist, and she grew up with the internalised racial anxiety common to those of her parents' generation. If she used words of Bajan creole or spoke in a Bajan accent in the home, she records in her 2022 memoir *Just Sayin'*, her father would tell her: 'The only way you'll get anywhere in this country is if you speak proper English.' When as a child she used the Bajan slang for a suitcase, 'a grip', her father 'grabbed my upper arm and squeezed hard'. 'That's a grip,' he told her. 'What you want to pack is a suitcase.' She says: 'I never called it a grip again.'*

Blackman encountered the erasure of Black heritage, and the soft racism of low expectations, outside the home as well as in. At school, where she performed well, she conceived the idea of becoming an English teacher. That was kiboshed by a staff member who told her: 'Black people don't become teachers. Why don't you be a secretary instead?' An episode that found a fictional home in the first book of her series *Noughts & Crosses* was when as a child she asked her history teacher why he never mentioned black explorers, scientists or inventors: he told her there weren't any.

Blackman was a science fiction and fantasy geek: she collected comics, followed *Star Trek* and *Doctor Who* (for which she went on to write an episode), revelled in myth and fairytales. The library – especially when her gambling addict father walked out on the family when she was thirteen and their house was repossessed, leaving Blackman's mother and her siblings homeless and her

---

* Blackman, *Just Sayin'*.

precious comics spirited away by bailiffs – was a refuge, a place of escape and absorption.

> By the time I started secondary school in 1973, I must have read several hundred books. I remember wondering why none of the books I read featured Black children in them. Not one of them featured a Black child like me. In recent times I've heard some adults say that children don't notice these things. Well, that's nonsense. They do. This child did. [...] Every book was full of descriptions of characters with pale skin, milky skin, porcelain skin, alabaster skin, which blushed and flushed and turned red, and I would skim over those sentences. Such descriptions took me out of whatever story I was reading, not because the stories contained white protagonists, but because *all* the stories I read featured white protagonists. I was nowhere. By extension I was nothing.[*]

In adult life Blackman set out to change that, and centred Black protagonists in her work. Getting published in the first place, though, took heroic determination. As *Just Sayin'* sets out, she had more than her fair share of obstacles to overcome. As well as going through the day-to-day racism of the 1970s and 1980s, she experienced the intense stigma of childhood poverty, conscious of the stink of the family's single paraffin heater clinging to her clothes. She suffered a sexual assault in her early teens; a medical condition, sickle cell disorder, which doctors predicted would kill her by the age of thirty (flare-ups of the condition continue to be so debilitating that she considered turning down the role of Children's Laureate); and she miscarried a desperately wanted daughter.

Not for nothing is one of the chapters in her memoir called 'Perseverance' (others include 'Loss' and 'Anger'; also, 'Wonder' and 'Love'). Persevere she did – and one of the things that kept her

---

[*]   Ibid.

going was meeting her heroine Alice Walker, author of *The Color Purple*, at a bookshop signing in London. She asked Walker to sign her book 'Don't give up!' She took writing course after writing course, bought 'every how-to-write book I could find',* tried her hand at all manner of styles and at writing for all different ages. She even had a bash at writing a Mills & Boon.

The turning point came when she was browsing in the Puffin bookshop in the 1980s and her childhood unease with the lack of representation was re-triggered: 'I practically lost my eyesight trying to find a Black child – any Black child – on a book jacket.' She turned her attention seriously, then, to writing for children: 'Maybe I could try to write all the books I would've loved to read as a child.'† She immediately signed up for a beginners' 'Writing For Children' course, whose tutor Elizabeth Hawkins she credits as a formative influence.

She had collected eighty-two rejection letters before her first collection of stories for children, *Not So Stupid!* (1990) was accepted for publication. In short order two more books found publishers, and she packed in her job as the project manager in an IT company to write full time. Still, she was grafting. When the publishers of her first novel, *Hacker* (1992), expressed reservations about it, she rewrote it so thoroughly that the only thing it had in common with the first draft was the title. It went on to win two major prizes.

She had dozens of books in print by the time she came to write the books that would make her internationally famous. In *Noughts & Crosses* (2001) she wrote the first of a six-strong series (not including a trio of in-universe novellas) that was not just to have Black protagonists, but whose central subject matter was race. It was an alternative-universe dystopia set in a parallel version of

---

*   Ibid.

†   Ibid.

Britain in which the historic power relations between Black people and white people were reversed. She has said it 'wasn't so much a book I wanted to write as a book I needed to write'* – inspired by a reckoning with events in her own past, a desire to take racism 'head-on' as a subject, and the aftermath of Stephen Lawrence's murder in 1993.

The dominant race in the world she invented for the books were the Black 'Crosses', who had historically enslaved the white population ('Noughts') and continued to enjoy a systematic structural advantage (though it was to shift in its nature over the course of the books). The parallel or inversion wasn't exact – the situation in that first book was more like the American South during the Civil Rights era mixed, with its paramilitary Liberation Militia, with a flavour of 1970s South Africa. The first Nought children are being admitted into schools previously reserved by law for Crosses. There is spontaneous crowd violence and reactionary political rhetoric of exactly the sort that attended desegregation and 'bussing' to school districts in the American South. There's a divide – though not much developed – between the militant leadership of the Liberation Militia, which plants bombs in shopping centres, and the peaceful-protest route taken by Alex Luther; a sort of Malcolm X vs Martin Luther King stand-off. From about the fourth book onwards, though, we're a generation on and the political environment is something much more like twenty-first-century Britain.

In some ways that first book is a good test-case for what it might mean to think about 'young adult' as a genre: not as a type of story that contains more 'grown-up' material, but as one that packages its grown-up material in a children's story. It contains a startling measure of sex, suicide, mental illness and violence. Yet its narrative shape is still something very like a fairytale.

---

*   Author's Introduction to *Noughts & Crosses* (Penguin, 2017).

Sephy is a princess archetype – the daughter of a Cross family privileged even by the standards of her own race; Callum, her childhood friend and will-be lover, is a Nought whose mother had worked as a nanny for Sephy's parents. Their mothers Meggie and Jasmine are friends – but the power difference between them comes to the surface when they have a falling-out. Callum's mother at a stroke loses not only her friend, but her job – and with it her family's stability and prospects for the future. Sephy and Callum continue to meet in secret – and try to maintain their public friendship in the face of institutional and peer-group disapproval at school. As a counterfactual, it's worth wondering what the books might have been like had Blackman made Callum, the male lead, a Cross and Sephy a Nought, with patriarchy reinforcing rather than cutting against the racial power dynamic.

As it stands, it's a good old-fashioned love-across-the-barricades story, with the satisfactions of melodrama. Sephy's racist politician father is a classic bogeyman: a cross between Bluebeard and Old Capulet, with a dash of Enoch Powell. Jasmine is, at least in this book, a wicked ice-queen, a snob and a cruel drunk intent on poisoning Sephy's relationship with Callum. (Her redemption arc, over the course of the following book, comes to cast her more complicatedly as a victim of abuse.) But the thematic underpinnings, and the world it supposes, are considerably more adult than the story it tells. Childish bodywork; adult engine.

Over the course of the six books of its main sequence, *Noughts & Crosses* tracks the way that the experience of racial inequality in a society manifests itself in everything from high politics to everyday life. A whole range of racial topoi are explored – from the fetishisation of Black hair by white people to the arguments over racial profiling or 'stop and search' policies, racial pay differentials, the rise of 'Nought Lives Matter' and racist heckling at football grounds – sometimes in the foreground and sometimes incidentally. In this world, Cross aesthetics dictate how the world is run – you can't get pink sticking plasters, and Nought women use collagen fillers to plump their lips,

sunbeds or melanin tablets to darken their skin and padded knickers to give them more curvaceous bums.* Heavy metal – a musical
style invented by Noughts – has been appropriated by Cross artists.

Above all Blackman shows virtuosically how the psychological
experience of trauma plays out: how hatred is internalised and then
projected outwards as violence. It's notable that – as she writes
in her memoir – the character in the books with whom she most
directly identifies is not the Black girl but the white boy, Callum.
His teenage rage, she writes, was hers. Probably the most compelling
and memorable character in the series is Callum's brother Jude. He
experiences racial trauma: his brother's death at the end of book one
and, more subtly but noticeably, the way that his mother's sacking
makes it impossible for him to continue his education. His response
is to conceive a categorical hatred of all Crosses. Jude goes on to
become a villain of Voldemortian proportions, eventually grooming
his niece Callie Rose as a suicide bomber, but Blackman – as when
she depicts his love affair with a Cross girl whom he goes on to
murder – troubles to show how he gets there.

> She smiled at me. Total trust, love and devotion. It was too much.
> I was dying in it. I clenched my fists and hit her. Her whole body
> fell backwards. She looked up at me, too shocked to even cry out.
> Her eyes, so warm and rich that I just wanted to pour myself into
> them, were now stunned and hurt. But the love was still there. I
> knelt down and hit her again. And then I couldn't stop. I punched
> her over and over again before leaping to my feet. And even then
> I couldn't leave her alone. I kicked out with all the rage erupting
> inside me. She had no right to make me care about her. I'd show
> her, I'd show both of us that she meant nothing to me. I kept
> hitting her over and over, even when she was screaming at me to
> stop. Even when she stopped screaming.

---

* This may not sound quite as counterfactual now as it did in the mid-1990s.

The progress of the story across the books is a strange one. They increase a little in structural complexity, and they jump from genre to genre – they are connected less by a continuous story (Blackman originally thought she was done with the series after book four) than by their shared world and its themes. *Noughts & Crosses* is a forbidden romance tale with a harum-scarum plot driven by Callum's involvement with the Liberation Militia. *Knife Edge*, which Blackman has described as the 'bleakest' of the series, depicts Sephy's life as a single mother with borderline mental illness – grief mingling with post-partum depression – alongside Jude's Anakin Skywalker-style move to the dark side. *Checkmate* – in which Jude grooms the teenage Callie Rose to be a suicide terrorist – is something like a spy novel. *Double Cross* is a gangland thriller. The paired books that bring the story to a close – *Crossfire* and *Endgame* – are a kidnapping caper that morphs into a legal drama, pivoting on a dinner-party murder mystery that tips its hat to Golden Age crime. The principal protagonists of the earlier novels come to be background figures in the later ones – Callie Rose is front and centre in the middle books in the series, before herself (somewhat) giving way to her much younger half-brother Troy.

Blackman, incidentally, is every bit as ruthless as J.K. Rowling would go on to be about killing off her characters. They are shot, blown up, run over, hanged, electrocuted, or walk in front of buses. The books are each prefaced by a family tree (like *Star Wars*, this is very much a dynastic saga), and with each successive book, more and more twigs on that tree are marked 'Deceased'. Emotions are operatic, and the prose tends to the purple:

> Silence reigns for too long. Despair, like icy hands, steals round my chest to hug me, squeezing and freezing by degrees, making it hard to catch my breath. It's a struggle to think clearly, what with the sheer dread bubbling up inside.

The melodramatic tenor of the writing means that the reader sometimes gets whiplash; characters swerve at the turn of a page or two
between enmity and alliance, and the psychological subtlety of the
books' themes is only unevenly transferred to the characterisation.
The need to give *Endgame* a satisfactory resolution stretches psychological and moral plausibility to its limits: sentiment requires the
adult Tobey to reunite with his teenage sweetheart Callie Rose, and
he does; but not before the novel has shown him to have committed
any number of unforgivable sins, including blackmail (of Callie
Rose herself), bribery, racketeering and – it's suggested – murder.
He's a bad man, and we have to more than half forget it to buy the
happy ending.

But what Blackman sometimes lacks in finesse she more than
makes up for with her storytelling verve and her world-building.
The books are excitingly plotted and packed with incident, and the
defamiliarising decision to reverse the racial polarity in her Albion is
a brilliant stroke. Here is a way of shaking up an audience's unexamined assumptions (above all, of the white person as a default human)
and causing them to consider the world afresh. If the love stories
in the books are predictably, if sometimes tragically, resolved, the
race stories are not. It won't escape the attention of bright children
that the game after which the series is titled is an unwinnable one.

Blackman persuasively creates a society in which 'blanker' can
have the force of the N-word, and there's a powerful scene in that
first book where Sephy is forced to confront the pain that her use
of it causes her best friend. One of the social media testimonies
printed inside later editions of the book says: 'Reading *Noughts
& Crosses* was the first time I could relate to anything I had ever
read.' Another: 'Made me see the world through a different lens.'

The public reaction to the books says, too, something about
the enduring anxieties about what might or might not be suitable
for children. We can, perhaps, discount the outright instances of
racist abuse that Blackman received and continues to receive (after
some remarks on diversity she made as Children's Laureate were

misquoted, she was deluged by racial invective). But parents at various times rejected the themes of her books as too adult. 'Some people,' she wrote, looking back at *Checkmate*, 'didn't feel that a girl being trained to be a suicide bomber was a suitable topic for a novel for young adults. I disagreed then and I disagree now.' The battles that Judy Blume fought two decades before need to be refought, it seems, in each generation – and at the time of writing, conservative America is engaged in another paroxysm of book-banning across the United States.

Blackman isn't a one-trick pony, either. Her overarching interest in race and representation doesn't preclude her addressing other difficult issues. Her 2010 novel *Boys Don't Cry*, for example, is a story of underage pregnancy – its teenage protagonist, Dante, finds himself literally holding the baby after a girl with whom he had a drunken one-night stand shows up with his infant daughter and then does a runner. It also contains a shockingly brutal queer-bashing perpetrated by a closeted gay young man; Blackman's special excellence may not be her reading of race so much as her acute sense, here as in Jude's story, of how socially sanctioned hatred is internalised, and the damage that it can do.

In her memoir she describes a mother asking her to contact her daughter's school to request that her own books be removed from the shelves, and reports: 'Most of the books I've written for teens have been criticised by adults regarding their suitability. No teen has ever contacted me or told me that they thought the subject matter of my books was too much for teens to handle. Ever. If my books and any resulting dramatisations make some adults nervous or uncomfortable then maybe I'm doing my job right.'

And there, perhaps, is a crux. Children's and especially YA books, in this prominent author's framing, are there to do more than just entertain. They are leading children away from their parents; providing a path for their emotional and moral growth into a wider, scarier world where their parents are nervous to follow.

This Is Not a Fairytale

JACQUELINE WILSON

*The Illustrated Mum; The Bed and Breakfast
Star; Dustbin Baby; Bad Girls; The Cat
Mummy; The Suitcase Kid; Clean Break;
Secrets; Love Frankie; The Primrose Railway
Children; Four Children and It; The Magic
Faraway Tree; Double Act; The Story of Tracy
Beaker; The Dare Game; Jacky Daydream*

T HE NEGLECTED ASPECTS OF THAT WIDER WORLD, IN
terms of family dynamics and social class rather than
race, were further explored by another prolific writer
who, though a generation older than Blackman, also hit her stride
in the 1990s. Jacqueline Wilson (1945–) was a disciple of Noel
Streatfeild, a reader of girls' comics and magazines like *Sunny
Stories, Girl, Girls' Crystal* and *Chicks' Own*, and a devourer of
the sort of 'children's books in the 1950s [that] sprouted veritable
forests of treehouses'.

Enid Blyton got me reading fluently and reinforced my desire to
write, though I knew right from a very early age that I wanted
to write very different sort of books. I wanted to write books that
didn't seem to exist yet – books about realistic children who had
difficult parents and all sorts of secrets and problems; easy-to-read
books that still made you think hard; books with funny bits that

made you laugh out loud, though sometimes the story was so sad it made you cry too.*

She made good on that intention. The books she was to go on to write tell stories including a heavily tattooed mother suffering alcoholism and bipolar disorder (*The Illustrated Mum* (1999) – a witty riff on a Ray Bradbury title that will whizz over the heads of eleven-year-olds), child homelessness (*The Bed and Breakfast Star* (1994)), infant abandonment and the legacy of suicide (*Dustbin Baby* (2001)). They encourage their readers to explore and empathise with the experience of bullying and shoplifting (*Bad Girls* (1996)), coming to terms with death and bereavement (*The Cat Mummy* (2001)), divorce or parental abandonment (*The Suitcase Kid* (1992)); *Clean Break* (2005)) or violence and abuse (*Secrets* (2002)).

Wilson is in the empathy trade. Her books are usually first-person narratives, introducing her readers to the inner lives of her characters – and allowing the more sophisticated of them to perceive the things that those characters don't know, as well as the things they do. They are set in a recognisably contemporary, usually urban, English working- and middle-class world. The frequently challenging subject matter is leavened by the humour of the telling, a tendency for kindness to triumph even by unexpected impulse, and by the cartoony illustrations of her long-time collaborator, Nick Sharratt. They are framed carefully for younger readers. Her books keep off the third rail of sex and drugs – even her first novel to deal expressly with homosexuality (*Love Frankie*, 2020) describes a chaste romance between two girls.

These books have connected with her pre-teen readers in a way that puts her in the company of J.K. Rowling and Enid Blyton. No fewer than four of her novels appeared in a 2003 BBC poll, with three-quarters of a million respondents, of the best-loved novels of

---

* Wilson, *Jacky Daydream*.

all time, and she was the most borrowed author from British libraries for most of the 2000s. At the height of her fame, she sat signing
books after an event in a bookshop in Bournemouth at the head
of an eight-hour queue. It's a feature of the children's publishing
industry that, when an author wins big, they really take off: the
school playground has long been the cradle of a word-of-mouth
virality that adult publishing had no way of rivalling (or didn't, at
least, before the advent of social media).

Her relationship with her audience follows the model established
by Blyton and Judy Blume. Her postbag is as formidable as her
signing queues. She writes in *Jacky Daydream*, for instance: 'Many
children write to me to tell me about their pets. They're very special
to them. [...] They nearly always mention their pets before their
parents and brothers and sisters, as if they're much more important.
[...] I often get the most touching tear-stained letters, telling me
that some beloved hamster or white rat has died.' Like E. Nesbit,
another of her obvious ancestors, she has made something of a
brand of her personal flamboyance – her hands are festooned with
chunky rings set with semi-precious stones, and she claims to buy
a new one for every novel she completes.

A theme of this book has been how many and enduring are the
threads that connect the children's writing of each generation with
its successors – the echoes and allusions and retellings that take
place. Jacqueline Wilson is secure in her place in the canon. She has
paid direct tribute to her predecessors by reimagining or extending
their work – as in *The Primrose Railway Children* (2021), which plays
off E. Nesbit's classic, or *Four Children and It* (2012), which brings
Nesbit's Psammead into the twenty-first century and introduces it
to a group of children who have an inkling of what they're dealing
with because they have already read *Five Children and It*.

Wilson's work is at once an entry in the long canon, then, and a
modern reimagining of it. Her 'woke' rewrite of Enid Blyton's classic
series, *The Magic Faraway Tree* (2022), even earned the disapproval of
the *Daily Mail*, which harrumphed that 'children reading her novel

will now be subject to a gender equality lecture instead of learning how people behaved and thought in the past."* When Moon-Face suggests that Silky the Fairy can help him out with some domestic chores while the boys do something more interesting, Mia jumps in to reprove him. Perhaps more telling of the temper of the times, though, is the change Wilson makes to the idea of children being unsupervised. In Blyton's original, her protagonists would roam overnight on their adventures without their parents taking much of an interest. Wilson's child adventurers return home before their parents have had time to finish a cup of coffee. The early-21st-century parent, as Wilson acknowledges in her work, sees something more sinister and less magical than pixies lurking in the hedgerows at night.

You can find a subtler kinship in other of Wilson's books with writers of the recent and the more distant past. *Double Act* (1995) tells the story of a pair of twin girls called Ruby and Garnet who first revel in, and then steadily and painfully dissent from, their similarity. It's a subtle story of growing pains, and the bitter-sweet process of finding your own place in the world. The dominant twin, Ruby, has ambitions for them both to be actresses; the shyer twin, Garnet, is dragged reluctantly in her wake. The dynamic between them shifts uneasily and sometimes painfully, until both enter for a scholarship to a fee-paying school and, to Ruby's mortification and anger, Garnet wins the place and she doesn't. There are echoes in the dynamics of the book of the Noel Streatfeild of *Ballet Shoes* and even, perhaps, of the ambitious stage mother and shy daughter in Judy Blume's *Deenie*. Its burden is that, as you grow up, you have to make accommodation with reality; and that love wins out. The girls learn to accept and support each other's differences, as well as to accept the stepmother who makes their widowed father happy, but whom they both loathe at first.

---

* James Gant, 'Jacqueline Wilson admits Enid Blyton "wouldn't be that thrilled" about her woke rewrite of *The Magic Faraway Tree* as author's society says it's a "pity" new "gender equality" version has been commissioned', *MailOnline*, 12 January 2022.

In keeping with her compact with her readers, Wilson's 2007 memoir *Jacky Daydream* was written, like Blackman's, with a simplicity that makes it available to be read by the child audience for her novels: 'I knew right from the start I didn't want to write a memoir for adults. I write for children and so I wanted my autobiography to be for children too.' She doesn't gloss over the profound social and emotional anxiety that characterised that childhood, though. An only child, she was bright and, as the title indicates, prone to seeking refuge from the world in her imagination. She had much to seek refuge from.

The childhood she describes is one strikingly remote from the world of her books; even in her lifetime, ideas about childhood changed fast. The popularisation of progressive ideas about child development by Benjamin Spock's *Baby & Child Care* (1946) and its many successors such as Penelope Leach's *Your Baby and Child* (1977) still lay in the future. Of the moments after her birth, she writes, 'They didn't bother about mothers and babies bonding in those days. They didn't give us time to have a cuddle or even take a good look at each other. I was bundled up tightly in a blanket and taken off to the nursery.' She adds: 'Fathers didn't get involved much with babies in those days.'

Her working-class parents Harry and Biddy (he a naval draughtsman; she a clerical officer in the Admiralty) had met and married in their early twenties after a chaste short courtship. 'It wasn't as if you had much choice,' her mother told her later. 'There weren't many men around, they were all away fighting. I'd got to twenty-one, and in those days you were starting to feel as if you were on the shelf if you weren't married by then. So I decided your father would do.'

They were painfully ill-matched. Wilson recalls childhood family holidays in Clacton – she'd become so overexcited on arrival that she'd have bilious vomiting attacks; like Blackman, childhood illness was a constant – being blighted by her father Harry's rages:

It's so strange, because when I was bright and bouncy he'd frequently snap at me, saying something so cruel that the words can still make me wince now. I was always tense when he was around. I think Biddy [her mother] was scared of him too at first. She used to cry a lot, but then she learned to shout back and started pleasing herself.

There was always at least one major row on holiday, often more. They'd hiss terrifying insults at each other in our bedroom and not speak at the breakfast table. My tummy would clench and I'd worry that I might be sick again. I'd see other families laughing and joking and being comfortably silly together and wish we were a happy family like that.*

She became aware that her mother was having an affair with a man she knew as 'Uncle Ron'. He and his wife shared evenings out and even a family holiday with Biddy and Harry. Wilson still doesn't know if Harry ever knew what was going on under his nose – and as a child she carried the burden of the secret: 'I didn't *like* my dad and he could be incredibly alarming and unkind, but I always felt sorry for him.' Only at his eventual funeral did the appearance of two unexpected 'aunties' indicate that Harry, too, had sought comfort elsewhere: 'They both told me – separately – how much my dad had loved me and been proud of me. I was astonished. I couldn't remember him saying anything of the sort to me. In fact several times he'd told me he couldn't stand me. Perhaps they were just being kind and felt it was the polite thing to say at funerals.'

But as long as that unhappy marriage lasted, divorce was out of the question.

It was considered shameful, barely socially acceptable. It was the reason why so many incompatible couples stayed together. They

---

* Ibid.

didn't want to go through the public disgrace of a divorce. I thought this odd even then. In fact I used to pray my own parents would divorce because there were so many screaming fights now. Sometimes I was caught up in a quarrel too, both of them yelling at me, appealing to me, while I begged not to have to take sides. Sometimes I simply listened from my bedroom while they argued endlessly, whipping each other with cruel words, then slapping and shoving, hurting and hating.

You could see Jacqueline Wilson the novelist reacting, a generation later, against the repressive social conformity of the 1950s that had made such misery for Jacqueline Wilson the child. It was social pressure that forced her mother to carry her marital unhappiness, and the fear of being 'common' that drove so much of her childhood anxiety: 'Biddy and Harry and I hovered precariously between working class and lower middle class. Harry was a civil servant, we said "lav" instead of "toilet", we never dropped our aitches or said "ain't". I knew I had to live up to our aspirations.'

Like Blackman, she was of a generation for which that meant passing the eleven-plus. Harry tried to coach her in maths ('"Are you a MORON?" he'd shriek, his fist thumping the page.')* and Jacqueline failed the first time she took the exam – a bad head-cold meant the letters on the paper swam before her – and was terrified to admit the result to her mother. She passed a retake, but left grammar school at sixteen for technical college and was set (according to the expectations of her mother) to train in shorthand and typing for secretarial work. Answering a D.C. Thomson advertisement for teenage writers, though, took her to Dundee and work on the new girls' magazine *Jackie*. By the age of twenty-two she was married and had a daughter. (Wilson's own rebellion against the conformity of her childhood was a slow burn. Her marriage broke down

---

*   Ibid.

when she was in her early fifties, and she has now been living with a female partner for two decades. Keeping her private life private, though, she didn't come out until 2020 when her 111th book *Love Frankie*, about a same-sex crush, was published.)

Throughout her marriage and early motherhood, though, her output was unceasing: she continued to write, 3,000 words of journalism in the morning and 1,000 words of fiction in the afternoon. The torrent of stories she had been turning out from childhood, wondering even then 'if any of my stories in my Woolworths exercise books would ever get published', continued unabated. She went back to take an English A level at the age of forty, having 'always felt a bit inadequate not having been to university, so I felt I had to prove something'.*

At the end of each chapter of *Jacky Daydream*, Wilson links episodes from the narrative of her real life to incidents and characters in her fiction: 'Which of my books starts with a heavily pregnant mum trying to find a new home for her daughters?' As well as being a canny self-plugging technique, this insistently draws the connection between the fictional worlds Wilson is describing and the real world that her readers inhabit. Wilson has always drawn material for her writing omnivorously from her own life and the world around her. She had already published dozens of books when she created what was to become her breakthrough character, Tracy Beaker, in *The Story of Tracy Beaker* (1991), which was also the book that began her long-running association with the illustrator Nick Sharratt.

The character was inspired by photographs Wilson saw in her local paper of children in care seeking foster-parents. She found herself imagining what it would be like to be 'advertised' in this way – and 'how would you feel if no-one at all came forward to meet up with you'. Tracy Beaker was born. The first name came quickly to the author – 'a perfect modern street-wise bouncy sort

---

* Ibid.

of name'. 'Beaker', prosaically enough, came to Wilson as she was rinsing her hair in the bath with a plastic Snoopy beaker.

'Modern, street-wise, bouncy.' Orphans have a long history in children's literature – but Wilson was doing something very different from both the romantic image of orphanhood that runs through the history of fairy stories and the sentimental Victorian one given life by Dickens. Tracy Beaker is a child of the modern care system, a child of the sort who had until then seldom been depicted in modern children's writing. She is angry, damaged, violent, cynical, boastful, a compulsive liar and often hard to love; a McDonald's-era descendent of the truculent Mary Lennox in *The Secret Garden* (a book Wilson has praised, saying in childhood she was 'thrilled to read about irritable, spoiled children for a change, totally understanding why they behaved badly'). But she is also fiercely resilient and energetic.

On the opening pages of *The Story of Tracy Beaker* (in the conceit of the story, she is writing about herself in an exercise book, and she begins with a quiz-style 'About Me' section), she introduces herself as 'the star' of a children's home she calls 'the Dumping Ground', and she says: 'I don't have a dad. I lived with my mum when I was little and we got on great but then she got this Monster Gorilla Boyfriend and I hated him and he hated me back and beat me up and so I had to be taken into care. No wonder my mum sent him packing.' Tracy has been twice fostered and twice returned to the system:

> I've had two. There was Aunty Peggy and Uncle Sid first of all. I didn't like them much and I didn't get on with the other kids so I didn't care when they got rid of me. I was in a children's home for a while and then I had this other couple. Julie and Ted. They were young and friendly and they bought me a bike and I thought it was all going to be great and I went to live with them and I was ever so good and did everything they said and I thought I'd be staying with them until my mum came to get me for good but then... I don't want to write about it. It ended up with me getting turfed out THROUGH NO FAULT OF MY OWN. I was so mad I smashed

up the bike so I don't even have that any more. And now I'm in a new children's home and they've advertised me in the papers but there weren't many takers and now I think they're getting a bit desperate. I don't care though. I expect my mum will come soon anyway.

As she goes on to reveal, the second family had fostered her when they had not expected to have any children of their own. When the foster-mother became pregnant, they decided they wouldn't be able to cope keeping Tracy, and her record counts against her ('When Julie and Ted first fostered you, we did tell them a bit about your background,' her social worker explains, 'and the trouble you had in your first foster home. You know, when you shut the baby up in the cupboard—'). Here's truth to life: older children and 'difficult' children are harder to foster, and as their disappointment compounds they become more difficult.

Transience is Tracy's constant. She describes early on the bond she formed with 'a lovely little baby at this other home [...] She really liked me, little Camilla. She got fostered quick as a wink. I begged her foster mum and dad to bring her back to see me but they never did.' Her self-reliance is defensive. Her arch-enemy is Justine Littlewood, whom she hates because Justine stole her best friend Louise: 'Of course I could always get Louise back again as my best friend, easy peasy. But she's lost her chance. I don't want her now.' The needle between Tracy and Justine manifests in real mental cruelty and physical fights; Wilson doesn't swerve the social viciousness of damaged children.

Her most constant relationship, now, is with her 'stupid old social worker Elaine', and, being an intelligent child, she sees through Elaine – especially Elaine's ostentatious, by-the-book patience: 'she sighed again and her lips moved for a moment or two. That's her taking a deep breath and counting up to ten. Social workers are supposed to do that when a child is being difficult. Elaine ends up doing an awful lot of counting when she's with me. When she got to ten she gave me this big false smile.' Of social workers in general,

Tracy is contemptuous: '"I guess you're feeling really angry and upset today, Tracy," they twitter, when I've wrecked my bedroom or got into a fight or shouted and sworn at someone, so that it's obvious I'm angry and upset. They do this to show me that they understand. Only they don't understand peanuts. They're not the ones in care. I am.'

There's a piercing moment when Tracy is, as often, literally misunderstood: 'Jenny [a member of staff at the Dumping Ground] caught me happily sniffing nail varnish one day, and do you know what she thought? Only that I was inhaling it, like glue sniffing. Did you ever? I let her think it too. I wasn't going to tell her I just liked the smell because it reminds me of Mum.'

Ah, Tracy's mum. Tracy has a photograph of her mother (the one who let her be taken into care rather than give up an abusive boyfriend). Tracy's mother is pretty and blond (Tracy is ordinary-looking and sometimes spotty and has hair that is 'dark and difficult and sticks up in all the wrong places'), and Tracy fantasises, and boasts to the other children and to her readers, that the only reason she doesn't come to visit is that she's in Hollywood being a movie star. Or she rationalises that her mother has lost her address: 'I bet she's been trying and trying to get hold of me, but she doesn't know where to look.' Poignantly, the reader knows that she only half believes her own lies.

She badgers a visiting writer, Cam, who befriends her, into taking her out for lunch at McDonald's – but when the day comes she tries to back out because she's worried that her mum will come to take her out and she won't be there. Cam cajoles her into coming, but: 'I *still* felt bothered about my mum, even though I knew it was silly. I knew she almost definitely wouldn't be coming. I knew deep deep down that Justine was maybe right about her. But I still worried.' Those epithets 'almost' and 'maybe' are perfectly pitched. Likewise, Tracy's insistence that she doesn't ever cry; she suffers from hay fever.

Wilson's great gift in the Tracy Beaker books is to make Tracy a convincing psychological study – often in ways that are more subtle than her younger readers will quite clock – while also speaking directly to those child readers. Tracy's bravado leads her into entertaining capers and scrapes; but older readers will see the fragility behind it. Hers is the egotism of the fragile ego; the pre-emptive 'screw you' of the damaged child who'd rather get her retaliation in first than risk disappointment.

Here, in a way, are the standard tropes of so many children's books – a child being adventurous and naughty, a child exercising independent agency in the world, adults proving incompetent or malign – but with an extra emotional torque on them: the sense that these things aren't the fulfilment of a fantasy but the painful realisation of a truth. But the book isn't without fantasy: Tracy fantasises constantly and lies constantly.

The book's antagonistic relation to the oldest children's form, the fairy story, is explicit: 'Once upon a time there was a little girl called Tracy Beaker. That sounds a bit stupid, like the start of a soppy fairy story. I can't stand fairy stories,' writes Tracy. 'They're all the same. If you're very good and very beautiful with long golden curls then, after sweeping up a few cinders or having a long kip in a cobwebby palace, this prince comes along and you live happily ever after. Which is fine if you happen to be a goodie-goodie and look gorgeous. But if you're bad and ugly then you've got no chance whatsoever.' Here, then, is an anti-fairy story.

Tracy's defiant last words in that book are: 'This started like a fairy story. And it's going to finish like one too. Happily Ever After.' But it's given ironic distance by the fact that the fairytale ending is one she's predicting rather than one she has already achieved: 'Next Saturday. When I see her. When she tells me that she's thought it all over and she wants to be my foster mum.'

What Tracy predicts – in part thanks to the strength of her will – comes true. Cam does foster her, and, as *The Dare Game* (2000) opens, Tracy is living in her flat. But the happy after isn't a happy ever after, and the fantasy collides with reality. The shine has come off her kind, unglamorous new foster-mother. Cam, for her part, is weepy and depressed: Tracy is unmanageable, ignores boundaries, steals from her purse and bunks off school.

Tracy resents that Cam earns peanuts as a writer, that her box bedroom is smaller than the one she had in the Dumping Ground, and that life is not the never-ending succession of goodies to which she believes she's now entitled. 'Cam wouldn't always take me out for treats and buy me stuff: stuff I seriously need, like designer clothes, else I get picked on by poisonous girls like [schoolmate] Roxanne.' She 'can be a boring old meanie when it comes to money'.

Why can't Cam write books that make money, where 'all the women are beautiful with heaps of money and designer outfits and all the men have dynamic jobs and are very powerful'? 'Cam just laughs at me and says she can't stick those sort of books. She says she doesn't mind not being a successful writer. *I* mind. I want a foster mum I can show off about. I can't show off about Cam because nobody's ever heard of her. And she's not pretty or sexy or glamorous. She doesn't wear any make-up and her hair's too short to style so it just sticks straight up and her clothes are *awful* – T-shirts and jeans all the time and they're certainly *not* designer.'

Wilson uses the books to cast a sceptical light, then, on the messages that television and the wider culture send children. The furniture of Tracy Beaker's world is of real brands (DKNY, KFC), real celebrities (Sharon Stone, Alan Shearer, Barney Harwood) and real TV shows (*Basil's Swap Shop*). The last decades of the twentieth century had seen consumer culture mushroom: Tracy Beaker lives in the backwash of the era of 'Loadsamoney', *Dallas* and *Dynasty*, Thatcherism and their literary cheerleaders in the high days of the so-called 'sex and shopping' novel. Tracy is devoutly materialistic. As were her real-world contemporaries; a staple of tabloid newspaper stories from the early 1990s onwards has been that of children being bullied at school for wearing off-brand clothes. (One of the totemic must-have accessories for schoolchildren, Nike's Air Jordan trainers, launched in the US in 1984.)

Unfortunately for Tracy, she is surrounded by well-meaning, knit-your-own-yoghurt liberals whom Wilson (though she of course takes their part) doesn't mind sending up: when Tracy visits her social worker Elaine's house for the first time she reports a toe-curling Valentine's card from 'this ultra-weedy guy with thick glasses', 'several framed mottoes [...] like "You don't have to be mad to work here but it helps" and a poem about an old woman wearing purple and some long drivelly meditation about Listening to your Inner Child'. Cam's friends are Jane ('you should see the size of her bum!') and Liz ('I was worried at first because she's a teacher'), the latter of whom delivers 'this boring old lecture about Caring not being the same as Spending Money and it was almost as if she'd morphed into Mrs Vomit Bagley [Tracy's teacher]'.

Tracy's cynicism banishes any potential piety from Wilson's narrative: she's constantly second-guessing and seeing through the forms of adult goodness. When Elaine warns that Tracy meeting her mother (who does reappear in *The Dare Game*) will be hard for Cam, Tracy sneers: 'Well. That's what being a foster mum is all about, isn't it? Taking a back seat when necessary. Encouraging all contact with natural families. I've read the leaflets.' These are knowing books about a knowing child; but self-knowledge eludes her. 'I don't know why I'm going on about this sad stuff when I'm HAPPY HAPPY HAPPY.'

That word again. Wilson doesn't let the Tracy Beakers in her work off the hook – nor the adults who are, falteringly, responsible for them. But she gives them something. If her endings are seldom conventionally happy, as she said in a 2020 interview, 'I suppose I'm trying to show that there are different ways of being a happy family.'* Like Malorie Blackman, Wilson is a writer who turns otherness – the quality that for so long excluded writers and characters from the charmed circle of children's writings – into exactly the thing that makes them belong.

---

*   Lisa Allardice, 'Jacqueline Wilson: I've never really been in any kind of closet', *Guardian*, 4 April 2020.

XI

BACK TO THE FUTURE

J.K. Rowling · Philip Pullman

OLD POTIONS IN NEW BOTTLES

THE PRESENT, FOR LITERARY HISTORIANS, IS A MOVING target: the twenty-first-century canon has yet to take shape. Since I took issue with Martin Amis in my introduction, it seems only fair to quote him again here, this time approvingly: 'There is only one value-judgement in literature: time.'* I don't propose, therefore, to close this book by scampering through the new arrivals section of my local children's bookshop making guesses at who will last.

But I would like to address two writers from just before the turn of the millennium who have already had an unignorable effect on the children's writing that was to follow: J.K. Rowling and Philip Pullman. The success of their work transformed the market yet again. Both wrote books that were as eagerly consumed by adults as by children and teenagers; and between them they heralded another swerve towards high fantasy after a period in which realism had quietly dominated.

As the millennium approached, the world of childhood underwent a change no less drastic than the one two centuries before that paved the way for modern children's writing in the first place. The last generation of children to have been born before the internet existed have grown up. Their successors are the so-called digital natives.

---

* Mira Sethi, 'The Weekend Interview: Martin Amis: Islam and the Limits of Permissible Thought', *Wall Street Journal*, 28 December 2012.

Children's writing, as I've argued, has always existed in a continuum with other forms of entertainment and media – sometimes competitive, sometimes collaborative. The digital age has seen a positive explosion of those other media. There's more entertainment, and more entertaining entertainment, available to children than at any other time in history.

It is everywhere, all at once: games, music, film, television, social media, and hybrid forms of all these things. But it doesn't just supersede what came before. It also encompasses it. We all now carry the digital equivalent of the Great Library of Alexandria in our trouser pockets. So it isn't necessarily so strange that, in pointing the way to the future, these two writers dig as deeply as any recent children's writers have into the past.

A Sorting-Hat World

J.K. ROWLING

Harry Potter and the Philosopher's Stone;
Harry Potter and the Chamber of Secrets;
Harry Potter and the Prisoner of Azkaban;
Harry Potter and the Goblet of Fire; Harry
Potter and the Order of the Phoenix; Harry
Potter and the Deathly Hallows; Harry Potter
and the Half-Blood Prince; Fantastic Beasts
and Where to Find Them; Quidditch Through
the Ages; The Tales of Beedle the Bard

THE CLOSING YEARS OF THE TWENTIETH CENTURY bring this story round in a neat circle, back to that enchanted summer afternoon in Oxford nearly a century and a half ago. The story of the writing of the first Harry Potter novel has become no less of a fairytale than the origins of *Alice's Adventures in Wonderland*. Part 'Cinderella'; part 'Bluebeard'. The story is a myth within a myth. We see Joanne Rowling, a young single mother in desperate poverty, settling at a corner table in Nicolson's café in Edinburgh, rocking her baby daughter to sleep with one hand while, eking a single cup of coffee out for hours, she writes the story of a boy wizard, longhand, with the other.

It's an irresistible image, and it played to advantage in early publicity for the books. It is grounded in fact. At the time she wrote *Harry Potter and the Philosopher's Stone*, though it had been seven years or more in gestation, Joanne Rowling really was a penniless single mother. She had flown to Scotland from Portugal just months after the birth of her daughter Jessica and the breakdown of her relationship with Jessica's father.

She was twenty-seven, living on £70 a week in a tatty rented flat in Edinburgh of which she later said: 'The best you could say about the place was that it had a roof. If I concentrated hard enough maybe I'd be able to block out the sounds of mice behind the skirting board.' She wrote in cafés while her daughter was asleep – Nicolson's, now a fixture on the Potter tourist trail, was part-owned by her brother-in-law – though the story was embroidered over the years. It has passed into legend that she wrote in cafés because she couldn't afford to heat her flat. 'I wasn't in search of warmth,' she later said. 'I was just in search of good coffee.'

The semi-fictional Harry Potter origin story, though, had two resonances. One was mythological – rags to riches; Cinderella among the embers; the nameless peasant girl in 'Rumpelstiltskin' in her dungeon spinning straw into gold. The other was contemporary: to do with how families, and childhood itself, were conceived. In 1993 John Major's Conservative government had launched the so-called Back to Basics campaign, a Dursley-pleasing affirmation of cultural conservatism in which 'respect for the family' had a central role.

Major's frontbench colleagues gave speeches attacking 'young women [who] have babies with no apparent intention of even trying marriage or a stable relationship with the father of the child' and 'benefit-driven' single parents.* The killing of a toddler, James Bulger, by two scarcely older boys that year – both the killers were children of single mothers – gave this rhetoric a darker edge. In the Britain of the mid-1990s, the Enid Blyton vision of childhood was a long way away. Rowling remembers shuffling to the counter to collect her weekly benefits, ashamed that others in the queue would see and judge her.

---

* John Redwood, speech reported in the *Daily Telegraph*, 3 July 1993.

That low was not what her beginnings would have predicted. Born in 1965, Joanne Rowling grew up in a happy, just-about-managing middle-class family, the oldest of two children, in the Forest of Dean, Gloucestershire. Her parents were young when they married – both just twenty; they had met the year before on a train heading north from King's Cross station. Pete Rowling was on his way to a posting with the Royal Navy and Anne was in the Wrens. Anne was pregnant with Joanne when they went to the altar. The couple both left the navy and settled in Gloucestershire, and Pete apprenticed on a factory production line. In 1974 they scraped together enough to move to a stone cottage in the pretty village of Tutshill.

E. Nesbit said, 'Only by remembering how you felt and thought when you yourself were a child can you arrive at any under-standing of the thoughts and feelings of children.'[*] Affirming her kinship with Nesbit, Rowling has said: 'I remember vividly what it felt like to be eleven and every age up to twenty and I think you could make a good case [...] for preventing anybody who doesn't remember what it felt like to be a child from writing a children's book.'

As has often been assumed, Rowling put a lot of her child self into the bookish, eager-to-please, sometimes priggish Hermione Granger. 'Hermione was very easy to create because she is based almost entirely on myself at the age of eleven. She is really a caricature of me. Like Hermione I was obsessed with achieving academically, but this masked a huge insecurity. I think it is very common for plain young girls to feel this way.' She has described herself as 'the epitome of a bookish child – short and squat, thick National Health glasses, living in a world of complete daydreams, wrote stories endlessly and occasionally came out of the fog to bully

---

[*]   E. Nesbit, *Wings and the Child: or, the Building of Magic Cities* (Hodder & Stoughton, 1913).

my poor sister and force her to listen to my stories and play the games I'd just invented.'*

But Harry Potter – orphaned, impetuous, rebellious, fearful, courageous – is also one of the literary horcruxes among which J.K. Rowling partitioned her soul. Joanne was fifteen when her mother Anne was diagnosed with the incurable and progressive disease multiple sclerosis. Over the following decade the disease steadily and cruelly went about its work, leaving Anne – who had worked as a lab assistant at her daughter's school – jobless and wheelchair-bound. She died in 1990 at the age of forty-five. The original premise of the Harry Potter books, their emotional core, the reason that Harry is – in Rowling's shiver-making phrase – 'The Boy Who Lived', is a mother's love. 'I know why you couldn't kill me,' Harry tells Voldemort. 'Because my mother died to save me.' When Harry looks into the Mirror of Erised, which shows the onlooker the 'deepest, most desperate desire of our hearts', it's his dead parents he sees, waving to him.

As her mother's health declined, the bookish child went through a fragile adolescence – in the course of which she shed her Hermione-like nerdiness to take up smoking, rock guitar and a gothy style. 'Home was a difficult place to be,' she told Sue Lawley on *Desert Island Discs*.† Yet she did not neglect her schoolwork; she became head girl and narrowly missed out on a long-shot place at Oxford, going instead to Exeter to study modern languages.

Rowling, as a young woman, drifted. After leaving university in 1987 with a middling degree, she lived in London and then, following a university boyfriend, in Manchester. She did a succession of bitty jobs – a secretarial course, temping work, a stint in an entry-level position at the charity Amnesty International. It was while looking glumly out of the window of a train from

---

* *With Great Pleasure*, BBC Radio 4, 25 May 2000.
† *Desert Island Discs*, BBC Radio 4, 10 November 2000.

Manchester to London, on the way back from a flat-hunting trip, that the idea for the story that was to make her name came into her head:

> All of a sudden the idea for Harry just appeared in my mind's eye. I can't tell you why or what triggered it. But I saw the idea of Harry and the wizard school very plainly. I suddenly had this basic idea of a boy who didn't know who he was, who didn't know he was a wizard until he got his invitation to wizard school. I have never been so excited by an idea.[*]

It was 1990: seven years before the book would make its way into print, and just a few months before her mother's death between Christmas and New Year. It was an inflection point. Her life in Manchester came unrooted, the relationship with the boyfriend ended, and the tin hat was put on her situation when she lost several precious mementoes of her mother in a burglary. She did a geographical, answering an advertisement in the *Guardian* for people to teach English in the Portuguese city of Porto.

This new start brought the second crisis in her life. The Bluebeard part: dark materials. Five months into her time in Porto, Rowling met a young Portuguese man, Jorge Arantes, and soon fell pregnant. They lost the child to a miscarriage, but they decided to try for another baby and to marry. She was pregnant with her daughter Jessica when they married. Though she didn't speak extensively about that period in her life until years later, she included a sour private joke in *Harry Potter and the Prisoner of Azkaban*. The divination teacher Professor Trelawney (usually a comical character) has a vision: 'That thing you are dreading – it will happen on Friday the sixteenth of October.' Rowling's wedding day in 1992 was Friday 16 October.

---

[*]   Sean Smith, *J.K. Rowling*.

The marriage lasted little more than a year. Arantes was violent and controlling towards Rowling, refusing to let her have her own house key and using the manuscript of her book (by this stage she had the first three chapters of *Harry Potter and the Philosopher's Stone* written and the rest in draft) as leverage in case she tried to leave him.

'He knew what that manuscript meant to me because at one point he took the manuscript and hid it and that was his hostage,' she said in 2023. She took steps to preserve it, and would take 'a few pages of the manuscript into work every day – just a few pages so that he wouldn't realise anything was missing – and photocopy it [...] gradually in a cupboard in the staff room, bit by bit, a photo-copied manuscript grew and grew and grew, because I suspected that, if I wasn't able to get out with everything, he would burn it or take it or hold it hostage.'*

In November 1993, Arantes beat her and threw her out of the house into the street at five in the morning. The following day, she returned with a policeman – 'Officially the police could not do anything but I convinced them to come with me. I thought they might frighten him' – and convinced Arantes to hand over her baby daughter. She went into hiding, frightened that he'd come after her and their child. Two weeks later she fled Portugal for good and headed to Edinburgh to be near her sister.

'I knew two or three people, and I was incredibly lonely. I was really angry,' she later said. 'I never expected to mess up so badly that I would find myself in an unheated mouse-infested flat, look-ing after my daughter. And I was angry because I felt that I was letting her down.'† The following year, Arantes appeared unex-pectedly in Edinburgh. She was frightened enough of him that she applied for, and was granted, a restraining order – which was

---

*   Interview with Megan Phelps-Roper, in 'The Witch Trials of J.K. Rowling' podcast, The Free Press, February 2023.
†   Simon Hattenstone, 'Harry, Jessie and me', *Guardian*, 8 July 2000.

made permanent in 1995. That summer, she filed for divorce and started the struggle to get her life back on track, studying towards a PGCE – and working on the manuscript of *Harry Potter and the Philosopher's Stone*.

The first three chapters of that manuscript found their way to an agent, Christopher Little, whose name Rowling had found in the *Writers' and Artists' Yearbook*. Little's office junior Bryony Evens by chance plucked it from the reject basket, started to read it, and was impressed. She showed it to a freelance reader, who in turn – after writing to Rowling for the full text – brought it to Little's attention. Though he didn't as a rule represent children's authors, he saw something in it. Twelve publishers turned it down before Bloomsbury's children's publisher, Barry Cunningham, made an offer. The rights to *Harry Potter and the Philosopher's Stone*, which would go on to be the third best-selling book of all time, went for £1,500. And, at her agent's urging, Joanne Rowling became J.K. Rowling (the K was for Kathleen, her grandmother's name).

The book was published to little fanfare, in an edition of just 500 copies. The second stroke of luck came three days after the UK publication, when Rowling heard that an auction was being conducted for US rights. Scholastic paid $100,000 for it – and at once, the single mother from Edinburgh became a person of interest to the media on both sides of the Atlantic. The legend was in place.

If you were writing a Whig history of children's books, you could see the Harry Potter stories as a natural terminus. Not only did their success transform the reception of children's writing in this country and around the world, but the writing of them deftly combines the most attractive elements of what has gone before. They are a fantastically adept mash-up of some of the most enduring tropes and genres in children's writing. Those who criticise them as unoriginal, or have sneered at Rowling's unambitious prose, have, it seems to me, missed the point.

Originality isn't, and never has been, the vital ingredient in children's writing. It's welcome when it's there, of course, but many if not most of the greatest children's books consciously and openly lean on their predecessors. They repurpose fairytale motifs, they namecheck or adapt writers of the generation with whom their authors themselves grew up – Kipling in Nesbit; Nesbit in Lewis – and they swim happily in the great torrent of school stories, portal fantasies, pirates and witches and explorers that lead up to their publication.

Rowling is emphatically a writer of that kind: steeped in, and determined to amalgamate, the long traditions of fantasy and school stories. A.S. Byatt, around the launch of *Harry Potter and the Order of the Phoenix* (2003), paid Rowling the (backhanded) compliment of calling the nascent Potterverse 'a secondary secondary world, made up of intelligently patchworked derivative motifs from all sorts of children's literature'.* That's surely right; though she points in my view to a central strength of those books rather than a weakness. Rowling is one of the great magpies.

For a start, she took the boarding-school story – a genre that until then seemed to have had its last gasp around the middle of the twentieth century – and put it right back at the centre of the contemporary canon. She did this in a very trad way. Hogwarts, with its grand halls and suits of armour, its arcane rituals and old-fashioned clothes, resembles an early modern boarding school more than it does a twentieth-century one. Even in the Muggle world, Harry Potter's universe is one seemingly untouched by mobile phones, the internet, modern brands or celebrities.

As I mentioned in a previous chapter, Rowling tips the cap to the Molesworth stories in borrowing 'Hogwarts' and 'Scrimgeour'. Probably by chance – the shape of the mythological set-up – it also echoes the X-Men: what, after all, is Hogwarts but another version of Professor Xavier's school for gifted youngsters, the divide between mutant and human echoed in the divide between wizard

---

* A.S. Byatt, 'Harry Potter and the Childish Adult', *New York Times*, 7 July 2003.

and Muggle? Other predecessors include Jill Murphy's series set in a school for witches, starting with *The Worst Witch* (1974) and (an acknowledged influence) T.H. White's *The Sword in the Stone*. Harry, like Wart, is a weedy and isolated figure who comes to discover that fate has marvellous and painful things in store for him, and who grows to his full powers under the tutelage of a kindly and eccentric wizard. Rowling learned too, I fancy, from White's ability to turn on a pin, tonally: as I've written, White's retelling of Malory is distinguished by its swerving from one paragraph to the next between epic grandeur and screwball comedy. J.K. Rowling makes the same swerves. And like every school story ever, it has sporting rivalry, swots, mean teachers and kind ones, rule-breaking adventures, pranks and larks, a tuck-shop, and – in the weaselly form of Draco Malfoy and his thuggish sidekicks Crabbe and Goyle – bullies.

All the greatest hits of children's writing through the ages have a place, among them the encyclopaedic info-dump qualities that are such a central part of the appeal of children's books since *Orbis Pictus*. The natural history facts and figures, and the practical knowledge, we find in *The Water-Babies* and Willard Price's *Adventure* stories are, in Harry Potter, applied to a wild bestiary of mythic creatures. You learn, along with the book's protagonists as they go lesson to lesson, about the ingredient list for a Polyjuice Potion, the safe cultivation of mandrakes, the care and feeding of dragons and blast-tailed skrewts, and how to clear a garden of gnomes (you pick the little brutes up, whirl them till they're dizzy and throw them lustily over the hedge).

Does she skimp on the mouthwatering depictions of food? She does not. Perhaps the archetypal instance – Kenneth Grahame's Joycean picnic of 'coldtonguecoldhamcoldbeefpickledgherkins-saladfrenchrollscresssandwichespottedmeatgingerbeerlemonadeso-dawater' has its echo in the regular feasts at Hogwarts. When Harry first arrives at wizarding school, the tables groan with 'roast beef, roast chicken, pork chops and lamb chops, sausages, bacon and steak, boiled potatoes, roast potatoes, chips, Yorkshire pudding, peas, carrots, gravy, ketchup [...] apple pies, treacle tarts, chocolate eclairs and jam doughnuts, trifles, strawberries, jelly, rice pudding...' Her punctilious attention to what the children were eating, though, Rowling has said, wasn't directly inspired by Grahame so much as by Elizabeth Goudge, whose *The Little White Horse* (1946) she has described as 'more than any other book a direct influence on the Harry Potter books [...] The author always included details of what her characters were eating and I remember liking that.'*

On the fantasy side, Byatt discerned echoes of Roald Dahl, *Star Wars*, Diana Wynne Jones and Susan Cooper. Ursula K. Le Guin, as Pottermania took hold of the world, grumbled publicly that 'when so many adult critics were carrying on about the "incredible originality" of the first Harry Potter book, I read it to find out what the fuss was about, and remained somewhat puzzled.'† She herself had told the story of an alone-in-the-world boy wizard discovering his true powers at a wizarding school in *A Wizard of Earthsea* (1968), complete with a scar that throbbed in the presence of dark forces and a Malfoy-like school rival.

Harry Potter isn't so much a portal fantasy as a *portals* fantasy: the rabbit-hole at King's Cross station, Platform 9¾, is one of a whole plethora of magical apertures in the books to be discovered and unlocked – from the entrance to the Chamber of Secrets in Moaning Myrtle's neglected bathroom to the password-locked portraits leading to the house dormitories in Hogwarts or the network of fireplaces accessed through 'floo powder'. But where Rowling follows Cooper, Garner and the Kipling of *Puck of Pook's Hill* is that the wizarding world isn't a separate universe you access through a wardrobe or a magic rail platform; it is an older, deeper, magical order of things that invisibly overlays our own. Events

---

*   Lindsay Fraser, 'Harry Potter – Harry and Me,' *Scotsman*, November 2002.
†   'Chronicles of Earthsea', *Guardian*, 9 February 2004.

in the magical world impinge on the disenchanted world of the Muggles. They share a geography. As a reader, you can fantasise that the world of Harry Potter would be all around you, were you only able to see it.

The *Harry Potter* books, then, are not just a tale of a set of magical shenanigans. They are a fantastical vision of Britain itself. The Dursleys – 'respectable', cruel, repressed and socially snobbish – are one version of Middle England, one model of an English family; the Weasleys – scruffy, boisterous, poor but happy – are another. Their home in the Devon village of Ottery St Catchpole is in the direct lineage of Bilbo Baggins's hobbit-hole and Badger's comfortable home in *The Wind in the Willows*:

> It looked as though it had once been a large stone pigsty, several storeys high and so crooked it looked as though it was held up by magic (which, Harry reminded himself, it probably was). Four or five chimneys were perched on top of the red roof. A lop-sided sign stuck in the ground near the entrance read *The Burrow*. Round the front door lay a jumble of wellington boots and a very rusty cauldron. Several fat brown chickens were pecking their way around the yard.

'Crooked'; 'lop-sided'; 'jumble'. This is the England of G.K. Chesterton's 'rolling English road' or Hopkins's 'Pied Beauty'. It is countryside not town, bricolage not planned construction: an England whose history builds up higgledy-piggledy, animated by human warmth: make-do-and-mend. It's a nostalgic image.

The magical world is a more exciting shadow version of the workaday world around us. It's a world in which (in keeping with Rowling's relentless punning) you can get around on a Knight Bus, the dull state comprehensive is replaced by a Gothic boarding school with Latin tags (*draco dormens numquam titillandus*: never tickle a sleeping dragon), and in which – heavens-to-betsy – the postal service, thanks to owls, actually works. That world reflects our own in the proverbial funhouse mirror – allowing Rowling to comment on snobbery, racism, tabloid journalism (in the form of the dishonest and prurient Rita Skeeter), the tediousness of government bureaucracy in the form of the Ministry of Magic, and liberation politics (legal slavery is no longer an issue in modern Britain, but Hermione's 'House Elf Liberation Front' can stand in for any number of social justice movements).

Roald Dahl is also present. The books could have been written with the injunction I quoted in a previous chapter in mind: '[Children] love being spooked,' wrote Dahl. 'They love suspense. They love action. They love ghosts. They love the finding of treasure. They love chocolates and toys and money. They love magic.' The Dursley family, with whom the orphaned hero lives so miserably, are pure Dahl. They belong not only to Dahl's era – the buttoned-up suburbia of Privet Drive, and the stout, moustachioed paterfamilias, could be from anywhere from the 1950s to the 1970s – but also to his idiom. They are two-dimensional adult authority figures whose physical grotesquerie echoes their moral standing. Vernon and Petunia resemble Matilda Wormwood's parents in temperament if not in respectability, while fat-necked, spoilt, pig-like Dudley is a malign Augustus Gloop.

The father of modern fantasy is a presence in the text, too. He could hardly fail to have been. Rowling in young womanhood was a dedicated reader and rereader of Tolkien – her battered copy of *The Lord of the Rings* was among the books she took with her when she travelled to Portugal to work as an English teacher, and her biographer Sean Smith crisply enumerates some of the echoes or borrowings:

> Aragorn, Butterbur, Mugwort, Wormtongue and Bilbo Baggins contrast [with] Aragog, Butterbeer, Muggles, Wormtail and Dudley Dursley. Both heroes [...] are naive orphans with unpleasant relatives: Harry has the Dursleys and Frodo the Sackville-Bagginses. Both Tolkien and Rowling employ a friendly mentor or father

figure who allows the hero to grow but is ready to step in and rescue if necessary. Harry has Dumbledore, Frodo has Gandalf. The enemy in both cases is a 'Dark Lord' [who] has been crippled and is coming back to power slowly. [...] Both Wormtongue and Wormtail reveal their true colours as close but ultimately weak acolytes of the Dark Lord [...] *The Lord of the Rings* has the black, hooded Ringwraiths while *The Prisoner of Azkaban* introduces the black, hooded Dementors.*

In the first Harry Potter book, Harry encounters the Mirror of Erised, which shows its viewer his or her heart's desire; in *The Fellowship of the Ring*, Frodo meets the Mirror of Galadriel. And so on. *Star Wars*? Here is another story in which the fate of the galaxy rests on a family struggle: another Dark Lord, another orphaned boy whose origins are more portentous than he begins to understand, another process of training under a series of father figures; a final clash between cosmic forces of light and darkness. Under the skin, the books trade in deeper mythic archetypes. They are a latency fantasy: Harry, with his meagre meals of scraps and his cupboard under the stairs, is as the stories open a shock-haired, male Cinderella. Even Voldemort storing the fragments of his soul in 'horcruxes' has a folktale antecedent: the Russian folktale 'Koshchei the Deathless' has its protagonist hide his soul in a series of nested objects (a needle inside an egg inside a duck inside a hare chained in a box on an island). By the end – in which Harry essentially gives his own life up in a sacrificial salvation, only to return – it's not too much to see Rowling as drawing on the power of the Christian story itself.

Rowling freely plunders the whole history of fantasy to give us her own versions of goblins and pixies and unicorns, hippogriffs and werewolves and phoenixes. The magical power of anagrams

---

* Sean Smith, op. cit.

('Tom Marvolo Riddle' becomes 'I Am Lord Voldemort') and incantatory effect of true names (Voldemort is 'He Who Must Not Be Named'), which is there in 'Rumpelstiltskin' as it is in *A Wizard of Earthsea*, also take their place in the stories. The Killing Curse – 'Avada Kedavra' – is a good homophonic joke on 'Abracadabra' – a version of which is found in magical writings from two millennia ago. Here is a classic instance of Rowling's balance of the comical and the sinister – the implication, perhaps, that a Muggle tribe-memory of real magic has been unknowingly domesticated as the banal cliché of the stage magician.

Prose-wise, Rowling's writing isn't setting out to dazzle its readers with unexpected similes or original turns of phrase. She doesn't have the sentence-by-sentence or conceptual sophistication of a T.H. White or a Le Guin. It's all at the service of her story: and when it comes to plotting and pacing, to the mix of comfort and excitement, and to the changing balance of humour and darkness in the books, she does her work as well as or better than any children's writer.

But as much as these books looked affectionately backwards over the canon of children's literature and gathered it into the folds of their wizarding robes, they also did something that was both subtle and original. They grew with their audience. The seven books cover seven school years. If Harry Potter's notional reader was, like Harry, just turning eleven in the first book, he or she would be just turning seventeen in the opening pages of *Harry Potter and the Deathly Hallows*. (In fact, the books were published over a decade, with two-year gaps between the last four, so he or she would be twenty-one – but the rough principle holds.)

Not only did the characters change and develop over the course of the series, but so did the storytelling. Rowling's directness of style remains a constant, but the books become longer and more complex in structure, and more adult in theme. The Harry Potter of the first book isn't yet even remotely a sexual creature. But as he goes through adolescence he goes through the likely adolescent experiences of his readership – he gets a crush on the rival Quidditch player Cho Chang in *Harry Potter and the Goblet of Fire*, and kisses her in *Harry Potter and the Order of the Phoenix*.

The series also goes on to supply its orphaned hero with a panoply of models of parenthood. James and Lily Potter are sainted in memory; Harry becomes uncontrollably enraged when his parents' memory is insulted. But a succession of father and mother figures is presented (in contrast to the anti-parenting of the Dursleys). To the question of what it is to be a parent, and what it is to be a family, *Harry Potter* supplies many answers. Dumbledore, Hagrid, Sirius Black, Remus Lupin, Arthur Weasley and even Severus Snape are all at various points contrasting models of parental authority; none of them are plaster saints. On the distaff side the contrastive figures of Minerva McGonagall and Molly Weasley – one a figure of stern formal integrity; the other a little furnace of warmth and love – supplement the memory of Lily Potter. A PG-13 moment in the final book – where Molly kills the dark witch Bellatrix Lestrange with a shriek of 'Not my daughter, you bitch!' – gives cuddly Mrs Weasley her mother tiger moment. A mother might give her life to save her children, as Lily Potter did; but a mother might also be prepared to take one.

Ever since Peter Pan's declaration that 'to die would be an awfully big adventure', most adventure stories for younger children have steered clear of dealing directly with death on the page. It'll be in the background – all those orphans have to be orphaned somehow – but not part of the story. In the first book, that precept is followed. So when, as part of the publicity campaign for *Harry Potter and the Goblet of Fire*, it was let slip that one of the characters was going to be killed, it was a very big deal in the fandom (the victim, spoiler alert, was the relatively peripheral Cedric Diggory). By the time the series came to a close, Rowling had become positively slap-happy about killing off her characters. The consensus seems to be (I confess I haven't counted myself) that no fewer than 158 characters buy the farm in the course of the story – among them Dobby the House-Elf, Severus Snape, Fred Weasley and Hedwig the owl. The Battle of Hogwarts in the final book has a body count of more than fifty.

The stakes get higher. As incarnated in the Dursleys of the early books, fear of the Other manifests as the semi-comical prejudice of the small-minded bourgeoisie. Harry takes pleasure in giving the Dursleys a fright by muttering incomprehensibly under his breath, knowing that they fear his ability to cast spells as much as they hate it. But their prejudice against the wizarding community has a darker shadow in the Death Eaters' contempt for Muggles and their exterminatory hatred of the 'mudblood' and Muggle-born. I think Rowling expects her readers to make the connection. The Dursleys despise something that's more powerful than they are: Voldemort despises something that's less powerful than he is. We hop, over the course of the books, from small-mindedness to eugenics and, in all but name, genocidal fascism.

The close-up cruelty ratchets up, too. The first great step-change is the appearance of the Dementors in the third book, *The Prisoner of Azkaban*. These apparent cousins of Tolkien's Ringwraiths are employed by the Ministry of Magic as prison guards at the wizarding prison of Azkaban. They feed leech-like on happiness and leave in its wake an icy despair: 'The cold went deeper than his skin. It was inside his chest, it was inside his very heart…' The kiss of a Dementor can permanently suck out the victim's soul. They are genuinely scary – and it's been said that for Rowling they were an objective correlative for the period of depression she underwent after she returned to the UK with Jessica after the great crisis of her own young adulthood. These emanations of the Dark Arts are nevertheless employed by the (supposedly benign) Ministry of Magic, and later defect to Voldemort; we could read that as a pert commentary on the criminal justice system and a sense of the deepening mistrust of institutions that the books evince as they go on. By *Harry Potter and the Order of the Phoenix*, Hogwarts itself has been infiltrated by the loathsome Dolores Umbridge – a pious supremacist whose signature punishment is the black quill, a cursed writing instrument that cuts the lines that its victims are forced to write into their skin. The Rowling who invented this torture device was taking her cue not from Molesworth or Enid Blyton but from the Kafka of 'In the Penal Colony'.

The structure of the books changes and loosens, too, and their complexity grows. The first couple in the series establish what looks to be a pattern: they open in the summer holidays, and the main action takes place in the bounded space of Hogwarts during term-time and closes with order restored. Dumbledore and the grown-ups are essentially omnipotent. If you've been turned to stone, the fifth act will see you good as new. More ambiguous adult institutions such as the Ministry of Magic and their actions in the wider world are in the background: the stories take their cues from the reassuring regularity of the school year. But that steadily crumbles and dissipates. The last two books are all about politics and all about war. The structures and routines that keep children safe have been blown to smithereens. Hogwarts is no longer a refuge. Torture and death and betrayal are routine, and their consequences permanent. Like a child moving towards adulthood, the books take Harry out of safe harbour and into a more dangerous world.

That's not to say that these books aren't, for the most part, morally black and white: the basic set-up is friendship and selflessness versus an expressly fascist will-to-power. There's a fierce sense throughout of which side has the right; but the protagonists cannot trust institutional norms, or even appearances, to judge which is which. Institutions are to be trusted only inasmuch as they are run by trustworthy individuals: the Ministry of Magic is corruptible; Dumbledore's Hogwarts is not, but only as long as he remains in charge. Normative authority is the creepy old caretaker Filch, skulking the corridors with his cat Mrs Norris, in search of fun to spoil and miscreants to snitch on. Rules are to be broken *ad lib* as long as it's the goodies doing it.

With this in mind far and away the most psychologically interesting character arc is that of Severus Snape, the potions teacher who starts his life as a boilerplate meanie but whose back-story broadens and deepens the reader's understanding of his motivation: bullying, thwarted love, multiple betrayals and a final ambiguous redemption. Snape becomes a study in Auden's gloomy prediction of how those 'to whom evil is done' will tend to respond, but without Auden's apparent fatalism. Snape comes good in the end.

The *Harry Potter* books did something else. They stopped. As much as the *Harry Potter* stories, in their constellation of characters and their open-ended world-building, resembled myths, they also in one important respect resembled fairytales: they came to a close. Despite the unimaginable financial rewards available to Rowling had she chosen to keep Harry, like Anthony Buckeridge's Jennings or *Just William* or *Biggles*, as an infinitely extendable franchise, she chose to tell one story. She had let it be known from very early on that she had already written the last chapter of the last book, longhand in a Summit notepad; and it was kept (once the success of the first books had made it seriously valuable) in a yellow folder in a safety-deposit box in the Edinburgh equivalent of Harry's vault at Gringotts.

These books were planned. They aren't individual entries in an infinite series; the story has an overall shape, and its architecture is formidably careful. Their long gestation – she was making notes for the series years before the first book was finished – means that she was able to leave a trail of breadcrumbs. She seeded little details that would later turn out to be significant. Ron Weasley's pet rat Scabbers is introduced with artful casualness in the first book; and only in *Harry Potter and the Prisoner of Azkaban* do we discover that he has been a wicked wizard in magical disguise all along. We don't learn for quite some time where Hagrid got the motorbike on which he dropped Harry at the Dursleys' in book one. You could contrast the slapdash way in which Richmal Crompton couldn't remember Ethel Brown's age or keep the names of the Browns' neighbours straight.

Rowling did drop a single stitch though. In *Harry Potter and the Goblet of Fire*, Harry is fighting a duel with Voldemort when he accidentally casts a spell that causes the Dark Lord's wand to spit out, in reverse order, spectral images of the people he has killed. Harry's father, James, comes out before his mother, Lily – when, according to the established story, he died in the process of trying to help his wife and child escape. Fans speculated as to whether Rowling was setting up some crafty plot twist, but she eventually admitted it was a mistake due to 'late-night writer's fatigue'; the text was corrected in later editions.

Rowling didn't leave the mythos she'd created entirely alone. She enriched the canonical timeline with prequels and sequels. She supplied the story for a fabulous theatrical production, *Harry Potter and the Cursed Child* (2016), which is set two decades after the events of *Harry Potter and the Deathly Hallows*, and follows Harry's son Albus (he's married, again spoiler alert, to Ginny Weasley) and Draco Malfoy's son Scorpius to Hogwarts, and a series of time-travelling adventures that stitch back through the events of the novels. In 2008 she wrote an 800-word prequel story on a postcard to raise money for the writers' charity English PEN (it raised £25,000 at auction but was lost in a burglary in 2017). She wrote three further in-universe 'non-fiction' books, *Quidditch Through the Ages* and *Fantastic Beasts and Where to Find Them* (both 2001), and a fairy-story collection, *The Tales of Beedle the Bard* (2008), also for charity (the first two were Comic Relief fundraisers, the third was originally auctioned, for The Children's High Level Group – now Lumos – the year before general publication in a limited edition of seven handwritten copies; the first copy went for £1.95 million). With excellent postmodern tricksiness, these were all books that themselves appeared as books in the main Harry Potter story.* Rowling is a much more sophisticated and deliberate writer than some of her detractors will tend to recognise.

---

* Harry reads a library copy of *Quidditch Through the Ages* in *Philosopher's Stone*, *Fantastic Beasts* is a Hogwarts textbook, and Dumbledore leaves Hermione a copy of *The Tales of Beedle the Bard* in his will.

The original seven books may have been helped off the launch-pad by that very marketable origin myth and given a boost by the newsworthy advance for the US edition, but none of that was what sent them into the stratosphere: they sold, and continued to sell, because children themselves adored them. Time and again, it was said of them what was said of the only comparably successful children's writer of a previous generation, Enid Blyton: 'they got children reading'. In the ultimate pre-digital space for word-of-mouth, the school playground, they went viral before virality was something we really talked about.

They were the first children's books, in fact, that really bedded into the birth of the digital age. In their ostensible trappings, they seemed to be a great reaction against the latest wave of modernity. They described a Muggle world that seemed frozen in the middle of the second half of the twentieth century – even the Ford Anglia that a besotted Arthur Weasley stashed away, and in which Ron and Harry fly to Hogwarts at the beginning of the second book, dates back to 1960. Its magical world combines the already outdated trappings of a retro boarding school with the olde-worlde mock-medieval furniture of Lewis, Tolkien, and every sword-and-sorcery story that derives from them.

So in that sense, they were proof that these classic storytelling techniques could hold their own in the world of Nintendo and YouTube. But they also thrived in that world like nothing else before them. I'm reminded a little of the way that, in adult literature, we think of William Gibson's *Neuromancer* (1984), Neal Stephenson's *Snow Crash* (1992) and David Foster Wallace's *Infinite Jest* (1996) as having been defining works of the internet age, when all three anticipated rather than reported it. *Harry Potter* is not about the internet age – if anything, it's a retreat from it into the comforting certainties of an imagined past – but it's *of* the digital age.

These books' playground virality segued into online virality as their readers came of age with the internet. Harry Potter caught the first great wave of online fan fiction. A theme of this study has been the fugitive, endlessly plastic, impossible-to-contain nature of children's stories: that like the myths they draw on they spill out constantly into different shapes, that they are remade and reimagined. They not only inspire and become TV adaptations, films, comics, boardgames, computer games, Lego sets and every imaginable permutation; they also inspire children to write their own stories.

As fan fiction became a big thing, Harry Potter fan fiction became the biggest thing in fan fiction. *Star Trek* aficionados had been publishing their own in-universe stories in fanzines since as early as the 1960s, and these migrated naturally onto early internet message boards. But the website fanfiction.net, which became the global hub for the explosion in fan writing, first came online in 1998, the year after *Harry Potter and the Philosopher's Stone* was published. Its fans, as they grew into young adulthood, seized the opportunity to respond to and extend Rowling's world that it and sites like it offered.

Rowling, at once generously and shrewdly, encouraged this. Bloomsbury owned the rights to the books (and, as we'll see, policed them ferociously). Warner Brothers, in completing the film deal for the properties, also took control of what would turn into a staggering merchandising operation. Rowling's intellectual property was locked down tight as far as commercial exploitation went. But if children and young adult fans wanted to write their own stories in the Harry Potter universe and share them with each other for free, that was fine by her. Other authors, such as Anne Rice of *Interview with the Vampire* fame, took a markedly different approach, pinging off legal threats to fan writers who used their characters in fan fiction. Rowling discouraged pornographic work but for the most part looked kindly on readers interacting in this way with her property.

A whole ecosystem of fan-run websites dedicated to the lore of the Potter universe proliferated, chief among them a site called *The Leaky Cauldron*, which came online in 2000. Rowling is known to

have monitored the site, albeit usually anonymously, and period-
ically used its reach as a means of engaging her fanbase. In 2011,
Rowling went further, launching a website called *Pottermore* that
offered various interactive widgets and was proposed as a home
for some of her 18,000 words of surplus unpublished material
related to the franchise. It ran games and competitions, and offered
digital access to sections of the published works. The site was
shuttered in 2019 and its content largely absorbed into a new site,
WizardingWorld.

That fan engagement was just one of the things that helped
Rowling's stories to drive a wholesale transformation in the market
for children's books. The *Harry Potter* series is a publishing phenomenon as much as it is a literary one. It sits at the heart of what
has been tentatively called a third golden age of children's writing,
and gave children's writing a central place in the culture.

When Bloomsbury first agreed to publish *Harry Potter and the
Philosopher's Stone*, for £1,500, they gave Rowling lunch in Soho,
where her new publisher Barry Cunningham told her wanly: 'You'll
never make any money out of children's books, Jo.' Indeed, my
understanding is that Bloomsbury had been on the point of shut-
tering its children's division altogether around the time that they
signed Rowling. Her success turned all that on its head.

I don't propose, here, to deliver a catalogue of sales records
broken, territories sold into and first edition prices, or dwell too
much on the uncontrollable hysteria around the launch days for
every book from *Goblet of Fire* (which almost produced a riot at
King's Cross station) onwards. But some details stand out. The
secrecy of the launches was so tightly policed that even translators
for foreign editions didn't get a whiff of the text until the English-
language launch day. In countries where English is widely spoken
as an additional language, translators worked around the clock in
teams to get the foreign-language editions finished, because every
day that the French or Dutch edition wasn't in bookshops the
English-language edition was cannibalising its potential sales. In

China, Rowling shared a publisher with Chairman Mao; the 600,000 boxed sets they produced of the first three books in translation was the biggest first printing there since the Revolution.

Publishers usually bust a gut to persuade the media to take an interest in their books and bookshops to stock them. With *Harry Potter*, it was the other way round. Newspaper reviewers were sent copies of the books by motorcycle courier at midnight: they were expected to read all night and file the next morning so that their reviews could feature on the following day's news pages. When in 2003 the *Sun* was offered a pre-launch copy of the first three chapters of *Harry Potter and the Order of the Phoenix* by a forklift driver at the printers, they calculated that enraging the publishers wasn't worth the scoop. They phoned the police and instead made a story out of setting up the sting operation that led to his arrest.

The economics of the books got seriously strange. Supermarkets discounted the titles so heavily that they lost money on every copy sold; independent bookshops took to restocking from Tesco, where they could pick up stock more cheaply than from wholesalers or even the publisher. And when, around the launch of *Deathly Hallows*, the supermarket chain Asda accused Bloomsbury of 'blatant profiteering' and 'attempting to hold children to ransom' by pricing the book at £17.99, Bloomsbury cancelled Asda's order of half a million hardbacks. 'If they want their 500,000 books, they'll have to come and make peace with us,' they said. 'It could be good news for all their disappointed customers, because they don't have to go to a soulless Asda shed to buy their book.'* It took Asda less than a day to make a grovelling reversal.

At the end of the nineteenth century, there was no clear and stable distinction between children's books and those written for adults; they shared bestseller lists, such as they were, and they shared a

---

* 'Twenty years of Harry Potter – the 20 things we have learned', *Guardian*, 26 June 2017.

readership. As the twentieth century progressed, children's writing became, for the most part, a separate literary and publishing domain, and the story of its development across that century is the story of its flourishing in that niche. But at the very end of the twentieth century, we seemed to be returning to where we were at the end of the nineteenth, though from the other direction. Adults were reading children's books; to the extent that – to save the blushes of commuters – 'adult editions' of the Harry Potter books were published in 2007 with 'sophisticated' covers in sombre shades of grey, designed to make them look less like children's books.*

That crossover appeal didn't prevent their vast cultural footprint from provoking the old anxieties that adults have always had about children's writing – particularly in the culturally and religiously conservative parts of the United States. The book-burners and censors against whom Judy Blume had struggled in the 1980s rallied to denounce Harry Potter a generation later. They are always with us, and always have been. Children's writing is powerful magic, and those who fear that magic will always seek to control it. In several places in the US, copies of Rowling's books were burned by fundamentalist Christians who believed they were encouraging children to take up witchcraft. 'Behind that innocent face is the power of satanic darkness,' said pastor Jack Brock of the Christ Community church in Alamogordo, New Mexico, in 2001. 'Harry Potter is the devil and he is destroying people.'

Latterly, the cultural left has also taken issue with Rowling's books. It has been pointed out that the characters are overwhelmingly white and heterosexual. This is perhaps in keeping with Rowling's mid-twentieth-century inspirations, most of which, as I've previously discussed, tend to be racially and sexually homogenous,

---

*   The cross-generational appeal of the *Harry Potter* franchise even extends to its merchandising. A typical review for Mattel's now discontinued Nimbus 2000 Vibrating Broom on Amazon read: 'I'm 32 and enjoy riding the broom as much as my 12-year-old and 7-year-old.'

and as Anglocentric as the Potter books are. The foreign characters in the book do get somewhat stereotypical names – Viktor Krum, Seamus Finnigan, Fleur Delacour and Cho Chang. The goblins who run Gringotts Wizarding Bank have even been denounced as anti-semitic stereotypes; though it's worth noticing that the hook-nosed semitic figures of which Rowling's critics complain are drawn from the imagery in the films rather than their descriptions in the books.

No doubt, had she known that her work would attract the almost theological scrutiny it has, Rowling would have thought harder about some of the thinner representations that her novels contain. She has said that she thinks of Dumbledore as having been gay and welcomed the casting of a Black actor as Hermione Granger in *The Cursed Child*, pointing out that Hermione's race isn't specified in the books. It's not really a debate for these pages. For what it's worth, it seems to me that to ask a children's book, no matter how beloved, to be entirely free from stereotypes (or even jokes that lean on stereotypes), or to faithfully and without exception represent the whole range of human diversity, is a lot to ask it to carry. Imperfect though they may be, the central moral message of these books is the fight against 'othering', bullying, eugenics and racism.

Even less a debate for these pages is Rowling's gender-critical intervention in the twenty-first-century argument over trans rights. It's not an issue that has anything to do with her children's writing (unless you count – bit of a stretch – the prefect Percy Weasley catching his brother Ron leaving Moaning Myrtle's domain and exclaiming in shock: 'That's a *girls'* bathroom!'). Except, perhaps, in one respect. The reaction against the books from the progressive left has differed from the reaction from the reactionary right not just in ideological character, but generationally: the pushback, here, is coming not from parents who disapprove of Rowling's books but from young adults who grew up adoring them.

There's a case, which seems to me convincing, that it's the very generation that grew up with the Harry Potter books that has most enthusiastically embraced so-called 'cancel culture'. The extreme reaction against Rowling by those who have decided that she's transphobic – which extends to the boycotting of her books and the intellectual property that flows from them just because of their association with the author's opinions – looks a little bit like the product of a generation whose ardent *Harry Potter* fandom shaped its understanding of the world.

Cancel culture takes a sorting-hat view of human nature: the hat peers deep into your soul, and after no more than a minute – though usually instantly – it assigns you a moral identity. A generation primed to take a goodies-vs-baddies worldview, energised by the books' sense of an apocalyptic struggle between good and evil, and seeing no need to put aside childish things, has turned with some decisiveness on the author of those books when it decided she was on the other team. The revolution, in other words, has eaten not its children but its parent.

But the revolution, for a generation that has carried a children's-book worldview into young adulthood, has continued. Young adult fiction, and children's fiction read by adults, has continued to thrive, as has fan fiction. Publishers always being in search of the last big thing, the influence of *Harry Potter* on both what has been written and how it has been published is incalculable. After the swerve into something like social realism described in the previous chapter, the pendulum swung decisively back in the early years of the twenty-first century.

The ostensibly adult soft-porn franchise *Fifty Shades of Grey* started life as online fan fiction for Stephanie Meyers's YA vampire series *Twilight* (originally published 2005–8). Fantasy and SF novels aimed at adolescents have been everywhere. In addition to *Twilight*, it's near impossible to imagine the successes of G.P. Taylor's *Shadowmancer* series (began 2003), Rick Riordan's *Percy Jackson & The Olympians* (began 2005) or Suzanne Collins's dystopian science-fiction *Hunger Games* (begun in 2008) in a world in which *Harry Potter* had never happened. Some of those writers were candid in acknowledging the debt. G.P. Taylor said in 2005: 'I got a copy of *Harry Potter*, counted the number of words that were on the page, measured the width of the margin, counted the number of chapters in the book, how many pages were in the book and set my computer screen up so that it would have 468 words on the page. My chapters were the same length as the *Harry Potter* chapters; I thought, "This must be how you write a book."'[*]

*   James Francken, 'A Writer's Life: G.P. Taylor,' *Daily Telegraph*, 14 August 2005.

Darkness Visible

PHILIP PULLMAN

Northern Lights; The Subtle Knife;
The Amber Spyglass; La Belle Sauvage;
The Secret Commonwealth; Daemon Voices

THE OTHER GREAT CROSSOVER FANTASY SERIES OF THIS third golden age owed no direct debt to *Harry Potter*. Philip Pullman's *Northern Lights* (1995) was first published two years before *Harry Potter and the Philosopher's Stone*. The success of the subsequent volumes in the *His Dark Materials* trilogy no doubt benefited from the spotlight swinging onto fantasy literature for children, but Pullman got under way quite on his own. Like the *Harry Potter* books, Pullman's work looked knowingly backward over the fantasy writing of the past, and like those books they took it in a quite new direction. Indeed, if Harry Potter can be seen as a summum of what came before, *His Dark Materials* can be seen as an overthrowing.

Philip Pullman (1946–) was a schoolteacher in Oxford when the first volume of the trilogy that made his name arrived in print, and it's a book that wears its connection to a children's classic of the past on its sleeve. *Northern Lights* is a direct riposte to the evangelical Christianity of C.S. Lewis's Narnia books, and it draws much of its energy from its engagement with Lewis. As the former Archbishop of Canterbury, Rowan Williams, has said shrewdly, 'In a peculiar way, Philip Pullman's *His Dark Materials* is quite a tribute to Lewis – because, although Philip loathes the Narnia stories, he clearly recognises that there is enough imaginative bounce and energy in them to demand a serious response.'*

Pullman reacted to Narnia – which he first encountered as an adult and read with an accordingly sceptical eye – with a version of the enduring anxiety about the influence that children's stories can have on their impressionable audience. He has called the Narnia books 'wicked': 'I find them very dodgy and unpleasant – dodgy in the dishonest rhetoric way – and unpleasant because they seem to embody a worldview that takes for granted things like racism, misogyny and a profound cultural conservatism that is utterly unexamined.'† Speaking at the Hay Festival in 2002, he said he saw in Lewis's fiction 'a peevish blend of racist, misogynistic and reactionary prejudice; but of love, of Christian charity, [there is] not a trace.' But rather than ban or burn them, he set out to write something better – a thrilling, high-concept adventure story animated by a fierce loathing for the institutional manifestations of religion, and the will-to-power that drives them.

Pullman's work is for a higher age-group than that of Rowling. Pullman himself doesn't consider it a children's story, and it can be and is read by adults without the need for a blush-saving alternative cover design.‡ It draws its title from a line in the second, still more influential, literary predecessor to which it responds: *Paradise Lost* (1667). In Book Two of Milton's epic poem, Satan escapes from hell and prepares to journey across the dizzying vastness of Chaos:

> ...this wilde Abyss,
> The Womb of nature and perhaps her Grave,
> Of neither Sea, nor Shore, nor Air, nor Fire,

---

* Sam Leith, 'C.S. Lewis's Literary Legacy: "Dodgy and unpleasant" or "exceptionally good"?', *Guardian*, 19 November 2013.
† Ibid.
‡ I first heard of the excellence of *His Dark Materials* from a friend before Pullman was widely known, and was surprised when, asking after it in a bookshop, I was directed by a shop assistant to the children's section.

> But all these in thir pregnant causes mixt
> Confus'dly, and which thus must ever fight,
> Unless th' Almighty Maker them ordain
> His dark materials to create more Worlds,
> Into this wild Abyss the warie fiend
> Stood on the brink of Hell and look'd a while.

That turbulent passage indicates some of the complexity of Pullman's ambition in the book. Chaos is a site, for Milton, of creation *and* destruction, its formless elements at ceaseless war with themselves unless and until God ordains them 'his dark materials to create new worlds'.

Among the central mysteries of the multiverse of *His Dark Materials* is Dust – which in one of the constituent worlds of Pullman's multiverse is analogous to the undetectable dark matter hypothesised by modern physicists as the *sine qua non* of the universe's existence in the form it takes. Pullman's imaginative multiverse grapples to bring together concepts in theology and in theoretical physics, which puts these sophisticated books in a territory that straddles the science fiction and fantasy genres. As a character in the third book puts it, 'Dust is only a name for what happens when matter begins to understand itself.'

Dust is the fundamental grounds of existence – and it is the material form of consciousness itself. As such it is associated with free will, and the Church accordingly seeks to conceal and if possible destroy it. The story's villains have forgotten, or want others to forget, that 'from dust ye came and to dust ye must return': that every sentient creature in the multiverse, *including God* (or 'the Authority') himself, is a product of Dust.

Accordingly, the Authority, we discover in the final book, is not an omnipotent and benevolent higher being, still less the immortal creator of the universe. He was the first Angel to form from Dust, and conned those that came after into believing him to be apart from and above the creation. By the time we meet him he is a feeble, geriatric, half-mad creature encased in a protective box, and whose powers are exercised on his behalf by a tyrannical regent. The 'fallen Angels' – those who rebelled against the Authority and its sublunary Magisterium – are the heroes of this story. If Milton was (as William Blake said) 'of the Devil's party without knowing it', Pullman is fully and consciously signed up to the Devil's party – though in the service of a stridently moral liberal worldview.

This is intellectually chewy material. But – did I mention? – it is also an extraordinarily involving adventure story and a virtuoso feat of world-building that cross-shades its fantastical inventions with plausibly built-out edifices of science, politics and organised religion. Perhaps the most memorable and original peculiarity of the books is the existence of 'daemons': animal familiars who accompany each character and are in some sense embodied representations of their souls. To be separated from your daemon causes agonising pain, and there's a profound taboo on making physical contact with another person's daemon. These daemons change form in children but become fixed in their shape when the child goes through puberty. One of the books' principal antagonists, the wonderfully sinister, 'sweet-faced' Mrs Coulter, has a golden monkey as a daemon.

In recognition of his debts to his predecessors in the canon, from Lewis and Milton and (in the second trilogy) Spenser to the *Boys'-Own*-style adventure stories whose narratives he echoes, Pullman has said that he sees his own daemon as a corvid: 'I think she's a raven. She belongs to that family of birds that steal things – the jackdaws, the rooks, crows and magpies – and I admire those birds.'*

The trilogy's first protagonist, introduced in *Northern Lights*, is eleven-year-old Lyra Belacqua, who inhabits a steampunk version of Oxford and goes on to travel to the Arctic north (and the titular aurora) in a hot-air balloon, to encounter mercenaries, giant bat-like

---

* Response to Frank Cottrell-Boyce in 'Interview: Philip Pullman', *Observer*, 22 October 2017.

'cliff-ghasts', flights of witches and – something you never saw in even C.S. Lewis's least mimsy moments – an honest-to-goodness armoured bear:

> Out there climbed Iorek Byrnison, the bear in armour. Without it he was formidable. With it, he was terrifying. It was rust-red, and crudely riveted together: great sheets and plates of dented discolored metal that scraped and screeched as they rode over one another. The helmet was pointed like his muzzle, with slits for eyes, and it left the lower part of his jaw bare for tearing and biting.

In battle, Iorek is even more thrilling:

> The armoured bear at the charge seemed to be conscious of no weight except what gave him momentum. He bounded past Lyra almost in a blur and crashed into the Tartars, scattering soldiers, daemons, rifles to all sides. Then he stopped and whirled round, with a lithe athletic power, and struck two massive blows, one to each side, at the guards closest to him [...] Iorek struck again, twisting to one side, slashing, snarling, crushing, while bullets flew about him like wasps or flies, doing no harm at all.

Iorek Byrnison is one bear to which you'd have no hesitation in surrendering your marmalade sandwich.

Pullman's great flourish in the trilogy, after the construction of this fully imagined world, is to pull focus to embed it in a wondrous multiverse. The second book, *The Subtle Knife* (1997), opens in a version of Oxford that is recognisably our own: no airships, no daemons, no flicker-lit grand halls, only 'a loop of road in a modern estate with a dozen identical houses'. Lyra is nowhere, and we meet instead twelve-year-old Will Parry, struggling to get by with a mentally ill mother and a father who has been missing for years after setting off on an exploratory expedition to the Arctic Circle.

As the story goes on it becomes clear that the fantasy universe of the first book isn't a 'fictional' alternative world; our world is just one of a whole constellation of universes that coexist (as, indeed, many quantum theorists believe may actually be the case). Will, when he becomes the bearer of the titular knife, wields a magical object that can cut windows between those universes through which he and Lyra are able to step, and their quest in due course takes them into a third space, Cittàgazze, still stranger than either of the worlds so far introduced. The movement of these books is always towards enlargement: an enlarged vision of the world, an enlarged vision of human possibility, and a struggle against the mental straitjackets into which power seeks to confine its subjects.

It's little wonder that Pullman hesitates to identify as a children's writer at all. His project in *His Dark Materials* is, in some sense, an assault on the nature of children's literature itself – or, at least, the species of children's literature that seeks to fetishise childhood innocence, to set childhood in amber or to portray growing up itself as a tragic fall from grace. Pullman rejects alike Milton's puritan theology (with its doctrinal emphasis on the danger of knowledge and of original sin) and the controlling nature of the Magisterium, which stands in Lyra's world for the Church. The shocking revelation in the first book is that the 'Gobblers' – operatives of the secretive 'General Oblation Board' run by Mrs Coulter – are torturing prepubescent children by amputating their daemons in a process they call intercision, a sort of spiritual castration (it's at one point expressly connected to the Church's creation of castrati) that leaves its victims near catatonic with trauma:

> The little boy was huddled against the wood drying-rack where hung row upon row of gutted fish, all as stiff as boards. He was clutching a piece of fish to him as Lyra was clutching Pantalaimon [her own daemon] with both hands, hard, against her heart; but that was all he had, a piece of dried fish; because he had no daemon at all. The Gobblers had cut it away. That was *intercision*, and this was a severed child.

[...]

Her first impulse was to turn and run, or to be sick. A human being with no daemon was like someone without a face, or with their ribs laid open and their heart torn out: something unnatural and uncanny that belonged to the world of night-ghasts, not the waking world of sense.

Dust is drawn especially to human beings as they reach the age of puberty. The fall from innocence, knowledge of good and evil, sex… all the things that religious authorities or children's stories in general, and C.S. Lewis in particular, anathematise: these are the things that Pullman's stories present as vital to human flourishing and human freedom.

Pullman built out his fictional multiverse further by embarking on a second trilogy, *The Book of Dust*, whose events sandwich the timeline of *His Dark Materials*. *La Belle Sauvage* (2017) is a prequel in which Lyra appears as an infant; *The Secret Commonwealth* (2019) revisits her in adulthood. The boundary-pushing incidents of sexual violence in both books – not to mention their continuing preoccupation with politico-religious violence and their generic experimentation (*La Belle Sauvage* is half spy caper, half Spenserian dream-vision) – are continuing evidence that Pullman is interested in taking his readers a long way from the breadcrumbed path.

In his essay collection *Daemon Voices: Essays on Storytelling* (2017), Pullman writes eloquently about what connects the children's writers of the present to the storytellers of the past – and how the heart of the thing never changes and never will.

'Most of all,' he says, 'stories give *delight*. […] They bewitch, they enchant, they cast a spell, they enthral; they hold children from their play, and old men from the chimney corner. The desire to know *what happened next*, or *whodunit* […] is passionate and universal. It transcends age and youth; it ignores education and the lack of it; it beguiles the simple and enchants the wise. It was as enchanting in the fire-lit cave as it is in the seminar room.'

XII

A THOUSAND WORDS

Janet and Allan Ahlberg · Munro Leaf and
Robert Lawson · Margaret Wise Brown and Clement
Hurd · Dr. Seuss · Eric Carle · Maurice Sendak · Judith
Kerr · Raymond Briggs · Oliver Jeffers · Jonny Duddle ·
Anthony Browne · Julia Donaldson and Axel Scheffler

PICTURE BOOKS

MOST GROWN-UP BOOKS DON'T HAVE PICTURES NOW-adays. Children's books very often do. Illustration is an unignorable part of the history of children's writing, and one that deserves a library of books to itself. What I can offer here will only, therefore, be a brief overflight. As I wrote in a previous chapter, Lewis Carroll's Alice would not be what she was without Tenniel;* nor Barrie's Peter Pan without Rackham; nor Milne's *Winnie-The-Pooh* without E.H. Shepard. Dr. Seuss is as distinctive for his drawings as for his verse. The Gruffalo we see in our minds' eye is the Gruffalo drawn by Axel Scheffler, whose partnership with Julia Donaldson is arguably even closer than that between Roald Dahl and Quentin Blake. Janet and Allan Ahlberg, Dave McKean and Neil Gaiman, Chris Riddell and any number of writers, Hoffman, Belloc, Richard Scarry, Judith Kerr, Emily Gravett... The list of children's books whose words are, cliché though it is, inseparable from the drawings that accompany them is a very long one.

But it also has a history. If illustrations are nowadays the preserve of children's books, they were not always so. Victorian novels, published as was standard in serial form, often came with drawings. The illustrations of Phiz (Hablot Knight Browne) and Cruikshank

---

* In Noel Streatfeild's *Ballet Shoes*, Pauline wears a ribbon in her hair to play Alice. Her teacher tells her she looks 'ridiculously Tenniel'.

are deeply bound up with what we now think of as 'Dickensian';
Sherlock Holmes would never have had his cape and deerstalker
were it not for Sidney Paget's drawings in the *Strand*. At the beginning of the nineteenth century, novels came without illustrations,
or with illustration limited to a frontispiece. Advances in wood
engraving and steel engraving around the turn of the century,
though, made it easier and cheaper for publishers to combine
images with printed text. Writers like Walter Scott and Jane
Austen, originally published without pictures, were reissued in
illustrated editions, and by the 1860s book illustration approached
the status of high art.

But as the twentieth century wore on, fashions changed. By
mid-century, adult fiction generally didn't have pictures but children's books generally did. And – thanks to a further advance in
printing technology, the increasing ease and cost-effectiveness of
printing full-colour illustrated paperbacks – there flourished a
subgenre, the large-format children's picture book, which now
represents the average child's first reading experience. Beautifully
illustrated children's picture books throng libraries and bookshops
today. They are, I think, almost a genre in themselves now – the
books that parents read to children too young to read, and in
whose friendly pages those children will in time take their first
steps reading to themselves. Some of the most distinguished and
enduring work in children's writing and illustration has been
done in that genre.

You could see *Orbis Sensualium Pictus* as a very early example;
and as a token of the way in which at least one strand of the
genre has its roots in educational material: illustrated primers,
hornbooks* and ABCs. But by the twentieth century – helped
along, you could speculate, by the success of Beatrix Potter, or

---

* A hornbook was a tablet, looking a bit like an optician's paddle, on which letters
of the alphabet would be written out for children to learn by heart. They'd been an
educational tool since medieval times.

Kipling's *Just So* stories, which are framed and indeed written as stories to be read aloud and in which the text encourages you to examine the pictures – they were emerging from that straitjacket and taking on an identity as narrative vehicles for young children. As Janet and John or Biff, Chip and Kipper testify, the didactic and the narrative roles often continued to go together; but the picture books that endure have tended to be the ones whose words are chosen according to literary criteria rather than synthetic phonics.

Allan Ahlberg (*Each Peach Pear Plum, Peepo!, Burglar Bill, Cops and Robbers, The Runaway Dinner*) once told me that he thought he was probably the best paid writer by the word in the country. It's precisely because these books have so few words in them that the choice of words matters so much. Structure is a huge thing in these books: repetitions, refrains, the rhythm of spreads and page turns, the shape of the story. A B C – aka alphabetical order – is a structure; as is counting, which gives shape to everything from Dr. Seuss's *Ten Apples up on Top!* to Eric Carle's *The Very Hungry Caterpillar.* Or there's the cavalcade structure that you can see in *Hairy Maclary from Donaldson's Dairy, The Elephant and the Bad Baby, The Runaway Dinner*, or any number of variations or retellings of 'The Gingerbread Man'. Often, they borrow a structure from established folklore or nursery rhyme. Michael Rosen's *We're Going on a Bear Hunt* is the retelling of a traditional folktale; the magnificent poetic daisy-chain of *Each Peach Pear Plum*, illustrated by Allan Ahlberg's late wife Janet, passes the reader hand over hand through a succession of traditional folktale characters: 'Each peach pear plum / I spy Tom Thumb / Tom Thumb in the cupboard / I spy Mother Hubbard / Mother Hubbard down the cellar / I spy Cinderella…'

Because they are designed to be read to very young children, these also tend to be books where the double form of address – the writer's and illustrator's awareness of a simultaneous audience of adults and children – is especially stark. The best of them are not only scores for voice, directing the interaction between readers and read-to, they also offer, in either words or images or both, something for adults to take an interest in too.

—————

An early example, Munro Leaf's *The Story of Ferdinand* (1936), beautifully illustrated by Robert Lawson, is a case in point. It tells the story of a Fotherington-Thomas of a big and brawny teenage bull living in the Spanish countryside who declines to join in with the violent butting and fighting of his peers. He'd rather just sit quietly in a field under his favourite cork tree and smell the flowers. Unfortunately, human talent-spotters from the bullfight circuit show up just after he has been stung on the bottom by a bee. They see him stamping and raging, decide he's clearly the fiercest bull in the field, and cart him off at once to Madrid. There, he flatly refuses to fight, instead sitting in the middle of the bullring and enjoying the scent of the ladies' flowers. No matter how they goad him, he refuses to fight. Defeated, the proud and ridiculously dressed picadors and matadors return him to the countryside. As the book closes, Leaf writes: 'And for all I know, he is sitting there still, under his favorite cork tree, smelling the flowers just quietly. He is very happy.'

It's enlivened by details primarily designed to please its adult readers – the cork tree, whimsically, has actual wine corks dangling from it like fruit; there's a splendidly deadpan illustration of Ferdinand (who 'grew and grew until he was very big and strong') inspecting a dead tree marked with lines showing his height at one week, three months, a year and two years, as a fond parent might mark a kitchen doorframe; and Lawson includes a carefully realistic representation of the Ronda gorge. It speaks to adults in more dramatic ways, too. Gandhi is on record as having loved the book, and its pacifist message was so enraging to the ridiculously-dressed-matador types that it was banned in Franco's Spain and burned in Hitler's Germany.

Quite something for a book whimsically scribbled, according to legend, onto a yellow legal pad in less than an hour. Munro Leaf wanted to help jolt his illustrator friend out of a thin patch by giving him something to draw, and 'dogs, rabbits, mice and goats had all been done a thousand times'*: so, Ferdinand was born. He's never been out of print.

—

Heading the post-war explosion of children's picture books came Margaret Wise Brown's extraordinary *Goodnight Moon* (1947), hauntingly illustrated by Clement Hurd. Here is a miasmically strange and *unheimlich* picture of the liminal space between waking and sleep, in which elements of the picture vanish and reappear. There's a lot to look at, and puzzle over, and the text interacts eccentrically with the images. Yet it also has a rigorous structure: alternating coloured double-page spreads showing a whole room, with floating, greyscale images focusing on objects in the room, and time progressing in exact ten-minute intervals. There are visual rhymes and echoes, and aural rhymes and echoes. Not for nothing is the pay-off: 'Goodnight noises everywhere.'

Its opening image shows a little rabbit in pyjamas, tucked up in bed but still awake, in a room too large to be cosy. An enormous window has the curtain pulled back to show a field of stars. There's a fire in the fireplace and three logs in a basket; a clock on the mantel. A balloon floats above the bed. There are two framed pictures on the wall, one above the fire, one above the bed. A telephone and a clock sit on the chest of drawers on the near side of the bed; a circular bedside table on the other side bears a lamp, a bowl with a spoon in it, and a couple of other objects. The centre of the floor (you can only, at this point, see

* Quoted in Karen MacPherson, 'Hitler banned it; Gandhi loved it: "The Story of Ferdinand," the book and, now, film', *Washington Post*, 12 December 2017.

the right half, or two-thirds, of the room) is covered with a vast empty round rug.

The text opposite reads:

> In the great green room
> There was a telephone
> And a red balloon
> And a picture of –

You turn the page. There's a close-up of the picture above the fireplace: 'The cow jumping over the moon'. On the facing page there's a close-up of the picture above the bed: 'And there were three little bears sitting on chairs.' The lurid orange-and-green palette of the previous spread has gone: the pictures are rendered in shades of grey. The words rhyme, and scan in an off-kilter way. You notice, maybe not on first reading, that in the picture of the three bears (sitting glumly on chairs in a more or less bare room) there's a picture on the wall. The picture-within-the-picture appears to be a copy of the picture of the cow jumping over the moon.

The next spread shows you the left-hand two-thirds of the room, off-page in the previous spread.

> And two little kittens
> And a pair of mittens
> And a little toyhouse
> And a young mouse

The fireplace, still in frame, is as it was. You can see the left-hand side of the nursery: a bookcase is against one wall, and a huge doll's house beside it. There's a second window, also with the curtain drawn back, the very top of a full moon just peeping up in the bottom left-hand corner. There's a rocking chair with someone's abandoned, half-finished knitting on it. The mittens, alongside a pair of socks, are neatly pegged on a clothes-horse. But time has, apparently, passed; a pair of kittens are now sporting in the middle of the rug, where there were none before. And that young mouse has appeared, too – over by the basket of logs, so far unmolested by the cats.

Page turn. Another pair of isolated images abstracted from the larger scene face each other, again colourless. 'And a comb and a brush and a bowl full of mush': it's the bedside table we saw in the first spread, with the mysteriously uneaten porridge, a comb and a hairbrush, in a cone of light from the lamp. 'And a quiet old lady who was whispering "hush"': it's the rocking chair again and, yikes, an old rabbit-lady is now sitting in it, the knitting on her lap and her ball of wool lying on the floor at her feet. Where did she come from?

Boom, new page: just two words. 'Goodnight room'. We can now see the whole room. Rabbit-lady is there. The kittens are now playing with her wool on the rug. The moon in the window has risen just a bit. The mouse hasn't moved. The baby rabbit is still awake, and is now looking over at the old lady in the chair. A new framed picture has appeared behind her, above the bookcase. It's black and white and appears to show a rabbit, standing in a river in waders, casting a fishing line. On the end of the line is a carrot. There's a baby rabbit – his prey? – right where he's casting it. On the riverbank there is a broken tree. God alone knows what's going on there.

The next spread follows the rhythm of the previous: two single pictures in grey wash on facing pages. 'Goodnight moon'; 'Goodnight cow jumping over the moon'. The first image is the full moon in the window of the real-world room; the second, of course, the crescent moon in the painting, with the cow sailing unmoving over it. As the story, or incantation, progresses, there's more subtle movement. The balloon sinks slightly; the moon in the window, page by page, rises. When we say, 'goodnight mittens', they are alone on the clothes-horse; on the following page, the socks have reappeared in time to be bid goodnight themselves. The clocks continue to creep on in increments of ten minutes every two pages.

Details of the picture continue to shift. The mouse vanishes, reappears, vanishes again. The goodnights continue. 'Goodnight little house / And goodnight mouse / Goodnight comb / And goodnight brush / Goodnight nobody [this one accompanied by a blank page] / Goodnight mush.' Specifics jostle with vast abstracts. 'Goodnight to the old lady whispering "hush"' gets a spread on its own; the knitting rabbit has a shushing paw raised to her mouth; the cats sit calmly at her feet watching her; the baby rabbit in his pyjamas seems to be settling.

'Goodnight stars / Goodnight air' – and the final full-room spread – 'Goodnight noises everywhere'. The moon is full in the window. The old lady has departed with her knitting and the cats sleep curled together on her rocking chair. The rabbit is sleeping. The whole room is washed, now, with darkness. But, again a little spookily, the lights are on in the windows of the doll's house. There's enough detail and enough mystery in this little book to engage, and re-engage, adult readers and child readers again and again.

And that out-of-nowhere line: 'Goodnight nobody'. Brr. Some of the spreads and lines in children's picture books can, in isolation, give their adult readers a satisfying chill. In Judith Kerr's *The Tiger Who Came to Tea* (which I'll look at in more detail soon) there's a haunting figure, which children seldom notice, walking hunched over in apparent misery, in the night-time street scene that in most ways seems to be the happiest tableau in the book. In Dr. Seuss's *Green Eggs and Ham* (1960), the train on which Sam-I-Am hounds and pesters his breakfast-averse quarry at one point hurtles into a tunnel. The page is a wash of blue shadow, only that radioactive ham still glowing green. 'Say! In the dark? Here, in the dark! Would you, could you, in the dark?' It's a whisper from somewhere else. Would you, could you, in the dark?

Dr. Seuss, the alias of Theodor Geisel (1904–1991), is another unignorable mainstay of this vast genre – a creator whose breathtaking facility with light verse (remember A.A. Milne: 'it is the work of a light-verse writer taking his job seriously') meshes wonderfully with the wildness of his line as an illustrator. Like so many creators here, Dr. Seuss deserves (and has had) a book to himself, so I can't begin to cover the range of his work. But I'd like to note how he stands in a line of descent that includes the Lewis Carroll of 'Jabberwocky': these works are triumphs of sound over sense. Their surrealism is unexpected, but it isn't random; it's underscored by an iron sense of the rhythm of the verse. He isn't fitting a world or a story into verse, but letting the verse itself dictate the story.

Look at *One Fish Two Fish Red Fish Blue Fish* (1960) – that first line a percussive series of trochees where the dyads one/two and red/blue are different qualities (number and colour) united by the rhyme of blue with two. Objects and situations seem to emerge according to rhyme or metre. That doesn't mean his (usually anapaestic) metre is regular, though: Geisel, a child of the jazz age, writes jazz poetry – and often capitalises words to indicate where he wants the reader to hit a particularly emphatic stress.

Fox in Socks (1965) is maybe the pinnacle of his achievement in verse as pure noise. He slows the reader down (often with tonguetwisters) and speeds the reader up (with an easy bit) at will. Take this sequence (illustrated, of course, with a blithe man in a hat, alongside a funny-looking duck, licking the surface of a pond): 'Luke Luck likes lakes. / Luke's duck likes lakes. / Luke Luck licks lakes. / Luke's duck licks lakes.' A tricky but regular rhythm is established for that quatrain, with a tight mesh of rhymes and assonances but each line ending with 'lakes'. Then he wrong-foots you: 'Duck takes licks / in lakes Luke Luck likes. / Luke Luck takes licks / in lakes duck likes.' Syllables you expect to be there are elided to trip you up. Fragments of the previous quatrain are plonked into a different rhythmic context; assonances (you get 'takes' instead of 'lakes') are false friends.

The adult reader limps through to the end of the quatrain and turns the page to find Mr Knox voicing his own complaint: 'I can't blab / such blibber blubber! My tongue isn't / Made of rubber.' That's easy to pronounce, as is the Fox's chiding rejoinder: 'Mr Knox. Now / come now. Come now. / You don't have to / be so dumb now…' You thank goodness for the respite. But that is just the pause at the crest of a rollercoaster. The Fox stares into Knox's eyes like a hypnotist before plunging him into the thickets of the 'three cheese trees' through which 'three free fleas flew'.

The story's climax relies, after a great pause for breath when the worm turns and the beleaguered Knox finally establishes some authority with a line of pure prose: 'Now wait a minute, Mr Socks Fox!', on a great skittering musical run of syllables – 'When a fox is in the bottle where the tweetle beetles battle with their paddles in a puddle on a noodle-eating poodle' – followed by a final series of staccato crashes on the keyboard: 'THIS is what they call… a tweetle beetle noodle poodle bottled paddled muddled duddled fuddled wuddled fox in socks, sir!'

Yet oddly, for a writer for whom meaning sometimes seems to be the proverbial bone the burglar throws to the dog, Dr. Seuss's work proved no less politically contentious than Munro Leaf's. Born to a German-American family in Massachusetts, Theodor 'Ted' Geisel adopted his pen-name (he originally pronounced it in the German manner, as 'Zoiss') as an undergraduate so he could continue contributing to his university magazine after being barred from doing so for being caught drinking gin during Prohibition. He made his living as an ad-man before his books for children started to take off, and worked as a political cartoonist (he was a New Deal Democrat) and government propagandist during the Second World War.

His political engagement didn't end when he sat down to write for children. Though he warned that 'kids can see a moral coming a mile off', the political and social import of many of his books for children is unignorable. 'Yertle the Turtle' (1958) is an anti-authoritarian allegory about a hubristic turtle king who tries to build a tower of turtles so that, as lord of all he surveys, he can see further and survey more; he's brought down when the lowest turtle in the pile burps and the whole assemblage collapses, leaving the turtles 'free [...] as turtles, and maybe all creatures, should be'. 'The Sneetches' (1953) satirises antisemitism, while *How the Grinch Stole Christmas* (1957) and *The Lorax* (1971) attack commercialism and environmental despoliation.

In the 1970s he even repurposed his book for early readers *Marvin K. Mooney Will You Please Go Now!* (1971) as political satire ('Richard M. Nixon Will You Please Go Now!').* You can see the extent to which his work, and its implications, were in the blood-stream of America's growing generations by the fact that – reaching, a little – a tagline from *Horton Hears A Who!* ('A person's a person, no matter how small') was co-opted as a slogan by anti-abortion activists. (Geisel's widow objected to this, and donated to Planned Parenthood.) 'I'm subversive as hell,' Geisel said.† A fun fact for those of a childish disposition: Ted Geisel's first work for children was a collection of sayings called *The Pocket Book of Boners* (1931).

———

Undoubtedly up there with Dr. Seuss in terms of popularity and influence is *The Very Hungry Caterpillar* (1969), the best-known book by Eric Carle (1929–2021). This is among the very simplest of children's picture books, but it continues to resonate in its simplicity. Carle, like Judith Kerr and illustrator Jan Pieńkowski, was a child of the Second World War. Born in New York to German émigrés, he moved back to Germany when he was six years old: just in time

---

* Art Buchwald (syndicated column), July 1974.
† Jonathan Cott, *Pipers at the Gates of Dawn: The Wisdom of Children's Literature* (Random House, 1983).

for his father to be drafted into the German army and captured by the Soviets. The young Carle, aged fifteen, was conscripted into digging trenches on Germany's Western defensive Siegfried Line. He saw bombs landing and fellow workers killed just a few feet away from him. He was in his early twenties, and still traumatised by his wartime experience, when he returned to America after the war to work in commercial illustration.

The Very Hungry Caterpillar – whose protagonist, represented in Carle's colourful collage images, eats his way through an ever-greater succession of foods day by day before getting a well-deserved tummy-ache – originally wasn't going to be a caterpillar at all; he was going to be a worm. Seldom since Gordon Lish took the blue pencil to Chandler has an editorial intervention been so important: Carle's editor Ann Beneduce said that nobody really finds worms cute, and suggested he make his hero a caterpillar instead. Which, of course, gave Carle the book's vital fifth-act twist, when the caterpillar (now a very fat caterpillar) turns into a beautiful butterfly like an insectoid Ugly Duckling.

The Very Hungry Caterpillar really does have everything. As well as its visual attractiveness, the book has the comic quality that the caterpillar's food starts out being the sort of thing caterpillars might plausibly eat (it's fruit from Monday to Friday) but come the weekend he goes nuts on ice-cream, cheese, lollipops, pickles and all sorts of foods it's unlikely an average caterpillar could obtain, let alone digest. On rereading, children will have the memory-game/counting-game pleasure of anticipating what comes next. It has that fairytale transformation – so it's heading somewhere. Finally, and maybe even best of all for very young children, the book has actual holes in the pages. The caterpillar seems to have eaten through the very book itself. This was expensive and difficult to arrange back then (the book had to be printed in Japan) but it undoubtedly contributed hugely to its success.

To talk a little more about structure, pagination in children's picture books is absolutely everything. Formally, they behave like the poems they often are – with a page-turn working as a particularly emphatic line-break. To take a representative and outstanding example of how text, image and page-turn can work together, look at the opening sentence of Maurice Sendak's *Where The Wild Things Are* (1963): 'The night Max wore his wolf suit and made mischief of one kind and another his mother called him "WILD THING!" and Max said "I'll EAT YOU UP!" so he was sent to bed without eating anything.' Writing that sentence down doesn't begin to give a sense of its effects as part of the book – its relationship with Sendak's wonderful drawings, with the white space around the words, and with the rhythm of the page-turns.

'The night Max wore his wolf suit and made mischief of one kind' – page turn – 'and another' – page turn – 'his mother called him "WILD THING!" / and Max said "I'LL EAT YOU UP!" / and he was sent to bed without eating anything.' The pagination, the line-breaks, the shouting all-caps dialogue... this is poetry, not prose, and it works in concert with the images: a series of frozen tableaux of domestic chaos, funny but a little alarming (Max is seen in the second illustration mid-air, chasing a Scotty dog with a fork).

It's a book that combines the mythic with the domestic, and the lilt of the poem gives it a haunting stateliness. It's a dream-narrative, and a timeslip narrative; the monsters Max meets are perfectly poised between the comical and the (just slightly) scary. Max makes the time-hallowed journey into the strange – the safety of his bedroom gives way to a forest, and then to Max's journey in his boat 'through night and day / and in and out of weeks / and almost over a year / to where the wild things are'.

But Max – even Max at home, in his wolf suit – is half a figment of the wild itself. First he's frightened of the monsters; and then (after he tames them with the magic trick of staring unblinking into their terrible yellow eyes) they are frightened of him, calling him 'the most wild thing of all'. The centrepiece of the book is the wordless 'wild rumpus' – again, frozen tableaux; there's no movement in this book's pictures at all – after which Max, a capricious monarch, sends the wild things to bed without their supper. Eating, in excellently Freudian fashion marrying love and consumption, is the thread that runs through the book.* Max threatens to eat his mother; the wild things, when Max proposes to leave them, threaten to eat Max: 'Oh please don't go – / We'll eat you up – we love you so!'

And it's the smell of food that lures Max back from his lonely eminence. It seizes him with wanting 'to be where someone loved him best of all'. The journey is reversed, and Max finds himself back 'in the night of his very own room/where he found his supper waiting for him' – page turn – 'and it was still hot.' Max moves, in terms of the two freedoms I've mentioned in my introduction, from freedom to back to the safety of freedom from. The story is a resonant muddle of safety and danger, love and violence, as intriguing and haunting to an adult reader as it will be to the child read to.

The later works in Sendak's sort-of-trilogy, *In the Night Kitchen* and *Outside Over There*, are even more peculiar and sinister than his best-known work. Children's picture books, much more than the 'chapter books' now written for older children to read to themselves, address a dual audience. These are books that will most likely be read, at least the first time, by an adult to a child. Many even contain jokes directed at adults. Will most children register that the trio of identical bakers in Sendak's later book *In the Night Kitchen* (1970) all look like Oliver Hardy?

Sendak's own childhood was shadowed by the Holocaust. Born in 1928, he grew up in Brooklyn to immigrant Jewish parents

---

* There's a famous story Sendak told of getting a fan letter from a child and writing back with a drawing of a Wild Thing: 'Then I got a letter back from his mother and she said: "Jim loved your card so much he ate it." That to me was one of the highest compliments I've ever received. He didn't care that it was an original Maurice Sendak drawing or anything. He saw it, he loved it, he ate it.'

whose families were all but wiped out in the camps, and, as he later narrated it, he was 'unhappily reminded endlessly of my good fortune' from the age of ten. If he was late coming up for supper his mother would rebuke him with 'Leo and Benjamin and the other children who were my age who could never come up for supper and were good to their mothers but now they were dead [...] You're in mourning all the time. [...] I hated them. I hated them because they blighted my life. I hated them for dying.'* He described, too, the violence that his traumatised parents visited on each other. In that context, perhaps, we can read the comforting ending of *Where the Wild Things Are* as compensatory fantasy.

Similarly, we can read the chillier narrative of the third book in the trilogy, *Outside Over There* (1981), as a refraction of his own anxieties. It tells the story of a little girl whose baby sister is stolen by goblins (Sendak referenced the Lindbergh kidnapping case). Its set-up is one where the family home is anything but safe: the father is away at sea; the mother, catatonic with some unnamed grief, stares trancelike into the middle distance. Ida, the older sister, is *in loco parentis* (as was Sendak's own older sister) and she loses the baby, learning of its disappearance only when the substitute, made out of ice, melts in her arms. Ida is playing with magic that she barely understands – she makes a terrible mistake when she climbs backwards out of the window. The resolution remains as mysterious and as precarious as the progress of the plot.

Judith Kerr (1923–2019) was, like her contemporary Sendak, a writer and illustrator whose early life was indelibly marked by the chaos of mid-twentieth-century Europe. She was born in Berlin. Her German-Jewish father Alfred, a prominent writer and broadcaster, had been outspoken in criticising the nascent Nazi party, and

---

* *Fresh Air*, National Public Radio, 30 October 2003.

in 1933 he fled Germany for Prague on the eve of Hitler coming to power after being anonymously tipped off that the Nazis planned to confiscate his passport and place him under arrest. The day before the elections that were to install Hitler as chancellor, Judith, her mother and brother too fled the country – as it turned out, not a moment too soon – first for Switzerland, where they joined Alfred; and after a stay in Paris to the UK, where Judith spent the rest of her long life.

The story of that flight as a refugee is told in Kerr's children's novel *When Hitler Stole Pink Rabbit* (1971) – in which Judith herself appears in third-person perspective as 'Anna'. Originally written to explain to her then eight-year-old son what her own childhood had been like, it's a bravura child's-eye view of the experience: true to her partial understanding of what's going on around her (when she hears there's a price on her father's head, she fears that he'll be killed by coins being dropped on his head), and of the way the things that loom large to a child are recorded.

Forced to choose only one toy to take, Anna leaves her battered but beloved Pink Rabbit in favour of a more newly acquired toy on the grounds that she's barely had the chance to play with it yet. Only when she's in Switzerland does she bitterly regret it: 'For a moment she felt terribly sad about Pink Rabbit. It had embroidered black eyes – the original glass ones had fallen out years before – and an endearing habit of collapsing on its paws. Its fur, though no longer very pink, had been soft and familiar. How could she ever have chosen to pack that characterless woollen dog in its stead? It had been a terrible mistake, and now she would never be able to put it right.'

Here is a child grasping, as if for the first time, an irreversible change in her world: regret at a mistake that cannot ever be undone. That child/adult perspective is delicately handled again, later in the book, when Anna records her father's recurring nightmares of trying to leave Germany and being stopped at the border by the Nazis: 'It seemed terrible to lie in bed listening to Papa and then

knowing that in his dreams awful things were happening to him.'
She prays ('although she did not exactly believe in God') that she
could have nightmares instead of her father: magical thinking; a
child, in an insecure and frightening situation, trying in some sense
to parent her parent. She herself does have a terrible nightmare,
just as her father's stop: 'Anna never told anyone, but she always
felt that it was she who had cured Papa's nightmares.' Two further
books chronicling Kerr/Anna's girlhood and young womanhood
followed, forming what came to be known as the *Out of the Hitler
Time* trilogy.

It's her picture books, though, on which her enduring reputation rests. She always thought of herself as an artist first and a
writer second. The *Mog* series, beginning with *Mog the Forgetful
Cat* (1970), described the adventures of an absent-minded cat in a
family based closely on her own (the children in the family were
given her own children's middle names; their surname, Thomas,
was the given name of her husband, the screenwriter Nigel Kneale).
Unlike most cats, the *Mog* series lasted for fifty years – though
when *Goodbye Mog* (2002) killed Mog off it caused a serious stir.
'Mog was dead tired,' it begins – and it introduces death and grief
to an audience of young readers in whose stories such things had
seldom if ever appeared.

Her very first picture book, *The Tiger Who Came to Tea* (1968),
may nevertheless be the one of hers that lives for ever. As the story
opens, it's an ordinary afternoon in Sophie's house. She's having tea
with her mummy, a stay-at-home housewife with sensible shoes, a
blue cardy and her hair in a bun. There's a ring at the door. Sophie's
mummy speculates anxiously about who it could be, ruling out the
milkman (already been), boy from the grocer (comes a different
day) and Daddy (has his own key).

Notice how beautifully the people who aren't at the door – the
cheery uniformed milkman with his milk-float, the errand-boy
with a wicker basket on his bicycle and an advert on the crossbar,
the father in overcoat and tie and hat – locate the action in the late

1960s. Sophie opens the door. It's a bloody great tiger, the height of the doorframe. And a talking tiger, at that. It says: 'Excuse me, but I'm very hungry. Do you think I could have tea with you?' Sophie's mother invites it in. What starts as a decorous sit-down with cakes and biscuits and proper china (1968, remember) soon takes an alarming turn.

'Owp!' says the tiger in big letters, swallowing the whole plate of sandwiches at once. Down the hatch go the buns. And the biscuits, the cake, the contents of the teapot, all the milk in the milk jug, 'and then he looked round the kitchen to see what else he could find'. Everything he finds, he eats, gobbling up the supper as it cooks on the stove, pillaging the fridge, ravaging the cupboards for dry goods and tins, and washing it down with milk, orange juice, all Daddy's beer (uh-oh), and, in the line that transfixed me and transfixes, I think, every reader: 'he drank all the water in the tap'.*

This tiger, though, is the least threatening tiger that any reader has ever seen. He's unsettling, yes – what he represents is unsettling. He's a creature of unruly appetite, whose adventures are framed with the elaborate courtesies of a not-quite-planned tea party. It's not just that he eats everything in sight. It's that, at least initially, he's offered cakes and buns and sandwiches in a very civilised manner. English politeness, strained not quite to breaking point, is a theme of the book.

But there's no fear at any point that he's going to do what most tigers in stories would threaten to do, i.e. eat Sophie and Sophie's mummy. The tiger smiles constantly, but in not one of the pictures does he show a tooth. He laps at the tap and at the supper on the stove like a cat, and pours tea merrily into his mouth directly from the pot. In the first of the book's double-page spreads, Sophie is giving this enormous apex predator a cuddle – while it greedily

---

* 'That was the one bit that the publishers thought perhaps should come out, because they said, "That's not very realistic, is it?"' – Kerr, interview with author, 2018.

eyes a string of onions hanging on the wall. Finally, abruptly, and with a polite 'Thank you for my nice tea. I think I'd better go now', the tiger vanishes, never to return.

It's a book about a semi-exciting, semi-alarming home invasion, much like Dr. Seuss's *The Cat in the Hat* (1957), where the unruly energy of the interloper leaves anxiety in its wake. The house is chaos. There's no water for Sophie's bath and no food for the family supper. What's Daddy going to think? The aftermath of the tiger's visit bathes Sophie (and the reader) in the reassurance she craves. Instead of being angry, and showing none of the scepticism you might expect at Sophie's mummy's explanation for how the house came to be in the state it is, Sophie's daddy takes them all out to supper.

A gloriously atmospheric double-page spread shows how 'they all went out in the dark, and all the street lamps were lit, and all the cars had their lights on, and they walked down the road to a café', Sophie walking between her parents with a Red-Riding-Hood coat on over her nightie. They have sausages and chips and ice-cream, and the next day they restock the pantry – as well as (the book's other whimsically surreal touch) buying a giant tin of tiger food in case their visitor returns. The bonds of family are affirmed; order is restored. The devouring machine has done no permanent harm.

Many critics have wondered whether the story is some sort of allegory. What does the tiger represent? Is this story really about sexual frustration: an animalistic disruption of the domestic anomie of the 1960s housewife? Is it really about addiction? Is it really about Nazis – a suggestion made by those who remember Kerr as the author of *When Hitler Stole Pink Rabbit*? Judith Kerr lived to be ninety-five. When I visited her that time a year or so before her death in her home in Barnes, west London, I asked her then what the book was really about, and Judith Kerr told me what she had always told interviewers: 'It's about a tiger who came to tea.'

Kerr's career spanned something of a boom-time for children's picture books, whose alumni are almost too numerous to mention: the husband-and-wife partnership of John Burningham (1936–2019) and Helen Oxenbury (1938–), the outstanding Shirley Hughes (1927–2022) of *Dogger* (1977) fame, and Helen Nicoll (1937–2012) and her Polish-born illustrator Jan Pieńkowski (1936–2022), whose books for very young children introduced a rival Mog as one of the witchy trio Meg, Mog and Owl. Of the same generation was David McKee (1935–2022), author of the *Elmer the Patchwork Elephant* series and, most memorably, that rebuke to the distracted modern mother, *Not Now, Bernard* (1980), whose protagonist is swallowed whole by a monster without his mum so much as noticing.

I notice, looking over all these birth and death dates, that writing or illustrating children's picture books seems to guarantee you a good long innings. That many of the most successful writers of children's picture books also had refugee childhoods or wartime trauma (Jan Pieńkowski survived the Nazi firebombing of Warsaw) suggests that there may be something restorative and grounding for their creators in the orderly and simple worlds they conjure.

Everyone will have their favourite books from this period and in this genre. This is my book, for instance, so I reserve the right to indulge myself in tipping the hat to Judith Viorst's *Alexander and the Terrible, Horrible, No Good, Very Bad Day* (1972). It tells the story of the eponymous small boy, who wakes up with bubblegum in his hair and whose day goes downhill from there. He's a steaming engine of self-pity and outrage as everything that can possibly go wrong for him does, and over and over again he vows to emigrate to Australia. For years after we read it, when things were going wrong, members of my family would remind each other of the book's punchline: 'Some days are just like that, even in Australia.' This is one of the world's great truths. The older you get, the more you see Alexander through his parents' eyes as well as his own.

—

I mentioned how often these books address themselves to a double audience, the readers and the read-to. Raymond Briggs (1934–2022) is perhaps the most sophisticated author of children's picture books of that generation in this respect. *Fungus the Bogeyman* (1977) is a work of wan philosophical pessimism, filled with sophisticated literary jokes, masquerading as a child-delighting fantasy about things that go squelch in the night. The entirely wordless *The Snowman* (1978) (the film adaptation of which is now infallibly shown at Christmas on UK television) has a poignant ending – the snowman, spoiler alert, melts – which lands even more heavily with adults than with children. His grouchy and slightly potty-mouthed *Father Christmas* (1973) is funny to adults because it presents this mythic character as a recognisably ordinary man grumbling about his job, and funny to children because it presents a version of Father Christmas that adults don't usually present. His fantasia about nuclear holocaust, written towards the end of the Cold War, *When the Wind Blows* (1982), is something like a comic-strip version of *Threads*: barely for children at all.

The pay-off of Oliver Jeffers's *Stuck* (2012) is a simpler case in point: a children's story with adult gags. In it, a boy tries to knock his kite out of a tree but finds that everything he throws up after it (shoes, ladder, bucket of paint, long-distance lorry, lighthouse, house across the street, whale) gets stuck too. (In terms of its basic narrative shape, it's a variation on 'There Was an Old Woman Who Swallowed a Fly.') Eventually the kite falls down and, forgetting about everything else in the tree, he goes about his day merrily. The final panel shows the tree, at night-time, under the moon, cluttered with all these bizarre objects. Leaning out of the window of the fire engine (yup, one of those goes up too – a dry joke is that, when presented with a fire engine or a ladder, the boy chucks those in the tree instead of using them to climb the tree and retrieve the kite) is a fireman. He says: 'Hang on a minute, lads. I've got a great idea.' Not many four-year-olds can be expected to recognise a line from *The Italian Job*.

These books throw their adult readers a bone because they are designed to be read and reread. Their texts implicitly score an interaction between reader and read-to: the 'can you guess what happened next?' or the delicious anticipation of a page-turn. You notice more and more, in the best of them, as you reread. Jonny Duddle's *The Pirate Cruncher* (2010), for example, tells the story of a pirate crew who meet a mysterious fiddler who tells them of an island on which riches beyond belief can be found. The island itself, as they discover to their cost, is the lure for a pirate-eating sea-monster who takes their boat down whole. But it's only on rereading it and studying the drawings more closely that you notice that the fiddler is a puppet: you can see his strings; and just at the edges of the frame, in every picture, you can see the blue tentacles of the monster operating him.

That remarkable generation of 1970s and '80s children's picture books, be it said, is not without its inheritors. As well as Jonny Duddle and Michael Rosen, there is Jon Klassen's extraordinary and thrillingly funny/sinister work, beginning with *I Want My Hat Back* (2011), in which a rabbit who steals a bear's hat gets his comeuppance with extreme prejudice. Jill Murphy (1946–2012), probably best known for her *Worst Witch* series of chapter books about a school for witches, was also a deft author and illustrator of picture books for younger children. Her *Large Family* series, beginning with *Five Minutes' Peace* (1986), follows the travails of a family of elephants. *A Piece of Cake* (1989), in which Mrs Large worries she's fat and puts the family on an unsuccessful slimming drive, is particularly delightful. The mother elephant's boosterism ('You're off for a nice healthy jog round the park, followed by your tea – a delicious sardine with grated carrot') is nicely counterpointed by the thunderous expression of Mr Large as he jogs out of the door in the facing illustration.

Anthony Browne (1946–)'s exquisitely drawn and frequently spooky work has a particular emotional sophistication. It includes the Greenaway-winning *Gorilla* (1983),[*] about a lonely and neglected child whose toy gorilla comes alive; and *Into the Forest* (2004), a uniquely unsettling and dreamlike mash-up of fairytale characters ('Have you seen our Dad and Mum?' a pitiful Hansel and Gretel ask the protagonist as he walks by them), a mysteriously absent father (Browne's own father died suddenly when he was seventeen) and a mother seemingly catatonic with sadness.

———

Running in parallel, though slightly outside the remit of this study because they're usually periodicals rather than books, are comics. They are not quite picture books – they have a slightly different visual grammar, and children typically read them by themselves rather than being read to by adults. But there's overlap (you could certainly see *Struwwelpeter* as a comic) and there's influence. Maurice Sendak acknowledged the effect of Winsor McCay's comic *Little Nemo in Slumberland* on the surreal style of *In the Night Kitchen*.

These successors of the cheap illustrated magazines of the nineteenth century – literature for the less literate – flourished from the early years of the twentieth century. In *Mary Poppins Opens the Door* (1943), the 'Marble Boy' – a statue in the park that the children befriend – says of the reading matter he enjoys: 'Best of all are the coloured comics, especially the one called *Lot o' Fun*.'[†]

Modern comics had their big bang in 1938; the first appearance of Superman in the US and the first issue of the *Beano* in the UK.

---

[*]   Such is Browne's commitment to the largest primate that he was once hospitalised by a gorilla bite during the filming of a TV programme for kids.

[†]   *Lot o' Fun* was an English comic that published from 1906 to 1929. Comics had already become an established part of the mix of childhood reading.

Marvel and DC told straight-faced stories of superheroes in issue-length arcs. In the UK, the *Beano* and its many rivals and imitators over the years, such as the similarly long-running *Dandy*, *Beezer*, *Topper* and *Whizzer and Chips*, were comic anthologies, whose most popular and enduring strips were stories of British childhood, at once mildly subversive and deeply conservative.

Alongside the playground antics of that sort of anthology comic, there emerged post-war another distinct strand of British comics, one aimed at older children and with more adult themes and, typically, adult protagonists. The *Eagle*, launched in 1950, had as its flagship character Dan Dare: Pilot of the Future – a Biggles figure with zigzag eyebrows who flew spacecraft instead of aeroplanes. From 1961 onwards, *Commando* told one-shot war stories in small-format black-and-white paperbacks several dozen pages long, and in a realist idiom: a lot of stick grenades and screaming Messerschmitts and cries of '*Achtung!*' And in 1977, the science fiction anthology 2000 AD first appeared, and soon introduced the futuristic lawman Judge Dredd, a brutal and cynical figure whose response to a nuclear holocaust was to declare: 'Next time, we get our retaliation in first.'

Generations of children have also enjoyed two European *bandes dessinées*. The Belgian writer Hergé (pen-name of Georges Remi, 1907–1983)'s comic strip Tintin made its first English-language appearance in the *Eagle* in 1951. It was not until 1958 – three decades after Captain Haddock, Professor Calculus and the perma-quiffed boy detective first appeared in French – that Methuen embarked on translating Hergé's large back catalogue into English and publishing them in book form. Goscinny and Uderzo's vibrant *Asterix* series, about the adventures of a pugnacious rebel taking on the Roman army in occupied Gaul, was the other great continental import. Having come out in French at the end of the 1960s, they also first appeared in the English language in now-defunct British comics anthologies. The book-length albums were translated with superb wit, from 1970 on, by Anthea Bell and Derek Hockridge.

I don't have space, as I say, to treat comics in detail. But I mention them as part of the storytelling ecosystem in which all these other children's books have existed. Comics were, and remain, an important part of the imaginative worlds of childhood.

—

The pre-eminent genius of the children's picture book in our own age is also its best-selling practitioner. Julia Donaldson (1948–) strikes me as having one of the best ears for prosody since W.H. Auden. She doesn't, pun intended, put a foot wrong, from the jiggety-jig metre of *Tabby McTat* (2009) to the propulsive couplets and swinging internal rhymes of *Superworm* (2012). In terms of story construction, too, she's virtuosic. And her roots in the genre are deep. Her books are nursery rhymes at the same time as they are folktales: tiny, perfectly structured dramas with the musical integrity of songs.

Tyrannosaurus Drip (2007), for instance, tells at an anapaestic gallop the story of a herbivorous duckbill dinosaur whose egg rolls into a T rex nest and hatches there, to the confusion of all. It's an obvious riff on Hans Christian Andersen's 'The Ugly Duckling', and its climactic scene (in which the T rexes, crossing the river on a fallen log, catch sight of their own reflections in the water and take fright) is a callback to Aesop's fable of 'The Dog and its Reflection'. Like a song, it has choruses: 'And they hooted "Up with rivers!", and they hooted "Up with reeds!" / And they hooted "Up with bellyfuls of juicy water weeds!"'

Her first book – published after Methuen approached her to turn a children's song she had written for the BBC in 1975 into a book – was *A Squash and a Squeeze*, which describes how an old woman learns to appreciate the limited space she has by sharing her house with ever more and more animals. (It shares its basic premise with Ruth Orbach's 1974 picture book *One Eighth of a Muffin*: the root story is a Yiddish folktale – Donaldson's 'wise old man' is identifiably a rabbi, though not named as such – and other versions include *A Big Quiet House, It Could Always Be Worse* and *No Room For A Pup!*) Practically everything Donaldson has written – from the magnificently metafictional *Tiddler* (2007) to the plangently Odyssean *Stick Man* (2008) – has a special sort of fairy-dust.

Her signature work, *The Gruffalo* (1999), was a classic folktale, new growth from old roots; Donaldson has said she took her cue in part from a Chinese folktale called 'The Fox that Borrows the Terror of a Tiger'. Our old friend Vladimir Propp, be it said, would have loved it. Like all folktales, it sends us into the forest: 'A mouse took a stroll in the deep dark wood. / A fox saw the mouse, and the mouse looked good.' There, in twenty one-syllable words, she establishes some archetypal Aesopic characters, a deep dark wood, and what film producers like to call jeopardy.

As the mouse makes its progress through the deep dark wood, it encounters three predators in turn: a fox, an owl and a snake. Their exchanges are formulaic. Each predator tries to lure the mouse into its den. Each time the clever mouse tricks the tricksters and turns the tables: 'It's terribly kind of you, [fox/owl/snake], but no: / I'm going to have [lunch/tea/a feast] with a gruffalo.'

Each time, the mouse describes the gruffalo to his interlocutor, who has never heard of one, and adds a fresh trio of frightful characteristics before adding that he's meeting the gruffalo nearby and mentioning: 'And his favourite food is [roasted fox/owl ice-cream/ scrambled snake]'. The predators each scarper in terror, while the smug old mouse strolls on congratulating himself: 'Silly old [fox/ owl/snake]! Doesn't he know / There's no such thing as a gruffalo?'

Then, bam, peripetaeia. The mouse runs smack-dab into a creature that has all nine of the frightful characteristics that he has given to the gruffalo. The joke's on mouse: gruffalo exists. And mouse only got one thing wrong in his description of the creature, as its first words dismayingly confirm: '"My favourite food!" the gruffalo said. / "You'll taste good on a slice of bread!"'

The story could have ended, quite satisfactorily, with the mouse vanishing into the gruffalo's tum. Moral, perhaps: it's possible to be too much of a smart-arse. Instead, in the grand tradition of the trickster story, the mouse turns out to be even more of a smarty-pants than we first thought. Without an instant of hesitation, he gets over his surprise and – playing, resonantly, on the word 'good' – shoots back:

> 'Good?' said the mouse. 'Don't call me good!
> I'm the scariest creature in this wood.
> Just walk behind me and soon you'll see,
> Everyone is afraid of me.'

The gruffalo, laughing at the absurdity of it, humours the mouse and follows behind him. The poem, after this, unpacks like a Russian doll: there are formulaic encounters with snake, owl and fox again in reverse order. Each predator takes one look at the gruffalo and legs it.* Each time the mouse tells the gruffalo: 'You see? I told you so.' The gruffalo marvels aloud. Right up until the point that the mouse declares that 'now my tummy's beginning to rumble / My favourite food is gruffalo crumble'. And the gruffalo, too, takes to his heels.

It's a story that touches on the power of storytelling itself. The mouse is right at the bottom of the food chain, but he tells a story that puts him, effectively, at the top of it – and everybody else believes that story. It is a little millefeuille of dramatic irony. Even the clever mouse is wrong-footed for a moment, knocked off his pedestal as the hermeneutic apex predator, when he discovers that the lie he has been telling describes something that's real. Did he *imagine* the gruffalo into existence?

Part of the joy of *The Gruffalo* – as well, perhaps, as its value as an introduction to the world of adulthood – is that it's a tale of deception and predation told in language of elaborate courtesy.

---

* Or wings it, or bellies it, as the case may be.

Fox, owl and snake seek to lure the mouse with an invitation to eat; the mouse thanks them gratefully for the invitation, or greets them like old pals on their second encounter. Nothing is quite what it seems. Nobody, not even the gruffalo, is sincere. And Axel Scheffler's illustrations contribute hugely to taming this extraordinary, simple-yet-complex tale. His gruffalo isn't terrifying: it's cute. And Scheffler's visual Easter-eggs help draw the books into a sort of Donaldsonverse – the gruffalo's child, in the sequel of that name, carries Stick Man about under its arm; in other post-*Gruffalo* books you can spot gruffalo faces or visual motifs unobtrusively in the background.

Finally, look at the brilliant simplicity with which the final couplet closes the story, with its inverted echo of the opening couplet and with a caesura in the final line to be relished by every reader-aloud: 'All was quiet in the deep dark wood. / The mouse found a nut, and the nut was good.' The deep dark wood is now a place of calm and comfort rather than fear and threat, and the tissue of dangerous little deceptions gives way to unfalsifiable bodily reality. After all those imaginary meals, a real one. So real, in fact, you can taste it. Sweet as a nut.

Children's books, I argued in my introduction, are gateways to adult reading. *Picture* books are gateways to childhood reading. You hear them, first of all. Then you start making the connection between the familiar story and the words on the page. Then you start to read aloud. And in due course you can read them to yourself, before you move on and out, beyond them.

It is in their pages that most children will first encounter poetry – see how words can bounce and chime even without a musical accompaniment. Because they have so few words in them, those words matter. They need, as children know, to be 'just so'. They will remain with their readers and listeners for a lifetime.

Children's picture books are not just read, but reread, sometimes hundreds of times; and the most beloved of them will be returned to decades later: first, when their auditors become readers to their own children; and maybe for a second time, years after that, when, with a grandchild on your knee, you reach down a frayed paperback from a shelf and say: 'The night Max wore his wolf suit...'

And there you are, the years falling away: back at the beginning...

EPILOGUE

THIS LOVELY WORLD,
THESE PRECIOUS DAYS

IN SEPTEMBER 2023, THE UK's NATIONAL LITERACY Trust charity released a disheartening report. 'Children's writing at "crisis point" as enjoyment among pupils drops,' said one newspaper headline of its findings. 'More than half of UK children don't read in their spare time,' said another. The charity's annual survey of attitudes to reading in children aged between eight and eighteen found that 56 per cent of their respondents said that they didn't enjoy reading recreationally; a change for the worse of more than 15 per cent since 2016. Among boys the figure was higher than among girls. Among children on free school meals, the figure who didn't enjoy reading was more than 60 per cent. The charity called it 'an all-time low statistic since we began surveying children in 2005'.

As I reach the end of a survey of the history of storytelling to children, this looks like a bleak capstone. Was Pottermania – with children queuing outside bookshops overnight to get their hands on a hardback book – merely what stock market analysts call a 'dead cat bounce'? Will childhood reading become what it started out as: a luxury activity for the children of middle-class parents? Are the pages that precede this one not, after all, the celebration of a living artform but the overlong obituary of a soon-to-be-dead one? I hope and believe not.

As I've attempted to show, the human impulse to consume stories is ineradicable. The stories that children's writers have given us over the years have proved accordingly resilient, and endlessly available to reinvention. Media that were once seen as potential threats to childhood reading – television having been the last great panic in that direction – have, when used imaginatively, rubbed along with and even helped support it; not least because selling screen rights is a good way of keeping a writer solvent enough to keep writing. There's always room in the ecosystem for one more species.

I don't, though, brush off the idea that new media might be something to be concerned about; that they might present a threat to the habit of recreational reading. Social media, videogames and other products of the digital age are super-sticky and sometimes more than just figuratively addictive. Many of them are engineered to game the brain's rewards circuits in a way that even the most exciting television show cannot. Given a choice between another game of Fortnite and half an hour in a quiet chair reading *The Secret Garden*, it's futile to pretend that the average eleven-year-old isn't going to plump for Fortnite.*

So Fortnite and its successors are here to stay. But that doesn't mean that they can't and won't coexist with *The Secret Garden*. It seems to me important that they do. For all their many virtues – and I write as an unashamed lover of videogames – these digital forms are weak in many areas in which ink-on-paper storytelling is strongest. The defining feature of videogames is their interactivity. Even in the sort-of-storytelling ones, the story and world-building are secondary to the gameplay. That crate is there for a player to take cover behind in a shoot-out; this plot twist is there to set up a boss fight. The best can be narratively engrossing and even, sometimes, moving, but letting the player *do stuff* comes first. They can create thrillingly atmospheric worlds for players to explore, but they are worlds of surfaces, of predictable mechanics.

---

* If you don't know what this is, count yourself lucky – or ask an eleven-year-old. It's a hectic videogame in which everyone's trying to shoot everyone else.

A videogame will always struggle to do what fiction does, which is to allow yourself to envision what it might be like to be somebody else. Videogames can't match fiction in terms of emotional engagement, and they can't match fiction in terms of moral engagement. There's a different sort of interactivity involved in reading: the imaginative interactivity of taking black marks on a white page and creating a world from them in your own head. If you and I both play through a videogame, we will have experienced the same world on screen. If you and I both read *The Wind in the Willows*, we will have experienced different worlds: we will have visualised them differently, directed our attention and remembered them differently, and allocated our sympathies differently according to our own needs and predilections.

What's more, if we reread the same book years later, when we have ourselves changed, the books will have changed with us. That's why it's not just children who benefit from reading and rereading children's books. In *Why You Should Read Children's Books, Even Though You Are So Old and Wise* (2019), Katherine Rundell makes the case well, arguing that if we ignore children's books as adults we discard 'a casket of wonders which, read with an adult eye, have a different kind of alchemy in them': 'Read a children's book to remember what it was to long for impossible and perhaps-not-impossible things. Go to children's fiction to see the world with double eyes: your own, and those of your childhood self.'

Prose narratives invite and reward the sort of continuous attention that is ever more valuable in the distraction economy of the digital age. The tech writer Cory Doctorow has aptly called the internet 'an ecosystem of interruption technologies', and so it is. More than that, its communal spaces on social media are remorselessly competitive. Validation comes in the stark metrics of likes and reposts, and their implicit promise – especially seductive to anxious children trying to figure out who they are – is that if you act a certain way, think a certain way, consume a certain way, you'll look and feel happier. The paradox of social media is that it places you in a crowd of millions and makes you feel alone. Storybooks are paradoxical in the opposite way: you consume them alone, but the act of consuming them makes you feel less alone.

So children of all backgrounds can get pleasure and consolation out of reading; they just need to know that that pleasure is available, and how to access it. That requires a will. It won't just happen. It means that adults, who are themselves all too easily distracted by the constant bleating and pinging of their smartphones, need to do more than just command our children to read before we go back to Instagram or Twitter or the school WhatsApp group. We need to slow down, turn off, and enter the worlds of these books with our children during that foundational time when reading is a shared experience. It begins with putting your arm around a small shoulder at bedtime and starting: 'Now, O Best Beloved…'

For the other thing that the National Literacy Trust discovered in that report was that 'nearly three times as many children and young people who perceived their reading environment to be supportive said they enjoyed reading'. It's not that they read because they had parents or teachers who encouraged them to: it's that when their parents and teachers encouraged them to read, they *enjoyed it*. And at *three times* the rate of those whose parents and teachers did not.

God knows, the good material is all out there, and it's coming thicker and faster than ever. The years since the turn of the millennium have seen the flourishing of a new generation of talents in children's writing in every genre. To name but a few: Neil Gaiman's *Coraline*, Katherine Rundell's *The Wolf Wilder* and *Impossible Creatures*, Lemony Snicket's *A Series of Unfortunate Events*, Cressida Cowell's *How To Train Your Dragon*, Piers Torday's *Last Wild* series, S.F. Said's *Varjak Paw*, Louis Sachar's *Holes*, Michelle Paver's *Wolf Brother* books, Francesca Simon's *Horrid Henry*, Philip Reeve's *Mortal Engines* trilogy, Frank Cottrell-Boyce, the indefatigable Michael Morpurgo, Charlie Higson's *Young Bond* and Anthony Horowitz's Alex Rider books, Percy Jackson and Artemis Fowl, *A Good Girl's Guide to Murder*… Here are fantasy, science fiction, humour and adventure – and, thanks to the revived interest in children's writing, they are being published more ingeniously and confidently than at any time in the history of the industry. I can't claim to be extremely excited about David Walliams's work, but lots of kids – especially those who are reluctant to read at all – love him.

That points to the lesson we have to learn and learn all over again in each generation. To keep children reading – or at least to *start* them reading with enjoyment – you must go to where they are. My own younger son, the one who came with me to meet Judith Kerr, read reluctantly. He tended to find what they now call 'chapter books', i.e. the sort with blocks of text, boring. But when he came across Jeff Kinney's witty and humane illustrated series *Diary of a Wimpy Kid*, he was hooked. He pesters me, months ahead of launch, to know when the next one is coming out. In due course he developed the same relationship with Jamie Smart's *Bunny vs Monkey* series, and Louie Stowell's *Loki* books.

These books are halfway to being comics (he also adores *Calvin and Hobbes*). But rather than tut-tut at them for not being proper books, let's thank heaven for gateway drugs. It only takes one or two encounters with a book that you really, really enjoy for the hook to be set. For one generation, that meant Enid Blyton. For another, Roald Dahl. For another, J.K. Rowling. Often these were books of which their parents disapproved for reasons of style, or content, or both: but no matter. These were the books that enticed those children, for the first time, into the haunted wood.

I started this book by talking about my father. I'd like to end it by telling a story about my daughter. She's now fourteen years old. She was about eight when what I think of as the inciting incident took place for her. It was early evening, not long before bedtime. She was upstairs in her room, and I was downstairs in the kitchen, making supper.

I heard, suddenly, a yelp of distress from the house above – the sort of howl of pure pain that makes you drop a knife and bolt upstairs three steps at a time before you're even aware you're doing it. I thought – or would have, if I'd had time to think – that my accident-prone child had done herself another injury. I expected to find her bleeding, contused, black-eyed or bloody-nosed, and to spend the rest of the evening in the A & E department of north London's Whittington Hospital.

I slammed her bedroom door open. And there she was, sitting on the edge of her bed, crying as if she'd never stop. In her hand was a copy of *Charlotte's Web*. She'd just got to *that* bit. The bit that I cried at when I was a child, and that I would cry at again if I allowed myself to reread it. She couldn't understand why – in fact, she recovered enough to be nearly affronted – I was so happy.

But I was – because, in that moment, I knew that she'd got it. She had been brought to tears of real anguish by a series of words on a page, written by a timid man who'd lived and died on another continent years before she was even born, describing a series of events that never happened to a character who never existed. That's the power of children's writing, and it goes generation to generation, and it never goes away.

Further Reading

Ahlberg, Allan, *The Boyhood of Burglar Bill* (Puffin, 2006).

Ariès, Philippe, *Centuries of Childhood*, trans. Robert Baldrick (Jonathan Cape, 1962).

Blackman, Malorie, *Just Sayin': My Life in Words* (Merky Books, 2022).

Blyton, Enid, *The Story of My Life* (Pitkin, 1952).

Brayfield, Celia, *Writing Black Beauty: Anna Sewell and the Story of Animal Rights* (History Press, 2023).

Briggs, Julia, *A Woman of Passion: The Life of E. Nesbit, 1858–1924* (Hutchinson, 1987).

Burnett, Frances Hodgson, *The One I Knew the Best of All* (Frederick Warne & Co, 1893).

Burnett, Vivian, *The Romantick Lady (Frances Hodgson Burnett): The Life Story of an Imagination* (Scribner, 1927).

Byatt, A.S., *The Children's Book* (Chatto & Windus, 2009).

Cadogan, Mary, *Just William Through the Ages* (Macmillan, 1994).

Carpenter, Humphrey, *Secret Gardens: A Study of the Golden Age of Children's Literature* (Allen & Unwin, 1985).

Chambers, Roland, *The Last Englishman: The Double Life of Arthur Ransome* (Faber, 2009).

Coren, Michael, *C.S. Lewis: The Man Who Created Narnia* (Fitzhenry and Whiteside, 1996).

Coveney, Peter, *The Image of Childhood* (Penguin, 1967).

Cunningham, Hugh, *Children and Childhood in Western Society Since 1500* (Routledge, 3rd edn, 2021).

Dahl, Roald, *Boy: Tales of Childhood* (Jonathan Cape, 1984).

Dahl, Roald, *Going Solo* (Jonathan Cape, 1986).

Darton, F.J. Harvey, *Children's Books in England: Nine Centuries of Social Life* (Cambridge University Press, 1932).

Dennison, Matthew, *Eternal Boy: The Life of Kenneth Grahame* (Head of Zeus, 2018).

Dennison, Matthew, *Teller of the Unexpected: The Life of Roald Dahl, An Unofficial Biography* (Head of Zeus, 2022).

Dennison, Matthew, *'Over the Hills and Far Away': The Life of Beatrix Potter* (Head of Zeus, 2016).

Douglas-Fairhurst, Robert, *The Story of Alice: The Secret History of Wonderland* (Harvill Secker, 2015).

Fisk, Nicholas, *Pig Ignorant* (Walker Books, 1992).

Fitzsimons, Eleanor, *The Life and Loves of E. Nesbit* (Duckworth, 2019).

Gavin, Adrienne E. and Humphries, Andrew F. (eds.), *Childhood in Edwardian Fiction* (Palgrave, 2009).

Hahn, Daniel, *The Oxford Companion to Children's Literature* (Oxford University Press, 2nd edn, 2015).

Hart-Davies, Rupert (ed.), *The Autobiography of Arthur Ransome* (Jonathan Cape, 1976).

Hunt, Peter, *An Introduction to Children's Literature* (Oxford University Press, 1994).

Hunt, Peter, *The Making of Lewis Carroll's Alice and the Invention of Wonderland* (Bodleian Library, 2020).

Jubber, Nicholas, *The Fairy Tellers: A Journey into the Secret History of Fairy Tales* (John Murray, 2022).

Lancelyn Green, Roger, *Tellers of Tales: Children's Books and their Authors from 1800–1968* (Edmund Ward, 1946).

Lawson, Valerie, *Mary Poppins, She Wrote: The Life of P.L. Travers* (Simon & Schuster, 2006).

Lear, Linda, *Beatrix Potter: A Life in Nature* (Allen Lane, 2007).

Lerer, Seth, *Children's Literature: A Reader's History from Aesop to Harry Potter* (University of Chicago Press, 2008).

Locke, John, *An Essay Concerning Human Understanding* (Thomas Bassett, 1689).

Locke, John, *Some Thoughts Concerning Education* (A. & J. Churchill, 1693).

McVeigh, Jane, *Richmal Crompton: Author of* Just William (Palgrave Macmillan, 2022).

Mack, Edward C. and Armytage, W.H.G., *Thomas Hughes: The Life of the Author of Tom Brown's Schooldays* (Ernest Benn, 1952).

Maunder, Andrew, *Enid Blyton: A Literary Life* (Palgrave Macmillan, 2021).

Milne, A.A., *It's Too Late Now: The Autobiography of a Writer* (Methuen, 1939).

Milne, Christopher, *The Enchanted Places: A Childhood Memoir* (Methuen, 1974).

Nicolson, Juliet, *The Great Silence: 1918–1920: Living in the Shadow of the Great War* (John Murray, 2009).

Propp, Vladimir, *Morphology of the Folktale*, trans. Laurence Scott (Mouton & Co, 1958).

Pullman, Philip, *Daemon Voices: Essays on Storytelling* (David Fickling Books, 2017).

Quintilian, *Institutes of Oratory*, trans. H.E. Butler (Loeb Classical Library, 1921).

Renton, Alex, *Stiff Upper Lip: Secrets, Crimes and the Schooling of a Ruling Class* (Weidenfeld & Nicolson, 2012).

Rousseau, Jean-Jacques, *Emile, or On Education* (1762), trans. Barbara Foxley (E.P. Dutton & Co., 1948).

Rundell, Katherine, *Why You Should Read Children's Books, Even Though You Are So Old and Wise* (Bloomsbury, 2019).

Smallwood, Imogen, *A Childhood at Green Hedges: A Fragment of Autobiography by Enid Blyton's Daughter* (Methuen, 1989).

Smith, Sean, *J.K. Rowling: A Biography* (Michael O'Mara, 2001).

Stone, Lawrence, *The Family, Sex and Marriage in England 1500–1800* (Weidenfeld & Nicolson, 1977).

Sturrock, Donald, *Storyteller: The Life of Roald Dahl* (Harper Press, 2010).

Sturrock, Donald (ed.), *Love from Boy: Roald Dahl's Letters to His Mother* (John Murray, 2016).

Thwaite, Ann, *A.A. Milne: His Life* (Faber, 1990).

Thwaite, Ann, *Beyond the Secret Garden: The Life of Frances Hodgson Burnett* (Duckworth, 2020).

Townsend Warner, Sylvia, *T.H. White: A Biography* (Jonathan Cape, 1963).

Westall, Robert, *Children of the Blitz: Memories of Wartime Childhood* (Penguin, 1985).

Westall, Robert, *The Making of Me: A Writer's Childhood* (Catnip Books, 2006).

Wilson, A.N., *C.S. Lewis: A Biography* (William Collins, 1990).

Wilson, Jacqueline, *Jacky Daydream* (Doubleday, 2007).

Zipes, Jack, *Sticks and Stones: The Troublesome Success of Children's Literature from Slovenly Peter to Harry Potter* (Routledge, 2002).

Acknowledgements

The author would like to thank the many people who wittingly and otherwise gave me information, encouragement or ideas, among them Lynn Barber, A.S. Byatt (sadly missed), Jenny Colgan, Matthew Dennison, Robert Douglas-Fairhurst, Roy Foster, Georgia Garrett, Tanya Gold, Michael Moorcock, Marcus Nevitt, Ruth Scurr, Piers Torday and Frances Wilson. Thanks to my agent Toby Mundy, without whom this book wouldn't have happened; and the best of editors, Cecilia Stein, without whom it wouldn't have been any good. The whole extraordinary team at Oneworld – too many to name, but you know who you are – have worked marvels. And I'm honoured to have Paula Clarke Bain as my indexer. A flexible day job has also been a huge help: thanks to Fraser Nelson and the incomparable Clare Asquith. Thanks, too, to the raiding team of Always Lost, who kept me cheery during the hermit-like writing phase.

I could not have written this book at all without the love and support of my wife, Alice, who put up with all that time I spent reading children's books, and my own children Marlene, Max and Jonah, whose tastes have helped to shape mine.

Index

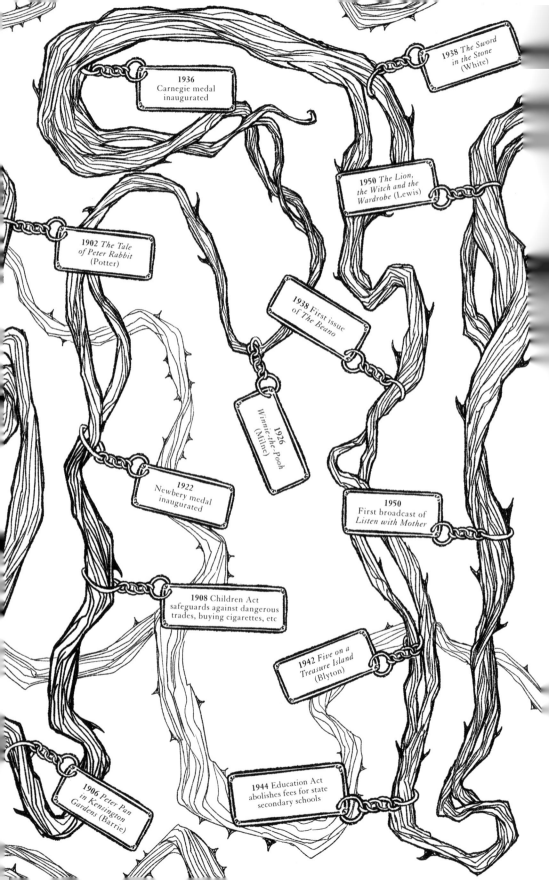

1938 *The Sword in the Stone* (White)

1936 Carnegie medal inaugurated

1950 *The Lion, the Witch and the Wardrobe* (Lewis)

1902 *The Tale of Peter Rabbit* (Potter)

1938 First issue of *The Beano*

1926 *Winnie-the-Pooh* (Milne)

1922 Newbery medal inaugurated

1950 First broadcast of *Listen with Mother*

1908 Children Act safeguards against dangerous trades, buying cigarettes, etc

1942 *Five on a Treasure Island* (Blyton)

1906 *Peter Pan in Kensington Gardens* (Barrie)

1944 Education Act abolishes fees for state secondary schools